# Decentralization and local democracy in the world

**First Global Report by United Cities and Local Governments**

UCLG wishes to acknowledge the Support of:

Generalitat
de Catalunya

Diputació
Barcelona
xarxa de municipis

Région
PAYS DE LA LOIRE

DEXIA

Cities Alliance
Cities Without Slums

# Decentralization and local democracy in the world

## 2008

**First**

**Global**

**Report**

A co-publication of the World Bank and United Cities and Local Goverments

United Cities and Local Governments
Cités et Gouvernements Locaux Unis
Ciudades y Gobiernos Locales Unidos

THE WORLD BANK

© 2009   United Cities and Local Governments
         Avinyó 15
         08002 Barcelona - Spain
         Telephone: +34 933 428 750
         Internet: www.cities-localgovernments.org
         E-mail: info@cities-localgovernments.org

1 2 3 4 5 13 12 11 10 09

This volume is a product of an international network of experts associated with United Cities and Local Governments initiative. The findings, interpretations, and conclusions expressed in this volume do not necessarily reflect the views of the Executive Directors of The World Bank, nor all the members of United Cities and Local Governments.
The World Bank and United Cities and Local Governments do not guarantee the accuracy of the data included in this work. The boundaries, colors, denominations, and other information shown on any map in this work do not imply any judgment on the part of The World Bank and United Cities and Local Governments concerning the legal status of any territory or the endorsement or acceptance of such boundaries.

**Rights and Permissions**
The material in this publication is copyrighted. Copying and/or transmitting portions or all of this work without permission may be a violation of applicable law. The World Bank and United Cities and Local Governments encourage dissemination of its work and will normally grant permission to reproduce portions of the work promptly.
For permission to photocopy or reprint any part of this work, or queries on rights and licenses, please send a request with complete information to the to the Copyright Clearance Center Inc., 222 Rosewood Drive, Danvers, MA 01923, USA; telephone: 978-750-8400; fax: 978-750-4470; Internet: www.copyright.com.
All other queries on rights and licenses, including subsidiary rights, should be addressed to the Office of the Publisher, The World Bank, 1818 H Street NW, Washington, DC 20433, USA; fax: 202-522-2422; e-mail: pubrights@worldbank.org.

ISBN: 978-0-8213-7734-5
eISBN: 978-0-8213-7735-2

**Design and Layout**   MIS Productions
**Proofreaders**        William Bank & Judith Fiorilli-Connett
**Photos**              UCLG archives and Rafael Escudé, Antonio Lajusticia
                        & Francisco Ontañón

Library of Congress Cataloging-in-Publication Data

Decentralization and local democracy in the world : first global report by United Cities and Local Governments, 2008.
   p. cm.
 Includes bibliographical references and index.

ISBN 978-0-8213-7734-5 -- ISBN 978-0-8213-7735-2 (electronic)
1. Decentralization in government. 2. Local government. I. United Cities and Local Governments.
 JS113.D426 2008
 320.8--dc22

**Printed in the U.S.A.**

**Coordinated by the Research Network
on Local Government in Europe (GRALE)**

GRALE

**Under the scientific direction of Gérard Marcou,
Professor at the University Paris 1 Panthéon-Sorbonne, Director of GRALE**

# CONTENTS

# 1st UCLG World Report on Decentralization and Local Democracy in the World

## Foreword

This publication of the UCLG on Decentralization and Local Democracy comes at a timely moment. The world has just passed a significant threshold: it is now more urban than rural, with a greater number of people living in cities than at any time in history. Furthermore, over the next 30 years most world population growth will be in developing country cities. Highly visible megacities will continue to grow, but more slowly on the whole, while cities under 1 million in size are projected to absorb a population increase of nearly one half billion in the next 15 years.

This demographic shift constitutes the maturation of the urbanization process and poses a tremendous challenge for poor and middle income countries. The challenge is to provide the services that are essential to the health, education, prosperity, and well-being of people living in cities, and to do so sustainably in the face of global challenges such as climate change.

Many developing countries seeking to respond to the challenge posed by these demographic shifts will choose decentralization and local democracy in various forms as one tool to achieve basic social ends. Regardless of the degree of decentralization, in an increasingly urbanized world governance and management in cities and towns will take on heightened importance. The World Bank applauds the work of the UCLG in underscoring these key functions and we welcome this *Report* as input to our collective thinking on the subject.

While many of the problems facing cities and towns may be global, the solutions will, in large measure, be local and unique to the specific circumstances on the ground. Good solutions will result from a smooth collaboration amongst various levels of government that is crafted pragmatically to get results. We look forward to a strong partnership with UCLG.

**Katherine Sierra**
*Vice President, Sustainable Development*
The World Bank

# Preface

It is my great pleasure, as President of the World Organization of Local and Regional Authorities, to present the first **World Report on Decentralization and Local Democracy**, published in cooperation with the World Bank and Cities Alliance.

I hope that this *Report*, which is the first of its kind, will contribute to deepen and strengthen knowledge about the role of local governments in the contemporary world, and to enrich national and international discussions on the relationship between decentralization and development.

The present *Report* clearly shows that the world is undergoing a **quiet democratic revolution**. Therefore, even if important aspects of this process have yet to be accomplished, especially in countries in conflict (in the Middle East, Asia and Africa) local democracy is gaining momentum all over the world: from the African savanna villages, the highlands of Latin America to the *barangay* in the Philippines.

In a world where more than half of humanity now lives in cities, local authorities are also the key to the solution of major contemporary challenges of all kinds: democratic, as it is in the local sphere that the sense of citizenship is reinforced and identities are constructed to deal with globalization; environmental, since the preservation of our planet and the fight against global warming depends to a great extent on finding sustainable solutions to transform current models of production and consumption, particularly in the urban areas; economic, given that large amounts of wealth and opportunities, as well as extreme inequities are generated within the cities and in their surroundings; and, social, as it is at the local level where the grounds need to be set for creating social inclusion, managing cultural diversity and ensuring human security.

This publication follows the adoption by Member States of the UN Habitat Governing Council of the *International Guidelines on Decentralization and Strengthening of Local Authorities*: the first international cornerstone reference to "outline the main principles underlying democratic, constitutional, legal and administrative aspects of local governance and decentralization[1]".

Both the guidelines and this *Report* are the fruition of longstanding efforts by local governments and their partners which I hope will complement each other promoting the ownership and implementation of the *Guidelines* by States and local authorities all over the world. The *Report* constitutes the first stage of the **World Observatory of Decentralization and Local Democracy** project launched by United Cities and Local Governments and supported by the UN Habitat Governing Council.

I am convinced that this publication –the first of regular triennial reports– will enable United Cities and Local Governments to become "a major world source of information and intelligence on local government" as anticipated by its members.

**Bertrand Delanoë**
*Mayor of Paris*
*France*
President of CGLU

1. UN Habitat, 21st Governing Council, Decisions and Resolutions, Nairobi, 16-20 April 2007: Resolution 21/3.

# EDITORIAL PROJECT

## UCLG Steering Committee

- Jean Pierre Elong Mbassi, Secretary General, UCLG Africa
- Christopher Hoene, National League of Cities, USA
- Béchir Odeimi, Director of UCLG Lebanon and Jordan, Lebanon
- Josep Roig, Secretary General, Metropolis
- Rashik Sagitov, Secretary General, UCLG Eurasia
- Jeremy Smith, Secretary General, Council of European Municipalities and Regions (CEMR)
- Guillermo Tapia, Secretary General of FLACMA, Latin America
- Peter Woods, Secretary General, UCLG Asia-Pacific
- Selahatim Yildirim, Secretary General, UCLG Middle East & Western Asia

## Responsibility for the Publication

- **Director :** Elisabeth Gateau, Secretary General, UCLG
- **Overall Coordination:** Edgardo Bilsky, Director for Programs and Research, UCLG
- **Advisor:** Emilia Saiz, Director for Statutory Issues and Institutional Relations, UCLG
- **Support team from UCLG:** Hélène Abet, Dominique Arrestat, Mohamed Boussraoui, Orla de Díez, Sara Hoeflich de Duque, Grégoire Husson, Thomas Meekel, Olivia Paton, Marie Laure Roa, Virginia Molina, Marcus Mayr, Renske Steenbergen

## Scientific Direction

- Gérard Marcou, Professor at the University Paris 1 Panthéon-Sorbonne, Director of GRALE, France

## Editorial Committee

- Mustapha Adib, Professor at the Lebanese University and at the French-Lebanese University Center of Technology, Director of the Center for Strategic Studies in the Middle East (CESMO), Lebanon
- Alex B. Brillantes, Professor and Dean of the University of the Philippines, Eastern Regional Organization for Public Administration (EROPA), Philippines
- Adrian Campbell, Senior Lecturer at the University of Birmingham, School of Public Policy, United Kingdom
- Vincent Hoffmann-Martinot, Research Director of the CNRS, Director of SPIRIT (CNRS), Institute of Political Studies of Bordeaux, France
- Talia Iaroulovna Khabrieva, Professor, Director of the Institute of Legislation and Comparative Law of the Government of the Russian Federation
- Biram Owens Ndiaye, Director, Municipal Development Partnership, Benin
- Jefferey Sellers, Professor at the University of Southern California, USA
- Salvador Valencia Carmona, Professor at the Nacional Autonomous University of Mexico (UNAM), Director of the Center of Legal Research, Mexico

# ACKNOWLEDGMENTS

## Main authors[1] by chapters:

### Africa:

- Mustapha Ben Letaief, Professor at the University of Tunis 1, Faculty of Law, Director of the Public Law Department, Tunis
- Charles Nach Mback, Expert, Municipal Development Partnership, Benin
- Jean-Pierre Elong Mbassi, Secretary General, UCLGA
- Biram Owens Ndiaye, Director, Municipal Development Partnership, Benin

### Asia-Pacific:

- Andrew Nickson, Lecturer, School of Public Policy, University of Birmingham, United Kingdom
- Alex B. Brillantes, Professor and Dean of the University of the Philippines, Eastern Regional Organization for Public Administration (EROPA), Philippines
- Wilhelmina L. Cabo, EROPA, Professor at the University of the Philippines
- Alice Celestino, EROPA, University of the Philippines
- Nick Devas, Lecturer, School of Public Policy, Director of the International Development Department, University of Birmingham, United Kingdom

### Eurasia:

- L.V.Andrichenko, PhD, Institute of Legislation and Comparative Law of the Government of the Russian Federation
- Talia Ia. Khabrieva, Professor, Director of the Institute of Legislation and Comparative Law of the Government of the Russian Federation, Team leader
- V.I.Lafitsky, Professor at the Institute of Legislation and Comparative Law of the Government of the Russian Federation

- A.V. Pavlushkin, PhD, Institute of Legislation and Comparative Law of the Government of the Russian Federation
- A.E.Postnikov, Professor at the Institute of Legislation and Comparative Law of the Government of the Russian Federation
- N.V.Putilo, PhD, Institute of Legislation and Comparative Law of the Government of the Russian Federation
- Y.A.Tikhomirov, Professor and Vice-Director of the Institute of Legislation and Comparative Law of the Government of the Russian Federation
- V.A.Vasiliev, Professor at the Institute of Legislation and Comparative Law of the Government of the Russian Federation

### Europe :

- Gérard Marcou, Professor at the University Paris 1 Panthéon-Sorbonne, Director of GRALE, France
- Hellmut Wollmann, Professor emeritus at the Humboldt-Universitaet Berlin, Germany

### Latin America :

- Mario Rosales, Director of Studies, Association of Municipalities of Chile
- Salvador Valencia Carmona, Professor at the Nacional Autonomous University of Mexico (UNAM), Director of the Center of Legal Research, Mexico

### Middle East & West Asia:

- Mustapha Adib, Professor at the Lebanese University and at the French-Lebanese University Center of Technology, Director of the Center for Strategic Studies in the Middle East (CESMO), Lebanon

1. Alphabetic list. If a person is quoted several times, titles and functions are mentioned only with the first quotation.

### North America

- Jefferey Sellers, Professor at the University of Southern California, USA

### Metropolitan governance:

- Vincent Hoffmann-Martinot, Research Director of the CNRS, Director of SPIRIT (CNRS), Institute of Political Studies of Bordeaux, France
- Jefferey Sellers

### Conclusions

- Tim Campbell, PhD, Urban Age Institute, USA

### Postface

- Gérard Marcou

## Other contributors[2]:

### Africa :

Chabane Benakezouh (Algeria), Mustapha Ben Letaief (Tunisia), Hassan Ouazzani Chahdi (Morocco), Jose Chivava (Mozambique), Lilian Dodzo (Zimbabwe), Elogne Kadja (Côte d'Ivoire), Georges Kasumba (Uganda), Sylvana Rudith King (Ghana), Djenabou Kone (Guinea), Nadjombe Gbeou Kpayile (Togo), Aliou Maguiraga (Mali), Albert Malama (Zambia), Jossy Materu (Kenya & Tanzania), Charles Nach Mback (Rwanda), Issa Moko (Benin), Mahamadou Ndriandy (Madagascar), Nneka Udumma Nkpa (Nigeria), Jean Charles Simobang (Gabon), Enone Théodore (Cameroon), Ibrahima Thioye (Senegal), Khaled Zaki (Egypt), Bureau d'études & d'ingénierie Conseil CERDDEA (Niger), Cabinet Rammble Consultancy – Leola Rammble (South Africa)

### Asia-Pacific:

Andy Asquith (New Zealand), Chris Aulich (Australia), Bambang P.S. Brodjonegoro (Indonesia), Alice Celestino (Philippines), Chandra-nuj Mahakanjana (Thailand), Musharraf R. Cyan (Pakistan), Gao Xiao Ping (China), Mathew John (India), Nguyen Ngoc Hien (Vietnam), Park In-soo (Republic of Korea), Qiao Jingjing (China), Yasuhiro Sagawa (Japan), Arkaja Singh (India), Fauziah Swasono (Indonesia), Mike Tumanot (Philippines), Roger Wettenhall (Australia), Ahmad Jailani Muhamed Yunus (Malaysia)

### Eurasia:

L.V. Andrichenko (Russia), Alexander V. Batanov (Ukraine), N.A. Ignatyuk (Russia), Leïla T. Januzakova (Kazakhstan), Artur G. Kazinian (Armenia), A.V. Pavlushkin (Russia), A.E. Postnikov (Russia), N.V. Putilo (Russia), Vage V. Rafaelian (Armenia), Nizami Safarov (Azerbaijan), Akmal Kh. Saidov (Kyrgyz Rep., Tajikistan, Turkmenistan, Uzbekistan), Kiamran Shafiev (Azerbaijan), Edgar E. Shatirian (Armenia), V.A. Sivitsky (Russia), Paata Tzinovadze (Georgia), Grigorij A. Vasilevitch (Belarus), V.A. Vasiliev (Russia)

### Europe:

Yves Cabannes (United Kingdom), Adrian Campbell (United Kingdom), Carlo Iannello (Italy), Gerardo Ruiz-Rico Ruiz (Spain), Mayte Salvador Crespo (Spain)

### Latin America:

Luciana Albuquerque Lima (Brazil), Pino Alonso (Cuba), Paola Arjona (Colombia), Michel Azcueta (Peru), Felix Barrios (Guatemala), Juan Carlos Benalcazar Guerrón (Ecuador), Antonio Cararello (Uruguay), Salvador Valencia Carmona (Mexico), Fernando Carrión (Ecuador), Jesús María Casals Hernández (Venezuela, R. B. de), Rokael Cardona Recinos (Costa Rica, El Salvador, Guatemala, Honduras, Nicaragua, Panama), Daniel Cravacuore (Argentina), Ramón de la Cruz Ochoa (Cuba), Ruben Hernández Valle (Costa Rica), Carlos Eduardo Higa Matsumoto (Brazil), Eduardo Klin-

2.  The majority of the contributors mentioned below compiled the UCLG Country Profiles (2007). These profiles are available at: http://www.cities-localgovernments.org/gold/

ger (Dominican Republic), Antonio Moreira Maués (Brazil), Dalia Moreno López (Mexico), Andrew Nickson (Bolivia & Paraguay), Martha Prieto Valdés (Cuba), Mario Rosales (Chile), Alejandro Socorro (Cuba), Néstor Vega (Ecuador), Alicia Veneziano (Uruguay), José Luis Villegas Moreno (Venezuela, R. B. de.)

**Metropolis:**

Philip Amis (United Kingdom)

**Middle East & West Asia:**

Mustapha Adib (Lebanon), Najem Al Ahmad (Syrian Arab Republic), Mohammad Djalali (Islamic Rep. of Iran), Yeseren Elicin (Turkey), Mohammad Hachemi (Islamic Rep. of Iran), Adnan M. Hayajneh (Jordan), Aude Signoles (West Bank and Gaza)

**North America:**

Jean-Pierre Collin (Canada), Jefferey Sellers (United States)

---

**Special acknowledgments for financial and advisory support:**

Generalitat de Catalunya

Diputación de Barcelona

Pays de la Loire

INTRODUCTION

18   Decentralization and Local Democracy in the World

# INTRODUCTION

*"Local self-government denotes the right and the ability of local authorities, within the limits of the law, to regulate and manage a substantial share of public affairs under their own responsibility and in the interests of the local population".*
(European Charter of Local Self Government, Part I, Art. 3)

One of the goals of **United Cities and Local Governments** since its creation in 2004 has been to create a Global Observatory on Local Democracy and Decentralization "in order to analyze on a regular basis the advances and possible reverses to local democracy and decentralization around the world, to anticipate potential changes and to analyze the obstacles faced and the solutions required to overcome them" (UCLG Executive Bureau, June 2005).

This *First Global Report*, as we present it today, is one of the results of that initiative. It is also the first global attempt to offer a comparative analysis of the situation of local authorities in every region in the world. The local elected representatives who are members of the governing bodies of UCLG share certain core values regarding local governance issues and support the principle of subsidiarity, whereby decisions should be made at the level of government closest to the citizens. This *Report* will contribute to deepening reflection of these values.

The *Report*, drawn up by a network of experts and university academics on every continent, under the scientific direction of GRALE (Research Group on Local Administration in Europe)[1], is not intended to be exhaustive, although a majority of states around the world are examined. Among the countries that were not included in the *Report* were those with insufficient information sources and/or failed states lacking local institutions or affected by armed conflict. The *Report* focuses strictly on the municipal level (or equivalent), or the intermediate tier of government when it is the main level responsible for local government. Relations between the local level and other levels of territorial administration are also taken into account.

The *Report* takes readers through the seven regions of the world, defined in accordance with the continental sections that make up the structure of UCLG. Each chapter deals with three main themes:

a) the evolution and development of territorial structures;
b) powers, management and finance;
c) local democracy.

An eighth chapter examines the forms of governance of the metropolises, where rapid growth presents significant challenges, particularly in countries of the global South and above all in Asia. This chapter is of particular interest to the metropolitan section of UCLG.

---

1.  GRALE is an international scientific network attached to the Centre National de la Recherche Scientifique (French National Science Research Center) in Paris. It was set up in accordance with an agreement between the following French universities and other bodies: the Paris 1 Pantheon-Sorbonne University, the University of Reims-Champagne-Ardenne, l'Institut d'Etudes Politiques (the Institute of Political Studies) at Aix-en-Provence, the French Ministry of the Interior, the French National Assembly, the Inter-Ministerial Delegation on Regional Development and Competitiveness and the Compagnie Générale des Eaux. Dozens of research centres in France and abroad are members of the network. The eight specialist academic centres that are GRALE partners are: CESMO (Centre d'Etudes Stratégiques du Moyen Orient – Center for Middle-East Strategic Studies) in Lebanon, the Institute of Comparative Law and Legislation in Moscow, Russia, the Institute of Political Sciences in Bordeaux, France, the EROPA (Eastern Regional Organization for Public Administration) in the Philippines, the Partnership for Municipal Development in Benin, the Autonomous University of Mexico, the University of Birmingham in the United Kingdom, and the University of Southern California in the United States.

Drafting the *Report* raised numerous methodological and practical difficulties. In the comparative work, the terms used and above all the concepts they express often conceal different meanings and connotations that simple translation does not uncover. In-depth analyses are required, notably of the essential notions: "The *Global Report* calls for, and at the same time makes possible, an effort to clarify the essential notions," as expressed by Gérard Marcou, the scientific co-ordinator, who raises the key question as to "What do we understand by decentralization, local democracy or even local self-government?" An attempt to clarify these matters is given in the postface to the *Report*.

As the *Report* clearly shows, in the last 20 years decentralization has established itself as a political and institutional phenomenon in most countries around the world. These countries have local authorities, consisting of local assemblies elected by universal suffrage and an executive, both of which are expected, to different degrees, to respond to their citizens. As is shown by widespread legislative or constitutional reform, the global process has resulted in wider recognition of the role and position of local authorities as well as a significant increase in their powers and financing, notwithstanding the many differences between countries. The emergence of new political leadership at the local level is reflected almost everywhere in the creation of associations of elected members or local authorities in more than 130 countries (virtually all members of UCLG).

"The notions of '*autonomía local*', 'local self-government', '*Selbstverwaltung*' and '*libre administration*' have gradually become the norm in territorial administration in every region.

However, the picture that emerges from the research contains sharp contrasts. In many countries, these reforms are either very recent or are facing difficulties in their implementation. Two issues come into view of particular concern for local authorities, especially in countries of the South: financing and staff.

Hence, the fundamental issues and questions of the growing debate are: What happens to local autonomy when the level of financial autonomy is deficient or non-existent, given the tendency of central governments to absorb a larger share of the resources? What is the adequate proportion of local authorities' own resources and state transfers? What happens when interventions by higher tiers of government within the state weaken the ability of local authorities to freely choose the ways they manage their services and administrative structures? More broadly, to what extent do decentralization and subsidiarity enable local authorities and their communities to improve access to services and to work towards development? Moreover, how can we guarantee good quality services expected by citizens?

These debates explain the rising interest among local authorities and international organizations in the definition of the universal principles that serve as a reference on a worldwide scale. The approval by UN-HABITAT of the *Guidelines on Decentralization and the Strengthening of Local Authorities* in April 2007 was a major step forward in this direction, for which UCLG has worked very hard.

The *Guidelines* recognize that sustainable development is made possible by "the effective decentralization of responsibilities, policy management, decision-making authority and sufficient resources, including revenue collection authority, to local authorities, closest to, and most representative of, their constituencies." The *Guidelines* are conceived as guidance on reforms but do not impose a uniform, rigid model. The guidelines integrate notions of governance and democracy, representative democracy and participative democracy; they define the principles that govern the mandate of locally elected authorities and the powers and responsibilities of local authorities, based on subsidiarity. The *Guidelines* also call for the introduction of constitutional and legislative guarantees to protect local autonomy and to ensure that local authorities have sufficient human and financial resources to meet their responsibilities. The *Guidelines* draw their inspiration from the *European Charter of Local Self Government*, to which the European section of UCLG contributed. The Charter, adopted in 1985 by the Council of Europe and today ratified by 46 countries, is the first document of a legal nature at an international level concerning the status and rights of local authorities[2].

The *Global Report* will allow the reader to consider the problems that may arise in the implementation of these principles and the way in which these difficulties may be surmounted. We therefore invite local authorities and their national, regional and international associations to engage in action with UCLG in order to:

- Circulate this *Report* and to press ahead with the dialogue with states on the implementation of the *Guidelines on Decentralization and the Strengthening of Local Authorities.*

- Ask national governments to support the adoption of the *Guidelines on Decentralization and the Strengthening of Local Authorities* by the General Assembly of the United Nations.

- Ensure that the principles of the *Guidelines* are supported by the regional institutions in every continent, thereby contributing to their implementation by member states.

- Contribute to furthering global reflection on local government systems of financing and management of human resources, which UCLG intends to pursue.

We would like to thank the experts and university academics who have contributed to this *Report*, in particular GRALE, which has co-ordinated the work and ensured the scientific quality of the project as a whole.

Mention must also be made of the support given by UCLG's regional and metropolitan sections, which, through their secretariats, have constantly defended the direction and approach of the project.

We would also like to express our gratitude to those institutions and local authorities that have contributed to the production of this *Report*, in particular the *Generalitat de Catalunya*, for their continued support throughout the project, the *Diputació de Barcelona*, the *Conseil Régional du Pays de la Loire* and the *Groupe DEXIA*.

Without the commitment and collaboration of all these partners, the *Report* would not have been possible.

**World Secretariat**
*United Cities and Local Governments*

---

2. *The European Charter of Local Self-Government focuses mainly on the following principles:*
   - *Regulation and management of a substantial share of public affairs by local authorities, through local elected representatives and citizen participation;*
   - *Right of local authorities to exercise their initiatives with regard to any matter included in their powers and responsibilities and not assigned to any other authority;*
   - *Selection and recruitment of local government staff according to merit and competence;*
   - *Conditions of office of local elected representatives to allow free exercise of their functions;*
   - *Local authorities' financial resources to correspond to the responsibilities determined by the constitution and law, of which they may dispose freely within the framework of their powers;*
   - *Administrative supervision of local authorities only to be carried out according to procedures determined by the constitution or by statute;*
   - *Entitlement of local authorities to belong to an association for the protection and promotion of their common interests;*
   - *Legal protection of local self-government*

# Africa

Mustapha Ben Letaief

Charles Nach Mback

Jean-Pierre Elong Mbassi

Biram Owens Ndiaye

## I. Introduction

Africa encompasses some 31 million square kilometers and, according to recent estimates, houses a population of more than 933 million.[1] This rapidly growing population (2.5% per year), characterized by its extreme youth (median age: 20), is a mosaic of peoples speaking many languages. Moreover, the region is subject to rapid urban development; the rate of urbanization in African countries ranges from 40% to 70%. There are thirty-four metropolises with more than one million inhabitants; most are beset by the rapid growth of impoverished suburbs, as well as deficiencies in infrastructure, public transportation and basic urban services. Literacy rates on average range from 40% to 60%. Civil disorder and military conflict are commonplace in a few regions, and in some countries a sizeable percentage of the population suffers from pandemics such as HIV/AIDS, malaria and tuberculosis.

In economic terms, after some 20 years of implementing structural adjustment policies, African countries are becoming financially sound again, achieving an average annual growth rate between 4% and slightly more than 6% in 2005. Despite these positive signs, Africa is still economically underdeveloped. With nearly 15% of the world population, Africa accounts for only 2% of world trade, and receives only 3% of direct foreign investment. (China received about 22% of foreign investment). Of the world's 47 least developed countries, as identified by the United Nations, 18 are in sub-Saharan Africa. The New Partnership for African Development (NEPAD) has not yet been able to attract significant aid and investment to the continent, or to mobilize African savings of which 40%, according to experts, is invested outside Africa. Nevertheless, some of the measures taken by the international community, especially the enhanced Heavily Indebted Poor Countries Initiative (HIPC), should help to increase the financial and policy capacity of public authorities and local governments in certain countries, especially in combating poverty, providing access to services and improving living conditions.

There has been a substantial rise in the number of democratic political systems since the 1990s, in marked contrast to the 1950s and 1960s, the two decades following African independence. During that time, one-party political systems predominated, and access to state power was often gained by means of *coups d'etat*.

In some areas, political and institutional systems remain fragile. Considerable tension still exists in parts of Central Africa (Democratic Republic of Congo, Central African Republic and Chad), West Africa (Côte d'Ivoire, Liberia, Guinea Bissau, Sierra Leone and Togo) and East Africa (Ethiopia/Eritrea, Somalia and Sudan).

Most political systems are now multi-party, and leaders are chosen by universal suffrage. Some categories of local officials (regional governors, *walis* in Algeria, Morocco and Tunisia, *mouhafidhs* in Arab Republic of Egypt, and government representatives in Cameroon) are still appointed. Over the past five years, Africa has seen 35 electoral contests, including 20 presidential elections, five parliamentary elections, four constitutional referendums[2] and six local elections.[3] The majority of states are unitary republics; three of these, Ethiopia, Nigeria, and South Africa have federal systems. Lesotho, Morocco and Swaziland are kingdoms. Comparisons of constitutional systems reveal the predominance of presidential systems. South Africa has a mixed parliamentary and presidential system, Niger has a semi-presidential system and Morocco has a constitutional monarchy.

The table below provides baseline data on the geographic, political and economic position, and territorial organization of African countries.

*The majority of states are unitary republics, but there are also three states with federal systems (Ethiopia, Nigeria and South Africa) and three kingdoms (Lesotho, Morocco and Swaziland)*

1. Internet world stats http://www.internet worldstats.com/stats 1.htm.
2. Algeria, Egypt, Kenya, Mauritania, Tunisia.
3. Data current at 20th December 2006.

Table 1    Geographic, Political and Economic Position and Territorial Organization of Each Country

| Country Population / land area | Political system | Type of state | Regional level | Provincial level | Supra communal level | Municipality/Metropolitan level |
|---|---|---|---|---|---|---|
| **Algeria** 33.4 m / 2,381,741 km² | Presidential | Unitary | | 48 Wilaya | | 1541 municipalities |
| **Benin** 8.2 m / 112.622 km² | Presidential | Unitary | | | | 77 municipalities |
| **Cameroon** 16.3 m / 475,412 km² | Presidential | Unitary | 10 regions | | 2 metropolis 11 districts | 11 urban municipalities 316 rural municipalities |
| **Arab Republic of Egypt** 76.7 m / 1,001,450 km² | Presidential | Unitary | | 26 Mouhafasats (both decentralized and deconcentred structures) | 217 cities and Luxor (Special Status) | 4617 towns |
| **Gabon** 1.4 m / 267,670 km² | Presidential | Unitary | | 47 departments | | 50 municipalities |
| **Ghana** 21.1 m / 238,540 km² | Presidential | Unitary | | | 166 district assemblies | |
| **Guinea** 9.5 m / 245,860 km² | Presidential | Unitary | | | | 38 urban municipalities 303 rural municipalities (CRD) / 1 city (Conakry) |
| **Côte d'Ivoire** 179 m / 322,463 km² | Presidential | Unitary | 19 regions | 58 departments | | 197 municipalities and 2 cities: Abidjan with 10 municipalities and Yamoussokro with town councils |
| **Kenya** 35.1 m / 580,370 km² | Presidential | Unitary | | 8 provinces including the City of Nairobi | | 175 Local Authorities (municipal councils, town councils and county councils) and 3 cities: Nairobi, Mombasa and Kisumi |
| **Madagascar** 18.6 m / 587,051 km² | Presidential | Unitary | 22 regions (Faritany) | | | 1557 municipalities, including 45 urban municipalities, 3 cities with special status: Antananarivo with six districts- Nosy Bé - Sainte Marie |
| **Mali** 13.9 m / 1,267,000 km² | Presidential | Unitary | 8 regions | | 49 cercles Bamako district (with six town councils) governed by special regulations | 703 municipalities |

AFRICA

| Country Population / land area | Political system | Type of state | Regional level | Provincial level | Supra communal level | Municipality/Metropolitan level |
|---|---|---|---|---|---|---|
| Morocco 32.2 m / 446,550 km² | Constitutional Monarchy | Unitary | 16 regions | 49 provinces 13 prefectures (urban areas) | | 1497 municipalities |
| Mozambique 19.8 m / 801,590 km² | Presidential | Unitary | | 10 provinces | | 33 urban municipalities 1042 localities (rural municipalities) |
| Niger 13.2 m / 1,267,000 km² | Semi Presidential | Unitary | 8 regions* (with Niamey) | 36 departments* | 4 urban communities | 265 municipalities, including 213 rural and 52 urban and 5 sedentarized nomadic groupings |
| Nigeria 131.5 m / 923,770 km² | Presidential | Federal | 36 Federated States | | | 774 municipalities |
| Senegal 11.4 m / 196,722 km² | Presidential | Unitary | 11 regions | | | 67 municipalities, 43 innercity municipalities (in 4 cities), 2 metropolitan point authority, 321 rural municipalities |
| South Africa 47.4 m / 1,221,041 km² | Mixed parliamentary and presidential | | Federal | 9 regions | 47 municipal district councils | 231 including 6 metropolitan municipalities |
| Tanzania 38.8 m / 945,090 km² | Presidential | Unitary | A self-governing unit that is not federated, Zanzibar | | 92 rural district councils | 1) 22 urban councils, 92 rural councils, 3 townships; 2) within the districts: 10,075 registered villages |
| Togo 6.15 m / 56,790 km² | Presidential | Unitary | 6 regions* | 30 préfectures* | | 30 urban municipalities |
| Tunisia 10.100 m / 163,610 km² | Presidential | Unitary | 24 governorates (Wilaya, (both decentralized and deconcentred structures) | | | 264 municipalities |
| Uganda 34.2 m / 241,040 km² | Presidential | Unitary | | | 79 districts | 1 city council, 13 municipalities in urban areas - 87 town councils |
| Zambia 10.6 m / 752,614 km² | Presidential | Unitary | | | 54 rural district councils | 1) urban areas: 4 city councils, 14 urban district councils 2) rural areas: none |
| Zimbabwe 13.01 m / 390,760 km² | Presidential | Unitary | | | 58 rural district councils | 1) urban areas: 6 city councils, 28 urban councils, 10 municipal councils, 8 town councils, 4 board councils 2) rural areas: none |

*Regarding territorial organization, this table highlights only local governments in these countries and not the administrative jurisdictions.*

*\* Provided by the law, regions, departments or prefectures, as well as rural municipalities in Niger, have not been established by norm.*

The view of decentralization in African governments seems to fluctuate between regarding it as a technique of administrative organization and –more rarely– as a genuine long-term policy. If decentralization is a policy, it can help to change the operation of existing political systems. If, on the other hand, it is thought of primarily as an administrative technique, it is likely to lead only to rationalization of administrative structures and their effectiveness.

In practice, decentralization in Africa has most often been conceived and implemented as an administrative technique. Indeed, when colonial powers controlled most of Africa, they often sought to disrupt traditional ties in order to consolidate their centralized power. In some cases a colonial power did try to preserve an existing administrative model, but this approach too was adopted primarily to strengthen colonial power, rather than foster self-governance. Predictably, local populations perceived the few decentralized structures set up by colonizers as tools for reinforcing the colonial presence. In all countries in the region, this colonial legacy of an *ad hoc* and often contradictory combination of centralization and decentralization formed the foundation of post-colonial territorial administration. Following independence, embryonic national administrations relied on the familiar centralized model as they confronted urgent problems of resources, administrative management and the establishment of state structures. The continuation of centralized power was seen as expedient not only to control data and policy orientation, but also to deal with the shortcomings and failures of new governments struggling to establish national authority.

This explains why, particularly in francophone African countries, the centralizing model inherited from the colonial power

*In practice, decentralization in Africa has most often been conceived and implemented as an administrative technique*

was adopted. For internal territorial administration, however, the preferred approach tended more toward decentralization, though not to an extent that could undermine an overarching philosophy of centralization. Decentralization was still feared and deliberately avoided if it threatened to move beyond administrative technique toward political substance and any democratic content. The concern of the new governing elites was to consolidate their power. From this perspective, the quest for national unity –seen as a way of combating potentially damaging tribal, local or regional affinities– was given a high profile. Modernization, economic development and national unity became the favoured slogans.

In African countries, the concepts of political and administrative decentralization developed along the lines of the French *déconcentration* –state representatives at the local level rather than locally elected bodies. From the outset they were strategic instruments intended primarily to ensure uniform administration of the territory by the central government. The ideal of centralization predominated for a long time, relegating the more democratic model of decentralization to the back burner.

The constraints on putting decentralization into practice have been apparent for a long time, though such restrictions have occasionally undergone nominal modifications to disarm critics. For the most part, such superficial alterations, however highly approved or formally enshrined in the legal system, amounted to little more than cosmetic palliatives.

Today, the legal status of decentralization policies in most African countries is stipulated in one of two ways: explicitly in a constitution, or by lower-level laws and regulations. To date, less than 40% of African constitutions mention local governments as a specific level of governance. In countries where decentralization and local governments are defined in statutes of a lower rank than the constitution, three main tendencies can be seen. Some countries have relatively elaborate legislation with many regulations, decrees and ordinances for implementation. This model is found primarily in francophone countries. The profusion of statutes complicates the implementation of decentralization and slows things down, causing substantial delays between confirmation of legality, and actual enforcement; delays of 10 years are not unusual. The second legislative tendency involves a relatively small number of laws and regulations on decentralization. Typically, only about half a dozen statutes cover the various aspects of implementing decentralization. The majority of countries in this category are former British colonies. Somewhere between the French and British models is North Africa, where there has never really been a major break in the decentralization policy. The process there seems to have taken root in the colonial era, and has progressed to this day with a kind of slow, sometimes imperceptible, continuity. Some of the earliest North African statutes date back to the middle of the 19th century (Tunisia, 1858). However,

there have been major territorial reforms, including the 1984 Algerian law, and Morocco's 1996 constitutional reform and 1997 law on regions. Despite the long experience of North African countries with decentralization, the autonomy of local government there is still restricted overall in relation to the central state.

A complex picture thus emerges of multiple historic, sociological, cultural, economic, political and legal influences in African governments. Nevertheless, movement toward decentralization and local democracy can be discerned.

The first major tendency, if not an actual trend, is quantitative. Since independence, in nearly every part of the continent there has been noticeable, continuous growth in the number of local governments and in the territory they administer. This growth is especially noticeable in the African urban environment. Diversification and a more refined and complex hierarchy of structures and territorial tiers of decentralization can also be seen.

The table below compares population figures, rates of urbanization and the number of local governments by African region.

## Table 2    Local Governments: Demography and Urbanization

| Regions | Population (millions) | Rate of urbanization (%) | Municipalities (number) |
|---|---|---|---|
| North Africa | 154 | 62 | 4200 |
| West Africa | 264 | 40 | 3000 |
| Central Africa | 98 | 47 | 1000 |
| East Africa | 245 | 31 | 1900 |
| Southern Africa | 148 | 36 | 1300 |
| Africa as a whole | 909 | 38 | 11400 |

**Source:** PDM, 2006.

The second major tendency is qualitative, an increasing acceptance of the substance of decentralization as a policy.

Although in most African states decentralization has long been regarded primarily as an organizational and administrative management technique, it now seems to be gaining true political substance in many countries. However slowly and gradually, decentralization is gaining recognition as an effective way to give increasingly robust independent decision-making powers to local governments. This gradual consolidation of local electoral legitimacy also enhances the credibility of the decentralized authorities. This trend is by no means dominant; in some areas decentralizing activities seem to be mixed with traditional systems and, as in Algeria, challenged to the point where it is virtually non-existent.

*In East and Southern Africa, the history of decentralization is closely related to the end of social and political crises*

Many countries, especially Niger, Senegal, South Africa and Uganda, have already undertaken decentralizing reforms in the organization of state and public life. These countries have organized local elections, and have seen local authorities emerging as new public authority figures alongside national authorities. Admittedly, in most of these countries, the division of public authority has caused problems. In part, this may simply be because such a major institutional change can be absorbed only slowly by many incumbent national authorities.

Implicitly, implementation of the decentralization process has rarely been properly planned. While North African countries have a longstanding policy of decentralization, the pace of implementation there is not altogether uniform. In West and Central Africa, apart from Senegal and Burkina Faso, there is no real plan to implement decentralization. Rather, moves to decentralize in this region seem to rest on policy announcements made in the speeches by heads of state. In East and Southern Africa, the history of decentralization is closely related to the end of recent social and political crises. There, implementation of decentralization has a high priority in government action plans and seems to be subject to a pre-established, regularly assessed timetable. The most exemplary case is South Africa, where the end of the apartheid policy imposed a new approach to governance that involves the entire population in public management at all levels. This policy of transformation is enshrined in the Reconstruction and Development Program (RDP) whose entire philosophy can be summed up in the slogan "A better life for all." With the Local Government Transition Act (1993), adopted to govern the transitional period, the Municipal System Act (2000) and the Municipal Property Rating Act (2004), the South African government gave itself 11 years to set up a system of local governance that is almost revolutionary compared with previous practice.

Apart from South Africa, African governments have not relied on rigorous planning to implement decentralization policies. It is not surprising, therefore, that most of them have no mechanisms to assess the conduct and establishment of such policies. This is why United Cities and Local Government of Africa (UCLGA) is asking that local governance be included in the good governance criteria selected by the Peer Review Mechanism of NEPAD.

Despite resistance, decentralization is moving forward in the region. More substantial progress may be expected as the number of local governments increases, and their capacities are enhanced. Understandably, the various decentralization policies have not developed in the same fashion, or in accord with the same timetable. Implementation as well as the content of policies is strongly influenced by the historical context from which they emerged, and the administrative tradition inherited from the colonial era.

The third tendency consists of a relative increase in the responsibilities of local governments in many countries. In principle, this increase bears witness to greater decentralization, and fits within the logic of disengagement of the state and central administration. In practice, however, it has proved problematic and even counterproductive in the absence of any real transfer of powers and financial resources. In virtually all cases, the central government retains control of local funds and taxation, as well as its monopoly on foreign aid and financing.

The fourth tendency, which is still at an embryonic stage, looks to enlist local and foreign private-sector resources to provide and manage a certain number of urban services, such as the collection of household or industrial waste (Tunisia, Benin, Burkina Faso and South Africa), drinking water (Morocco), or urban transport and sanitation.

The fifth tendency, which is gradually taking shape, involves setting up networks of local authorities to foster decentralized co-operation. The creation of national associations of local governments, including the UCLGA, and the reinforcement of their role at the national level, reflects this tendency. Such associations provide tools to enhance the credibility of local authorities as relevant actors in the dialogue on development and co-operation in Africa. In South Africa, the association of local government authorities, SALGA, is recognized as a public institution. Elsewhere, national associations of local governments have the status of associations under private law, although some, such as the Association of Municipalities in Burkina Faso (AMBF), may be acknowledged as acting on behalf of public interest.

The sixth tendency now emerging and certainly varying from one country to another, is a modest relaxation of the control exerted over local governments. There is a discernible retreat from practices reminiscent of the exercise of power from the top down, and a move toward restricting oversight to strictly legal aspects, allowing greater local autonomy. However, it is also true that, in a few African countries, the situation is less fluid, and there have in fact been some setbacks.

These various movements, obvious and tangible to varying degrees, and often very gradual with pauses, checks and less frequently, qualitative leaps, can be seen (i) at the structural level, (ii) at the material and functional levels of responsibility and management, and (iii), more globally and substantially, in the progress and limits of local democracy.

## II. Changes at Structural Levels

Municipal structures emerged in the 19th century, particularly in Senegal, Egypt and Tunisia. In the 20th century, municipalities were established and gained ground in all colonial territories. Far from respecting principles of local participation, the system was designed to ensure the colonizers' control over the territory, and their ability to oversee the local population. Before independence, municipal administration in African colonies differed somewhat, depending on the model preferred by the controlling European nation: the French system of "communes," the British local government system, and Portuguese "municipios." In all cases, decentralization tended to be purely administrative. Few local bodies were elected; local executives were usually appointed and had only limited or consultative powers. Such decentralization also enabled administrators and colonists in rural areas to be governed by the same arrangements as their compatriots in colonial capitals and in Europe.

Overall, two systems, direct and indirect rule, predominated in sub-Saharan Africa. Direct rule was favored in countries colonized by France, Belgium and Portugal. Direct rule meant administrative oversight of colonial territory organized into "cercles," subdivisions and cantons under the responsibility of the colonial administrators. Local authorities played only a consultative role.

*In fact, changes in administrative structure went hand-in-hand with moves towards decentralization, which formed the core of all endeavors to modernize the State and with it public policy in Africa, supposedly leading to "local democracy" as a key pillar of the entire territorial administrative organization*

Indirect rule, established primarily in British colonies, allowed local people some freedom to manage their own affairs, such as the administration of justice or the collection of taxes –to be shared with the colonial government. Indigenous customs and authority were more or less ignored as long as local leaders protected the interests of the colonial power. This system sowed the seeds of future decentralization in these countries.

In North Africa, the colonial administrative process was more complex. In this region, 18th and 19th century colonial powers encountered many established state structures. For the most part, colonial municipal administration under European nations rested on old, indigenous structures, albeit heavily influenced by the recent, European occupying power. Both the British in Egypt and Sudan, and the French in Algeria, Morocco and Tunisia sought such accommodation.

When African countries achieved independence, the new governments chose to retain the structure inherited from the colonial power, rather than move immediately toward decentralization. From the outset, the old systems were seen as instruments for extending central power over local communities. It was not until the 1980s and the ensuing wave of democratization in the 1990s that a new direction gained momentum. Centralized African governments showed renewed interest in decentralization. Gradually, local governments began taking charge of more local matters. In fact, changes in administrative structure went hand-in-hand with moves toward decentralization in all endeavors to modernize the state. This widespread change in public policy in Africa was expected to lead to acceptance of "local democracy" as a key pillar of  territorial administrative organizations. Since the mid-1980s, several factors have pushed African governments toward economic liberalization and adjustment policies. These factors include: budget difficulties generated by shrinking resources, challenges to interventionist public administration systems, the resurgence of liberal ideas advocating the rehabilitation of market mechanisms, the disengagement of the state, and the changing roles of the public sector and private initiative. These new considerations implied taking part in globalization and international competition required genuine policies of reform and restructuring, and this rationale affected all subsequent reforms relating to local government and urban policy.

However, not all African countries chose the same route in adopting and implementing decentralization policies. In the majority of countries, decentralization policies were adopted following citizens' demands for increased participation. This was strongly expressed by local communities in pro-democracy movements during the 1990s. Because of the connection between democratization and decentralization, some people saw the adoption of decentralization reforms as a corollary to the democratization and liberalization that some financial partners of African governments were imposing as a condition for providing aid. In some cases, central governments made the adoption of decentralization policies appear to be the result of donor conditions. In Mali and Niger, decentralization was a response to local demands, including some violent demonstrations and threats of secession. In other countries, decentralization provided an opportunity to overcome or even eliminate the stigma of a previous political and administrative organization, as in the case of South African apartheid.

In North Africa, changes in local government structures seem to have come about more slowly, and the reforms to have been less thorough. In all countries in this region, the territorial administrative structure seems to be fixed, tied to the structure of the governorate (Wilaya in Algeria, Tunisia and Morocco, Mouhafadha in Egypt), which is more a tier of administrative decentralization.

Nevertheless, almost everywhere the decentralization option is perceived as progress and is expected to:

- Mobilize communities to work for sustainable local development and improved living conditions;
- Help democracy to take root and spread at the local level;
- Reform the state and rebuild the legitimacy of public institutions from the bottom up;
- Constitute the starting point for regional integration genuinely rooted in African realities.

To achieve this, local governments are being given general notional authority over the territory for which they are responsible. Some have exclusive powers as well as powers they share with other levels of public governance. In North Africa, the powers of local governments must compete with the central administration and various national public enterprises for service delivery (education, health, transport, sanitation, drinking water and electricity).

The theory and content of decentralization policies tends to be different in federal states and unitary countries. The decentralization concept also varies in accordance with the administrative tradition inherited from the colonial period. In federal states, local governments come under the remit of federated states; these federated states define the content of the local government system and its administration. This can lead to a wide range of methods of organizing local government —a circumstance which does not facilitate a comparative interpretation of local governance. In unitary states, the organization of local governments is usually the same throughout the national territory. However, the actual powers granted to local officials are, again, influenced by the administrative tradition inherited from the colonial era.

In francophone countries, the organization of local governments corresponds in principle to a division of powers between central and local authorities, the latter being represented by an elected deliberative body and an elected or appointed executive body. Municipal terms of office are usually similar to those of national institutions (four or five years) and re-election is allowed. In these countries, the municipal executive, mayor or top administrator typically has real decision-making power in local management, the powers of this office being defined by law. However, this nominal decision-making power is often restricted by the practice of pooling funds; that is, all public resources are held in the Treasury under the control of the Minister of Finance. Thus, the representatives of the Ministry of Finance, such as the comptroller and municipal tax collector, have effective power over local governments. Many mayors consider such fiscal power excessive because ministry representatives can block expenditure even if it has been committed in accordance with all laws and regulations. It is therefore a claim of national associations of local governments to relinquish or even suppress the principle of unified treasury. However in Senegal the law makes it possible to deviate from this rule:

local governments may be authorized to deposit all or only part of their available funds with the Treasury.

In countries with a British administrative tradition, local governments also have elected deliberative bodies; executive bodies are either elected or appointed. The terms of office of deliberative bodies are similar to those in francophone countries, but those of the executive body –one to three years– are shorter. Furthermore, re-election is not always permitted. Mayors generally have a ceremonial rather than executive role. Real executive power is actually held by another public official, the Town Clerk or Chief Executive Officer, who more often than not is appointed at the national level by the Minister for Local Government. As they do in francophone countries, national associations supporting local governments seek further decentralizing reforms in anglophone countries, including the establishment of true executive powers for mayors, and an extension of mayors' terms of office.

*More generally, African decentralization systems classify lower-tier local authorities according to their level of development or urbanization*

### Governance of major cities

Most countries on the African continent are experiencing a marked trend toward urbanization, the gradual movement of rural populations into the cities. This phenomenon is considered a vector of modernization and competitiveness, not only for cities, but also for the surrounding territories.

In most parts of Africa, the organization of major metropolises –particularly capital cities– tends to display specific features. Such features can be identified in political capitals such as Rabat (Morocco), Lusaka (Zambia), Dakar (Senegal), Tswane (South Africa), Yaoundé (Cameroon), Accra (Ghana) and Algiers (Algeria). Common elements are also apparent in big cities whose importance is determined by demographic or economic weight, such as Johannesburg (South Africa), Douala (Cameroon), Kumasi and Shama-Ahanta (Ghana). All such major cities are governed by distinct legal arrangements that constitute important organizational and managerial exceptions to the more common laws of municipalities.

> In Morocco, the new commune charter of October 3, 2002 made special arrangements for cities with more than 500,000 inhabitants. These cities are managed by a single commune with *arrondissements* that are not legal entities. Morocco modeled its system on the French political configuration of Paris, Lyon and Marseille (known as PLM Law).
> The Moroccan charter also decreed special status for the urban commune of Rabat, the capital, and the Mechouar communes where the royal palaces are situated.

Typically, major African cities are divided into sub-urban administrative units, which may be separate legal entities. The latter is the case for the urban *arrondissement* communes in Douala and Yaoundé in Cameroon. Sub-metropolitan communes created in this way are governed by the common law of municipalities. Conversely, in some countries sub-metropolitan units remain sub-municipal bodies without administrative autonomy; this occurs in Accra and Kumasi in Ghana, and Cotonou in Benin.

Elections also differ somewhat in major metropolises; the deliberative body is elected by direct universal suffrage, as for example in Algeria, Nigeria, Gabon and Madagascar. Those elected then appoint one of their fellow representatives as municipal executive. Another method of selection is appointment by indirect universal suffrage. Metropolitan councillors are elected by the deliberative bodies of the sub-metropolitan units; most candidates are members of that deliberative body, as is the case in Cameroon. As for the distribution of powers, sub-urban units are responsible for local community services, and are forums for participatory democracy. Federative services of importance to the entire city are provided by the larger, central government of the city.

Many African decentralization systems classify lower-tier local authorities according to their level of development or urbanization. For example, in decreasing rank of urbanization Cameroon has urban communities, urban communes under a special scheme, urban communes and rural communes. In South Africa, classification takes the form of an alphabetical hierarchy with category A, B and C municipalities. Such differentiation makes it easier to identify the most disadvantaged authorities and, through a process sometimes called equalization, to focus on their development with specific support policies.

The governmental variations observed in major cities point up the need to define the minimum common content of over-arching African decentralization policies. In fact, an African local government charter that addresses this need for more standardization is currently being mooted. The debate is being driven in particular by the United Cities and Local Governments of Africa (UCLGA) and the African Conference on Decentralization and Local Development (CADDEL).

## III. Responsibilities, Management and Finance

Undeniably, there is a trend toward strengthening the responsibilities of local governments. However, the transfer of responsibility may not be accompanied by a transfer of the money or other resources required to fulfill the added duties. Most African local governments continue to experience very serious financial constraints on their resources and powers.

The administrative capabilities of local governments are also restricted by a shortage of qualified personnel and the wherewithal to train employees properly. In part, it is this dearth of skilled officials that has lead to inefficient and ineffective local management, particularly in the areas of strategic planning, urban development, economics and social development. Lacking qualified personnel, some local and urban governments have turned to the private sector for help in the management of local affairs, public services and property. Recently, several African cities have also sought private assistance with modern information and communications technology.

### III.1. Responsibilities

One of the most important aims of decentralization is to provide an effective, appropriate response to the needs of local communities for public services. The density and efficiency of public services are among the most important indicators of the vigor of decentralization, and provide a vital source of legitimacy for local governments. Unfortunately, such services seem unsatisfactory in virtually all countries. The prerogatives of local governments also vary from country to country, with two notable tendencies:

- Increased responsibilities of local authorities for local services and urban management.

- More private-sector management of local public services by means of various forms of devolution, such as delegation, licensing and partnerships.

Table 3 shows that a majority of countries grant many important powers to local governments. The scope of responsibility covers social investment –infrastructure and social facilities, health, education, leisure–

and the provision of goods and services for education, health, culture, leisure, transport, water and sanitation. Local responsibilities also cover administration, urban planning and management, and local development.

Successful decentralization depends on the manner in which power is transferred to local governments. Invariably, transfer of authority provokes resistance from managers within larger regional and national ministries. In North Africa, transfer of power may be considered only nominal. In this region, national ministries typically

*The ministries concerned tend to bypass local governments in implementing sectoral policies. They are encouraged to a greater or lesser extent in this by the practices of development partners who are often in ignorance of the consequences of applying such policies*

retain control of local services, or delegate them to the private sector. Sectors such as education and health are managed directly by the corresponding ministries, while drinking water, sanitation and energy are either state monopolies, or are provided by private concerns. In virtually all cases, the private providers are under contract to the state, rather than to local authorities. This tendency can also be observed in West and Central Africa, although basic services there for education, health, water, sanitation and transportation are generally acknowledged as local concerns. Even so, the ministries in this region also tend to bypass local governments in implementing long-range sectoral policies. The ministries are often encouraged by their private partners to minimize larger policy discussions with local authorities. It appears to be of small concern to private developers how their pressure for increased central control might affect a national momentum toward decentralization.

Nevertheless, there are promising developments in several eastern and southern African countries, as well as a few anglophone countries in West Africa. In these countries, sectoral ministries are gradually disengaging from the implementation phases of their programs. The result: local governments are taking over the local departments that previously came under the territorial jurisdiction of sectoral ministries. This transfer of authority, seen in Ghana, South Africa and Uganda, necessitates changes in staff, budget resources, assets, and decision-making power. In these countries, central government defines strategic guidelines for sectoral policies regarding health, water and education. Local governments, however, are responsible for implementation. Wherever such territory-wide measures have been undertaken, as in the case of water and HIV/AIDS policy in Uganda, the effectiveness of these policies has increased substantially. However, the decentralization process is often hindered by national sector-based policies that tend to privilege deconcentration (limited transfer of responsibilities). One of the recurrent claims of African local authorities is that sector-based policies should be territorialized and thus more decentralized, as in Ghana, Uganda or South Africa, and that local authorities should be fully responsible for their implementation.

While public assertion of the new nominal powers of local governments is widespread, the actual transfer of real executive and operational powers is still rare. The challenge remains to resolve the problem of effectively transferring the real financial and managerial powers from the centralized ministries to local authorities. Financial management is, of course, the crucial factor.

### III.2. Financial Management

Local government finance comes from two main sources –local taxes and state grants. In some places, local governments share local tax revenues with the central government. The state also makes financial transfers to local governments in the form of con-

**Table 3** Responsibilities of Local Authorities

| COUNTRY | POWERS OF LOCAL GOVERNMENTS (COMMUNES/MUNICIPALITIES) | | | | | | | | |
| --- | --- | --- | --- | --- | --- | --- | --- | --- | --- |
| | Planning and support to the local economy | Drinking water, waste, sanitation | Security (administrative police and CID) | Town planning and habitat | Basic services (health, basic education) | Sport and leisure | Culture and tourism | Energy | Transport |
| Algeria | X | X | X | X | X | X | X | | |
| Benin | X | X | X | X | X | X | X | | X |
| Cameroon | X | X | X | X | X | | X | X | X |
| Egypt, Arab Rep. of | X | X | X | X | X | X | | | X |
| Gabon | X | X | X | X | X | X | X | | X |
| Ghana | X | X | X | X | X | X | X | X | X |
| Guinea | X | X | X | X | X | X | X | | X |
| Côte d'Ivoire | X | X | X | X | X | | | | X |
| Kenya | X | X | X | X | | | | | |
| Madagascar | X | X | X | | X | | | X | X |
| Mali | X | X | | X | X | X | X | X | X |
| Morocco | X | X | | X | X | X | X | X | X |
| Mozambique | X | X | | X | X | | | | X |
| Niger | X | X | X | X | X | X | X | | X |
| Nigeria | X | X | X | X | X | X | X | | X |
| Senegal | X | X | X | X | X | X | X | | X |
| South Africa | X | X | X | X | X | X | X | X | X |
| Togo | | X | | X | X | | | | |
| Tunisia | X | X (waste only) | X | X | | X | X | X | |
| Uganda | X | X | X | X | X | X | X | | X |
| Zambia | X | X | | X | X | | | | X |

ditional or unconditional grants, and other types of state financial contributions. The specific method of funding local development varies from country to country. The capacity to mobilize "own revenues" is one of the fundamental principles of decentralization.

### III.2.1. Local resource mobilization

Legislation allows African local governments to raise a panoply of resources in their own territory from direct or indirect local tax revenues, service tax, fees collected from the operation of services, economic activities or municipal asset management. Unfortunately, the law does not always list the necessary local government taxing powers to alter the volume of their revenues; which means that municipal incomes generally regarded as "own resources" are in fact controlled by central government.

This imbalance can be seen most clearly in the numerous countries that apply the French administrative model, where, in theory, there is a more diversified local taxation system, yet in practice, local governments remain devoid of taxing powers, as tax rates are set out in the law or imposed by central government. Local governments do not administer local taxation systems as such, rather they depend on taxes transferred from the state, which in some cases have become state-shared taxes (e.g. Côte d'Ivoire, Cameroon). The taxing powers of local governments in Gabon, Niger and Togo are the exception to this tendency. Except for local governments in Senegal, local governments are also not empowered to set service fees and tariffs. Only in exceptional instances can local governments collect duties on certain local services or activities (as in Togo, for example) with the prior approval of the overseeing state authority.

Local governments in anglophone countries generally enjoy broader taxing powers and greater freedom to set service rates and other indirect local tariffs; such as real es-

tate tax in Ghana, South Africa, Tanzania, Zambia and Zimbabwe, and service fees in the afore-mentioned countries and Nigeria. Nonetheless, local taxation in some countries is negligible (e.g. Nigeria and Uganda, where tax revenue as a percentage of total revenue dropped from 30% to 11% in five years after the removal of the more productive "graduated tax"). Local government powers to create indirect duties or tariffs on local activities are also exceptional (e.g. in Zambia and Mozambique). It is however, necessary to relativize the importance of these local taxing powers, bearing in mind the decisive control of central governments over revenue mobilization (such as the prior approval required for rates and tariffs in Zambia), the low levels of own source revenues (see the case of Ghana in Figure 1) and the percentage of own revenues making up a small share of the whole budget (30% on average, except in Zambia –77%– and South Africa -90%-).

The level of government responsible for collecting the revenues also varies between countries: in some locations the municipalities ensure the collection of taxes, while in others the state collects the taxes and later distributes the revenues among local governments. African francophone tax revenue systems are generally centralized, although some duties may be collected locally (e.g. Mali, Morocco, Senegal) and some countries may present certain exceptions to this rule (as is the case in Tunisia for the collection of certain taxes). However, regardless of the system in place the tax collection rates remain low in all the countries: approximately 50% in Kenya; lower still in Nigeria; 20% of real estate taxes in Tunisia (collected at the local level); and between 45-50% on average in Côte d'Ivoire or Níger (where the state ensures the collection of revenues).

The use of a shared tax system is slowly spreading as the main source of local government budget funding. Value Added Tax (VAT) is a major component of shared taxation. VAT has been established in almost all countries, and is divided between the state and local governments in proportions that vary from one country to another. In Morocco, for example, local governments have been receiving 30% of the revenue since 1986, and about 25% in Nigeria. In Mozambique, 75% of the vehicle tax and 30% of the tourist tax goes to the local governments. In Cape Verde, there is a set of unallocated taxes, and local governments receive 7% of that revenue.

The two most pressing problems arising from this tax system management are the terms of the division, which are often very unfavorable to local governments, and the regularity of payments. The manner in which the share allocated to local governments is distributed varies considerably. In some countries, there are legal rules about the timing and amount of fund transfers. However, in most countries the central administration has discretionary decision-making power; the state may take years to pay the agreed-upon share to the local governments. Typically, the local authorities have no legal recourse to counter such delays. Over and above these difficulties, shared tax systems cannot be considered to be own revenues, as local governments hold no power over setting the tax base and rate; these resources, from both a political and economic point of view, are similar to general transfers.

### III.2.2. State financial transfers to local governments

Grants are organized in many ways, and also vary from country to country. Similarly, the process of transferring grant funds varies. In general, transfers can be unconditional (local governments are given free use of revenues), or conditional, in which case central government transfers are either based on pre-established objective criteria or have a certain margin of discretion (for local spending).

The principles of intergovernmental transfers are sometimes listed in the Constitution (including procedures and calculating criteria). For instance, the Ghanaian Constitution envisages the existence of the District Assemblies Common Fund, which should receive 5% of the total national revenue, to be distributed among the districts through a for-

*However, in most countries the central administration has discretionary decision-making power; the state may take years to pay the agreed-upon share to the local governments*

mula approved by Parliament (art. 252). This is a unique case. Apart from practical difficulties, this system has increased the financial dependency of local governments on central government. The 1999 Constitution in Nigeria provides that at least 13% of the country's revenue accruing to the Federation Account derived from natural resources should be distributed among the states, based on a sharing formula that takes the principle of origin into account (in relation to the volume of production of each state). It is up to each state legislature to determine the amount of resources that will be distributed among local governments, and to institute a joint account between the Federation and the state where Federation and state contributions for local government transfers are deposited (art. 162). With no direct constitutional safeguards over the volume of revenues earmarked for local government transfers, the Federation decided to make direct transfers to local governments and allocated a portion of VAT for this purpose.

| Figure 1 | Local Resources/GDP |

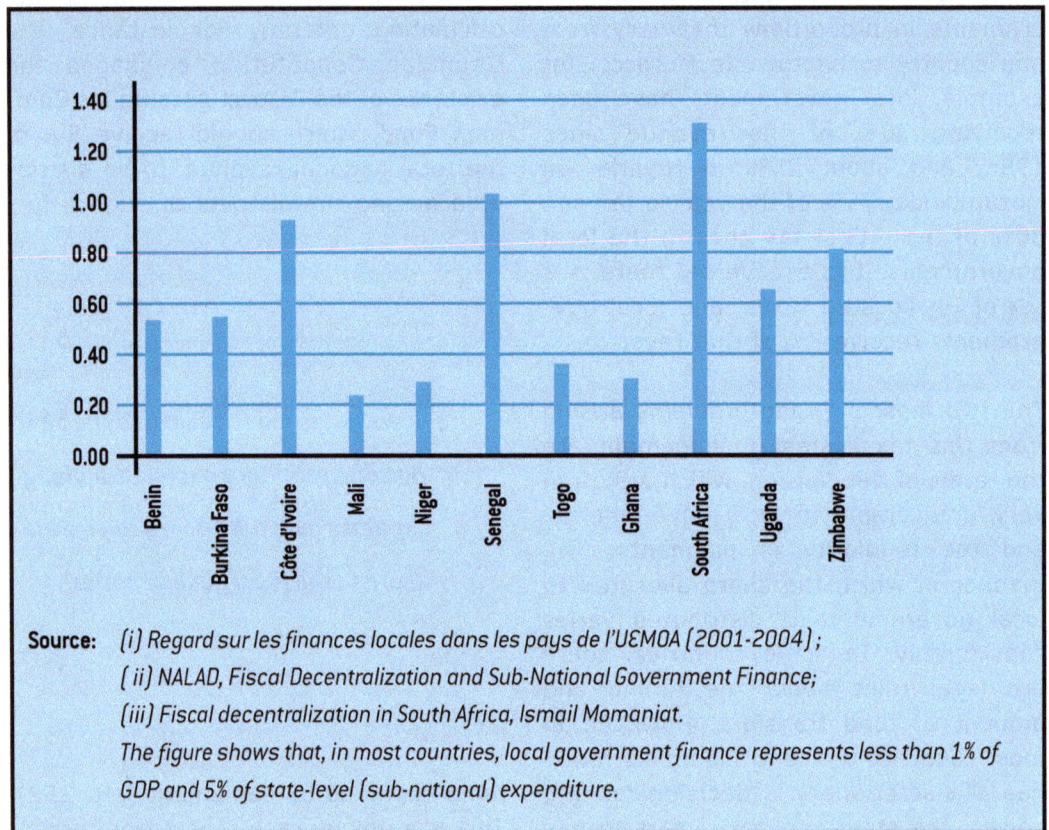

**Source:**    (i) *Regard sur les finances locales dans les pays de l'UEMOA (2001-2004);*
(ii) *NALAD, Fiscal Decentralization and Sub-National Government Finance;*
(iii) *Fiscal decentralization in South Africa, Ismail Momaniat.*
*The figure shows that, in most countries, local government finance represents less than 1% of GDP and 5% of state-level (sub-national) expenditure.*

Sometimes the law provides a formula for grant allocation. One of the best examples is that of South Africa governed by articles 213 and 214 of the Constitution. All money received by national government is paid into the National Revenue Fund (art. 213). The Division of Revenues Act provides annually for the equitable distribution of revenue amongst national, provincial and local spheres of government, and balanced division of tasks to be financed. The Act also defines the distribution of revenues amongst the provinces (regions), and finally, sets the amount of conditional purpose-specific grants for provinces and local governments, financed through the fund. The division of these grants are regulated by formulas that are also defined by law. Paragraph 2 of Article 214 in the Constitution contains the criteria to be applied to the revenue-sharing formula amongst local governments and provinces (in principle, the structure is determined every five years). While province finances depend essentially on transfers, local government finances mainly rely on own-source revenues (taxes, tariffs and service charges).

The situation in other countries is a lot less favourable. The guarantees offered to local governments to access revenues also vary from country to country. Sectoral grants are routine in some countries, usually conditional or purpose specific. These grants are easily controlled but involve central government monitoring of local governments. This is the case in Uganda and Zimbabwe. In Tanzania the government is likely to introduce calculation of grant amounts on the basis of fixed formulas. In Zambia, central government also transfers funds through sectoral grants that are not calculated through a set formula; these transfers represent only 3% of local budgets. In a second group of countries, central government transfers mainly consist of general disbursements to local governments for operations or transferred functions, while investments are covered by occasional grants. Global transfers offer local governments more freedom over spending, though the allocation criteria are usually vague, as in the case of Algeria, Tunisia, Gabon, Guinea, Côte d'Ivoire, Senegal and also in Kenya (where the global transfers are combined with a sectoral grant for road works). In Algeria, the allocation of the solidarity fund grant (95% of the resources from this fund) is managed with clear eligibility criteria: for communities where wealth indices are lower than the national average. Finally, there are countries that do not have an organized system of transfers: in Niger and Togo, intergovernmental transfers are intermittent and dependent on the political situation. Similarly, particularly in UEMOA (West Africa Economic and Monetary Union) and CEMAC (Economic and Monetary Community of Central Africa) countries, governments are often resistent to decentralizing the financial resources in keeping with the sectoral policies that absorb, even so, large flows of aid and public investment.

### III.2.3. The financial weight of local governments

Two indicators usefully measure the financial significance of local government: the share of the nation's Gross Domestic Product (GDP) allotted for local authorities, and the actual amount of money that comes under the control of local governments. Figure 1 (p. 40) shows the actual financial weight of local governments. The sample is small because reliable data were available only for certain years in certain countries. Even so, this sample of countries at different levels of development is quite representative.

In the UEMOA countries (West Africa Economic and Monetary Union), total municipal expenditure of the area amounted to FCFA 150 billion (€228 million) in 2004, i.e. 4.8% of State expenditure of around FCFA 3103 billion (€4.7 billion). A World Bank study on the experience of decentralization in 30 African countries revealed that expenditure controlled by local governments is around 10% in South Africa, between 5 and 10% in Nigeria, Uganda and Zimbabwe and between 3 and 5% in Kenya, Ghana, Senegal, Mozambique and Zambia. Generally speaking, the average ratio between local expenditure and national budget resources excluding donations is below 5% and the ratio between local expenditure and gross domestic product (GDP) less than 1%.

In addition, with the exception of South Africa and North Africa, local governments' resort to borrowing in other countries is at a very early stage.

In view of the weakness of their own income (the insufficient flow of intergovernmental transfers is further exacerbated by the allocation modalities and constraints on access to loan markets), it cannot be denied that African local governments will have trouble in meeting on their own the costs of their ordinary activities and the transferred powers, not to mention their responsibilities in local development and combating poverty.

One of the explicative factors is that own tax revenue and local finance depend on the macroeconomic framework –and central governments in sub-Saharan Africa face severe financial constraints. The poverty affecting large segments of the population places limits on the tax take. On top of this comes the frequent lack of political will to redistribute the tax to ensure a better support to local governments and more effective management of the fiscal chain particularly in the collection of taxes. One of the top priority claims of elected bodies is a better distribution of resources, with the aim of taking the share of own tax revenues in relation to GDP to 2% and increasing financial transfers by 5 to 10%, which would make it possible to double or even triple local resources, the current level of which jeopardizes the positive fallout expected from decentralization.

The weak financial capacity is exacerbated by persistent limitations and failings in administrative capacities and human resources.

### III.3.  Administrative Capacity

#### III.3.1.  Human resources

The advent of decentralization has revealed a shortage of trained personnel in African countries, all of which lack qualified staff in local administrations. This dearth of trained personnel makes it all the more difficult for local governments to handle additional powers transferred to or granted them.

*Some countries such as Morocco and Mali have opted to establish a territorial civil service, with the aim of making local jobs look more attractive and of conferring on local government staff all the advantages granted to state civil servants.*

A lack of information about the qualifications of local government staff members precludes a comprehensive accounting of staff numbers and skills. Still, data provided by several countries provide an instructive sample. Data from Benin, Côte d'Ivoire, Morocco, Senegal and Tunisia show a very low percentage of the population holding staff positions in local government. In these countries, the percentage of citizens in all levels of government ranges from 0.49% to 3.11%. At the local level it varies from 0.012% to 0.46%: below one staff member per 100 inhabitants. For the countries providing data the percentages are:

- Benin: 0.49% at the national level, 0.012% at the local level.
- Côte d'Ivoire: 0.69% at the national level, 0.029% at the local level.
- Senegal: 0.73% at the national level, 0.06% at the local level.
- Morocco: 1.7% at the national level, about 0.46% at the local level.
- Tunisia: 3.86% at the national level, 0.2% at the local level.

Remedies proposed to date fall into one of two categories: capacity-building within local governments themselves, and transferring state personnel to local governments.

Table 4 illustrates the position.

#### III.3.2.  Existence and level of training of the principal municipal officials

Most local governments need a minimum team to assist the mayor with his or her functions. This administrative core is made up of the secretary-general for general administrative and personnel management, the director of technical services, and the director of financial services. Municipalities in the major urban centers typically have such a team, or the means to recruit it.

The financial weakness of municipalities results in weaknesses in human resources and management skills in local government. This is a severe drawback for the implementation of decentralization policies. Strengthening project management capacities of local government should be a crucial part of all decentralization support programs.

#### III.3.3.  Status of local government personnel

The most common method for addressing this shortfall of personnel is to transfer state senior civil servants to local governments by secondment or by granting leave of absence. Consequently, in many countries the mayor's technical team is comprised of senior officials drawn from the state.

Some countries, such as Morocco and Mali, have established a territorial civil service with the aim of making local jobs look more attractive, and of conferring on local government staff all the advantages granted to state civil servants. This strategy is designed to stimulate interest in local jobs that are perceived as second-rate positions. In many countries, state civil servants regard appointment to local jobs as a punishment or a disgrace.

## Table 4 — Human Resource Situation

| COUNTRY | Number of state civil servants | Number of local government staff | Level of qualification | Legal system (public or private law, or mixed system)/ career job positions | Recruitment procedure (especially for higher positions) | Existing training programmes |
|---|---|---|---|---|---|---|
| Benin | 32,882 (1995) | 4000 from which 94% are support staff and 6% belong to management. | 7% qualified for conceptual and supervisory work. The remainder at average level. | Mixed legal system | Former employees of the prefectures redirected to communes | There is no specialist institution for training local officials |
| Côte d'Ivoire | 112,707 (1994) | 47,325 | Category A4 (engineers, administrators) Category B3 (administrative secretaries, senior technicians, bookkeepers) | Mixed system. Governed by the service regulations for public employees and the law establishing service regulations for territorial authority staff in the case of public employees and the labour code plus the law establishing service regulations for territorial authority staff in the case of other officials. | The line ministry appoints public employees. For other officials, each commune follows its own recruitment policy depending on analysis of the function and needs expressed. | Training is organized by development partners. Moreover, each commune organizes its own training plan. There is no training initiated by the line ministry. |
| Morocco | 537,166 | 145,736 | Senior management: 12,109 Middle management: 25,020 Junior staff: 31,382 Manual workers: 76,982 Other: 223 | Public and private law (employment contracts) | Competitive examination – secondment - automatic appointment by Ministry of the Interior | Regional training centres/Training division of the Ministry of the Interior/Elected local officials' initiatives |
| Senegal | 71,694 (2004) | 6846 | Approx. 3% senior officials / 4% middle management + 90% backup and support staff | Public law for seconded State employees and private law for staff recruited by local governments | Commune staff recruited at the discretion of the local authorities | Ad hoc training programmes depending on support from development partners |
| Tunisia | 390,000 including 80,000 manual workers | 25,000 including 18,000 manual workers | 54 % managerial staff, including 70% male and 30% female 26% junior staff | Public | Competitive examination or applications or qualifications - graduates of approved training centres | - initial training at training centres approved by the administration - further training - ongoing training to achieve promotion - advanced training courses - missions abroad |

*Various mechanisms have been tried to bring local people and community organizations into local public management, ranging from publicizing the meetings of local government bodies, required by law in many countries, to various types of debates and consultation between those bodies and local people*

Even secondment and other stop-gap strategies must be considered partial, short-term solutions. The essential issue is the lack of financial resources to pay for qualified, high-level staff in local governments.

The financial weakness of local governments leads inevitably to weak human resources and limited management capacity —both are grave handicaps in implementing decentralization policies in Africa. Building local government project management capacity should therefore be one of the priorities in all measures supporting decentralization and better local government in Africa.

## IV. Local Democracy

The following table gives a picture of local democracy in each country.

### IV.1. Local Political System

When putting democracy into practice at the community level, local governments often face the same difficulties as modern state systems —a variety of local, tribal and family loyalties and traditions that influence civic behavior. For example, there may be a tendency to reject the notion that "people from outside" might have a right to stand for election locally "when they are not from around here". In other places, such as Senegal, electoral law requires candidates to have party affiliation in local elections. This affiliation with established parties increases the risk that standing for election will have more to do with national party politics than with the needs and preferences of local voters. Despite such difficulties, local democracy has made undeniable progress. In many countries, one sign of increased vitality is an increase in turnover of municipal teams from one local election to another. This turnover is apparent even in countries where change in political power is rare at

parliamentary, presidential or central government levels. And indeed, the lively turnover of power increasingly seen in local elections remains almost unthinkable at top government levels in the majority of African nations.

Participatory democracy can be fostered only if the cultural bedrock already favors consultation, debate and participation in collective decision-making. In this regard the picture in Africa is mixed, with substantial progress in many countries but no movement in others, the latter including Egypt, Togo, Tunisia, Central African Republic and Chad. Overall gains in transparency and accountability remain fragile.

The first indicator of progress is the consensus regarding universal suffrage. Not only has the principle of election become widely accepted for local offices, but African local elections are also being held with a regularity unprecedented in the history of Africa[4].

Another indicator regards the possibility of holding several local mandates at the same time, or holding a local mandate alongside a national one. This is highly restricted and may even be entirely forbidden. In most countries political parties continue to monopolize local and national politics, but many countries do allow independent candidates in local elections. Those nations include Mozambique, Benin, South Africa and Mauritania. In Ghana political parties are excluded from local elections entirely; the list is open only to independent candidates.

### IV.2. Citizen Participation

Signs of progress toward representative democracy include publicizing official meetings and encouraging local people and community organizations to take part in open discussion of local issues. For example, in Zambia, residents are involved in the implementation of certain

4. For instance, with the exception of Mali, where elections have been postponed, the electoral timetable has been respected over the last three years in Burkina Faso, Niger, Guinea, South Africa and Mozambique.

**Table 5    Portrait of Local Democracy in Each Country**

| Country | MUNICIPAL COUNCIL | | | LOCAL EXECUTIVE | | | | | | DIRECT DEMOCRACY |
| --- | --- | --- | --- | --- | --- | --- | --- | --- | --- | --- |
| | Voting system (majority/ proportional or mixed) | Term of office | Rounds of voting | Method of appointment | Terms of office | Mayor | Collegiate | Rounds of voting | Vote of no confidence /removal from office | |
| Benin | Mixed (majority and proportional) | 5 years | 2 rounds | Indirect | 5 years | No | Yes | Several | Yes | No |
| Cameroon | Mixed (majority and proportional) | 5 years | 1 round | Indirect | 5 years | No | Yes | 2 for the Mayor and 1 for deputies | Yes | No |
| Egypt, Arab Rep. of | Relative Majority | 4 years | 1 round | Nomination | | | | | No | No |
| Gabon | Proportional | 5 years | 1 round | Indirect | 5 years | No | Yes | | Yes | No |
| Ghana | Majority | 4 years | 1 round | Indirect | 4 years | No | Yes | | | |
| Guinea | Majority | 5 years | 1 round | Indirect | 5 years | No | Yes | | Yes | No |
| Côte d'Ivoire | Majority | 5 years | 2 rounds | Indirect | 5 years | No | Yes | | Yes | No |
| Kenya | | 5 years | 1 round | Indirect | | | | | | |
| Madagascar | | 4 years | | Direct | 4 years | | | | | |
| Mali | Majority | | | Indirect | 5 years | No | Yes | | Yes | No |
| Morocco | Majority | 6 years | 1 round | Indirect | 6 years | No | Yes | | Yes | No |
| Mozambique | Proportional | 5 years | 2 rounds | Direct | 5 years | Yes | No | 2 rounds | No | No |
| Niger | Proportional | 5 years | 1 round | Indirect | 5 years | No | Yes | | Yes | No |
| Nigeria | Majority | 3 years | 1 round | Direct | 4 years | No | Yes | | Yes | No |
| Senegal | Mixed (Majority/ Proportional or mixed) | 5 years | 1 round | Indirect | 5 years | Yes | No | | Yes | No |
| South Africa | Proportional | 6 years | 1 round | Indirect | 6 years | No | Yes | 1 round | | |
| Tanzania | | 5 years | | Indirect | 5 years | No | Yes | | | |
| Tunisia | Mixed (predominantly majority) | 5 years | 1 round | Indirect | | Yes | Yes | 1 round | No | No |
| Uganda | | 4 years | 1 round | Direct | 4 years | Yes | Yes | 1 round | Yes | |
| Zambia | Mixed | 5 years | 1 round | Direct | 5 years | Yes | No | 1 round | | No |

development projects in basic service sectors, such as health and education. In Uganda, participation sometimes extends as far as cooperation agreements between the municipality and civil society associations; the latter are given responsibility for running a project or for monitoring and evaluating such projects. In some municipalities of Benin, Burkina Faso, Mali and Mozambique, elected officials increasingly use community radio to keep in touch with the local population and continue exchanging views with them about local development issues. These exchanges provide an opportunity for community and religious leaders, teachers and civil society activists to play a role in guiding local people, and in improving communication between officials and residents. To make local government bodies more representative, countries such as Ghana and Niger, Uganda and South Africa have been developing instruments to bring social, economic, or cultural forces into local councils, ensuring that all sociological components of the local community are involved in the local governance system.

To ensure the representation of women, several countries have set quotas by law. In Niger, at least 10% of seats on local councils are reserved by law for female candidates. In Mozambique, the representation of women within local bodies has risen from 23% after the 1999 elections to 28% in 2004. South African legislation favors a minimum of 50% female candidates on competing lists. In Uganda, the law requires that at least one third of local council seats should be occupied by women. Women are not, however, the only demographic group whose specific representation is promoted by decentralization.

## IV.3. Relationship between Central and Decentralized Government Authorities

In the majority of African countries, decentralization was imposed from the top down, making it more a tool used by central government to control territory and urban populations and ensure the continuity of its own structures and policy than a framework for teaching and empowering residents with the goal of strengthening independent local governments.

Consequently, despite constitutional or legislative provisions and safeguards, the autonomy of local governments is restricted by central government oversight of local government bodies and their actions. However, positive developments can be seen in many countries towards slackening controls and refocusing them on legal aspects.

Local administration in Africa rests essentially on two political pillars: a deliberative body, the council, and an executive body comprised of a mayor assisted by one or more deputies. Such local bodies exercise their functions under the control of the state. These features are the norm in all African countries where decentralization is on the agenda. The differences lie in the way local bodies are appointed, and the degree of freedom allowed by the state, which controls local government bodies and their actions. In West and Central Africa, state oversight of local governments is being relaxed. However, in North Africa central control over all the activities of local governments persists with little change. Former colonial systems of centralized control are giving way to models modified by independent governments. This is a positive development in principle even though important matters such as budgets and land allocation are still subject to old, colonial-style control. Neither is jurisdictional control properly organized.

Regarding the transparency of local management and accountability, many countries have enshrined classic control mechanisms in formal statutes. In such cases, councils adopt budgets and review and approve executive bodies' administrative and management accounts. These accounts must also be approved by supervisory authorities. In some countries, specialist institutions, such as the Committee on Local Government and Chiefs' Affairs in Zambia, monitor and oversee local government management. In Uganda, the amounts of financial transfers from central to local government, as well as the local development sectors for which the funds are intended, are made public. The government then encourages local people to ensure that the transferred amounts are used properly. More than that, the web site of the ministry for local government provides a public forum for discussion; citizens are encouraged to state their opinions on any aspect of local authority management.

However, in some countries, there is a large gap between legal procedures and methods of operation in practice.

## IV.4.  Role of Local Government Associations

Establishing associations of elected local bodies, often called Local Government Associations, (LGAs) has become the method of choice for advancing the mutual interests of local governments in Africa. Such associations exist in almost all countries on the continent. Membership may be restricted to mayors and deputy mayors, the municipal executive, or the local authority as an institution.

LGAs may sometimes be set up in accord with categories of local government (communes and cities, regions, rural communities) and typically have a three-fold charge:

- Representing member authorities speaking with a united voice,

- Providing capacity-building services to local governments,

- Defending and promoting the interests of their members.

LGAs provide a platform for exchanging views and discovering opportunities for members. Their aim is to promote decentralization by lobbying the state as well as international development partners. In many countries, they help to implement decentralization by bringing the point of view of local officials to the attention of higher government in reports and proposals.

However, LGAs also experience resource constraints in many countries. They have to rely on contributions from their members to cover costs. The uncertainty of such resources necessarily limits the scope of the LGA's efforts.

In eastern and southern Africa, LGAs are genuine administrative bodies, but some in West Africa and Central Africa have no office or permanent staff. Where resources are minimal, LGAs are less effective in implementing decentralization.

Regional LGAs have also been set up in Central, East and Southern Africa. Some of these regional organizations are more effective than others. For example, The Association of Central African Mayors (AMAC) presently exists in name only, but the association of East African local governments is comparatively dynamic, offering a regional platform for exchanges between elected officials from member countries.[5]

### IV.4.1.  United Cities and Local Governments of Africa (UCLGA)

The organization known as United Cities and Local Governments of Africa (UCLGA) is the Pan-African local government organization. The UCLGA represents a combination of three African local government organizations previously divided along linguistic lines: the African Union of Local Authorities (AULA) for local governments

5. *The East Africa representative on the UCLGA executive committee was appointed during an extraordinary meeting of that association, held in Kigali (Rwanda).*

*The UCLGA represents all local governments in*
*Africa and seeks recognition from the African Union*
*as the voice of African local governments within*
*the Pan-African organization*

from anglophone countries, the Union des Villes Africaines (UVA) for francophone countries and the União dos ciudades y Capitaes Lusofono Africana (UCCLA) for Portuguese-speaking countries.

This initiative reflects a recognition of increasing globalization, a comparatively new phenomenon that cannot fail to affect local governments.[6] The UCLGA founding congress took place in Tshwane in May 2005, marking the starting point of the unified African municipal movement. The UCLGA represents all local governments in Africa and seeks recognition from the African Union as the voice of African local governments within the Pan-African organization.

### IV.4.2. African Conference on Decentralization and Local Development (CADDEL)

In the spirit of African unity, African ministers set up a Pan-African platform for discussion and sharing experience on decentralization and local development in Africa.

Meeting in Windhoek, Namibia, at the second Africités summit in May 2000, African Ministers for Decentralization and finance

ministers decided to move the decentralization process forward in Africa by setting up a political body at continental level known as the African Conference on Decentralization and Local Development (CADDEL).

At that meeting, proponents of decentralization expressed the wish that the African Union should be the reference body for the new platform.

They set CADDEL the following objectives:

• Persuade governments to list decentralization among their priorities and push for greater awareness on the part of both leaders and citizens of the central role played by decentralization in the economic development process;

• Keep decentralization and local development on the national policy agendas of member states, and at continental level within the African Union;

• Make sure that African states maintain their commitment to the decentralization process;

• Act as liaison between the organization of African local government associations and their central governments for all issues involving decentralization and local development;

• Mobilize resources from development partners in order to implement decentralization and local development programmes.

6. The first Pan-African summit "Africities" took place in Abidjan (Côte d'Ivoire) in 1998, gathering together various African municipal unions. During the 2nd Africities summit organized in Windhoek (Namibia) in 2000, the three main municipal organizations agreed upon the creation of an African Union of Cities. In 2003 a first founding assembly took place, during the 3rd Africities summit, in Yaoundé (Cameroon). The common declaration of Yaoundé was adopted with the following principles:
· to promote to local authorities of Africa the founding congress of the association "United Cities and Local Governments"
· to set up the statutes of the new Pan-African organization
· to decide on the definitive name of the organization and prepare its founding congress.

## V. Conclusion

This overall picture of decentralization and local democracy in African countries shows significant progress at the strictly institutional level. No country now publicly opposes the implementation of decentralization policies. Local governments exist in all countries, and elections are held to elect local authorities

Not only are there more local governments covering ever-increasing areas, but the qualitative development of decentralization can also be observed in the form of more self-government and progress toward local democracy in more African nations. This trend is accompanied by an unprecedented increase in the responsibilities of local governments throughout most of the continent.

The extent of such progress must, however, be set against a number of persistent obstacles that continue to hinder a real progression of decentralization in Africa.

Difficulties remain within states concerning the transfer of financial resources needed to match the devolved responsibilities. Local governments also face difficulties in increasing their own resources (aside from state-transfers and grants) at a faster pace. Ensuring the availability of qualified human resources at the local level and improving public access to local services are also fundamental issues of concern.

Tangible progress needs to be made in two key areas: the transfer of responsibilities, with adequate human and financial resources, and entrenching a culture of citizen participation, transparency and accountability. These areas of complicated yet indispensable reform are crucial for progress to be sustained, and for its inherent democratizing ideas to take root. To this end it is essential that all involved parties continue to mobilize high-level political commitment at both national and Pan-African levels.

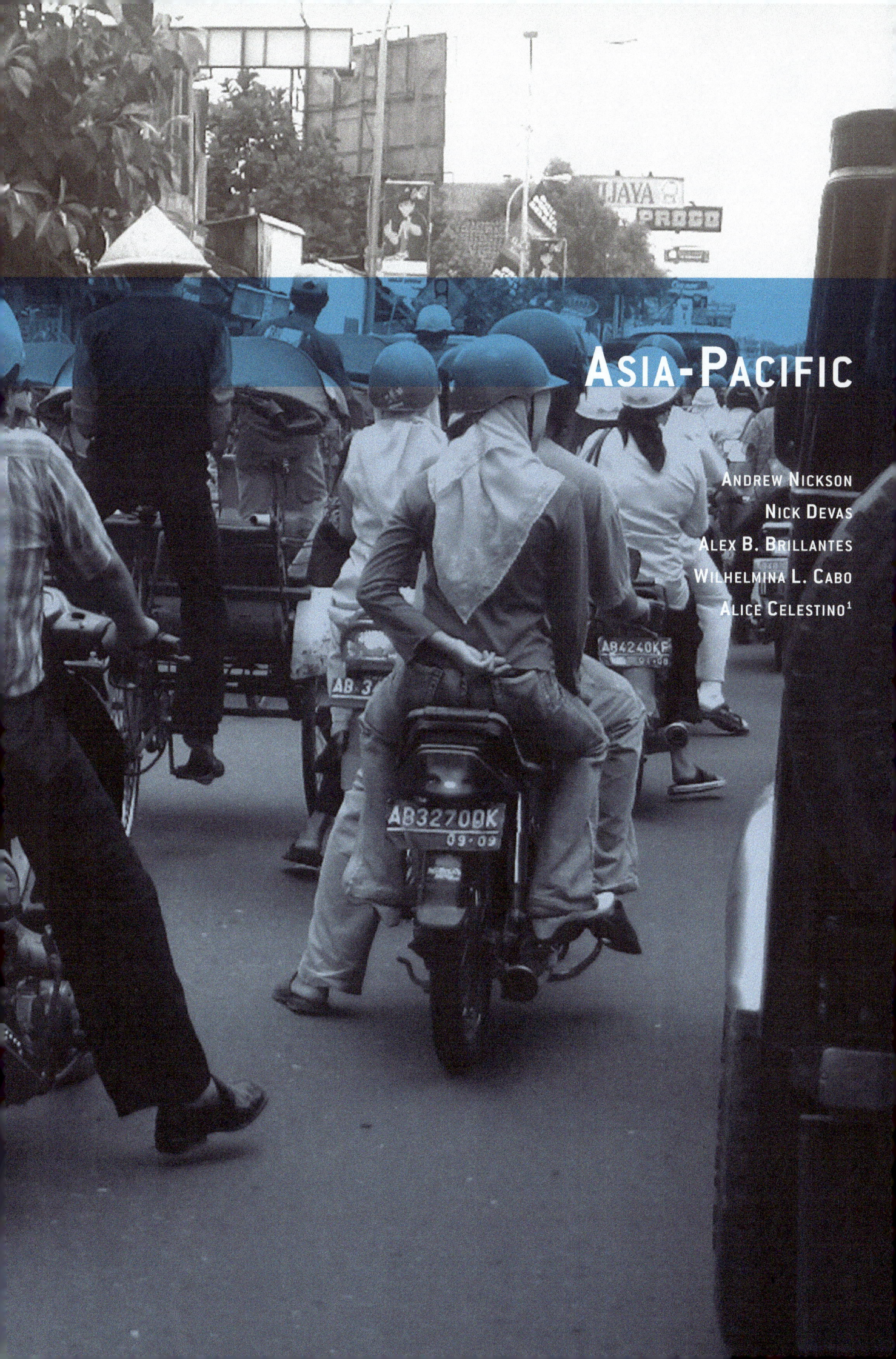

# Asia-Pacific

Andrew Nickson

Nick Devas

Alex B. Brillantes

Wilhelmina L. Cabo

Alice Celestino[1]

1. The final draft has been worked out by Andrew Nickson. The authors gratefully acknowledge the valuable research assistance provided by Mr. Jose Tiu Sanco, Ms. Frances Fatima Cabana and Mr. Prejean Prieto, research staff at the National College of Public Administration and Governance, University of the Philippines.

## I. Introduction

The Asia-Pacific region comprises an enormous variety in the size of nation states. This ranges from the two demographic giants of the world, China and India, which together account for one-third of global population, to the many island states of the Pacific that have less than 100,000 inhabitants. The region also displays a great variety in living standards, ranging from the high-income OECD countries of Australia, Japan, Republic of Korea and New Zealand to a number of the least-developed countries of the world, including Bangladesh and Nepal. It also includes some of the currently fastest growing economies in the world, notably China, India and Vietnam, as well as the country – Korea – that has experienced the most dramatic growth in living standards in the world during the period 1950-2000.

The Asia-Pacific region also embodies great diversity of historical experience. Many of the countries incorporated colonial models of governance to a greater or lesser extent - British, in the case of Australia, New Zealand, India, Pakistan, Sri Lanka, Malaysia and some of the Pacific islands, French in the case of Vietnam, Cambodia and Laos (but largely superseded by communist models in these countries), Dutch in the case of Indonesia and US in the case of the Philippines. Recent laws in Pakistan also reflect US, German and Japanese influences. The single-party communist system adopted by China, Laos, North Korea and Vietnam owes much to the Marxist-Leninist ideology of the former Soviet Union.

| Table 1 | Basic Development Indicators in the Asia-Pacific Region, 2004 | | | | |
|---|---|---|---|---|---|
| **Country** | **Population (millions)** | **Density People per sq. km** | **% Urban Population*** | **GNP per head (US$)** | **HDI Ranking** |
| Australia | 20.1 | 3 | 88.2 | 26,900 | 3 |
| China | 1,296.5 | 139 | 40.4 | 1,290 | 81 |
| India | 1,079.7 | 363 | 28.7 | 620 | 126 |
| Indonesia | 217.6 | 120 | 48.1 | 1,140 | 108 |
| Japan | 127.8 | 351 | 65.8 | 37,180 | 7 |
| Malaysia | 25.2 | 77 | 67.3 | 4,650 | 61 |
| New Zealand | 4.1 | 15 | 86.2 | 20,310 | 20 |
| Pakistan | 152.1 | 197 | 34.9 | 600 | 134 |
| Philippines | 83.0 | 278 | 62.7 | 1,170 | 84 |
| Korea, Rep. of | 48.1 | 488 | 80.8 | 13,980 | 26 |
| Thailand | 62.4 | 122 | 32.3 | 2,540 | 74 |
| Vietnam | 82.2 | 252 | 26.4 | 550 | 109 |

**Source:** *World Bank 2006; UNDESA 2006; UNDP 2006a.*

*\* Data is for 2005.*

This chapter reviews the results of twelve country case studies of decentralization and local democracy from the region: Australia, China, India, Indonesia, Japan, Malaysia, New Zealand, Pakistan, Philippines, Korea, Thailand and Vietnam (Table 1). The sample reflects the more developed and faster growing nations of the region but also those where there is a more active program of decentralization, albeit of widely varying patterns. The chapter draws on other published material on these countries as well as the authors' own knowledge of the region.

*The term 'local government' is generically used in all countries to refer to sub-state/ sub-provincial units*

The Asia-Pacific region embraces the most highly developed features of global urbanization and already contains 23 of the 40 largest metropolitan areas in the world (Table 2). Of the top 100 metropolitan areas, China has 15 (with a combined population of 96.2m), India has 9 (with a combined population of 80.1m) and Japan has 3 (with a combined population of 49.1m).

With such a diversity of population size, per capita income, historical experience and political system, it is not surprising that models of decentralization and subnational governance should also vary considerably. As a result of this lack of homogeneity, it is both difficult and questionable to make sweeping generalizations about the Asia-Pacific region as a whole. In fact, the recent experience of decentralization and local democracy in the region has been quite diverse. Nevertheless, there are some common themes and issues across the region, which are addressed in this chapter. Four of the sample countries –Australia, India, Malaysia and Pakistan– have federal systems of government that accord states a greater or lesser degree of autonomy. Since, within a federal system, local government is generally a state matter, this can produce a wide diversity of practice within a country with regard to local governance. This is certainly true in Australia and India but less so in Malaysia

and Pakistan. The enormous size of China means that, although it is a unitary state, there is a considerable diversity of practice among provinces. To a lesser extent, this is also true in Indonesia.

## II. Territorial Organization

### II.1. Delineating Local Governments

While local governments are generally understood as units of government responsible for providing direct services to inhabitants in a given territorial jurisdiction, their classification and location in the subnational government vary across the Asia-Pacific countries. The term 'local government' is generically used in all countries to refer to these sub-state/sub-provincial units. In a few countries, other terms are used such as 'councils' in Australia and New Zealand, and district administration in Malaysia. In Japan, the preferred term is 'local autonomy' to indicate freedom from central control in making decisions and self-responsibility in managing local affairs. Depending on population size, income and location, local governments in the region are variously categorized as wards, districts, communes, shires, counties, municipalities, cities, prefectures and provinces. And although all these forms are generally considered local governments, their classification also varies such that a municipal unit in one country (Indonesia) may be much bigger than an intermediate local government unit in another one (for example a province in the Philippines or Vietnam).

In federal countries like Australia, India, Malaysia and Pakistan, local governments in general comprise the lowest level of government. In these countries, local governments are a function of the intermediate level of government such as the states in Australia, India and Malaysia and provinces in Pakistan. While there may be some general provisions in federal constitutions concerning local governments, as

| Table 2 | Global Ranking of Metropolitan Areas in the Asia-Pacific Region |
| --- | --- |

| Rank | Name | English name | Country | Population | Remarks |
| --- | --- | --- | --- | --- | --- |
| 1 | Tokyo | Tokyo | Japan | 33,600,000 | (Greater Tokyo Area) incl. Yokohama, Kawasaki, Saitama |
| 2 | Seoul (Soul) | Seoul | Korea | 23,400,000 | incl. Bucheon, Goyang, Incheon, Seongnam, Suweon |
| 5 | Mumbai | Bombay | India | 21,600,000 | incl. Bhiwandi, Kalyan, Thane, Ulhasnagar |
| 6 | Delhi | Delhi | India | 21,500,000 | (National Capital Territory) incl. Faridabad, Ghaziabad |
| 9 | Shanghai | Shanghai | China | 17,500,000 | |
| 10 | Osaka | Osaka | Japan | 16,700,000 | (Osaka Metropolitan Area) incl. Kobe, Kyoto |
| 12 | Kolkata | Calcutta | India | 15,700,000 | (Kolkata Metropolitan Area) incl. Haora |
| 13 | Manila | Manila | Philippines | 15,600,000 | (Metro Manila) incl. Kalookan, Quezon City |
| 14 | Jakarta | Jakarta | Indonesia | 15,100,000 | (Jabotabek Metropolitan Area) incl. Tangerang |
| 15 | Karachi | Karachi | Pakistan | 15,100,000 | |
| 16 | Guangzhou | Canton | China | 14,700,000 | incl. Foshan |
| 19 | Beijing | Beijing | China | 12,800,000 | |
| 20 | Dhaka | Dacca | Bangladesh | 12,600,000 | |
| 28 | Shenzhen | Shenzhen | China | 9,150,000 | |
| 29 | Krung Thep | Bangkok | Thailand | 8,650,000 | |
| 30 | Wuhan | Wuhan | China | 8,650,000 | |
| 33 | Nagoya | Nagoya | Japan | 8,250,000 | |
| 36 | Tianjin | Tiensin | China | 8,000,000 | |
| 37 | Lahore | Lahore | Pakistan | 7,950,000 | |
| 38 | Chennai | Madras | India | 7,850,000 | (Chennai Metropolitan Area) |
| 40 | Bangalore | Bangalore | India | 7,350,000 | (BMRDA) |
| 41 | Hyderabad | Hyderabad | India | 7,150,000 | |
| 43 | Hong Kong (Xianggang) | Hong Kong | China | 7,100,000 | (S.A.R.) incl. Kowloon, Victoria |
| 44 | Taipei (T'ai-pei) | Taipei | Taiwan | 6,700,000 | (Taipei-Keelung Metropolitan Area) |
| 46 | Chongqing | Chungking | China | 6,200,000 | |

**Source:** *The principal agglomerations of the World (2007-09-03).*
*City population, http://citypopulation.de/World.html.*

in the case of India and Malaysia, it is generally left to the state or provincial government to determine the scope of local government in these countries. Thus, it is not surprising that perceptible differences in local government practices exist across the federated states within the same country. The system of election for local councils in Australia, for example, varies from state to state. In India, fiscal and administrative decentralization is unevenly implemented across the states compared with political decentralization, while local democracy is also at varying levels of development across the Indian states. In contrast, local government variation in Malaysia and Pakistan is slight.

*Each country of the region has made significant strides over the past several decades in the creation of a strengthened institutional framework in support of decentralization*

Local governments in unitary states comprise the only sub-national layers of government, thus putting local government directly under central government oversight. Theoretically speaking, unitary governments may incline towards centralism and constrain local autonomy. The experience in the region shows that this is not necessarily so. Robust local governments and local democracy exist in unitary systems like Japan, New Zealand and Philippines, as is also the case in federal Australia. China, though unitary, exhibits a variety of local government practices between provinces owing to the sheer size of the country. This is true to a lesser extent in Indonesia.

Local governments in all countries exercise powers by virtue of ultra vires. The powers, roles and responsibilities are set out in specific legislation or acts promulgated by national or state level government, with some countries having more or fewer local powers and functions assigned to them. Japan is markedly different on this as local governments in this country operate on the basis of the general competence principle. But as reforms continue to characterize intergovernmental relations in the Asia-Pacific countries, the      political and functional bases of local government continue to be redefined. Australia, for instance, is

moving to a less prescriptive approach in regard to the councils' roles and functions, albeit subject to greater public accountability and stricter requirements for corporate planning and reporting. The recent local government reforms, particularly the Local Government Act 2002, undertaken by New Zealand have broadened the responsibilities of local councils practically giving them the power of general competence. Philippine local governments have their powers and responsibilities specifically defined in the Local Government Code. Significantly, the general welfare clause in the Code allows local governments to do practically whatever they think will promote the well- being of people and community, limited only by expressed prohibition of law. In any case, the scope of powers and functions assumed by local governments in the region varies from country to country, and even among local governments within the same country. These practices had been shaped by the respective country's historical traditions, and increasingly by political, economic and fiscal considerations as evidenced by the decentralization programs being implemented by countries in the region. In most countries, local governments perform wide-ranging functions to address local needs and promote economic and social well-being of citizens and local areas. The functions of local governments in the region will be discussed at length in Section III.1.

## II.2.  Legal Framework for Local Government

The legal framework for local government in the Asia-Pacific region is contained either in national constitutions or in separate laws. Major local government legislation in the selected countries is shown in Annex 1. Most countries recognize local government in their constitutions as well as having separate laws for local government. However, local government in Australia is recognized not in the Commonwealth Constitution but in comprehensive Local Government Acts passed by individual state parliaments and in a few cases, references are also made in state constitutions. In New Zealand, which has no consolidated constitution, local government was greatly strengthened by national legislation in 2002 granting it general competence power in marked contrast to previous restrictions imposed by ultra vires. Despite not offering constitutional protection, local governments in both countries enjoy substantial powers and responsibilities that are not observed in several countries in the region that do provide constitutionally for local government autonomy.

Each country of the region has made significant strides over the past several decades in the creation of a strengthened institutional framework in support of decentralization. The framework is established variously in the basic law of the land and in separate national and state statutes and laws. This is the case whether a nation is a multi-party democracy, socialist country or military regime. Even when local self-governance is promoted as a national objective, central government still intervenes to introduce and sustain these reforms. Such was the case in India where the 1950 Constitution (Article 40) requires that "...states shall take steps to organize village panchayats and endow them with such powers and authority as may be necessary to enable them to function as units of local self-government," but left the legislation of local self-government to the states. Because the implementation of panchayats was uneven across the states, decentralization reforms were promoted by the 73rd and 74th constitutional amendments in 1992. These require states to hold elections for local bodies and to transfer fiscal and administrative responsibility for certain services and functions to local government in both rural and urban areas. As a result there has been a dramatic improvement in local democracy in many parts of India but the constitutional requirements for administrative and fiscal decentralization are still not complied with to the same extent by all states. This is also the case in Japan with article 92 of the constitution of 1946, followed by several instances of legislation to decentralize (namely 1947, 1995-1999).

Recent constitutions in the Philippines (1987, Article 10), the Republic of Korea (1987, Articles 117 and 118) and Thailand (1997, Article 78) all provide for local government autonomy, but the constitutions of China and Vietnam (see on the contrary: China, art.110; Vietnam: art.6). In the Philippines, the 1991 Republic Act (Law 7160)–also known as the Local Government Code– fleshed out the constitutional provisions concerning the principle of decentralization and local autonomy, transferring responsibility for the delivery of many basic services to local government and thereby fundamentally altering central-local relations. In Korea the 1987 constitution (Article 117) states that local governments "shall deal with matters pertaining to the well-being of local residents, shall manage properties, and may establish their own rules and regulations regarding local autonomy as delegated by national laws and decrees." However, this constitutional provision remained unfulfilled until July 1995 when the nation elected local government mayors for the first time in more than 30 years. Until then local governments were no more than local administrative districts of the central government. The heads of local governments (in effect, solely administrative authorities) were appointed by the central government, and their capacity for autonomous decision-making was virtually nonexistent. In Thailand the 1997 constitution requires the promotion of decentralization as a basic policy of the government and this was followed by basic legislation in 1999 in the form of the Decentralization Plan and Procedures Act. As of June 2003, eight enabling laws had been proposed in support of decentralization goals, four of which had been promulgated. More generally, more tasks does not mean more responsibility; in India the two higher tiers of local government are considered to be "implementing agencies of state government", also after the 1994 constitutional amendments[2].

2. G. Rao / N. Singh (2000), How to think about local government reform in India? Incentives and institutions, Berkeley, p.9; adde: G. Sethi (ed.) (2004), Fiscal decentralization to rural governments in India, World Bank, p.19

*Within the Asia-Pacific region, there has been a wide range of drivers of decentralization and of obstacles to such changes, but decentralization has generally been driven from the top*

Indonesia provides the most dramatic example of major legislative reform for enhanced local government autonomy. The 'big bang' decentralization took place on the basis of Regional Government Law 22 of 1999, which eliminated the hierarchical relationship between provincial and municipal governments. This significantly shifted resources and responsibilities from the central and provincial levels to urban (kotamad-ya) and rural (kabupaten) municipalities. Under Regional Autonomy Law 32 of 2004 these district governments were assigned 11 obligatory functions while provincial governments were given a secondary role. In line with these expanded responsibilities a major shift of staff resources (about 2.5 million civil servants, of whom about three-quarters were teachers or health workers) took place from the central and provincial governments to the districts during a short transition period (2000-2001). Law 33 on Fiscal Balance between Central and Regional Government in 1999 (later amended by Law 25 of 2004) provided a new intergovernmental fiscal framework for general allocation grants (DAU), which represent block grants to finance the administrative and other costs associated with newly decentralized functions (rather than the earmarked grants of the past). Under the previous centralized system, social and public service indicators of some major resource-producing regions were weak, and to redress this imbalance, these regions were now provided with a share of the revenues generated. Local governments were also granted the power to levy their own taxes supported by regulations on the type of taxes and service charges permissible and maximum tariffs (ADB 2006b). However, to date the legal framework and division of responsibilities among levels of government remains unclear.

## II.3.  Evolution of Local Government Structures

A great variety of historical experience has influenced the evolution of local government structures in the Asia-Pacific region, ranging from the intermarriage of longstanding local traditions of self-governance to organizational forms imported through the colonial experience and Marxist-Leninism. Traditions of community or grassroots self-governance have long existed in the region, though not necessarily in the more sophisticated organizational forms of local government that exist today. For example, in Korea, local government was founded on the basis of informal, voluntary organizations for the purpose of promoting mutual assistance among citizens as well as the strengthening of community ethics (Sproats 2003). In Japan traditional customary institutions are still functioning today in the form of an extensive network of voluntary neighborhood associations that in practice operate as subcontractors of local government. In those countries that came under foreign rule, these old systems underwent a process of colonization that subsequently shaped the forms of local administration that are in operation today. However, national independence encouraged countries such as India and the Philippines to restore their traditional systems of governance, respectively known as panchayats and barangays, and to integrate them into the formal system of local government. During the immediate post-independence period in many countries, centralization was considered to be the most efficient way of achieving the goals of rebuilding national identity and attaining rapid economic growth. Notwithstanding, most of these countries subsequently initiated local government reforms as part of wider processes of improving public sector efficiency and democratization (Sproats 2003).

Within the Asia-Pacific region, there has been a wide range of drivers of decentralization and of obstacles to such changes. In some parts of the world, notably in Latin America during the 1980s and 1990s and in Central and Eastern Europe following the collapse of the Soviet Union, there was a widespread demand from citizens for local democracy and for greater citizen control over local affairs. This has not generally been the case in Asia, where decentralization has more often been driven from the top. In the case of China, decentralization has primarily been about economic reform, as part of the shift towards a market-based economy, and liberating the economic potential of regions and localities, rather than political engagement and local accountability. In Vietnam, the massive Doi Moi (renovation) process initiated in the late 1990s was also primarily about economic and administrative reform, including the devolution of management responsibilities. One feature of Doi Moi was to encourage and legitimize citizen participation in local decision-making as well as to strengthen transparency and accountability mechanisms at the commune level. In this sense, the creation of decentralized structures and processes is a manifestation of a wider movement towards democratization in the region as it provides the enabling context for broader citizen participation in local governance.

By contrast, the recent and quite radical programs of decentralization in the Philippines and Indonesia have been more overtly linked to 'bottom-up' processes of democratization. In the Philippines, the substantial devolution of responsibilities and resources to elected local governments was part of the radical reform agenda of deepening political participation and bringing political decision-making closer to citizens following the 1986 overthrow of the Marcos regime. Indonesia experienced one of the most radical decentralization programs in the world from 1999, shifting major functional responsibilities, resources and staff to local governments. This was partly a response to the highly centralized state under Suharto, which was blamed for many of the ills of the country. Whilst this program built on an existing structure of local government, the reforms devolved substantial decision-making powers to what had previously been little more than a system of deconcentrated local administration (albeit referred to in earlier legislation as 'local autonomy'). Nevertheless, the 'big-bang' decentralization was also strongly driven by the urgent need to satisfy the interests of the resource-rich outer islands

of Indonesia, which had long felt marginalized and were threatening to secede.

In some countries of the region there has been a noticeable cyclical movement to and fro between periods of centralization and decentralization. This has especially been the case in Pakistan, where local government reforms were introduced in 1960, 1979 and 2001. The main objective of the 2001 reform was an attempt by the military government at the center to reinforce its legitimacy and gain popularity across the country. But the institutionalization of local (non-party) political accountability has been thwarted to a significant degree by the continuing provincial control over local government and the difficulty of implementing the provisions for recall of officials (Cheema et al 2006). This was also, to some extent, the case with earlier failed attempts at decentralization in Bangladesh. In Thailand, communist insurgency during the 1970s and 1980s reinforced commitment to strong central control. Only since the 1990s, and despite strong opposition from the Ministry of Interior, have governments supported decentralization. By contrast, in Bangladesh and Malaysia there has been resistance from the center to any substantial decentralization that would strengthen the political role of local government. Thus local government in these countries may be regarded as more akin to local administration.

Decentralization is never a smooth process as there are many competing interests at play, some of which resist decentralization. Strong resistance can come from a central ministry that perceives that decentralization erodes its powers and resources. For similar reasons, central civil servants may resist decentralization, especially when it involves their reassignment to a sub-national level of government, as was the case for large numbers of civil servants in Indonesia and Thailand. Party political rivalry can also be a major obstacle, where parties position themselves by opposing proposals for de-

*By contrast, the recent and quite radical programs of decentralization in the Philippines and Indonesia have been more overtly linked to 'bottom-up' processes of democratization*

*There is a considerable variation in the Asia-Pacific region in both the number of tiers of local government and in the average population size covered by local government*

centralization. This is compounded by political competition at sub-national levels: ruling parties at the national level may get cold feet about decentralization if they perceive that the opposition may gain control of large numbers of the decentralized units. Three-way political conflicts among union, state and local governments in India were one of the main reasons for the 1992 constitutional amendments designed to protect the interests of local governments from excessive state interference. Such political conflicts continue to hamper effective decentralization in some Indian states.

Finally, the OECD countries in the region, Australia, Japan, the Republic of Korea and New Zealand, also emphasize decentralization as part of their ongoing administrative reform process. Australia, Japan and New Zealand have a long history of local government; so, recent experience here has been of relatively modest reform to deal with particular problems or changed circumstances. A series of reforms to local government acts in all the states of Australia expanded the general powers of local government during the 1990s. An Inter-Governmental Agreement in 2006 expanded local government responsibilities in the fields of planning, health, environmental protection and cultural activities. In New Zealand, the Local Government Act of 2002 granted local and regional government broad general powers.

In Japan, House and Diet Resolutions on decentralization were passed in 1993 based on the premise that the centralized administrative system was unable to cope with rapid developments at the local level. In 1995 a Law for the Promotion of Decentralization was passed, in 1998 a Decentralization Promotion Plan was initiated and in 2004 the Local Government Law of 1947 was amended to strengthen the administrative authority of cities.

In the Republic of Korea, a series of decentralization laws and policies were intro-

duced in the 1990s that increasingly recognized the importance of local autonomy, including the introduction of direct election for local government executives. As in Japan, they were largely driven from the center. One writer has described the actual practice of decentralization in Korea as a "curious mixture of deconcentration and devolution" (Seong 1998:13). A unique feature of the process was the Saemaul Undong, a community-based movement established during the rule of President Park Chung Lee in the 1970s. Although these were mobilized 'top-down' by central government, they eventually laid the foundation for a variant of 'citizen participation' that made a significant contribution to Korean rural development.

## II.4. Tiers and Size of Local Governments

There is a considerable variation in the Asia-Pacific region in both the number of tiers of local government and in the average population size covered by local government. The territorial organization of local government in selected countries is presented in Table 3. Two of the four federal nations in the case study countries have a single tier of local government below the state level (Australia and Malaysia) while Pakistan has a triple tier and India has a single tier in urban areas and a single, double or triple tier in rural areas, depending on the state. Of the eight unitary nations in the sample, four have a two tier system of local government (Indonesia, Japan, Thailand and New Zealand), while three others have a three tier system (Philippines, Korea and Vietnam) and China has four subnational government layers. Furthermore, what is a local government tier is not always clear, especially when there is a combination of modern local government structures and of traditional or customary institutions, as is usual in a lot of countries of the region at the village level. Even the material evidence of such basic criteria as the exercise of public and budgetary power may be uncertain.

**Table 3**  Territorial Organization of Local Government in the Asia-Pacific Region

| Country | Type of government | Type of state | Federated units, regions or territories with special rights | Regional / provincial level | Upper level of local government | Lower level of local government |
|---|---|---|---|---|---|---|
| **Australia** | Costitutional and parliamentary democracy (Governor general representing the Queen as head of State, Prime Minister as chief of government) | Federal | 6 states and 2 territories | | | Single Tier: 703 councils variously described as cities, municipalities, shires or districts with 7 differents local authority systems. The Australian Capital Territory (ACT) of Canberra has its own local government system |
| **China (2006)[2]** | Communist state (President as chief of state, Premier as head of government) | Unitary | Not applicable | **1) Provincial level: 34 units** <br> -23 Provinces, <br> - 4 large cities directly under central government <br> - 5 autonomous* regions: Inner Mongolia, Guangxi Zhuang, Tibet, Ningxia Hui, Xinjiang Uygur <br> -2 special administrative regions: Hong-Kong, Macao <br><br> **2) Regional level: 333 units:** <br> -283 cities of regional level <br> -17 regions (diqu) <br> -30 autonomous prefectures (zi zhi zhou) <br> -3 unions (meng) | **District level: 2,860 units** <br> -1,463 districts (xian) <br> -369 cities with district right <br> -856 inner city districts in larger cities <br> -117 autonomous* districts (zi zhi xian) <br> -49 ethnic banners (qi) <br> -3 autonomous* banners (zi zhi qi) <br> -2 special zones <br> -1 forest zone | **Township level: 41,040 units** <br> -14,119 townships (xiang) <br> -19,369 boroughs (zhen) <br> -10 joint township boards (qu gong suo) <br> -6,355 inner city wards <br> -1,088 ethnic townships (min zu xiang) <br> -98 tribes (sumu) <br> -1 ethnic tribe <br><br> -644,000 village committees (85% of villages) and 71,375 urban neighborhood committees (70% of neighborhood communities-2004) are not local authorities |
| **India** | Parliamentary Democracy (President as chief of state, Prime Minister as head of government) | Federal | 28 states and 7 union territories | \*Urban areas: Single Tier: 3,694 urban municipalities <br> \*Rural areas: Single, dual, or triple tiers depending on state, 246,977 rural councils comprising of: <br> - 459 zilla panchayats (district: third tier), <br> - 5,930 panchayat samitis (block: second tier) <br> - 240,588 gram panchayats (village: first tier) | | |
| **Indonesia** | Republic, presidential government (President is both the chief of state and head of government) | Unitary | 2 special districts: Aceh, Papua | 33 provinces (including special districts) Capital district Jakarta | Single Tier: 450 units (2006) <br> - municipalities (urban): Kotamadya (2004:91) <br> - regencies (rural): Kabupaten (2004:349) <br> - Villages (Desa): (pop. approx. 70,000). Their organization and functioning are the responsability of the provincial authorities (law n° 22/1999). | |
| **Japan** | Constitutional Monarchy with a Parliamentary Government (Emperor as chief of state, Prime Minister as head of government) | Unitary | Not applicable | 47 prefectures | 1,820 municipalities. 779 city councils, 844 town councils and 197 village councils | |
| **Malaysia** | Constitutional Monarchy (Paramount Ruler as chief of state, Prime Minister as head of government) | Federal | 13 states 3 federal territories | | 144 local government units (depending on population): <br> - 10 city councils, <br> - 36 municipal councils for large towns <br> - 98 district councils (areas with small urban centers) | |

2. *Data on China from: Quio Jing (2005). La réforme de l'administration chinesse face aux rites confucéens, Thesis, University Paris 1, Panthéon-Sorbonne. (P. 125) (unpublished). Updated by Dr. Qiao.*

| Table 3 | Territorial Organization of Local Government in the Asia-Pacific Region (cont.) |

| Country | Type of government | Type of state | Federated units, regions or territories with special rights | Regional / provincial level | Upper level of local government | Lower level of local government |
|---|---|---|---|---|---|---|
| New Zealand | Costitutional and parliamentary democracy (Governor general representing the Queen as head of State, Prime Minister as chief head of government) | Unitary | Not applicable | 12 Regional Councils 4 unitary district councils | 74 Territorial Local Authorities (TLA) including among which: - 4 unitary district councils), - 15 city councils, - 54 district councils, Chatham Islands Council Community boards: created by TLA at their discretion: 150 in 2006 in 50% of TLA | |
| Pakistan | Republic, presidential government (President as chief of state, Prime Minister as head of government) | Federal | 4 provinces | 111 district units including: - City districts: - Large metropolitan areas - Federal capital district (no self-government) | 396 sub-district units: - Tehsil in districts - Town Municipal Administration (TMA) in city districts | 6,125 union administrations |
| Philippines | Republic, presidential government, (President is both the chief of state and head of government) | Unitary | Autonomous region of Mindanao | 83 provinces | 120 cities 1501 municipalities | 41,982 villages (barangays) |
| Korea, Rep. of | Republic, presidential government (President is both the chief of state and head of government | Unitary | Special autonomous province of Jeju | 9 provinces 6 metropolitan cities Seoul (special metropolitan city) | 230 municipal units: Seoul: 25 Metropolitan cities: 49 Provinces: 75 cities 81 rural districts | Lower municipal units (wards): Dong (urban), Erp/Myeon (rural) differentiated according to population: Eup = larger unit in rural areas (over 50,000, Eup may become a city) Seoul: 522 Dong Metropolitan cities: 689 Dong; 10 Eup / 36 Myeon Provinces (incl. Jeju): 942 Dong, 213 Eup, 1,112 Myeon |
| Thailand | Constitutional monarchy (King as chief of state, Prime Minister as head of government, at present provisional military government) | Unitary | | 75 Provincial Administrative organizations Bangkok Metropolitan Administration | 1,129 municipalities (cities and boroughs) Pattaya City Council 6,744 Sub-district (tambon) Administrative Organizations (rural) | |
| Vietnam | Communist government (President as chief of state, Prime Minister as head of government) | Unitary | Not applicable | 59 provinces 5 centrally controlled cities (including the capital city) | 662 district units, among which: 25 provincial towns, 42 urban districts (in centrally controlled cities), | 10,776 municipalities: 1,181 wards (urban areas) 583 district towns (rural district centres) 9,012 communes (lower units in urban and rural areas) |

**Source:** *UCLG Country Profiles (2007).*
   *Autonomous areas means a special administrative regime based on the recognition of special rights for ethnic groups.*

The average population size of local governments in the region is shown in Table 4. The relevance of this ratio depends very much on whether the lower tier is devised as a rather large jurisdiction adequate to perform a number of functions, or whether it is closer to settlements and has to maintain a link with the people. Both may exist in the same countries; then, the significance of the ratio depends on the distribution of functions. We have indeed to take in to account that some countries have a two tier local level (most Indian states, Pakistan, Philippines, Korea, Vietnam), whereas others have only a single tier local level (Australia, Indonesia, Japan, Malaysia), and exceptionally three tiers in some Indian states and in China. To make a comparison, we have to take in to account the functions of these levels. Indeed, major local government functions are usually exercised at the upper local level in countries with a two tier local level. Therefore, the upper level has to be taken for the comparison with countries having a single tier local level. Conventionally, we call it a district whatever its name in the respective countries.

This table is probably misleading in some respects. It overlooks the role of the provincial state administration, with its local branches in Thailand, which allows a higher degree of fragmentation. It underestimates the role for the people of lower level municipal administrations, and its value in terms of local democracy (for example in India or the Philippines). However, the high ranking of the ratio suggests decentralization at the meso level rather than at the local level (for example in Indonesia, Pakistan and Korea), and a low profile at the municipal level.

**Table 4    Average Population Size of Local Governments in the Asia-Pacific Region**

| Country | Population (m) | Number of local governments | Average size of local government |
|---|---|---|---|
| Australia | 20.1 | 703 | 28,592 |
| China | 1,296.5 | 2,860 | 453,147 |
| India | 1,079.7 | 9,624 | 112,115 |
| Indonesia | 217.6 | 450 | 483,556 |
| Japan | 127.8 | 1,820 | 70,220 |
| Malaysia | 25.2 | 144 | 175,000 |
| New Zealand | 4.1 | 73 | 54,931 |
| Pakistan | 152.1 | 396 | 384,091 |
| Philippines | 83.0 | 1,621 | 51,300 |
| Korea, Rep. of | 48.1 | 230 | 209,010 |
| Thailand | 62.4 | 7,874 | 7,924 |
| Vietnam | 82.2 | 662 | 124,169 |

**Source:** *Table 1 and Table 3.*

The changing 'shape' of territorial organization in the region reflects two very dissimilar processes under way. In the high-income OECD case study countries, the number of local governments has fallen in recent years as a result of amalgamation promoted by central government in pursuit of economies of scale in service delivery. In Australia, as a result of state policies, the number of local authorities diminished by 200 in the last 30 years. In Japan, an amalgamation policy from 2001, encouraged by the central government to capture these scale economies, reduced the number of local governments from 3,229 to 1,820. In New Zealand, a major territorial reform in 1989 dramatically reduced the number of local governments from 830 by creating an upper tier of 12 regions in addition to 74 lower-tier local governments. In Korea, the central government's efforts to consolidate local governments in

*In lower income countries, in order to support*

*the development of democracy and the legitimacy of political*

*leaders, local councils or authorities elected by the residents*

*have been restored, but at the same time major functions*

*have been devolved upon the intermediate level*

1994 and 1995 was undertaken not only to realize economies of scale but also to correct the much-criticized manner of demarcating the boundaries of local governments. As a result of this reform, the number of local governments was reduced from 265 to 241 (including autonomous districts and rural districts in Seoul and metropolitan cities). The boundaries of rural districts and secondary cities were redefined to form urban-rural integrated cities separated from newly created urban districts.

In lower income countries, the picture is much more contrasted. In order to support the development of democracy and the legitimacy of political leaders, local councils or authorities elected by the residents have been restored, but at the same time major functions have been devolved upon

the intermediate level. This is typical for Chinese reforms: village committees are directly elected in more than 644,000 Chinese villages every three years. The committees deal with the lease of land and the management of local affairs; however, main responsibilities are carried out at the province and county levels. The same movement can be seen in Vietnam. The number of communes has increased by 265 units between 2000 and 2004. The vitality of traditional village institutions is supported by the government and some administrative tasks can be delegated to them by the people's committee of the commune. Even so, the key levels of local government are provinces and districts. Similar trends can be observed in the non-communist countries. For example, the Indonesian reform of 1999 resulted in the transfer of important responsibilities to local governments, but in the form of very large municipal units (on average near 450,000 inhabitants), whereas villages are the framework of citizen participation. In the Philippines, there is less concentration of local government functions at the upper level; nevertheless, the municipal governments are still relatively large, with more than 50,000 inhabitants on average. The barangays, communities of pre-colonial origin reshuffled by law at the time of the Spanish colonization, constitute an avenue of participation and of access to some administrative service rather than a government level.

In several other lower income countries, there has been a process of municipalization with more tasks transferred to a local level closer to the inhabitants while nevertheless endowed with some administrative capacity. The major example is India, although the situation may vary considerably from one state to another: the lowest level, the gram panshayat, has to manage pre-school and primary education, provide some local services (libraries) and amenities (sport, leisure) and support local agricultural and economic development. In Pakistan, too, although the sub-district level is crucial, union administrations are local government units of a fair size and some capacity. In Thailand, the reforms of 1999 and 2003 resulted in municipal-level consolidation in cities and boroughs and in the upgrading of sub-district administrative organizations into units of local self government. These units subsumed the headmen that until that time had been elected by the people but subordinated to the provincial administration. These reforms represent an important step towards the generalization of municipal government in Thailand – although the government system as a whole remains rather centralized.

The very rapid pace of urbanization in Asia – a seven-fold increase in urban population since 1950 (ADB 2006a) – presents huge challenges for urban governance. At the same time, decentralization policies in many countries are increasingly putting these challenges into the hands of local governments (ibid. p.4). Although city and urban municipal governments are often some of the longest-established local governments in these countries (some going back over a century) they have generally been unable to keep pace with the demands of urbanization. A city or municipal government often covers only the historic core that spawned a vast metropolitan area. Although its boundaries may, in some cases, have been enlarged, this has very rarely been sufficient to keep pace with the rapid urban expansion.

As a result, the urban periphery is often governed by a multiplicity of smaller municipalities, town and village councils, without any overall system of metropolitan-wide management. The available fiscal resources are often concentrated in the core city, while the poorly served periphery (where many of the poorest live) is governed by various municipal and village councils that have access to minimal resources. This fragmentation of urban governance presents huge problems in the financing

and management of infrastructure and services across the city.

A few metropolitan areas (Metro Manila, Bangkok, Tokyo) have a functioning metropolitan level of government and in China strong municipal governments that encompass large rural hinterlands have always governed the largest cities. In Australia, most of the metropolitan populations live outside central cities and informal cooperation about planning has served as a means of metropolitan governance. Uniquely, the city government of Brisbane encompasses the whole metropolitan area (ADB 2006a). In New Zealand, 12 local governments representing the largest cities and peripheral districts in the six biggest metropolitan regions have joined with local government associations to develop joint strategies to address governance issues.

Elsewhere, there may only be some form of coordinating mechanism between the various municipal governments. But it rarely has the power or resources to tackle metropolitan-wide infrastructure and service needs. For example, in Jakarta, the remit of the city government (DKI) covers only what was the metropolitan area until around the 1970s. In recent years four additional city governments have been created in the adjoining areas where most new development has taken place. Although there is a planning framework for the whole metropolitan region (Jabodetabek), this has to operate on the basis of consensus among the constituent authorities.

A further complication is the multiplicity of agencies involved in urban development, infrastructure and service provision. This has been a particular issue in India where there has been a long tradition of special purpose agencies (SPAs). Thus, in a city such as Bangalore, there is a plethora of SPAs in addition to the state government, the municipal government and the municipal and village governments in the surrounding area. The SPAs include the Bangalore Development Authority, the Bangalore Water and Sewerage Board and the Karnataka Slum Clearance Board (Devas 2005). This leads to overlaps, gaps and the lack of a coordinated response to the needs of the rapidly growing population. In many large cities of the region, endemic political conflict between the various levels of government –municipal, state and central– make metropolitan coordination even more problematic.

## III. Powers and Responsibilities, Management and Finances

### III.1. Functions of Local Government

As in other parts of the world, local governments in the selected countries of the Asia-Pacific region have multiple roles to

*Education is the most notable service delivered by local government in the region. The only exceptions are Australia, New Zealand and Malaysia, where basic education remains a state or central government responsibility*

perform: service delivery, governance, planning and community development, and regulation and supervision. Table 5 provides a profile of the functions that are the responsibility of local government. Generally speaking, all countries have decentralized some basic services to this level, including planning, education, provision of social and health services, water supply, public transport and business development support. In Indonesia, the 2004 decentralization legislation (Law 32) devolved a comprehensive list of 16 obligatory functions to local government.

Education is the most notable service delivered by local government in the region. Local governments in China, Japan, India, Indonesia, Pakistan, Vietnam and the Philippines are involved in the delivery of basic education, ranging from preschool to secondary school. The only exceptions are Australia, New Zealand and Malaysia, where basic education remains a state or central government responsibility. Some aspects of health and welfare services are delivered by local government in most countries in the region except for Australia and New Zealand, where these functions remain with the state and central government respectively. In Korea, health and social welfare accounted for 31% of total local expenditure in the consolidated local government budget for 2007. In the Philippines, health and welfare services have been fully devolved since 1992. Water supply is primarily a local government responsibility in several countries of the region (e.g. Australia, Japan, Indonesia, Pakistan and Vietnam). By contrast, electricity supply remains a central government responsibility throughout the region except in China where it is a municipal responsibility.

In New Zealand, under the influence of New Public Management (NPM), there has been a dramatic increase in private sector participation in local service delivery. The 1989 Local Government Act requires local authorities to "give due consideration to the advantages and disadvantages of different delivery options" in the provision of local services. This led to a large increase in contracting out and by the mid-1990s 75% of all services were delivered by private contractors (Boston 1996). In India, the pressure on recruitment, together with the spread of NPM initiatives at the state level, has also encouraged many local governments take up new activities and service provision arrangements through public-private partnerships, but corresponding systems of contract supervision and 'public service comparators' are still not very well developed.

In addition to the functions listed in Table 5, many local governments in the region also perform some public works functions such as road construction (e.g. Australia,

| Table 5 | Services Delivered by the Local Governments in the Asia-Pacific Region |
|---|---|

| Country | Planning | Basic education | Basic social welfare | Basic health services | Water supply | Electricity supply | Public transport | Business development support |
|---|---|---|---|---|---|---|---|---|
| Australia | Yes | No | No | No | Yes | No | Yes | Yes |
| China | Yes | Yes | Yes | Yes | Yes | Yes | No | Yes |
| India | Yes | Yes | No | Yes | Yes | No | Yes | Yes |
| Indonesia | Yes | Yes | Yes | Yes | Yes | No | Yes | Yes |
| Japan | Yes | Yes | Yes | Yes | Yes | No | Yes | Yes |
| Malaysia | Yes | No | No | No | Yes | No | Yes | Yes |
| New Zealand | Yes | No | No | No | Yes | No | Yes | Yes |
| Pakistan | Yes | Yes | Yes | Yes | Yes | No | Yes | Yes |
| Philippines | Yes | No | Yes | Yes | Yes | No | No | Yes |
| Korea, Rep. of | Yes | Yes | Yes | Yes | Yes | No | Yes | Yes |
| Thailand | Yes | Yes | Yes | No | Yes | No | Yes | Yes |
| Vietnam | Yes | Yes | Yes | Yes | Yes | No | Yes | Yes |

**Source:** *UCLG Country Profiles (2007).*

India, Pakistan and Philippines) and even airports (Australia). In most countries of the region local government also has a responsibility for environmental protection although its powers of enforcement tend to be severely limited. China is the only country where local governments in autonomous regions perform functions normally reserved for central government (e.g. judicial administration, scientific research, unemployment benefits and pensions).

A number of local governments in the region engage directly in business activities. This is especially so in China and Vietnam, where local governments are major producers of industrial goods. In New Zealand, the 2002 Local Government Act enabled local governments to create a

Local Authority Trading Enterprise (LATE). These companies, in which the local governments may hold 50% or more of the equity, employ their own staff and are subject to company taxation. They operate in activities such as public transport, shopping malls, cinemas and car parks as well as water utilities, property management and quarrying. Some provinces in the Philippines own major facilities such as convention centers and shopping centers that are managed as 'profit centers' to provide additional sources of local revenue. Elsewhere, at the very least, local governments provide support services for business development activities. The most common commercial activity of municipalities is the operation of local public enterprises such as markets, slaughterhouses, bus terminals and car parks.

**Table 6**    Relative Size of Local Government Expenditure and Income in the Asia-Pacific Region

| Country | Total public expenditure a) as % of GDP b) € per capita | Local public expenditure (local and meso level only) a)% GDP b)€ per capita | Ratio local public expenses/total public expenses | Ratio local public investment exp/ total civil public investment expenditure | Tax shares + general grants as % of the total LG Income | Local tax revenues (= tax revenues subject to a local tax power) as % of total LG income |
|---|---|---|---|---|---|---|
| Australia | a) 37% | a) 2% | 7% | 6% | 52% | 38% |
| (2005) | b) €11,486 | b) €276 | | | | |
| China | a) 27% | a) 22% | 81% | n/a | 32% | 29% |
| (2004) | b) €291 | b) €235 | | | | |
| India | a) 19.1% | a) Karnataka: 2.9% | Karnataka: 18.5% | n/a | Rural panchayat: 90% (all India average) | Urban local bodies: 60% of revenues from property tax (all India average) |
| (2002) | b) n/a | b) n/a | | | | |
| Indonesia | a) 19% | a) 6% | 33% | 36% | 70% | <10% |
| (2006) | b) €189 | b) €62 | | | | |
| Japan | a) 22.9% | a) 12.3% | 53.6% | n/a | 69% | 34% |
| (2004) | b) €7,243 | b) €3,903 | | | | |
| Malaysia | a) 27% | a) 4% | 13% | 11% | 35% | 26% |
| (2003) | b) €1,152 | b) €155 | | | | |
| New Zealand | a) 42% | a) 3.9% | 9.4% | 16% | 68% | 56% |
| (2005) | b) €9,693 | b) €380 | | | | |
| Pakistan* (2005) | a) 18.5% | a) 2.6% | 14% | n/a | 90% | 10%** |
| Korea, Rep. of | a) 36% | a) 16% | 44% | n/a | 53% | 34% |
| (2005) | b) n/a | b) n/a | | | | |
| Thailand | a) 21% | a) 2% | 9% | 15% | 45% | 12% |
| (2002) | b) €376 | b) €34 | | | | |
| Vietnam | a) 24% | a) 11% | 48% | 51% | 44% | 24% |
| (2002) | b) n/a | b) n/a | | | | |

**Sources:** *IMF 2006; OECD 2005; World Bank 2004, 2006; and country profiles; + Add. Sethi (2004); Weist (2004). UCLG Country Profiles (2007)*
*\* Estimates based on own calculations [sources: Cyan, M. (2006); ADB/DfID/WB (2004)].*
*\*\*Estimate including all own revenues.*

## III.2. Local Government Finances

The relative economic size of local government varies widely across the region, as shown in Table 6. In China, the different tiers of local government play a major role in service provision and local economic development. Local governments manage some 80% of state-owned enterprises. As a result, they account for 81% of public expenditure and 22% of GDP. In Japan, local governments have wide functional responsibilities and account for over half of total public expenditure and 10% of GDP. In Indonesia, as a result of the recent 'big bang' decentralization, local governments now account for one-third of total public expenditure. By contrast, despite their long-established traditions, local governments in Australia and New Zealand have quite limited responsibilities and account for less than 10% of public expenditure and around 2-4% of GDP. The size of local government in Vietnam has risen rapidly in recent years – more than doubling in absolute size and increasing from 40% to 48% as a share of total public expenditure from 1997-2002. Nevertheless, until it implemented the 2004 State Budget Law, Vietnam was formally one of the least decentralized countries in the world, with local governments essentially carrying out deconcentrated functions at the behest of the central government (World Bank 2005:87). For the biggest countries of the region, global data hide enormous disparities between regions and between local governments.

Local governments of the selected countries in the Asia-Pacific region are all equipped with powers of taxation, as shown in Table

| Table 7 | The Scope of Local Tax Powers in the Asia-Pacific Region |
|---|---|
| **Country** | **Major local taxes** |
| **Australia** | Property |
| **China** | Collective enterprise, agricultural and real estate |
| **India** | Property, octroi (tax on goods entering the municipality) |
| **Indonesia** | Hotel and restaurant, entertainment, advertisement, electricity (street lighting), non-strategic and non-vital mining, parking, groundwater and environment. In addition, proceeds from taxes on land and property, motorized vehicles, vehicle transfer and fuel are shared with provinces. |
| **Japan** | Individual inhabitant, business, local consumption and automobile, property tax, city planning tax, local tobacco tax |
| **Malaysia** | Property |
| **New Zealand** | Property |
| **Pakistan** | District/city: education, health, vehicles (excluding motor vehicles) Tehsil: services, property and sale of property |
| **Philippines** | Property, business, amusement, sand and gravel, printing and publication, franchise and community |
| **Korea, Rep. of** | Property, business, acquisition, registration, license, inhabitant, farmland, butchery, leisure, tobacco consumption, urban planning, regional development, motor fuel and local education |
| **Thailand** | Property, land and building, land development, signboard, slaughter duties, swallow nest duties, tobacco, petroleum and hotel |
| **Vietnam** | Land and house, natural resources (excluding those on petroleum activities), license, land use rights transfer and land rent. |

**Sources:** *UCLG Country Profiles (2007).*

*National Tax Service of the Republic of Korea (2006).*

*Weist (2001).*

7. Property taxation is by far the major source of local taxation; in Japan it accounts for 46.2% of own tax revenues (before the "Trinity Reform"); in Australia this accounts for 100% of own-revenue and in New Zealand for 91% of own-revenue. In both countries, as well as in China, local governments also have discretion over the rate of property taxation whereas elsewhere this tends to be determined by central or state government. In some countries, business (or enterprise) taxation is also a major source of own-revenue. Municipalities throughout the region also collect taxes on hotels, restaurants and places of entertainment. Some local taxes are peculiar to a specific country. For example, city governments in Japan impose an urban planning tax, Pakistani municipalities impose health and education taxes and Chinese munici-

*Ideally, the financial resources at the disposal of a local government – whether from its own sources[3] or from grants and transfers – should be sufficient to cover all services that it is mandated to deliver*

palities impose collective enterprise and agricultural taxes. In Indonesia since 2004, municipalities may impose a tax on surface water. Together with the existing local tax on groundwater, this authority is part of the government's effort to curb environmental damage from over-exploitation of water resources.

In China, Indonesia and Vietnam, the proceeds of some locally collected taxes are shared with higher tiers of government. In China, revenue from personal income tax, product tax, business tax and joint enterprise tax are all shared between central and local government. In Vietnam, local governments have no taxing powers at all. Instead, they share with central government the proceeds

from VAT, corporate income tax, income tax on high-income earners, special consumption tax on domestic goods and services, and gasoline and oil tax. Other tax revenues are exclusively assigned to them, namely land and housing taxes, natural resource taxes (excluding petroleum), license tax and land use rights transfer tax. In Indonesia, local governments share the proceeds of taxes on land and property, and on motorized vehicles and fuel with provincial government. Many municipalities also levy user fees and charges that comprise a minor part, typically less than 10%, of their total own-source revenues.

While local governments all have their own tax sources, the degree of fiscal autonomy also varies considerably between countries. The more developed countries, such as New Zealand and Australia generate a substantial share of their revenues locally and are hence less reliant on intergovernmental fiscal transfers. The share of grants in total local government revenue has fallen in both Australia and New Zealand in recent years - from 23% in the 1980s to 16% in the late 1990s in Australia and from 18% to 10% over the same period in New Zealand (OECD 2001). In Japan the local finance reform ("Trinity Reform") 2005-2007 replaces targeted subsidies by tax revenues (transfer from the national personal income tax upon the individual inhabitant tax, however for a lower expected yield) and the global tax grant, until now a major equalizing transfer from central budget, is being reduced drastically. By contrast, in lower-income countries of the region such as India, Indonesia, Pakistan and Thailand, local governments (outside the major urban centers) generate a much smaller share of their total revenues from local tax sources (typically 10-30%) and hence are heavily reliant on central transfers and grants. In Thailand, according to the 1999 Decentralization Plan and Procedures Act, local governments were to be allocated at least 20% of the national government budget by fiscal year 2001 and at least 35% by fiscal year 2006. The latter goal has not yet been reached and these targets have been the subject of heated debate. However, the degree of local fiscal autonomy is not necessarily a function of the overall income level of the country. For example, Japanese local government only raises 34,4% of its total income from own-taxes while local governments in China receive only 32% of their incomes from grants and shared taxes of central government. This disparity reflects the very strong role that local government in Japan plays as an 'agent' of central government in the delivery of services, especially education and social welfare, which are financed by earmarked inter-governmental fiscal transfers. In contrast, the much stronger practice of fiscal decentralization in China through the mechanism of revenue sharing is counterbalanced by extreme political centralization.

Ideally, the financial resources at the disposal of a local government –whether from its own sources[3] or from grants and transfers- should be sufficient to cover all services that it is mandated to deliver. This is not the case in India, Pakistan and the Philippines. In these countries own-source revenues of local governments plus transfers received are together insufficient to fund the delivery of local services, suggesting the need for the devolution of extra tax powers in order to correct this imbalance. By contrast, the strength of municipal associations in the OECD countries of the region has ensured that the corresponding extra revenues required to comply with new mandates have accompanied the devolution of new responsibilities to local government. In Australia, such 'cost shifting' to local government was a central point of a 2006 Inter-Governmental Agreement between the Local Government Association and the federal government. In New Zealand, it has been one of the major issues that contributed to successive waves of local government reform from 1989 onwards. Complicating this

problem is the issue of 'unfunded mandates,' namely the predilection of central government to legislate further responsibilities that involve an additional fiscal burden on local government. This is so in the Philippines, where local government is required to pay additional incentives and allowances to devolved health sector employees and allowances to national government public servants (e.g. judges and police) whose offices lie within its jurisdiction. These unfunded mandates have put a strain on the finances of local government and are a burning issue in the discourse on central-local relations in many other countries in the region.

Borrowing is another source of local government funding. In the past, central governments in most countries of the region have limited the access by local government to capital markets because of the inherent risk that over-borrowing may lead to macro-economic instability. In Korea the size of local government outstanding debts from bond issues hardly changed during 2000-2006 because of the strong control exercised over local borrowing by central government. In China, the central government placed strict limits on the power of local governments to borrow, but the latter often found ways to avoid these controls by obtaining loans through their municipally owned enterprises. Today some central governments in the region are increasingly encouraging larger municipalities to borrow. In Japan, loans are no longer subject to authorization, but only an understanding with central government, since April 2006. In India, several of the larger cities have issued municipal bonds and in the state of Tamil Nadu arrangements have been made for smaller municipalities to join together to issue bonds. Of course, municipal borrowing depends on a functioning capital market as well as the repayment capacity of municipalities. In the Philippines local governments are legally enabled and encouraged to tap financial markets and other non-traditional sources of finance in order to make them less

3. Own sources: resources levied directly by local authorities.

ASIA-PACIFIC

reliant on central grants. However, very few have yet attempted to tap private capital markets. Some local governments have used variants of the build-operate-transfer (BOT) schemes and other forms of private sector participation in order to fund major investment projects, although interest in these has waned somewhat following the East Asian financial crisis.

Borrowing from commercial banks has been minimal because of the lack of collateral or guarantees. Loans from government financial institutions (GFIs) have been far more common because these GFIs serve as the depository banks for the local governments for their intergovernmental transfers. Hence GFIs can always withhold these central transfers in the event of default on loan repayment by the local governments. A drawback, though, is that such arrangements can encourage irresponsible lending. In Indonesia, most borrowing by local governments has been from the central government, often involving on-lending of donor funds. In New Zealand, a 1996 reform eased the process of loan approval but also placed new legal restrictions on it. In place of central government approval, localities were required to specify explicitly the purpose and beneficiaries of a borrowing measure and to budget accordingly so as to cover operating expenses. In Australia, local government borrowing is coordinated by a national Loan Council that allocates and regulates debt among the states. In Korea, the size of outstanding local government debt from bond issues hardly changed during 2000-2006 because of the strong control exercised over local borrowing by the central government.

### III.3. Administrative Capacity of Local Government

Data on the share of local level personnel in total public sector employment for selected Asia-Pacific countries is shown in Table 8. The share ranges from highs of 92% and 77% in China and Indonesia respectively to lows of only 7% and 10% in Malaysia and New Zealand. Most local government personnel in the region have permanent positions with tenure protected by law although chief executive officers in New Zealand are recruited on seven-year renewable contracts.

The institutional and policy frameworks for recruitment, as well as the organizational responsibilities in undertaking recruitment processes at the local level, are shown in Table 9. Specific laws govern local public service in most countries of the region. In Japan, the Local Public Service Law defines the criteria for recruitment of local government personnel as well as a position classification system, remuneration and benefits, hours of work, disciplinary matters and training. In the Philippines, local government personnel are covered by civil service laws and by the rules and regulations of the Civil Service Commission (CSC), the central agency for public sector personnel. In addition, the 1991 Local Government Code has provisions regarding personnel administration. The Code mandates all local governments to design and implement their own organizational structure and staffing pattern, taking into account their service requirements and financial capacity. It also provides for the mandatory appointment of certain posts at every tier of local government and the creation of a Personnel Selection Board in each local government unit to assist the local chief executive in the fair selection of personnel for employment and promotion. Notwithstanding these safeguards, problems such as nepotism and associated non-compliance with the merit principle in recruitment and promotion are endemic in the local public service system in many countries of the region.

The degree of influence by higher tiers of government in the selection of local government staff remains considerable in the region. In China, the committees of the Chinese Communist Party choose,

*The degree of influence by higher tiers of government in the selection of local government staff remains considerable in the region*

| Table 8 | Size of Local Government Personnel in the Asia-Pacific Region |

| Country | Local government personnel | Total public sector personnel | Share of local government personnel in total public sector employment |
|---|---|---|---|
| Australia | 147,500 | 1,357,600 | 11% |
| China | 5,000,000 (est.) | n/a | 92% |
| India | n/a | n/a | n/a |
| Indonesia (2006) | 2,781,476 | 3,635,816 | 77% |
| Japan | 1,432,494 | 2,311,920 | 62% |
| Malaysia | 58,000 | 829,000 | 7% |
| New Zealand | 21,680 | 227,220 | 10% |
| Pakistan | n/a | n/a | n/a |
| Philippines (1999) | 390,561 | 1,445,498 | 27% |
| Korea, Rep. of (2006) | 345,989 | 611,219 | 56% |
| Thailand | n/a | n/a | 20% |
| Vietnam | n/a | n/a | 60% |

Source: *UCLG Country Profiles (2007): Figure 7.1.*

manage, discipline and dismiss civil servants, including those in local government. The recruiting body is likewise responsible for the discipline and dismissal of appointees. At the other end of the spectrum, in Australia and New Zealand, local councils appoint the Chief Executive Officer (CEO) but all other staff are employees of the CEO. In Pakistan, provincial authorities largely determine the appointment of senior local government personnel, with district and city establishments composed basically of seconded federal and provincial civil servants. In Indonesia, despite a radical decentralization reform, the central government still exercises substantial control over local government staff appointments. In India, selection and recruitment of local government staff is done by either the local authorities themselves or by a state level body concerned with recruitment. Local government in Malaysia can recruit, train, promote and discipline their personnel and even manage pensions but all these actions require approval by state government. Local budgets are also subject to state supervision.

In Thailand, the strong vertical connections between local officials and officials of the central government (especially in the Department of Local Administration of the Ministry of Interior), who handed out jobs, have been dismantled and personnel decisions are now largely under the power of the local executives. Bureaucrats resident in Bangkok often resist transfer to the provinces, which involves moving and possibly less authority and lower pay. However, transfers to local governments are more attractive for provincial officials given that provincial offices and district offices have lost authority as a result of decentralization and the transfer does not require a change in residence.

**Table 9** Institutional and Policy Frameworks for Recruitment Processes and Human Resource Development at the Local Level in the Asia-Pacific Region

| Country | Staffing regime (public or private law, career or job positions) | Recruitment procedure, especially for high-level positions | Institutional arrangements for training of local government staff |
|---|---|---|---|
| Australia | Public law | Recruitment by individual local government unit | Organized and funded by individual local government units |
| China | Civil servant law | Annual competitive exam at national and local levels | Organized and funded by local government |
| India | Largely by public law | Central and state level staff, selected by examination, are assigned to senior LG posts. | Not mandated by law but organized by central and state governments |
| Indonesia | Public law with career positions | Central government still exercises control over recruitment, which is generally by competitive exam with senior LG posts filled by promotion of career-based officers. | Implicitly mandated by law and organized by central and local government |
| Japan | Local public service law for full-time positions, career positions | Competitive exams for all local governments | Regulated by local public service law and implemented by each local government |
| Malaysia | Local councils have recruitment boards, supervised by Public Service Commission. | By local government subject to approval of state level government | National Institute for Public Administration (INTAN) acts as training arm of the Public Service Commission. |
| New Zealand | Fixed-term seven year contracts for Chief Executive Officer (CEO) and tenure for other personnel | Staffing levels determined by each CEO who recruits and acts as legal employer of all other staff | Local Government New Zealand provides limited professional training |
| Pakistan | Federal, provincial and local civil service cadres under civil service acts | Centralized recruitment by merit through Public Service Commission with provincial cadres assigned to senior posts in local government | Various public sector training institutions |
| Philippines | Civil service law and rules, 1991 local government code and civil service rules and regulations | By individual local government | Local Government Academy, Dept of Interior and Local Government and Centre for Local and Regional Governance, UP-NCPAG |
| Korea, Rep. of | Local public service law for full-time positions | Central government staff assigned to local government. Other staff recruited by competitive examination or on contract basis | Local Administrator Formation Institutes (LATI); Other public sector training institutions |
| Thailand | Strong central government control relaxed with recent rapid devolution of personnel responsibility to local government | Central government sets broad national standards for hiring, firing, recruiting, and setting salaries and benefits in local governments. Personnel decisions are now largely under the power of local executives. | Central government and provincial responsibility |
| Vietnam | Regulated by 2003 Ordinance on Cadres and Civil Servants | Central government staff assigned to local government. Other staff recruited by competitive examination or on contract basis | National Academy of Public Administration and Provincial and District-level Political Schools |

**Source:** *UCLG Country Profiles (2007) and Brillantes 2006.*

The most far-reaching management reforms affecting local government in the region have been in New Zealand where the 2002 Local Government Act requires both annual and long-term plans as well as systematic consideration of outcomes for local communities. It also prescribes principles for public consultation including transparent presentation of proposals, options and procedures. Most Australian states have introduced systems of performance management for local government, including performance indicators and other benchmarking strategies. In particular, the introduction of accrual accounting has had a major impact on local government management because of the requirement to value assets and make adequate provision for depreciation. Elsewhere in some countries of the region, significant decentralization programs have created severe strains on the management capacity of local governments as they try to cope with the administrative challenges caused by the rapid transfer of central government responsibilities and personnel.

The challenges of limited capacity and resources that all local governments face are amplified in urban areas. The problems of urban management are more complex and the potential for disaster (natural and man-made) is greater. Environmental problems are particularly severe, with inadequate capacity to treat human and industrial waste, severe contamination of water sources and serious air pollution from both industrial activity and the rapid growth of motor vehicles. Although city governments may be better able to recruit qualified staff compared to rural local governments, their capacity to regulate development and to effectively control environmental risks remains quite limited. Similarly, although city governments may have access to much greater fiscal resources than rural governments, their need for resources is also much

greater, since infrastructure and services are likely to be much more expensive. In turn, inadequate physical infrastructure is often a major impediment to industrial development and urban economic growth, on which national economic development depends.

In its report on urbanization and sustainability in Asia (ADB 2006a), the Asian Development Bank identified a number of examples of good urban governance in 12 countries in the region. These include: innovative approaches to revenue mobilization and capital financing; improved administration and performance-oriented management; increased availability of information and transparency of decision-making; greater citizen participation in decision-making; collaboration between municipalities within the metropolitan area or economic sub-region; serious attempts to tackle environmental problems and effectively enforce pollution controls; significant programs to address urban poverty, and support to community-based service improvements. However, such initiatives have been the exception. In all such cases, local leadership has been the critical factor: leadership that is committed to reform and to improving municipal conditions, is effective in mobilizing support for such initiatives and is responsive and accountable to local citizens. Developing such civic leadership across the region remains a major challenge.

Decentralization reforms and associated greater local level autonomy require major capacity building and training interventions for local government personnel in the Asia-Pacific region (Brillantes 2006). As shown in Table 9, such training and capacity-building programs in the selected countries of the region often form part of each country's overall civil service and policy frameworks. It is noteworthy that Korea, a country that has emphasized knowledge management as a core element of the development process, is

*Decentralization reforms and associated greater local level autonomy require major capacity building and training interventions for local government personnel in the Asia-Pacific region*

*Corruption in the public sector, including local government, is a global concern*

pursuing capacity building in the public sector through the establishment of separate specialized training institutes for central and local government personnel, respectively the Central Officials Training Institute (OTI) and the Local Administrators Training Institute (LATI).

In the context of the current decentralization reforms in the region, attitudinal change among central government officials is necessary to mitigate the new challenges and difficulties faced by local government personnel. In Japan, this process is encouraged by intergovernmental personnel exchanges, whereby central government personnel from the Ministry of Home Affairs are regularly seconded to local government, a practice that is not at all common in New Zealand. Apart from enabling these officials to appreciate the perspectives of the 'locals' and hence decentralize their own ways of thinking, this is also a way of building the capacity of local government through the expertise that is shared with them. In this respect, there is growing interest in encouraging joint training institutes of public administration for both local and central government personnel in order to promote cross fertilization and collaboration between the different tiers of government. Given the continued thrust towards decentralization in the region, the relative merits of separate training institutions for national and local government employees (as in the case of Korea and the Philippines) and joint training institutions deserve attention.

## III.4. Integrity and Corruption

Corruption in the public sector, including local government, is a global concern. Developed and developing countries alike are bedeviled with corruption issues. The annual Corruption Perception Index (CPI) published by Transparency International reveals that some of the case study countries in the region (Indonesia, Pakistan, Philippines and Vietnam) are near the bottom of the ladder and strongly suggest that corruption in these countries is perceived as a major problem. On the other hand, New Zealand is ranked as the least corrupt country

in the world while Australia is ranked ninth (Transparency International 2006). Although the CPI does not directly pertain to corruption at the local level, local governments are not exempted from this negative perception. In fact, there is a widespread perception in both China and Indonesia that decentralization has increased corruption. Indeed decentralization can increase the problem of corruption, or at least spread it around much more widely, making it more difficult to manage. On the other hand, democratization and the strengthening of civil society may simply expose corruption to more public view, so that citizens perceive that the problem has increased even when it has not.

Many developing countries of the Asia-Pacific region have serious problems with corruption. This is much less significant in the richer countries such as Japan, Australia and New Zealand, because of both the much higher rates of staff remuneration and the well established arrangements for public scrutiny and control in these countries. In New Zealand, the State Services Commission has since 1988 elaborated and monitored a Code of Conduct for public ethics and conflicts of interest in local as well as central government. The national Auditor-General enforces these rules and criminal charges can be brought in the event of breaches. Elsewhere, corruption can seriously erode the availability of resources for local service delivery and can prevent citizens, particularly the poor, from gaining access to these services.

Several countries in the region have introduced new mechanisms to curb corruption, including greater transparency of decision making. In Malaysia, improvements in local government recruitment procedures and remuneration, together with e-governance initiatives, have been designed to improve ethical standards and the transparency of local service delivery. In the Philippines, the Transparent Accountable Governance Project involves a 'conduct of lifestyle' check on public officials and procedural reforms in local government transactions (procurement, administration of local public enterprises, property tax administration and business permitting and licensing). In India, many states have appointed a Lokayukta (ombudsman) to combat corruption and malpractice in government, including local government. In Japan, there were a reported 92 cases of corruption in 2004 at the municipal level. Measures to combat corruption include strengthening the external audit system and check up and reform of the accounting process. But elsewhere (e.g. Pakistan, Philippines and Indonesia) the capacity of central government to monitor and audit local governments remains a major concern. For example, reports from the Philippine Center for Investigative Journalism point out that up to 70% of local health funds disappear as a result of corruption.

## III.5.  Central-Local Relations

Local governments in the selected countries operate under a legal framework that is defined by higher levels of government. In unitary nations such as China, Indonesia, Japan, Korea, New Zealand, Philippines, Thailand and Vietnam, central governments prescribe the powers and functions of local government. In federal systems such as Australia, India, Malaysia and Pakistan local governments are answerable to the state or provincial government. In Australia, state and territory ministers for local government may dissolve local councils and appoint administrators to carry out all local government functions. When this happens, the ministers usually have to hold public inquires into the alleged failings of the concerned council that justified the intervention. Even state constitutional provisions that restrict these powers can be amended relatively easily (CLGF 2005:29). In New Zealand the 2002 Local Government Act gives the minister for local government the power to initiate review of local governments for mismanagement or deficiencies in council decision making. In India there are no special avenues for intergovernmental relations and there is no formal representation of local government in the state structures (CLGF 2005:106).

Generally speaking, local governments as self-governing institutions are both accountable to their citizens and to the higher levels of government of which they are agents. In Pakistan, local political accountability remains problematic because of the control functions that the provincial government continues to exercise over local government on matters such as local personnel management and local finances. Local governments are also helpless in influencing grant-aided programs in their jurisdiction because these are usually determined by provincial and national legislators. By contrast, in Indonesia, decentralization fundamentally altered the direction of accountability. Prior to the 1999 reforms, local government was answerable primarily to the central government, but after the introduction of direct elections of provincial and local government executives and legislatures, the direction of accountability shifted markedly towards the local electorates.

In most of the selected countries, national or state level agencies perform general oversight of local government with regard to audit and probity. Nevertheless, the extent of this 'upward' accountability of local government to higher levels of government differs markedly among countries in the region. In China and Vietnam, local governments have a dual subordination, both sectorally (to central government ministries and agencies) and territorially (to the people's councils). The people's councils are themselves subject both to supervision and operational guidance from the national level and to guidance and inspection from sector ministries and agencies of central government. In India, state sectoral agencies often perform functions that overlap with local government functions and preempt local government responsibility[4].

In contrast to many countries in the region, central government ministries and agencies in Japan do not have direct control or supervision over local governments but may only provide information and suggestions. However, the Ministry of Home Affairs exercises *de facto* central fiscal supervision and control by way of the model budget that it presents to

*Local governments in the selected countries operate under a legal framework that is defined by higher levels of government*

4. Sethi (ed.), 2004, (pp.15-16.)

*Even when major decentralization reforms have taken place, the power of central government may still prevail over local government*

the local governments every year. When the central government disapproves of their decisions or policies, local governments can appeal to the Dispute Settlement Commission; however, authorities almost always prefer further discussions. A similar situation exists in Korea, where, despite their significant size, local governments have far less autonomy in practice than suggested by legislation. The lack of clarity over the division of responsibilities with central and provincial governments –two-thirds of enacted local government responsibilities are exercised jointly with provincial government– is especially true in the case of education, where local governments deliver services as agencies of central government. Provinces and metropolitan city governments enjoy considerable supervisory authority over local government (cities, rural districts and autonomous urban districts).

Even when major decentralization reforms have taken place, the power of central government may still prevail over local government. In India the state-level Local Government Minister may dissolve elected bodies and govern them directly for up to six months. However elections must be held within six months in order to reconstitute the municipality. By contrast, in the case of the Philippines the dissolution of local elected bodies is prohibited, even by the highest level of government. Such a process can only be carried out 'from below,' either through regular elections or through the recall process, whereby the voters themselves decide on the fate of the elected officials. The principle here is that elected officials are solely accountable to the citizens who elected them.

In Thailand, the Ministry of the Interior is perceived as the strongest opponent of decentralization. By pointing to local weaknesses in administrative capacity and personnel, the ministry has attempted to stem the loss of its authority. The ministry argues that it needs to retain the extensive supervisory powers that it exercises over local governments through the provincial administration under its control. Local governments are subjected to auditing by the ministry once a year. The ministry can also intervene to terminate or modify local po-

licies if it believes they contradict or threaten national policies or interests. As a result, provincial governors and district officers still retain considerable authority over local government.

### III.6.  Local Government Associations

The development of local governments undoubtedly depends to a large extent on the "local hands" that mind these communities. Yet there are situations when local governments need to look beyond their parochial concerns and be more forward-looking and pro-active in their orientation. Oftentimes, local governments would need some kind of mechanism that can work for their mutual interests and more significantly, to represent their collective interest in dealing with higher levels of government and external institutions such as donor agencies. In this respect, local government associations have become the instrument that local governments in the region adopt to advance their mutual interests. These associations perform diverse functions   for local governments.

One significant role that these associations perform is to act as representative and advocate of local government interests in  higher levels of government. Australia has perhaps one of the longest existing national local government associations in the region. Established in 1947, the Australian Local Government Association (ALGA) sits as member in the Premiers Conference[5] and Council of Australian Government and various ministerial councils, intergovernmental committees[6] and specialist advisory bodies. The association has helped shape the reform agenda in 1990s such as National Competition Policy and reviews of intergovernmental relations. At the state level are also found local government associations that link the councils in intergovernmental forums, negotiations, and cooperative efforts in general and specific areas of activity. As in Australia, local governments in New Zealand have formed the Local Government Association of New Zealand representing the interests of 86 member local authorities. Since 2000 when the central government-local government forum was initiated, the association has consistently represented

5.  *Member states of the Federation (Translator's note).*
6. *Gathering together the different levels of local representatives (Translator's note).*

local government in discussing common issues and coordination of public services. Membership in Australian and New Zealand local government associations is voluntary but councils in the two countries have chosen to be members because of the actual and potential contributions that the associations give to the councils. The senior local authority officers in this country have also formed themselves into a national professional body called Society of Local Government Managers. Other associations in the sub-region, recently created, are the Fiji Local Government Association and the Papuasia New Guinea Urban Local Level Association.

In the Philippines, the Union of Local Authorities in the Philippines (ULAP) is a national body, established in 1997, that is composed of various leagues at the provincial, city, municipal and barangay (village) levels. These leagues represent their respective interests and serve as mechanisms to articulate issues that directly concern them and to secure solutions. The ULAP seeks to unite members to pursue genuine autonomy for all local government units. Various groups of elected local officials (such as vice mayors, women mayors and young legislators) and professional local government staff (such as treasurers, assessors and planners) also have their respective national associations. In Indonesia, six independent associations representing specific levels of local government were created in 2001, following the Local Government Law 1999/22: the Association of Indonesian Municipal Councils (ADEKSI), the Association of All Indonesian Regency Legislative Councils (ADKASI), the Association of Indonesian Provincial Councils (ADPSI), the Association of Indonesian Municipalities (APEKSI), the Association of Indonesian District Governments

(formerly APKASI – now BKKSI) and the Association of Indonesian Provincial Governments (APPSI). They lobby the National Parliament and the central government to advocate local issues and interests. The associations also serve as a forum for discussing common interests and forging partnerships among local governments. Local government associations are more closely linked with the central government in Malaysia, (the Malaysian Association of Local Authorities or MALA), Vietnam (the Association of Provincial Cities of Vietnam, renamed the Association of Cities of Vietnam or ACVN) and Thailand (the National Municipal League of Thailand or NMLT). The youngest associations are the Provincial Association of Commune/Sangkat Council (PAC/S) and the National League of Communes and Sangkat (NLC/S) established in August 2006 in Cambodia.

India has several local government associations including the All India Council of Mayors, representing the municipal corporations, and the Nagar Palik Pramukh Sangthen, representing the other urban municipalities. Unlike Australia, New Zealand and the Philippines, these associations are not recognized in law. Many Indian states have City Manager Associations for urban local government officials. Despite the existence of these associations, local governments have no formal representation in state government structures; meetings and dialogues with state level institutions happen on an ad hoc basis and by specific local government. After several years of effort, an Association of Local Governments was established in India in 2006. In Bangladesh, Nepal and Sri Lanka national associations of local governments were created in the mid-1990s[7]. By contrast, there is no local government association in Pakistan.

*Local government associations work for the mutual interests of local governments and represent their interests in dealing with higher levels of government as well as external institutions such as donor agencies*

7.  There is ADDC/N, the Nepalese Association of District Development Committees (founded in 1995); MuAN, the Municipal Association of Nepal (established in 1995) and NAVIN, the National Association of Village Development Committees. Following the establishment of ADDC/N, a new impetus was given to the collective strength of DDCs and decentralization supporters for speeding up the process toward decentralization. After four years of hard struggle, a new Local Self-Government Act was enacted in 1999, which can be regarded as a milestone in the gradual but steady movement toward decentralization. Sri Lanka has the National Chapter of Mayors (NCM) created in 1997, the United Urban Councils Association (UCA) and the Pradeshiya Sabhas Association (PSA) created in 2002. Bangladesh gained local government associations in 2003 when both the Municipal Association of Bangladesh (MAB) and the National Union Parishad Forum (NUPF) were established.

*Beyond*
*representation to*
*higher levels of*
*government, local*
*government*
*associations*
*advance their*
*respective*
*concerns*
*and interests*
*internationally*

In Japan, there are no formal associations of local governments that represent local government interests. But there exist a number of elective position-based associations such as Japan Association of City Mayors, Association of Town and Village Mayors, National Association of Chairpersons of City Councils and the National Association of Chairmen of Town and Village Assemblies. These organizations cooperate with the National Governors' Association and the National Association of Chairpersons of Prefectural Assemblies in presenting and negotiating policy alternatives with central government. In China, local governments are represented by the China Association of Mayors, created in 1991. In the Republic of Korea, the new course in favor of decentralization has been accompanied by the creation of national associations: the National Association of Mayors (1996) and the Governors Association of Korea, based on article 154, paragraph 2 of the Local Government Act (1999).

Another area where associations have played an important role is training and capacity-building for councils and local staff. In Australia, the state associations also act as employer bodies for councils in industrial relations. They also provide training and capacity-building projects for councils and deliver a number of specialist services such as general insurance, workers' compensation insurance and retirement income schemes for their member councils. The documentation and dissemination of local government best practices are increasingly becoming an important function that these associations fulfill for their members.

Beyond representation to higher levels of government, local government associations advance their respective concerns and interests internationally. This is especially true in Australia and New Zealand. Local government associations in these countries are members of regional and international organizations such as the Commonwealth Local Government Forum and the Asia-Pacific Regional Section of United Cities and Local Government Organizations. Additionally, several countries have developed local government organizations aimed at developing international cooperation with local governments abroad: in China, the Chinese International Friendship Cities Association; in Japan, the Council of Local Authorities for International Relations (CLAIR) and in the Republic of Korea the Korean Local Authorities Foundation for International Relations.

## IV. Local Democracy

Throughout much of the Asia-Pacific region, multi-party democracy is thriving at the local level. The mayor-council system is the norm across the region although local electoral practices vary considerably, including whether mayors are directly or indirectly elected (UNDP 2006b). In most countries citizens directly elect their local government legislatures (councils) as well as their executives (mayors), as shown in Tables 10 and 11 below. The major exception is Malaysia, where the state government appoints local councils and executives –although those appointed are intended to act as representatives of the local community. In Pakistan, an electoral college of lower tier council members selects the higher tier of local administration. In China and Vietnam, local communities elect their respective congresses or councils but the candidates are subjected to a prior screening process. These local councils in turn nominate representatives to higher level bodies at the town, county, city and provincial levels. In Vietnam, although candidates for council elections are usually members of the ruling Communist Party, there have been recent efforts to attract non-party members or self-nominated candidates to stand in local elections. In the 2004 local elections, non-party candidates won 312 seats compared to 25 in previous elections, spread among more than 10,000 municipalities.

## IV.1. Electoral Systems for Local Councils

It is generally believed that proportional representation (PR) electoral systems are the most representative because they tend to produce electoral results that are more reflective of actual voting patterns, whereas plurality-majority or 'First Past The Post' (FPTP) systems are thought to enhance accountability because they give voters a specific representative with whom to identify. However, this may not always be true. PR systems can concentrate power in parties rather than voters' hands, and having an identifiable representative in a FPTP system may not necessarily translate into greater accountability from this person to the electorate (UNDP 2006b).

**Table 10    Electoral Systems for Local Councils in the Asia-Pacific Region**

| Country | Electoral system for directly elected lower tier LG councils | Electoral system for directly elected upper tier LG councils | Terms of mandate and number of terms | Electoral turnout and trend |
|---|---|---|---|---|
| Australia | Mixed system – PR and FPTP | | 2 years (2 states), three years (3 states), 4 years (1 state) and 1-4 years in Northern Territory | Compulsory voting in 4 states. Elsewhere turnout is generally low, except where there is postal voting |
| China | Mixed system throughout. | Mixed system | 5 years | Declining |
| India | All LG councils (rural and urban, all tiers) have FPTP, single-member ward constituencies | | 5 years | Figures unavailable |
| Indonesia | All LG councils have PR 'open List' system | | 5 years with no limit on number of terms | Complete figures unavailable. |
| Japan | All LG councils have PR list system | | 4 years with no limit on number of terms | Declining, 56.23% (2003) |
| Malaysia* | Not applicable | | | |
| New Zealand | Mostly FPTP but STV in a few cases | | 3 years | 2001 – 50% 2004 – 52% |
| Pakistan | Union councils have FPTP + multi-member constituencies | Not applicable | 4 years | Figures unavailable |
| Philippines | Barangay councils have FPTP with block vote. arrangement | Municipal and city councils, and provincial boards have FPTP. | 3 years and maximum 3 terms | Approx. 80% |
| Korea, Rep. of | Korea: Direct council election by single round majority vote in the electoral districts, and by PR lists in local authority territories with unitary wards. | | 4 years | |
| Thailand | All LG councils have FPTP system. | | 4 years | 35.39% (Bangkok Met. Admin. Council) District (Council elections) |
| Vietnam | People's councils (commune, district and province) have FPTP and multi-member constituencies | | 5 years | 98.7% (2004) |

**Source:** *UCLG Country Profiles (2007) and UNDP (2006b).*

*Note: FPTP = First-Past-The-Post; PR = Proportional Representation; STV = Single Transferable Vote.*

*\* There is no electoral system for local government in Malaysia.*

The major features of the electoral system for local councils in selected Asia-Pacific countries are presented in Table 10. In most countries council members are directly elected according to the FPTP system via single-member constituencies, i.e. geographical areas at the sub-municipal level, known as 'wards' in Australia and Pakistan and as 'districts' in the Philippines. The only exceptions are Pakistan and Vietnam where the FPTP system is applied to multi-member constituencies. The Block Vote system is used for local elections in the case of barangays in the Philippines under which electoral districts are multi-member and voters are given as many votes as there are open seats in a legislative chamber. They can cast the full number of votes or as few votes as they like and the candidates with the most votes overall win the election. Uniquely, New Zealand conducts local elections exclusively by mail and in four states of Australia voting in local government elections is compulsory.

Only Indonesia and Japan rely exclusively on PR for local elections, a system that has tended to strengthen the power of national political parties over local political life. In 2004, Indonesia moved from a 'closed' to an 'open' list PR system, in order to reduce the power of national party executives to select local candidates. This electoral reform sought to provide voters with more 'voice' in deciding which individuals (as opposed to which parties) represent them in local government. New Zealand and Australia have a mixture of systems for electing council members, which includes FPTP, PR and single transferable voting.

### IV.2. Electoral Systems for Local Executives

The method of election of the local executive also varies from country to country within the region, but in many cases it also varies between the different tiers of local government within a country. The major features of the electoral system for the local executive in selected Asia-Pacific countries are presented in Table 11. Typically the local executive (or mayor) is directly elected (e.g. Japan, New Zealand and Philippines). Indonesia's two-round electoral system (ballotage) for local executives is designed to ensure that they have at least received a majority (i.e. more than 50%) of the votes. This aims to overcome one of the disadvantages of the FPTP electoral system, namely the likelihood of 'wasted' votes. In Indonesia and Pakistan, the heads and deputy heads of lower tier councils are directly elected, but on the basis of a joint ticket. In Indonesia this is on a party basis, while in Pakistan it is on a non-party basis. In India, the form of election of panchayat and municipal leaders varies from state to state, depending on state legislation. Hence, in a few states council members belonging to the party with an elected majority, indirectly elect the local executive. Australia has a mixed system –in three states the local executive is directly elected, in three states the council chooses between direct and indirect election and in one state citizens choose.

Where upper tier councils are themselves directly elected by voters (and not by electoral colleges), their local executives are invariably also directly elected by voters (e.g. India, Indonesia, Philippines and Vietnam). Similarly, where upper tier councils are indirectly elected, local executives are generally also indirectly elected. This is the case in Pakistan, which has a hybrid system of indirect elections for local executives. The leader (nazim) of any town (tehsil), district or city is indirectly elected by an electoral college consisting of all the union councilors[8] in their respective constituencies. They are thus indirectly elected by all union councilors (including the union council leaders (nazims) and deputy leaders (naib nazims) in their respective jurisdictions. However, naib nazims at the tehsil or district tiers are indirectly elected by their respective councils (from amongst themselves) and not by a wider electoral college.

The term of office of the local executive varies within the region –from a minimum of three years (e.g. New Zealand and

8. The union administrations council is the institution which brings together villages or neighborhoods which have their own elected organs. In Pakistan there are 6,125 union administrations that each form the basic municipal administration for an average population of 15.000.

Philippines) to a maximum of five years (e.g. Australia, China, India, Indonesia and Vietnam). Several countries place restrictions on the number of executive office terms – two in Indonesia and Thailand and three in the Philippines.

| Table 11 | Electoral System for Local Executives in the Asia-Pacific Region |

| Country | Directly elected mayors | Mayors elected by council | Mayor appointed by higher tier | Term of office of mayor | Maximum number of terms | Provision for citizen recall of mayor |
|---|---|---|---|---|---|---|
| Australia | In 3 states | In 3 states | No | 4 years | No limit | In some states |
| China | No | No | Yes | 5 years | No limit | No |
| India | In most cases | In case of samiti and zilla chairpersons | No | 5 years | No limit | No |
| Indonesia | Yes | No | No | 5 years | 2 terms | No |
| Japan | Yes | No | No | 5 years | No limit | Yes |
| Malaysia | No | No | Yes | n/a | n/a | No |
| New Zealand | In all cases | Only in cases of regional chairpersons | No | 3 years | No limit | No |
| Pakistan | Union nazim and naib nazim - on a joint ticket | Tehsil/district nazims elected by all UC members in their respective jurisdictions. Naib nazims at tehsil and district tiers chosen by their respective councils | No | 4 years | No limit | No |
| Philippines | Yes | No | No | 3 years | 3 terms | Yes |
| Korea, Rep. of | Yes | No | No | 4 years | 3 terms | Yes, with effect from July 2007 |
| Thailand | Yes | No | No | 4 years | 2 terms | Yes |
| Vietnam | No | Chair of People's Councils' Standing Committees indirectly elected by People's Councils. Chairs of People's Committees (Commune, District and Provincial) elected by People's Councils | No | 5 years | No limit | No |

Source: UCLG Country Profiles (2007).

### IV.3.  The Role of Political Parties

Partisan local elections are the norm in the Asia-Pacific region. The only significant exceptions are New Zealand and Australia where non-partisan or independent affiliation is the norm except in large cities. Attempts to 'de-politicize' local government have occurred in Pakistan and the Philippines, two countries where political parties are a vital part of political life at the national level. In Pakistan, political parties are banned from contesting local elections and in the Philippines they are banned from barangay elections but are allowed at all other tiers of local government. However, in practice political parties play a major role in local government elections in Pakistan by supporting candidates who are closely identified with one party or another.

In China and Vietnam, the only political party allowed to contest local elections is the ruling Communist Party. Independent candidates may stand for election in Vietnam but all candidates (whether Party on non-Party) must initially be screened by a range of institutions, such as the Fatherland Front, that are closely linked to the Communist Party of Vietnam. This effectively ensures that all candidates speak more or less the same 'political language' (that of the Party) and thus implies a limitation on any variation in the political programs of candidates. In China, free and direct elections of village committees have been introduced since 1987, and have become compulsory nation wide since 1997 (15th Communist Party Congress); in 2004 there were committees elected in 85% of villages and 75% of neighborhood communities in urban areas. From 1995 (first experience), township leading positions (governor, deputy-governor and sometimes the Party secretary) have been subject to a semi-competitive election procedure in the province of Sichuan and in some counties elsewhere. This semi-competitive procedure includes as a rule a kind of primary election among self-nominated candidates

by a broad selectorate (150 – 300 people), before approval by the party leadership at county level, and final direct election by the citizens among selected candidates. Although under Party control, these elections have already changed the relationships between villages and lower local government levels in favour of villages[9].

Local government elections throughout the region are hotly contested but are often marred by manipulation and cheating by competing parties. In most countries, local political parties are branches of national political parties. Independent candidates are prohibited in Indonesia but are allowed in the Philippines. Local and national elections are often synchronized, with local party branches receiving funds from their national headquarters to promote the electoral campaigns of candidates for national office. Throughout the region, politicians view local government as a stepping stone to national political office. However, as a result of decentralization reforms, issue-based local elections are increasingly transforming local politics.

### IV.4.  Citizen Participation in Local Governance

Local government is the closest tier of government to the citizens. As such it is the first entry point for people to gain access to and influence decision-making in government. In all the selected countries, citizen participation in local governance is increasingly gaining importance. The most common form of participation is through the electoral system. All countries allow local citizens to select to varying degrees the leaders who manage the affairs of the community, ranging from the consultative people's congress in Vietnam and China to the directly elected councils and mayors of Australia, India, Indonesia, Japan, Korea, New Zealand, Pakistan, Philippines and Thailand. The level of participation in local government elections varies considerably throughout the selected countries. The

9. Gunter Schubert (2003), «Democracy under one-party rule?», China perspectives n°46, March-April; Lai Hairong (2004), "Semi-competitive elections at township level in Sichuan province", China Perspectives n°51, January-February.

turnout is extremely high under the one-party communist government in Vietnam (98.7% in 2004) and China (80% in village elections in rural areas). Voting is compulsory in four states of Australia but in the rest of the country turnout in local government elections is generally low at around 30-40%, even where postal voting has been introduced. Elsewhere in the region the turnout ranges from a high of around 80% in the Philippines to 56% (2003), 52% (2004) and 47% (2005) in Japan, New Zealand and Pakistan respectively, and a low of 35% in Thailand's Bangkok Metropolitan Administration.

However, citizen participation in local governance is not merely confined to voting in local government elections. The presence of decentralized structures and processes has been considered one manifestation of a wider movement in the region towards democratization because it provides the enabling context for broader citizen participation and active civil society engagement in the democratic discourse. Ensuring the participation of civil society groups (NGOs and non-profit organizations), and business and the private sector in the local governance process is a continuing concern in the region. Such participation is a sine-qua-non for successful decentralization. How to overcome the so-called 'psychological divide' between government and civil society is a challenge that is being addressed in various ways by the selected countries of the region.

Japanese citizens have extensive powers to demand a local referendum – for example, on important issues such as US military relocation, nuclear sites and construction of industrial waste disposal facilities. They can demand formulation, improvement or elimination of ordinances, audits and even dissolution of the local assembly, as well as the dismissal of the mayor, council members or officials. In Korea, citizen participation has been greatly strengthened by three legislative reforms in the very recent past: the 2005 Local Referendum Act, confirming the

power of councils to hold referendums; the 2006 Act on the Local Ombudsman Regime and Local Petition against the abuse of local finance, and the 2007 Local Recall system, by which elected mayors and councilors may be removed from office by a local vote. In New Zealand around half of all municipalities have introduced some form of community board structure as a strategy for linking communities with the local council. Although these structures are authorized in the 2002 Local Government Act, the boards lack formal government authority or independent financial resources.

In the Philippines there has been a noticeable increase in citizen participation in local governance in recent years. The 1991 Local Government Code established new mechanisms of consultation and participation. Local referendums and recall of officials have been introduced and there were 29 recorded local recall elections between 1993 and 1997 (Teehankee 2002). The Code requires all municipalities to establish a local development council (LDC), with at least one-quarter of its members being representatives of non-governmental and civil society organizations. The LDC draws up a comprehensive development plan for approval by the council.

Attempts at promoting citizen participation often challenge powerful vested interests and are not always successful. The Gram Sabha (or assembly of all registered voters in a panchayat) is a key feature of rural local government in India, and it is mandatory for rural local bodies to hold Gram Sabha meetings where important decisions have to be approved. There is also an increasing emphasis on setting up user groups to take decisions and to participate in the management of public services. This is more controversial as it is often seen as a dilution of the institutional role of elected local bodies. Currently, urban local government in India does not have a corresponding institution to the Gram Sabha and does not offer any institutionalized role for citizens beyond voting at election time

*The presence of decentralized structures and processes has been considered one manifestation of a wider movement in the region towards democratization*

*In several countries much attention has been given to the villages, because of their roots in traditional patterns of social relations and as a legitimate basis, owned by the local people, for local development*

–although there are calls to build a ward-level platform for citizen engagement. As a step towards greater public accountability, India has recently enacted a Right to Information law, overriding earlier laws that protected government policies and decision-making from public scrutiny. Local government laws in some states contain their own Right to Information provisions, mandating what information must be placed in the public domain.

In Pakistan, a major objective of the 2001 decentralization reform was to institutionalize community participation in local governance. To support this objective, one-quarter of the local development budget is mandated for community organizations. Despite this, neither community organizations nor participation has increased significantly. Resource allocation for community organizations has become highly politicized within the local councils. Local government laws have also enshrined traditional dispute resolution within the formal system to facilitate citizen participation. But these mechanisms have proved ineffective in defending the interests of weaker and poorer members in the community.

In several countries much attention has been given to the villages, because of their roots in traditional patterns of social relations and as a legitimate basis, owned by the local people, for local development. Therefore barangays are promoted in the local government system of the Philippines. In Indonesia, the military government reorganized the villages in 1979 in order to integrate them in its ruling system. The decentralization reform of 1999 reversed this decision in order to revive villages in rural areas as a social structure, based on customary institutions and rules, that can help to integrate local people in the management of local government affairs. Surveys have shown that the village can play a role in local dispute settlement instead of official police and justice – unless formal authorities are involved in the conflict

(World Bank: 2004). However, other surveys show that, despite reforms, local people do not see much opportunity to participate in decision-making or even offer input in the decision-making process. (Alatas, Pritchett, Wetterberg: 2002). Perhaps better results will come in time.

Large city governments face particular challenges of representation and accountability. Their large size can mean remoteness from citizens and voters. In terms of responsiveness, much depends on the prevailing institutional and electoral arrangements. (Rakodi 2004). One way in which cities can retain a degree of responsiveness, particularly to the poor, is through a lower tier of government at the community level, such as the barangays in the Philippines, which have access to resources for local service and infrastructure needs (Devas et al 2004). However, with the exception of the OECD countries Australia, Japan, Korea and New Zealand, which have much greater resources and longer established traditions of local democracy, the cities of Asia-Pacific demonstrate huge problems of lack of responsiveness to the needs of their citizens, particularly the poor, and a woeful lack of accountability. Their lack of responsiveness can in large part be attributed to their inadequate resources, both human and financial. But it can also be attributed to weak, unaccountable and opaque administrative systems, political systems that are unrepresentative and repressive, and high levels of corruption. In addressing these problems, demands from civil society are increasingly forcing municipal governments to practice greater transparency and accountability (ibid).

### IV.5. The Political Representation of Disadvantaged and Minority Groups

Elite representation has tended to dominate the electoral systems in the Asia-Pacific region, even where PR has been the norm, and especially where upper tier local governments are indirectly elected. For this reason, many countries have taken affirmative action in order to promote the political representation of disadvantaged and minority groups at the local level. In principle, the democratic election of local government representatives gives all citizens a voice. But in practice, some electoral arrangements are more inclusive –particularly of women but also of minority groups and the poor– and so can produce outcomes that are more representative. To date there is no legislation in any of the selected countries in the region requiring that political parties ensure that a given percentage of their candidates for local election are representative of minority or disadvantaged groups. However, in Vietnam, the law states that the Communist Party should, when selecting candidates to stand for election, ensure that an appropriate number of women and ethnic minority people are elected to the People's Councils.

India, Pakistan and the Philippines have adopted electoral arrangements with quota systems and reserved seats for women and for disadvantaged and minority groups. India offers the most striking example in terms of the positive outcome of affirmative action in favor of women's and minority representation. Not less than one-third (including seats reserved for Scheduled Castes (SC) and Scheduled Tribes (ST), of seats and chairs on all local government councils in all states are reserved for women. As a result, over one million women are serving as local government councilors in India. SCs and STs also have reserved council seats – in the same proportion as the population of SCs and STs bear to the total population. The requirement that a proportion of senior positions must be reserved for women and minority groups has also had an empowering effect although the evidence of the impact is mixed, with states such as Kerala and West Bengal making much greater strides on this front than others (Blair 2000).

In Pakistan on directly elected village or neighborhood councils one seat is reserved for women and one seat is reserved for peasants and workers, while on directly elected union councils four seats are reserved for Muslim women, six seats (of which two are for women) for workers and peasants, and one seat for minority communities. For the indirectly elected zilla, tehsil and town councils, women must represent 33% of all members while peasants and workers must represent 5% and members of minority communities in the respective local government unions must represent a further 5%. The electoral college for filling these seats consists of the members of the union councils in each local government. However, a large number of the reserved seats remain unfilled or are simply not contested. Following the 2000-2001 elections, 17% of councilors at the union council level were women, 15% at the tehsil level and 11% at the district and city level (CLGF 2005:1183).

Strong traditions of local elite domination in many of the countries in the region mean that the achievement of more inclusive representation is a long-term process, although the growth of the civil society movement and its engagement with local government is helping. This has been particularly the case in the Philippines, where NGOs and civil society organizations enjoy quite a high degree of legal protection and rights within the local government system. The 1991 Local Government Code states that there must be three sectoral representatives in local councils at all tiers, i.e. one woman, one agricultural or industrial worker and one representative for the urban poor, indigenous cultural communities, disabled persons, or any other sector as may be determined by the council concerned. In addition, the Philippines has one of the most overtly 'pro-youth' local representational systems in the world. The Local Government Code provides for the establishment of youth councils, whose members are elected by persons between 15 and 21 years of age, in every barangay.

*Strong traditions of local elite domination in many of the countries in the region mean that the achievement of more inclusive representation is a long-term process, although the growth of the civil society movement and its engagement with local government is helping*

ASIA-PACIFIC

The presidents of these youth councils and of their federations represent the youth as ex-officio members at every tier of the local government system.

In Australia and New Zealand the rights of indigenous peoples to local self-government is a political issue, and one that is more about self-determination than about inclusion (Sproats 2003). In Australia, there is a long-standing difficulty in incorporating the aboriginal population within the formal governmental structures. In some regions, there are special local government areas to serve the needs of the aboriginal population in order to achieve a greater degree of representation for them. Although the Maori population in New Zealand makes up 15% of the total population, it accounted for only 6% of council members in 1998-2001. Despite the absence of affirmative action in both countries, female representation at the local political level is considerable. In 2000, 26% of council members in Australia were women and only 10% of councils had no women councilors. Some 15% of councils had a woman mayor, more in metropolitan areas (21%) than in rural councils (11%) (UNESCAP 2005a). In New Zealand, women accounted for 34% of city council members and 28% of district council members in 2004. In the same year four of the 16 city mayors and 12% of district mayors were women (UNESCAP 2005b).

## V. Conclusion

In considering the impact of decentralization and democratic local governance on service delivery, citizen voice, accountability and poverty reduction, it is important to bear in mind that, while some countries in the Asia-Pacific region have undergone significant decentralization of government functions (notably Indonesia, Philippines and some states in India, as well as some sectors in China, and to a lesser extent, Korea, Thailand and Vietnam), in other countries there have been more modest reforms to the existing system of local government (Australia, Japan – but significant on local finance system – and New Zealand). Decentralization and local governance also show widely differing degrees of local democratic control and accountability across the region. As such, it is difficult to make generalizations about such a wide range of experience, especially where decentralization is a comparatively recent phenomenon in comparison to other parts of the world. Nevertheless, two broad conclusions can be made about the impact of decentralization and local democratic reform in the region.

First, in terms of the impact of democratic decentralization on service delivery, there is a degree of support from within the region (e.g. Indonesia, Korea, Philippines and some Indian states) for the positive view that service performance improves when elections are introduced for local decision-makers, who are then obliged to become more responsive and accountable to local citizens. Decentralization should in principle open up political space for citizen participation and voice, and so create the potential for greater accountability of decision makers. In India, Indonesia, Pakistan and the Philippines, decentralization has indeed greatly increased the number of elected positions, thereby increasing the scope for democratic accountability. But traditions of patron-client relationships between local elites and citizens, which are strong in many countries in the region, can seriously undermine local democratic accountability.

Decentralization can open the door for 'money politics,' as is the case in Indonesia, where it is often money rather than accountability that counts (Hofman and Kaiser 2006). In China and Vietnam, local democratic choice of community leaders is beginning to be implemented at the village level, and citizens are increasingly willing to challenge and demand accountability from local officials. In Malaysia, where there is no direct line of accountability because local government councilors are appointed not elected, nevertheless striking innovations in terms of greater public access to information are under way that are intended to enhance local accountability. In many countries, particularly in the Philippines and some Indian states, local civil society organizations are increasingly ready to use that information to demand accountability. Meanwhile, in countries with well-established local administrative systems, such as Australia, Japan and New Zealand, much effort over the past two decades has gone into improving the management and efficiency of local service delivery, including the adoption of performance management and facilitation of citizen access to information through e-governance initiatives. These should have had a positive impact on local service delivery outcomes.

Second, the available data is insufficient to draw any firm conclusions yet with regard to the impact of decentralization on poverty reduction. In principle, in combination with an effective and equitable resource distribution system, decentralization should spread the benefits of growth around more widely and so help to reduce poverty. On the other hand, without such an equitable system for resource distribution decentralization can lead to an increase in inter-regional inequality. This is typified by China where economic reform generally, including economic decentralization, has greatly increased living standards and substantially reduced the numbers living in absolute poverty but at the same time has substantially increased inter-personal and inter-

*Decentralization and local governance also show widely differing degrees of local democratic control and accountability across the region*

regional inequality. In Indonesia, decentralization has increased the resources going to the local level, but this increase has been much greater in the resource-rich regions than elsewhere. While this may help to redress historic differences in the levels of development between regions, it may not do so in a manner that systematically addresses either poverty or inter-regional inequality.

In conclusion, it is clear that decentralization has become a major theme of governance reform throughout the Asia-Pacific region over the past decade and that decentralization has for the most part been accompanied by enhanced local democracy. But the forms and patterns of local governance have varied widely, as have the outcomes, reflecting the diversity of country contexts. While there are clearly a great many weaknesses in the current arrangements for decentralized governance in the case study countries, and further reforms will undoubtedly be required, it is hard to imagine that any wholesale return to a centralized system of governance would be either appropriate or politically acceptable.

| Annex 1 | Major Local Government Legislation in Selected Asia-Pacific Countries |
|---|---|

| Country | Year | |
|---|---|---|
| **Australia** | 1989 | Victoria: Local Government Act |
| | 1993 | New South Wales: Local Government Act |
| | 1993 | Northern Territory: Local Government Act |
| | 1993 | Queensland: Local Government Act |
| | 1993 | Tasmania: Local Government Act |
| | 1995 | Local Government (Financial Assistance) Act |
| | 1995 | Western Australia: Local Government Act |
| | 1999 | South Australia: Local Government Act |
| **China** | | No constitutional or dedicated legal basis exists for local government. The following laws are relevant for the role of sub-national governments: Comprehensive Fiscal Reform (1994), Budget Law (1995) and Tax Sharing System (1994) |
| **India** | 1950 | Constitution (Article 40) |
| | 1992 | 73rd and 74th Constitutional Amendments |
| **Indonesia** | 1974 | Law 5 on Local Autonomy |
| | 1975 | Law on Decentralization (decentralisatiewet) that established autonomous regions |
| | 1999 | Law 22 on Regional Government and Law 25 on Fiscal Balance between Central and Regional Government |
| | 2000 | Constitutional Amendment strengthening basis for decentralization |
| | 2004 | Law 32 on Regional Government (amended Law 22) and Law 33 on Fiscal Balance between Central and Regional Government (amended Law 25) |
| **Japan** | 1947 | Local Government Law |
| | 1993 | House and Diet Resolutions on Decentralization |
| | 1995 | Law for the Promotion of Decentralization |
| | 1999 | Global Decentralization Law |
| | 2004 | Revision of 1947 Local Government Law |
| | 2005-2007 | "Trinity Reform" of local finance |
| **Korea, Rep. of** | 1949 | Local Autonomy Act, amended in 1956, 1958, 1960 and 1961 |
| | 1986 | Local Autonomy Law |
| | 1987 | Constitution: Title V111 (Articles 117 and 118) on Local Autonomy |
| | 1990 | Revised Local Autonomy Law |

## Annex 1 — Major Local Government Legislation in Selected Asia-Pacific Countries (Cont.)

| Country | Year | |
|---|---|---|
| Malaysia | 1950 | Local Authorities Elections Ordinance |
| | 1952 | Local Councils Ordinance |
| | 1976 | Local Government Act |
| | 2003 | Smart Local Government Governance Agenda |
| New Zealand | 1989 | Local Government Amendment Acts No. 1 and No. 2 |
| | 1991 | Resource Management Act |
| | 2001 | Local Electoral Act |
| | 2002 | Local Government Act |
| | 2002 | Local Government (Rating) Act |
| Pakistan | 1959 | Basic Democracies Order |
| | 1960 | Municipal Administration Ordinance |
| | 1972 | Local Government Ordinance |
| | 1979 | Local Government Ordinances passed in each Province |
| | 2001 | Local Government Ordinances passed in each Province |
| | 2005 | Amendment to 2001 Local Government Ordinances |
| Philippines | 1959 | Local Autonomy Act |
| | 1960 | Barrio Charter Act |
| | 1963 | Revised Barrio Charter Act |
| | 1967 | Decentralization Act |
| | 1983 | Local Government Code (Batas Pambansa) |
| | 1987 | Constitution: Article 10 provides for local autonomy |
| | 1991 | Republic Act (known as Local Government Code) |
| Thailand | 1933 | Municipal Administration Act |
| | 1985 | Bangkok Metropolitan Administration Act |
| | 1991 | National Administrative Organization Act |
| | 1997 | Constitution: Article 78 provides for local autonomy |
| | 1997 | Provincial Administration Organization Act |
| | 1999 | Decentralization Plan and Procedures Act |

| Annex 1 | Major Local Government Legislation in Selected Asia-Pacific Countries (Cont.) |
|---------|------------------------------------------------------------------------------|

| Country | Year | |
|---------|------|---|
| Vietnam | 1958 | Law on Local Governments |
| | 1994 | Law on Organization of the People's Council and the Administrative Committees at All Levels of government |
| | 1996 | Ordinance on Concrete Tasks |
| | 1998 | Budget Law |
| | 2004 | Revised State Budget Law |

**Source:** *UCLG Country Profiles (2007) and Brillantes 2006; CLGF 2005; World Bank 2005.*

# EURASIA

T. Y. KHABRIEVA
(CHIEF RESEARCH GROUP)

L.V. ANDRICHENKO

V.A. VASILIEV[1]

1. *The authors thank professors A. Campbell and G. Marcou for their inputs in the discussion of this chapter.*

# I. Introduction

This chapter analyzes the formation, development and recent trends of local self-government in the states of the Eurasian region that were formerly member states of the Soviet Union: Azerbaijan, Armenia, Belarus, Georgia, Kazakhstan, Kyrgyz Republic, Moldova, Russia, Tajikistan, Turkmenistan, Ukraine and Uzbekistan.

Until the fall of the Soviet Union in 1991, all these countries shared a unified system of local government. The main characteristics of that system were that 1) local soviets (councils) were part of the state, 2) soviets at each level were subordinate to soviets at all higher levels, and 3) the executive at each level of government was nominally accountable to a representative council but in practice both representative and executive powers at each level were subordinated to the ruling party organization at that level.

Taken together these attributes of the Soviet system of sub-national government form a legacy that continues to influence the evolution of sub-national government in the successor states. In the early years of post-soviet transition this legacy was evident in terms of the practical difficulties caused by the collapse of the previous system. After 1991 there were difficulties due to overlapping functions and shared competencies, as well as the lack of a clear relationship between functions, responsibilities and resources, whether generated locally or transferred from higher levels. The removal of party control over the executive and representative powers opened a power struggle between the two branches in those countries in the region where genuine democratic elections were applied at sub-national levels.

However, it is at the level of ideas –the ideas that have informed the debate around local government reform in Eurasian countries– that the Soviet legacy can be seen to have enduring influence.

The legacy is most clearly evident in regard to the relationship between local government and the state. On one hand, Soviet-era centralist ideas continue to color the ruling elite's view of local autonomy. On the other, the advocates of local autonomy and decentralization often adopt excessively idealistic views of local government in their zeal to break with the institutional legacy of the Soviet period. The first group sees local government as an integral part of the state and entirely subordinate to higher-standing state bodies. The second group typically regards local government as a social institution created by the people of the local community and entirely separate from the state.

The 'social' or 'society' view has provided a basis for defending municipalities against excessive intervention from above. It was this view that inspired Article 12 of the Russian Federal Constitution, which declares that local self-government is not part of the state; this has been a central reference point in all debates on local government in the Russian Federation. At the same time it can be argued that the social view itself limits the role of local government by emphasizing its role in community representation at the expense of delivering services. The social view can encourage fragmentation into small municipal units that are powerful on paper, but not in practice (as occurred in several of the countries of Central and Eastern Europe after 1989).

However, as long as the 'state' view of local government remains influential in governmental circles, the social view is necessary as a countervailing force. The debate between these opposing views of local government tends to coalesce around the key issue of whether mayors are appointed or elected –or, in a non-mayoral system, whether the elected council has power over the executive. This matter is effectively the working litmus test of local autonomy. This can be seen in the recurrent debate within the Russian Federation regarding appointment of mayors. On sev-

*After the removal of party control over local government bodies, local government reforms have been driven by the struggle between Soviet era centralist ideas and advocates of decentralization based on the principle that local self-government is not part of the state*

*Three groups of countries can be distinguished:*

*1) where local government has been established as separate from the state power;*

*2) where the reform process is still not concluded;*

*3) where local issues are still in the hands of local state bodies, whereas local self-government exists only at the very lowest level*

eral occasions in recent years, draft legislation that would have introduced appointment rather than election of mayors has come close to adoption, only to be withdrawn at the final stage. This reflects the fact that proponents of both views of local government can be found at the highest levels of government. In the post-Soviet context the principle of local autonomy has often come into collision with that of regional autonomy. Nowhere more than in the Russian Federation from the early 1990s onwards has conflict between regional governors and mayors of regional capital cities shaped local politics and development, sometimes over many years. In this case regional governors have frequently supported the state view of local government, whereby local authorities would be subordinate to regional state bodies. Advocates of the social or non-state view of local government may, paradoxically, be found at the higher national or federal levels.

Most Eurasian countries have inherited in some form the Soviet territorial unit, the raion, consisting of a number of different settlements over a particular territory (much like a UK district). In most countries in the region this is where most local functions and services are performed. Initially much criticized as a legacy of the previous regime, the raion has proved difficult to replace. In Ukraine perhaps the most important of the reforms designed in 2005 (but not adopted, due to that year's split in the Orange coalition) was that which would have made the raions into genuine local authorities, with the executive reporting to the council; councils currently have no executive reporting to them. In Russia the reform of 1995 emphasized settlements rather than districts. As a consequence, many local functions were exercised by the state. The 2003 reform ended this anomaly, creating a two-tier system with raions as the upper tier to carry out those local functions that required economies of scale (in addition to certain delegated state functions, as in the German/Austrian model)

and leaving settlement-based municipalities to do the rest. In Georgia the municipal reform has transformed the districts (raiony) in municipalities and cities without subordination to any raion into self-governing cities. Raiony continue to provide the basis for central Asian local government systems, although local self-government (in the sense of local autonomy) is confined to the sub-raion level where there are few functions. In cases such as the local makhallas in Uzbekistan, services are provided at this level, but genuine autonomy is restricted.

Local self-government in the states of the Eurasian region has attained different levels of institutional development. In several states it exists as an independent institution; in others it is a structure combined with the institutions of state power. In this respect it is possible to distinguish three groups of countries.

In the first group are Russia, Armenia and Azerbaijan. In these countries local self-government is legally autonomous and institutionally separate from the structures of state power, and local government is seen as an institution through which the local community decides on local issues.

In the second group –Georgia, Kyrgyz Republic, Moldova and Ukraine– the process of the formation of local self-government is still not concluded. Reforms have barely been implemented, or simply have not been achieved up to now. The aforesaid trend in the development of local self-government has been changed neither in the course of the Ukrainian "orange revolution," nor in the course of the "revolution of roses" in Georgia.

The third group is composed of the states of Central Asia: Kazakhstan, Tajikistan, Turkmenistan and Uzbekistan. Local self-government there functions only on the lowest level, in small villages. In the main, local issues in this region are vested in local state organs subordinate to central

**Table 1**     General Information and Territorial Structure

| Countries | Territory (1000 sq. km) | Population (m) | Administrative territorial division (intermediate level) | Local units and tiers | Form of government |
|---|---|---|---|---|---|
| Armenia | 29.74 | 3.21 (census of 2001) | 10 regions<br>City of Erevan | 930 municipal units | Unitary state with mixed presidential-parliamentary government |
| Azerbaijan | 86.6 | 8.4 | Nakhichevan Autonomous Republic (Nagorno-Karabakh) *de facto* secessionist republic | 59 districts<br>11 district cities<br>2,757 municipalities | Unitary state with presidential government |
| Belarus | 207.6 | 9.75 | 6 regions<br>City of Minsk | 1.665 municipal units:<br>1) district (basic)<br>2) primary | Unitary state with presidential government |
| Georgia | 69.7 | 4.661 | 9 districts,<br>9 cities, Abkhaz and Adjar Autonomous republics | 1,017 municipal units | Unitary state with presidential government |
| Kazakhstan | 2.724 | 15.074 | 14 regions<br>3 cities | 1) 159 districts and 36 district cities<br>2) 45 cities, 241 boroughs, 2,042 rural circuits | Unitary state with presidential government |
| Kyrgyz Rep. | 198.5 | 4.823 (census of 1999) | 7 regions<br>City of Bishkek | 1) 40 districts and 10 district cities<br>2) 11 cities and 465 rural municipalities | Unitary state with presidential government |
| Moldova | 33.8 | 4,466 | 1 autonomous territorial entity – Gagauz Eri<br>1 territorial unit – Stinga Nistrului "Prednestrovye Moldavian" *de facto* Republic struggling for secession | 1) 32 districts and 3 cities<br>2) 907 municipalities and communities | Unitary state with parliamentary government |
| Russia | 17,075.2 | 142.893 | 84 Federation subjects. Russia is a federation comprised of 86 "subjects". These subjects have equal federal rights and an equal representation (two delegates each) in the council of the Federation, but with varying degrees of autonomy. For the composition of legal units see Table 1 (p 97) (member states at 01/03/2008) 21 republics, 47 oblast, 8 kraj 1 autonomous oblast 6 autonomous okrugs | 22.972 municipal units (at 01/01/2007)<br>1) 1,802 municipal districts, and 522 district cities<br>2) 19,892 rural municipalities and 1,756 urban municipalities | Federative state with presidential government |
| Tajikistan | 143.1 | 7.32 | 2 regions<br>1 autonomous region Nagorno-Badakhshan | 1) 58 districts and 23 cities<br>2) 47 towns, 256 settlements and 2,803 villages | Unitary state with presidential government |
| Turkmenistan | 491.2 | 5.37 (census of 2001) | 5 regions | 1) 50 districts<br>2) Several hundred cities, settlements and villages | Unitary state with presidential government |
| Ukraine | 603.7 | 48 | 24 regions<br>Autonomous Republic of Crimea<br>2 cities with the status of Regions (Kiev and Sevastopol) | 1) 490 districts and 176 cities with district status<br>2) 279 cities of district subordination, 884 urban municipalities and 28,573 rural settlements (however 10,227 councils) | Unitary state with mixed presidential-parliamentary government |
| Uzbekistan | 448.9 | 26 | 12 regions,<br>City of Tashkent<br>Autonomous Republic of Karakalpakstan | 233 urban municipalities<br>164 rural municipalities<br>About 10,000 local communities (makhalyas) | Unitary state with presidential government |

**Sources:** *UCLG Country Profiles (2007).*

*Several constitutions prohibit the dissolution of representative bodies of local self-government (municipal councils)*

government. Nevertheless, first steps of reform are in progress, aiming to increase the role of local self-government and to enlarge its functions.

Another model of local self-government has developed in Belarus with a peculiar combination of different elements of central state government, local state government and local self-government.

Table 1 describes the territorial structures of the countries of the region in relation with geographic and demographic data. It distinguishes the intermediate level of government (meso level) from the separate local (municipal) level; the latter may be organized with a single tier or two tiers (see below, section 1).

## II. Evolution of Structures

Territorial and institutional structures reflect both the introduction of new political and legal principles, and the legacy of the past.

### II.1. The Renaissance of Local Self-Government and Its Constitutional Basis

The first time the term 'local self-government' was used in the law of the USSR was in the "General Fundamentals of Local Self-Government and Local Economies," enacted on the wave of democratization at the end of the 1980s and the beginning of the 1990s.

After the collapse of the Soviet Union, each of the states has been independently developing its own model of local government. Nevertheless, the common heritage of the past is manifest in many current legal notions including: local self-government, local state government, local state administration, own and delegated powers, municipal budgets, municipal property, programs of economic and social development of municipal entities, local public service, premature termination of powers of representative bodies of local self-government and dismissal of heads of municipalities.

The constitutions of all states of the region contain separate articles, sections or norms devoted to local self-government and to guarantees of its realization. They proclaim that the rights of citizens to local self-government may not be restricted. The constitutions of several states, including Russia and Ukraine, stipulate that the rights of citizens to local self-government may be suspended only in the time of war or emergency. Constitutions regulate relationships between central and local governing bodies on such principles as: separation of state powers and powers of local self-government, organizational and functional independence of local self-government in the sphere of its competence, unity and integrity of state territory, combination of centralization and decentralization in the execution of state power, balanced social and economic development of territories, and responsibility of bodies and employees of local self-government to the state. Some constitutions, including that of Uzbekistan, prescribe that relations between central and local governments shall be built on the basis of subordination and mutual cooperation.

With the exception of Kazakhstan, all constitutions prescribe the principal powers of local authorities. Transfer of such powers to other entities and persons is not permitted. The constitutions of Russia and Kazakhstan proclaim the principle of separation of state and local governments.

Several constitutions, including Armenia's, prohibit the dissolution of representative bodies of local self-government (municipal councils). This serves as an important guarantee of their independence. In a number of states there are procedures for revocation and suspension of acts of local state entities and local self-government, and for the right of citizens to lodge complaints in courts against their decisions. Belarus and Uzbekistan provide examples of this system.

The constitutions of several states proclaim guarantees for the integrity of the boundaries of local territories; in particular a local referendum is required to change the boundaries of municipal units (Armenia). Although virtually all constitutions have detailed norms providing for the development of local self-government, in practice they have been implemented at different degrees.

## Stages of development

Local self-government in the states of Eurasia has achieved different stages of development. In several states it is functioning as an independent institution, in others as a structure combined with, or subordinated to state power. Again, the countries fall into three groups.

In the first group of countries, including Russia, Armenia and Azerbaijan, local self-government is independent: it is separate from the system of state-level government bodies; local representative bodies independently decide local issues.

In Russia the system of local self-government was launched in 1991 by the law "On Local Self-government in the RSFSR." Later the Constitution of the Russian Federation of 1993 guaranteed local self-government by providing that local self-government bodies shall be separated from the system of state power (article 12). In 1995 the federal law "On General Principles of Organization of Local Self-Government" was enacted. It proclaimed democratic fundamentals of local self-government, though they have not been fully implemented. Therefore in 2003 a new law was enacted "On General Principles of Organization of Local Self-Government" (Federal Law No. 131), which enlarged, in accordance with the requirements of the European Charter of Local Self-Government, the functions of municipal entities, and transferred some functions from member states to federal state bodies.

In Armenia, the present system of local self-government was formed on the basis of the Constitution of 1995. Between 1995 and 1997 the Parliament enacted laws "On Elections of Organs of Local Self-government," "On Local Self-Government," "Transitional Provisions for Regulating Relationships of Organs of Local Self-Government," "Organs of Territorial Government" and some other acts. This was the period of formation of the legal and institutional basis of the systems of state territorial government and local self-government. Local self-government was defined as the right and ability of communities to decide upon and take responsibility for local issues deemed to be in the interests of local populations.

In Azerbaijan the Constitution of 1995 contained a separate section devoted to local self-government. The constitutional requirements were implemented in 1999 in the laws "On the Status of Municipalities" and "On Elections to Municipalities," which laid down the basis of the system of local self-government in the republic. Later about 20 other laws were enacted, including "On Transfer of Property to Municipal Property," "On Municipal Service," "On the Status of Members of Municipalities," "On Fundamentals of Municipal Finances," "On Management of Municipal Lands" and "On Administrative Supervision Over Activities of Municipalities." All of these laws reinforced the organizational, legal and economic basis of local self-government.

In the second group of states –Georgia, Kyrgyz Republic, Moldova and Ukraine– the process of the formation of local self-government is still in progress.

The Constitution of Georgia of 1995 proclaimed the general principle that local issues have to be the responsibility of local self-governments, subject to an obligation to respect the sovereignty of the state. The procedure of formation and the powers of local self-governments and their relationships with state entities were regu-

*The constitutions of several states proclaim guarantees for the integrity of the boundaries of local territories; in particular a local referendum is required to change the boundaries of municipal units (Armenia)*

*The constitutions of the states of Central Asia acknowledge and guarantee local self-government. But on the whole, local matters are not the business of local self-goverment bodies*

lated by the "Organic Law" of 1997. During the municipal reform of 2000–2001, the powers of local self-government were significantly enlarged, but were not adequately supported by necessary material resources. This divergence was one of the main themes of debates in the last local elections held on October 5th, 2006.

In Kyrgyz Republic the basis for local self-government was established by the Constitution and laws "On Local Self-Government and Local State Administration," "On the Financial and Economic Basis of Local Self-Government," "On Municipal Property" and "On Municipal Service." The new stage of the reforms has been initiated by the "National Strategy On Decentralization of State Government and the Development of Local Self-Government in the Kyrgyz Republic for the Period till 2010." Nevertheless, local issues are still under the control of the state's local administrative entity.

In Moldova the democratic fundamentals of local self-government were laid down by the Constitution of 1994. In fact, the process was launched four years later with the adoption of the laws "On Local Public Administration" and "On Territorial-Administrative Organization." The division of the territory at the intermediate level has been changed twice: from districts (raion) to provinces (judete), and back to districts. The next stage of municipal reform started in 2003, when the Parliament amended the legislation by significantly enlarging the powers of local self-government. Nevertheless, many problems were not resolved. The material basis of local self-government is still not sufficient and its independence from state powers is not duly ensured.

In Ukraine the fundamentals of local self-government were shaped by the Constitution of 1996 and by the law "On Local Self-Government in Ukraine" (May the 21st. 1997). They proclaimed the principles of decentralization of public powers and the priority of territorial units or communities

known as gromada. But these principles have not been fully realized. Currently a mixed system exists, combining local state government and local self-government on the levels of districts (raion) and regions (oblast). On one side are provincial and district councils as elements of local self-government, representing the interests of territorial gromadas. On the other are state administrations of provinces and districts –local organs of state executive power vested with the executive functions of these councils. Such a combination of municipal and state structures actually derogates principles of local self-government, leaving it in the domain of state rule. Reform projects have faltered because of political divisions and are still pending.

The third group is composed of the countries of Central Asia –Kazakhstan, Tajikistan, Turkmenistan and Uzbekistan. In these nations local self-government functions only on the lowest level, in small villages variously called jamoaty, shakhrak and dekhot in Tajikistan, and makhalya in Uzbekistan. It is nevertheless necessary to note that these states are in the process of implementing reforms to increase the role of local self-governments and to enlarge their functions. In Kazakhstan, for example, recently approved legislation will introduce elections for municipal heads (mayors).

The constitutions of the states of Central Asia acknowledge and guarantee local self-government. Some laws of these republics contain original definitions of the notion of local self-government. Thus, the "Law of Uzbekistan On Organs of Self-Government of Citizens" defines local self-government as an independent activity of citizens in the solution of local issues in accord with their interests, historical development, national and spiritual values, local customs and traditions.

But on the whole, local matters in these countries are not the business of local self-government, an autonomous or quasi-independent body elected by local popular vote. Rather, control of local matters more often falls to what is termed "local state government" (Kazakhstan), "state power on local level" (Tajikistan and Uzbekistan) and "local state executive power" (Turkmenistan).

Another model of local self-government has been developed in Belarus. The "Law On Local Government and Self-Government in the Republic of Belarus" established a peculiar combination of different elements of central state government, local state government and local self-government. Local self-government—as opposed to the notion of a state-controlled local body –is defined as the organization and activities of citizens for independent solution of local issues, directly or through elected entities. This definition takes in to account the interests of the population, the development of administrative territorial units and the basis of own material and financial resources local government can generate or attract. But at each of the three levels (province, district or city with district rights, rural or urban municipality) executive powers are integrated in the system of the state executive power, even though they are, at the same time, bodies of local government. Local councils therefore do not have their own executive powers.

## II.2.  Territorial Organization and Territorial Reforms

The countries of the region have different forms of territorial organization of public power. As a rule, these forms are highly diversified, but not all countries have a clear hierarchy of territorial units with local self-government organs, as reflected above in Table 1.

Most countries have introduced or allowed autonomous territorial units in recognition of ethnic or regional peculiarities, sometimes with a dimension of conflict: Azerbaijan (Nakhichevan and Nagorno-Karabakh), Georgia (Abkhaz and Adjar

republics), Moldova (Gagauz Eri, "Predniestrovye Republic"), Ukraine (Crimea), Tajikistan (Nagorno-Badakhstan) and Uzbekistan (Karakalpakstan).

Russia is the only federal country in this region. However, several countries have an intermediate level of government on a rather broad scale, distinct from the local or municipal level of government. It is generally called oblast, here translated as "region" and it is found in Armenia, Belarus, Kazakhstan, Kyrgyz Republic, Tajikistan, Turkmenistan, Ukraine and Uzbekistan. Georgia also has such a territorial level (mkhare). The capital city and other main cities may have the status of province; that is, they are directly subject to the central government.

Usually the local government level (municipal level) is organized on two tiers, as reflected in Table 1. The most important is the district level, which is a rather small constituency, embracing a lot of villages but also some cities. Many municipal functions for small and mid-size cities are the realm of district-level powers; large cities are independent of the district-level authorities. Usually, the lower municipal level is much less significant with respect to its functions. This pattern can be compared with the German municipal organization (Kreis-district, and cities independent from a district) or to English districts; it was also used in the Soviet era. Now, such a two-level municipal organization can be seen in Azerbaijan, Belarus, Kazakhstan, Kyrgyz Republic, Moldova, Russia, Tajikistan and Ukraine. Only one municipal level, although it may be differentiated, exists in Armenia, Georgia and Uzbekistan. In Turkmenistan, local government institutions exist only at the district level. The level of local government autonomy varies considerably, even among similar countries.

In further detail, Russia, as a federative state, is composed of such member states (called "'subjects") as republics, lands (krai), regions (oblast), federal cities,

*Most countries have introduced or allowed autonomous territorial units in recognition of ethnic or regional peculiarities, sometimes with a dimension of conflict*

autonomous regions and autonomous cir-cuits (okrug). All member states of the Russian Federation have equal status. Local self-government in the Russian Federation is exercised in urban settlements and rural settlements formed as municipalities (pose-lenie), municipal districts (municipalnij ra-yon), district cities (gorodskoï okrug) and the territories of federal cities (Moscow and St. Petersburg).

In Ukraine the administrative-territorial or-ganization has a three-tier structure: the highest level includes the Autonomous Re-public of Crimea, regions (oblast) and two cities, Kiev and Sevastopol that have a special status. The next level, the upper municipal level, embraces districts and dis-trict cities. The lowest level includes city districts, cities of district subordination, towns, settlements and villages.

*Usually the local level is two tier, with the raion being still the key*

The territory of Tajikistan is divided in a descending hierarchy into provinces (veloy-ats), districts (nohiyas), towns of republican significance, towns of provincial significance, towns of district significance, settlements and villages (qyshloqs).

In the countries of Central Asia (Kaza-khstan, Tajikistan, Turkmenistan and Uzbekistan), local self-government plays a limited role. Organs of local state govern-ment exercise the principal functions. In Russia, Azerbaijan, Armenia, Georgia, Kyr-gyz Republic and Moldova, local self-gov-ernment has greater autonomy and is sep-arated from state government.

In the majority of countries of the region the majority of the population resides in cities and towns. Statistics show that, on January 1, 2006, 73% of the population of the Russian Federation resided in urban settlements and 27% resided in rural regions. Urban population slightly exceeds 70% of the population in Belarus, 68% in Ukraine and nearly 60% in Kazakhstan. By contrast, in Uzbekistan, at the beginning of 2006, 36% of the population resided in cities and 64% in rural regions. Rural

population prevails also in other states of Central Asia. The legislation of Kazakhstan (law of December 8th, 1993) distinguishes the administration of territories and of pop-ulated areas. Territories are provinces, dis-tricts and rural circuits; populated areas are cities, settlements and villages. This means that the municipal area is usually limited to the settlements, whereas areas between populated areas are administered by the upper level of government. The new law on local government of the Russian Federation is backing away from this conception, and the territory of each subject of the Federa-tion is divided into municipalities; only in areas of low density may the territory between municipalities be administered by the district government (law 131: article 11, paragraph 1).

A number of countries have implemented territorial reforms after the political change, aimed, inter alia, at improving state govern-ment (Belarus, Georgia, Kazakhstan, Moldova, Russia, Ukraine and Uzbekistan). Major goals and trends of territorial reforms were different. In a number of states they resulted in the enlargement of regional ter-ritorial units (Kazakhstan, Ukraine). In other states territorial reform was called upon to move the processes of public power closer to the general population (Azerbaijan, Arme-nia, Russia, Uzbekistan).

In the Russian Federation, territorial reform has been in the process of implementation since 2003. According to the Law of 2003, the subjects of the Federation have fixed boundaries of municipal entities, and have defined the status of appropriate local enti-ties as urban or rural settlements, munici-pal districts (municipalnii rayon) and dis-trict cities (gorodskoï okrug). The year 2005 was decisive in the establishment of the two-tier model of local self-government in Russia. The member states of the Russ-ian Federation have fixed the boundaries of 23,972 local entities, including 19,892 rural municipalities, 1,756 urban municipalities, 1,802 municipal districts and 522 district cities (January 1st 2007).

## Capitals and Metropolitan Areas

In the majority of countries, capital cities have separate legal status as provided by constitutions and laws (Belarus, Kazakhstan, Russia and Ukraine –see Table 1). In the Russian Federation the separate regime of Moscow is laid down by the Constitution and the law "On the Status of the Capital City of the Russian Federation." In Uzbekistan the separate legal regime of the capital city is provided only by the Constitution. By contrast, Baku, the capital of Azerbaijan, does not have any special regime.

Several states have metropolitan areas with special governance status. Under the Constitution of the Russian Federation two metropolitan areas –Moscow and St. Petersburg– have the status of the member states of the federation. Law provides for specific legal regulation of their local self-government forms. According to the charters of Moscow and St. Petersburg, local self-government is exercised by institutions of local self-government formed in appropriate city territories. The enumeration of local issues and sources of revenues of the local budgets of the municipal units are determined by the laws of Moscow and St. Petersburg, taking into account the necessity of preserving the unity of the cities' economic systems.

In Georgia, similar special forms of governance are applied to Tbilisi and Poti, in Belarus for Minsk, and in Kazakhstan for the cities of Astana and Alma-Ata. Expenditures of the capital cities are singled out in each republic's budget; the cities receive grants and subventions, transfers of property and state guarantees for investments. In Kazakhstan, separate governance rules are provided for Alma-Ata to support the development of the city as the region's international financial center. In Georgia, specific status is accorded Poti with the aim to create a free economic zone.

The following table lists the capitals and main cities of the countries of the region (2006).

| Table 2 | Capital Cities and Main Cities | |
|---|---|---|
| **Countries** | **Capitals and metropolitan cities** | **Population (thousand)** |
| Armenia | Erevan | 1,104 |
| Azerbaijan | Baku | 1,874 |
| Belarus | Minsk | 1,781 |
| Georgia | Tbilisi | 1,103 |
| Kazakhstan | Astana | 550 |
| Kazakhstan | Almaaty | 1,248 |
| Kyrgyz Republic | Bishkek | 799 |
| Moldova | Chisinau | 660 |
| Russia | Moscow | 10,425 |
| Russia | St. Petersburg | 4,581 |
| Russia | Novosibirsk | 1,397 |
| Russia | Nizhni Novgorod | 1,284 |
| Russia | Ekaterinburg | 1,308 |
| Russia | Samara | 1,143 |
| Russia | Omsk | 1,139 |
| Russia | Kazan | 1,113 |
| Russia | Chelyabinsk | 1,093 |
| Russia | Rostov-on-Don | 1,055 |
| Russia | Ufa | 1,030 |
| Tajikistan | Dushanbe | 647 |
| Turkmenistan | Ashkhabad | 828 |
| Ukraine | Kiev | 2,693 |
| Ukraine | Kharkov | 1,463 |
| Ukraine | Dnepropetrovsk | 1,047 |
| Ukraine | Donetsk | 994 |
| Ukraine | Odessa | 1,002 |
| Uzbekistan | Tashkent | 2,141 |

**Source:** *Inter-State Committee of Statistics of the Commonwealth of Independent States.*

## II.3. Evolution of Relationships between Central and Local Governments

Relationships between central government and local self-government are complex. As a rule, they cooperate closely. For instance, in Russia federal state institutions and those of local self-government have agreements of cooperation, and jointly participate in the realization of special programs.

Different state structures are responsible for local government matters. In the Russian Federation, a decree of the President established a specialized ministry –the Ministry of Regional Development of the Russian Federation– which is vested, inter alia, with the powers to determine and implement the policy of the state in the sphere of local self-government. In Moldova, the Agency of Regional Development performs such functions.

In other states, matters of local government lie mainly in the province of sectoral departments of appropriate state bodies. Thus, in Azerbaijan the Administration of the President has a division responsible for work with municipalities; the Ministry of Justice has formed a specialized center on matters of local self-government; in the Parliament there is a standing committee on regional issues.

## III. Functions, Management and Finances

In theory, resources have to be sufficient for functions (connexity principle); in practice functions are adjusted to resources, and adequacy depends on the financial capacity of the public budgets. However, much has still to be done to improve the financial system and the management in order to use scarce resources more effectively.

### III.1. Financial Management

The most acute problem of local government is the shortage of financial resources. This lack

*In theory, resources have to be sufficient for functions (connexity principle); in practice functions are adjusted to resources, and adequacy depends on the financial capacity of the public budgets*

of funds inevitably impedes the execution of local-government functions.

**Local taxes.** The principal indicator of financial power of local self-government is the right to impose taxes. In most countries of the region, the share of local taxes in the total revenue of local government is extremely low. Azerbaijan is an exception, with the share of local taxes and duties in municipal budgets reaching 24.5% (of this, 22.6% is attributed to local taxes).

In Armenia, local communities may levy only local fees and payments. Rates of local fees, within the frameworks prescribed by law, are set by municipal councils at the initiatives of heads of municipalities prior to the adoption of annual budgets. Rates of local duties are defined by municipal councils on the proposals of heads of municipalities in the sums necessary for exercising appropriate actions. On November 27, 2005, constitutional amendments were adopted permitting the imposition of local taxes.

The Constitution of Belarus (article 121) and annual laws on the republic's budget enumerate local taxes and duties that may be established by local councils of deputies. For instance, the law "On the Budget of the Republic of Belarus for 2006" prescribes the following local taxes and duties for the 2006 financial year: tax on retail sale, tax on services, special purpose duties, duties from users, duties from purveyors, and health-resort duties. The share of local taxes and duties in state revenues is about 2.1%.

The Russian Federation has only two local taxes: the land tax and the tax on physical personal property. Representative bodies of local self-government define, within the framework provided by the Tax Code of the Russian Federation, tax rates and the procedure and terms for paying taxes. Other elements of local taxation are prescribed by the Tax Code. According to preliminary data for 2005, local taxes comprise only 4.29% of revenues of local budgets. Local self-governments in the Russian Federation have been constantly losing their local, own sources of revenues. The Law of December 21, 1991 "On Fundamentals of the Tax System" provided for 23 kinds of local taxes and duties. Even so, in 1998 they yielded on average 12% of the total municipal revenues. Furthermore, local authorities could vary the rates within narrow limits for only eight of the 23. The same number of local taxes and payments was preserved by the initial version of the Tax Code of the Russian Federation enacted on July 31, 1998. Later this list was reduced to five in 2000. With the amendments of 2004 to the budget code, proposals to transfer the tax on vehicles to municipal budgets and to establish a local tax on retail sales were rejected, and two local taxes remain –the land tax and the tax on personal property.

In Ukraine, bodies of local self-government may establish, in accordance with law, local taxes and duties, which are allocated to appropriate budgets. Meetings of citizens may introduce local duties on the principles of voluntary self-taxation. In 2005, local taxes and duties comprised 2.4% of the general revenues of local budgets.

Local bodies in the states of Central Asia are not permitted independence in the tax and budget spheres. They are not able to define tax rates or other elements of local taxation. Tax rates and other elements of taxation are prescribed by central bodies for all taxes, including local levies. In Uzbekistan, the Cabinet of Ministers establishes local taxes and their rates. In Kyrgyz Republic, local taxes and duties may be introduced only by the Parliament. On the whole, local taxes account for an insignificant share in the revenues of local budgets.

**Tax shares.** In all countries of the region, tax shares accrued to local government on the revenue from national taxes are the main source of revenue for local budgets. This is generally a share of the local yield of the national taxes.

In Kazakhstan, law does not provide for a division of taxes between the republic and local governments. Local budgets receive 50% of the income tax on corporate entities, and 50% of the excises levied on certain specified goods. Income tax on personal property, social, land and transport taxes, and payments for the use of water and forest resources are wholly directed to local budgets. Certain kinds of duties are also considered tax revenues.

Reinforcement of the revenue base of local budgets is exercised by increasing the share of taxes left to local budgets at the expense of state taxes; such is the case in Uzbekistan and Kazakhstan, for instance. In Belarus, the share of state taxes and duties makes up more than 14% of local budget revenue. In Ukraine, since the adoptions of a new budget code in 2001, the personal income tax is fully devoted to local budgets of the respective levels (province, district, municipality) in proportions fixed by the law.

Since Russia is a federal country, the bulk of local budgets depends on the budget and the policy choices of the subjects of the Federation, within the framework designed by the Budget Code. The tax base of the subjects of the Federation has been strengthened in 2004 and 2005 with the transfer of the transportation tax and of the tax on assets of legal persons. Part of the current revenues of the subject has to be reallocated to local budgets. Laws of the subjects of the Federation grant additional assignments of tax revenues from regional budgets. As a rule, such assignments are to be made at uniform rates, except that differential assignments may be established in cases provided by law for the period from 2006 to 2008. In 2005, assignments of taxes comprised 36.7% of local budget revenues. The share of local budget revenues of the total budgetary funds of the Russian Federation (including regional and local) comprises 10%.

**Budgetary transfer.** Transfers have two main functions:
- bring revenues in line with spending requirements to accommodate disparities in the revenue base and in needs,
- compensate the costs of duties assigned to

*Local bodies in the states of Central Asia are not permitted independence in the tax and budget spheres*

*To provide subsidies for shared financing of investment programs and development of the public infrastructure of municipal units, the subjects of the Russian Federation may establish funds for municipal development*

2. Editor's note: according to definitions given by the Budgetary Code of the Russian Federation (art.6), grants are budgetary transfers to cover current expenditures; subventions are budgetary transfers aimed at financing specific expenditures (delegated functions), and subsidies are budgetary transfers as participation in the financing of specific expenditures.

local government by central or regional governments. Subsidies are specifically used for the latter purpose. Efficiency and equity require transparency and objectivity in resource allocation. Budgetary reforms in Russia, Ukraine and several other major countries in the region are oriented in that direction. However, in a number of countries, the grant allocation formula does not exist, or is too complicated and cannot be supported by appropriated data.

In Ukraine, the equalization grant for some 700 main local budgets is calculated by the difference between spending needs established from a formula devised by the central government, and the revenues from tax sharing. This also includes a coefficient determining the level of equalization. The only needs that are taken into account are those listed in the budget code, such as education, social care, and primary health care. Other functions (housing, basic service delivery, infrastructure, public transport) have to be funded on the basis of own resources; that is, local taxes and fees. Although the system is sound in its basic principles, it has been biased by modifications by the government and by multiple decisions affecting the resources and tasks of local governments. Nevertheless, a similar equalization scheme has been introduced at the district level for municipalities. In brief, the insufficiency of own resources leads to underfinancing of functions not taken into account in the distribution of resources between different local governments.

In Russia, more discretion is left to the subjects of the Federation than is permitted for Ukrainian regions in the matter of resource allocation to the local budgets. Basic resources are tax shares from personal income tax and shares of regional taxes as determined by laws of the subjects of the Federation. But the principle of equalization is similar: there is an estimate of needs based on expenditure standards, and an equalization grant to cover the gap between the revenues and the level of equalization required by the law. Part of the income tax is also involved in equalization. Grants are paid by the subjects

of the Federation through district funds for the support of municipalities, and through regional funds for the support of municipal districts and city districts. There is also a regional support fund for municipalities receiving contributions from the district funds. Grants are distributed among municipal units in accordance with the methods approved by laws of the subjects of the Federation, and in conformity with the requirements of the Budget Code of the Russian Federation. The provisions of the Budget Code exclude arbitrary distribution of grants. They have to be distributed among municipal units in an "automatic way." The situation varies considerably from one subject to another, and not only for geographic reasons, but also due to the mechanisms and levels of redistribution of resources between local governments, and whether the transfers are based on spending or needs estimates. On one hand the spending power is centralized, leaving only the management to local authorities (e.g. the regions of Novosibirsk and Tiumen), or on the other hand the expenditure responsibility is delegated (e.g.in the region of Lipetsk). However, the consequences of the reduction of social privileges by federal law 122 of 2004, and continuous shifts in the allocation of tasks since 2004 make any evaluation of the transfer and equalization system prohibitively complex.

To provide subsidies for shared financing of investment programs and development of the public infrastructure of municipal units, the subjects of the Russian Federation may establish funds for municipal development. Funds for mutual financing of high priority social expenditures may also be included in subject budgets. Municipal units may receive other forms of financial aid from the federal budget and from budgets of the subjects. The main requirement is the transparency of distribution of financial resources.

According to data from the Ministry of Finances, in 2005 budgetary transfers to local budgets totaled 52.5% of local budget expenditures. In the total volume of transfers 54% were subventions, 32% grants and 14% subsidies[2].

| Table 3 | Local Finance Indicators (Various Years) |
|---------|-------------------------------------------|

| Country | | Total public expenditure (% GDP) | Local public expenditure (% GDP) | Ratio of local on general public expenditures | Tax shares and budgetary transfers as % of the total income | Local tax revenues as % of total income |
|---------|---|---|---|---|---|---|
| Armenia | (2003) | 20.6% | 1.3% | N/A | N/A | N/A |
| Azerbaijan | (2003) | 17.8% | 0.2% | 27.5% (1999) | Subsidies: 10.4% | 22.6% |
| Belarus | (2004) | 48% | 19.3% | 40.1% | Basic level budget transfers: 45.6% | Local taxes and payments: 2,1% |
| Georgia | | 13.9% (2003) | 4.6% (2005) | N/A | N/A | N/A |
| Kazakhstan | (2004) | 22.1% | 10.8% | 48% | Transfers: 37.1% | Local gvt bodies may not establish taxes |
| Kyrgyz Rep. | (2005) | 28.7% | 3.4% | 12% | N/A | N/A |
| Moldova | (2003) | 25% | 7.2% | 29% | N/A | N/A |
| Russia | (2005) | 18% | 5.3% | 18% | Transfers to local budgets: 52.5% | 4.29% |
| Ukraine | (2005) | 45.2% | 11% | N/A | N/A | 2.4% |
| Uzbekistan | (2005) (estimations) | 32.5% | 23% | 55% | Subsidies covering budget deficits: 16.2% | N/A |

**Sources:** *Domestic sources, UNDP, World Bank as compiled by authors; data on Tajikistan and Turkmenistan are insufficient or not available. It could not be verified whether all data are calculated on the same basis, in particular due to extra-budgetary funds.*

The study of the dynamics of the correlation of expenditures of local budgets to GDP shows a downward trend. Thus, in the Russian Federation the share of GDP allocated to local budget expenditures was 6.5% in 2003, 6.2% in 2004, and 5.3% in 2005.

On January 1, 2006, the share of local expenditures in the general volume of public services consumed 18% of the consolidated budget of the Russian Federation, and 40% of the consolidated budgets of member states of the Russian Federation.

In other countries, too, transfers are an important part of local budgets. For instance, in Belarus the share of transfers in the general volume of revenues reaches 58%, depending on the kind of territorial units and the relationships between state local government and local self-government. In Uzbekistan, where law proclaims the principle of balanced local budgets, grants are used to cover deficits. In Kazakhstan, the share of grants is high and has a tendency to grow: in 2004 by 19.81%, in 2005 by 25.28% and in 2006 by 37.1%. A similar tendency can be observed in several countries, such as Ukraine and Georgia. This reflects the low buoyancy of tax shares compared to expenditure needs that are growing faster.

Financial provisions for certain state functions delegated to local self-government are made with the help of subventions transferred to local budgets from federal or regional budgets. Bodies of local self-government are responsible for the use of material and financial resources received by them for the execution of certain state powers.

Aggregate data on the local finances of the states of Eurasia is provided in Table 3. But such data have to be used with care. Due to the unstable economic situation of many of

*In Russia and most of the European part of the region, main local government functions are education, public health, social security, culture, local economy, sport and physical training and youth policy. In most of Central Asia, such functions are exercised by state executive entities integrated in a hierarchically centralized system*

the countries of the region, economic indicators are volatile; important differences in terms of GDP, and percentage of GDP may occur from one year to the next. Furthermore, changes in proportions may have different meanings, depending on other characteristics of the situation. For example, a diminution of the share of local government expenditure may be due to the centralization of expenditure, or to a sharp increase of GDP caused, for example, by an increase in oil prices.

*Functions*. The functions of local authorities are not clearly defined by law. Such ambiguity is explained primarily by an ongoing process of redistribution of powers among different levels of government. Nevertheless, it is possible to distinguish several models of function allocation.

*Main functions.* The main functions of local self-government in Russia and Armenia are to: provide participation of the population in local matters, ensure effective development of territories, provide public services, represent and protect the rights and interests of local self-government, manage municipal property and finances, protect public order and organize public transportation.

In Russia, in the course of the reform of local self-government, the functions of municipal units were enlarged, thus limiting regulation by subjects of the Federation. The law has reshaped the functions of municipal units, taking into account their nature and status. Law has also prescribed more clearly the economic basis of local self-government and specified the responsibilities of bodies and officials. Further, the law has introduced new schemes of economic inter-municipal cooperation and regulated more precisely the procedures for transferring certain state functions to local self-government. Today, the main responsibilities of local self-government are education, public health, social security, culture, local economy, sport and physical training and youth policy.

The same functions are transferred to the local level in several other states of the region. For instance, in Ukraine, health services, education and social protection represent more than 80% of local public expenditures. Furthermore, Ukrainian local authorities manage communal property and local finances, ensure development of appropriate territories, provide services to the population, ensure participation of the population in civic life, and protect public order.

In the majority of the states of Central Asia, such functions are exercised by state executive entities integrated in a hierarchically centralized system. Accordingly, state functions are distributed between different levels of the vertical structure. Regulatory functions belong to central administrations. The execution of laws is reserved for local authorities. As an example, in Kazakhstan the role of local government in health care and social aid remains significant. Kazakhstan local government expenditures in 2004 were: administrative functions 4%, defense 2%, police 4%, education 31%, health care 20%, social aid 7%, local economy 12%, transportation 6% and 14% for other lesser functions. In Uzbekistan, regional and city budgets represent 64.4% of all social spending, including 69.6% of all spending on education and 61.4% of all healthcare spending.

### III.2. Main Trends in Selected Competences

*Planning.* Planning is an important endeavor in all the states of the region. In Russia, it serves as a basis for federal, regional and municipal programs aimed at the development of municipal units. Instead of the former strictly centralized methods of governance that were characteristic of the Soviet period, Armenia and Russia apply new approaches to planning that exclude administrative mandates. The states of Central Asia retain, as a rule, centralized systems of planning for economic and social development.

**Education.** In the majority of states, responsibility for public education is divided between local state government and local self-government. The latter, as a rule, is entitled to deal with pre-school and basic education. Nevertheless, central state government establishes general legal norms in this sphere, and local self-governments put these norms into practice.

In Uzbekistan, education is centralized. For pre-school and basic education, central state organs approve standards, provide resources and supervise the execution of laws, while other levels are engaged in providing services and deploying resources.

In Tajikistan, local self-government is responsible for pre-school and elementary school institutions, while cities and districts handle secondary schools and colleges. In Ukraine, there is no strict separation of functions in education, which results in a confusion of powers between local state government and local self-government.

In Armenia, according to the law "On State Non-Commercial Organizations," the state reserves the role of founder of educational institutions. At the same time, as provided by the law "On Local Self-Government," all facilities of pre-school education were given to municipalities and became municipal property.

**Provision of social services.** In the majority of the states of Eurasia local self-government has fairly broad functions in the provision of social services. For instance, Russian law prescribes that local self-government is responsible for organizing social protection of the population, providing social assistance, establishing different social services and assisting institutions that provide social services.

In Armenia, social services administration is assigned to the state. But even there, local self-government has been empowered to provide social services through their own social programs. The same situation prevails in Tajikistan, where providing social services is handled on three levels: that of the republic, the region and the locale. Regional and local authorities are entitled to maintain the institutions that provide assistance at home.

In Kazakhstan, local state organs pay allowances and benefits to the unemployed, large families, orphans and single mothers. They also subsidize childbirth, housing and funeral expenses. Ukraine has made a clear separation of responsibilities in the sphere of social services. The law "On Social Services" (2003) establishes two spheres of state and community services financed by different budgets.

**Provision of public health services.** Nearly all states of the region have divided the responsibility for public health between state (national and provincial) government and local self-government. The exception is Ukraine where powers of local self-government are not clearly defined. In Russia and a number of other states, local authorities are responsible for providing medical first-aid, organizing medical aid in the "zone of first contact" with patients in hospitals, ambulances and medical posts, and organizing preventive medical services.

According to laws of Armenia, heads of municipalities are responsible for organizing and managing municipal health-care institutions. They promote improvement of sanitation and implement sanitary, hygienic, anti-epidemic and quarantine measures. In Kazakhstan, local state authorities administer public health. They assist local hospitals and general polyclinics, specialized clinics, tuberculosis hospitals, diagnostic centers and rural medical posts. They are also responsible for the prevention and treatment of dangerous infections. In Uzbekistan, public health is handled mainly by the state. Local self-government is responsible for organizing and maintaining medical posts.

The majority of states have a multi-level system for financing social services. As a rule, local state authorities and local self-governments do not have adequate financial resources for maintaining public services in the fields of education, public health and social aid, though total budgets grow constantly.

In Tajikistan, public health and social services are not handled by local governments. However, local budgets finance 7% and 8% of expenditure on social aid and education. Another model exists in Uzbekistan: 100% of expenditure on social insurance is covered by local budgets. Meanwhile, social aid, public health and education costs are financed as follows: about 20% by the state, approximately 50% by regional budgets, and 20% to 30% by district budgets. In 2005, Russian Federation local budgets financed 22% of expenditure on public health, 16% on social policy and 43% on education.

***Water, energy and public transportation.*** In Russia, responsibility for public transportation, and for providing water, energy, gas and heat falls to local self-government. Organs of self-government have received broad powers and may have appropriate objects in municipal property, which permit them to implement these functions. In Armenia, infrastructures of gas, energy and water supplies used for municipal needs may be transferred, according to the Law "On Local Self-government," to municipal property.

In Belarus, Ukraine and in the states of Central Asia, the functions of water and energy supplies and public transport are within the province of local state administrations. They are obligated to provide for the management and maintenance of local services, and to grant subsidies to users. Nevertheless, it is necessary to note that local budgets are not always able to provide adequately for the management and maintenance of these functions due to shabby condition and a shortage of financial means.

***Business development support.*** In Azerbaijan, Armenia, Russia and Ukraine, support to business development may be provided at all levels: by central, regional and local state bodies, as well as by local self-government. Several countries, including Russia, not only affirm the right of local self-government to support business development, they also provide necessary financial resources.

In the states of Central Asia, support for business development comes primarily from central state entities. Nevertheless, the role of local state authorities is also considerable. Local governing bodies are responsible for licensing economic activities at the local level, granting permission for construction of community nets and buildings, organizing tenders for the provision of social services, and managing the sale of community property.

A summary table on functions of local authorities is presented below (see table 4).

### III.3. Administrative Capacity

Efficient execution of powers by local authorities is determined not only by adequate financing, but also by a well-organized professional municipal or state local service.

***Municipal service.*** The notion of municipal service in the nations of Eurasia is applied to the level of local self-government. Unlike many other countries, the Eurasian countries generally do not include employees engaged in the sphere of education. Municipal service is regarded as a professional activity that has to be exercised independently of state bodies, regardless of political forces and results of local elections.

In all countries of the region, the executive bodies of city municipalities function on a more professional level. Rural territorial communities have far fewer municipal employees, and their knowledge of munic-

| Table 4 | Functions of Local Government (Intermediate and Local Levels) |
|---|---|

| Country | Planning | Education | Social services | Public health | Water supply | Energy supply | Public transport | Support of business |
|---|---|---|---|---|---|---|---|---|
| Armenia | Yes | No (with the exception of pre-school institutions) | No (with the exception of voluntary implementation of own municipal social programs) | Yes | Yes | Yes | Yes | Yes |
| Azerbaijan | Yes | No | Yes (in the spheres not occupied by the state). | Yes | Yes. | No | Yes | Yes |
| Belarus | Yes | Yes | Yes | Yes | Yes | Yes | Yes | Yes |
| Georgia | Yes | Yes | Yes | Yes | Yes | Yes | Yes | Yes |
| Kazakhstan | Yes | Yes (elementary, secondary and professional secondary education) | Yes | Yes | Yes | Yes | Yes | Yes |
| Kyrgyz Republic | Yes | Yes | Yes | Yes | Yes | Yes | Yes | Yes |
| Moldova | Yes | Yes | Yes | Yes | Yes | Yes | Yes | Yes |
| Russia | Yes | Yes | Yes | Yes | Yes | Yes | Yes | Yes |
| Tajikistan | Yes | Yes (pre-school and basic educational institutions) | No | No (though local budgets finance public health - 8%) | Yes | Yes | Yes | Yes |
| Turkmenistan | Yes | N/A | N/A | Yes | Yes | Yes | Yes | Yes |
| Ukraine | Yes | Yes | Yes | Yes | Yes | Yes | Yes | Yes |
| Uzbekistan | Yes | Yes | Yes | Yes | Yes | Yes | Yes | Yes |

**Source:** *UCLG Country Profiles (2007).*

ipal management and marketing is low. The improvement of the professional level of municipal employees is still an acute problem in the development of local self-government.

In Russia, there were in 2006 about 280,000 employees (on average, one municipal employee for every 500 citizens) (see table 5). According to Russian law, the municipal service is exclusively comprised of persons working in local self-government. Municipal institutions, such as schools and healthcare facilities are not regarded as bodies of local self-government and, as a result, their employees are excluded from municipal service. The legal status of municipal employees is established by federal laws, laws of member states of the federation and charters of municipal entities. The status of municipal employees and the guarantees of their employment are based in the main on general principles, applied to the state public service. Evaluation of the work of municipal employees is exercised on the basis of qualification exams and attestations. For non-execution or undue

| Table 5 | Staff of local government |
|---|---|

| Countries | Staff | Regime (public or private law, carrier or job positions) | Status (law or contract) | Recruitment procedure especially in higher positions | Training |
|---|---|---|---|---|---|
| Armenia | N/A | Public law; carrier and contract professional municipal service | Legal status is defined by the law "On Municipal Service" | Municipal employees are appointed by heads of municipalities | The law provides for organization of training courses |
| Azerbaijan | 25,000 (average 1 municipal employee for 300 citizens) | Public law; carrier and contract professional municipal service. | Legal status is regulated by the law "On Municipal Service" dated November 30, 1999 | Chairmen of municipalities appoint heads of branch departments on the basis of the decisions of municipalities; other municipal employees are appointed directly by heads of municipalities | N/A |
| Belarus | 22,000 at the end of 2005 | Public law; contract state service | Legal status is defined by the law "On State Public Service in the Republic of Belarus" | Municipal employees are appointed by heads of local government bodies on the basis of exams | Training courses |
| Kazakhstan | 46,546 | Public law; contract service | Activity of local bodies is regulated by legislation of state public service | Akims and heads of staff of regions, capital and city of Almaty are political, appointed state employees. The majority of employees of representative and executive bodies are carrier employees (according to results of contests and attestations). | N/A |
| Kyrgyz Republic | N/A | Public law; contract and carrier service | Legal status is defined by the law "On Municipal Service" | Municipal employees are engaged according to results of contests and attestations | N/A |
| Moldova | N/A | Public law; contract | Application of the law on the state civil service | Appointment and dismissal by the mayor or district head | N/A |
| Russia | Approximately 280,000 (average 1 municipal employee for 500 residents) | Public law; contract service | Legal status is defined by federal laws, laws of member states of the Russian Federation and by charters of municipal units | Heads of municipal units may be elected directly by population or appointed by representative bodies of municipalities. Other employees are appointed by heads of municipal units | Training courses |
| Tajikistan | N/A | Public law; contract service | Legislation regulating state public service | Employees of local bodies are appointed by heads of local administrations | N/A |
| Turkmenistan | N/A | Public law; contract service | Legislation regulating state public service | Employees of local bodies are appointed by heads of local administrations | N/A |
| Ukraine | 91,925 municipal employees as on September 1, 2006 | Public law; contract service | Legislation regulating state public service | Election and appointment of municipal employees | Staff reserves for appointment and promotion of municipal employees |
| Uzbekistan | N/A | Public law; contract service | Legislation regulating state public service | Appointment by higher bodies and heads of local gvt bodies | N/A |

**Sources:**  *UCLG Country Profiles (2007).*

execution of their duties municipal employees may by subjected to disciplinary punishments. The new federal framework law number 25 of March 2, 2007, establishes a new unified legal basis for the municipal public service. It is linked to the state public service, but clearly differentiated from the elected officials; it is aimed at professionalizing and stabilizing the corps of municipal public servants. The new law took effect on June 1, 2007, and has to be developed by laws of the subjects of the Federation.

Presently in Azerbaijan there are about 25,000 municipal employees: on average, one for every 300 citizens. In Belarus, state employees function on the local level. Their numbers comprise approximately 22,000 persons: on average, one for every 450 citizens.

***Integrity of elected officials and employees; prevention of corruption.*** Municipal authorities face the same danger of corruption as authorities do at other levels of public power. Mass media inform the public about criminal prosecution of municipal employees for bribes, thefts and other misuses of public functions.

Sociological inquiries conducted in one of the regions (oblasts) of Ukraine show that annually 60% of respondents witness at least one incident of corruption (15.69 % reported 'numerous,' 28.55% 'several' incidents of corruption).

A number of countries have adopted legal remedies to aid the struggle with corruption. For instance, the government of Armenia enacted the decree "On Anti-Corruption Strategy and Program of Implementation." It provides measures strengthening public control over bodies of local self-government, creating transparent procedures for forming local budgets and spending local funds. It emphasizes the necessity of holding local self-government officials personally liable for misdeeds.

Several states of Eurasia have ratified the UN "Convention against Corruption" and the European "Criminal Law Convention on Corruption."

***Management reforms.*** A number of countries, including Russia and Ukraine, have launched administrative reforms to improve the functioning of all chains of public management. The emphasis for local self-government is recruiting professional administrators with sufficient knowledge and experience to resolve most local issues. In recent years, the percentage of such employees in the system of local self-government has visibly increased. These changes were directly caused by replenishment and intensive education of municipal employees. The states of the region also adopted measures for the introduction of modern management technologies. Emphasis is placed on the importance of strict registration procedures and rapid responses to the requests of citizens.

The improvement of the quality of local services is also connected with further privatization of municipal property, in particular in the sphere of residential community economy.

## IV.  Local Democracy

A certain indicator of progress for local democracy is the increasing competitiveness of local elections at the levels where they are organized, even though this occurs only at the lowest level of governance in some countries. Electoral participation remains low in some countries, but is comparable to European countries in others. It is useful at this point to précis the legal status of local government bodies because this factor can have an impact on the relationships between elected bodies and the local administration.

The following table summarizes the basic institutional features of local democracy in the countries of the region.

*Mass media inform the public about criminal prosecution of municipal employees for bribes, thefts and other misuses of public functions*

## Table 6  Local Democracy

| State | Formation of local representative bodies | Local executive bodies | General features of electoral systems | Number of deputies (minimum and maximum) | Term of powers |
|---|---|---|---|---|---|
| **Armenia** | Elections of councils of municipalities | Big administrative territorial units are governed by bodies of local state government. Municipalities (villages, settlements, cities and quarter communities of Erevan) are managed exclusively by organs of local self-government. Heads of municipalities are elected. | In elections of bodies of local self-government, candidates are appointed exclusively at their own initiative, but most candidates are affiliated with different parties providing them appropriate support. In the elections of heads and councils of municipalities, majority electoral system applies. In 2005 elections, bodies of local self-government were formed in 829 out of 930 communities of Armenia. | Depending on the quantity of population, 5 to 15 members of municipal councils (5 members for municipalities not exceeding 1,000 residents and 15 members for municipalities totaling more than 20,000 residents) | Local self-government bodies are elected for a 4-year term. |
| **Azerbaijan** | Elections of members of municipalities | Heads of executive power of cities and districts (state local government) are appointed by the President and are responsible to him. Chairmen of municipalities (local self-government bodies) are elected; they direct activities of executive staff of municipalities. | Majority electoral system. In the 2004 elections 2,731 municipal bodies were elected composed of 21,613 members of municipalities. On October 6, 2006, by-elections were held with the aim to fill 1,941 vacancies in 604 municipalities | The number of members of municipalities is determined by law, depending on the quantity of population of municipalities | Members of municipalities are elected for a term of 5 years |
| **Belarus** | Elections of local councils. There are 3 territorial levels of local councils: primary, basic and regional | Chairmen of regional executive committees are appointed by the President of the Republic with consent of regional councils (by majority of votes of elected deputies). Appointment of chairman of district (city) executive committees is by chairmen of regional executive committees with consent of appropriate district (city) councils. Chairmen of district (city) committees may be appointed directly by chairmen of regional committees when his candidates have been twice rejected by appropriate district (city) councils | Majority electoral system. In the elections held on January 14, 2007, 1,581 local councils were elected comprising 22,639 deputies. Absolute majority of deputies were not affiliated with any party | | Local council members are elected for terms of 4 years. |

| State | Formation of local representative bodies | Local executive bodies | General features of electoral systems | Number of deputies (minimum and maximum) | Term of powers |
|---|---|---|---|---|---|
| Georgia | 1,017 local councils (sakrebulo) are elected | Local councils elect mayors. Local council of the city of Tbilisi elects the mayor from among its members for a term of 4 years. | In Georgia at the local elections of 2006, 69 local councils were elected in 4 self-governing cities, 60 municipalities, 4 communities in zones of conflict and one in the capital city, Tbilisi. A proportional electoral system was used in Tbilisi and a mixed electoral system in other constituencies. 1,733 councilors were elected under the new mixed electoral system | The council of city of Tbilisi is composed of 37 members: 25 members are elected in 10 multi-member majority election districts. Remaining 12 seats are distributed proportionally among the parties that gained 4 % of the votes in all 10 of Tbilisi's 10 districts | Local councils are elected for a term of four years. |
| Kazakhstan | Local self-government bodies are provided only at the lowest level, but they are still not formed. Elections to state local representative bodies of provinces, districts and cities of republican and district significance | Executive bodies of state local government (akims) have been until now appointed by the President of the upper akim. But they may be elected according to the procedure determined by the President. In 2005–2007, elections of akims have been gradually introduced in rural circuits, villages and settlements and as an experiment in several districts and city districts of Astana and Almaty | Majority electoral system is used for elections of state local representative bodies. Second round of elections is held when no candidate has received 50% of votes. Elections of lower akims in administrative units with population less than 5, 000 are held directly, with population exceeding 5, 000, indirectly through electors. | The number of deputies of local state representative bodies is determined with account of population of appropriate units in the procedure as specified by the Law On Local State Government. Representative bodies of Astana and Alma-Ata are composed of not more than 50 (city, 30, district, 25) deputies. | Local representative bodies and akims are elected for a term of 4 years. |
| Kyrgyz Rep. | Local self-government functions only at the lower level in small settlements. Bodies of representative and executive power are headed by hokims. | Executive bodies of local self-government are elected. Hokims (heads of state administrations) of districts are appointed and removed by the President with consent of appropriate local council, and after consultations with the Prime Minister | Proportional electoral system is used for elections of local councils. 6,737 members of local councils were elected at the elections of 2004. Majority electoral system is used for elections of heads of administrations of administrative circuits. In 2006, elections were held in 34 circuits with populations not exceeding 9,000 residents. | | Hokims of state administrations of districts are appointed for terms of 4 years. |
| Moldova | Local councils and mayors of local communities are elected. | In the elections held on June 3, 2007, 899 mayors of municipalities, towns, communes and villages. | 11,967 members of local councils were elected in 2007. A proportional electoral system was used for the elections of councilors, and a majority electoral system with a run off between the two top-scoring candidates for the elections of mayors. Second round of elections of 473 mayors was held on June 17, 2007. | The number of councilors depends on the size of the population. | Councilors and mayors are elected for 4-year terms. |

## Table 6    Local Democracy (Cont.)

| State | Formation of local representative bodies | Local executive bodies | General features of electoral systems | Number of deputies (minimum and maximum) | Term of powers |
|---|---|---|---|---|---|
| **Russia** | Representative bodies of local self-government are formed in units with populations exceeding 100 voters. When there are fewer than 100 voters, the powers of representative bodies are exercised directly by meetings of citizens. However the rights of a municipal authority can be exercised only for a unit of 1,000 inhabitants as a whole (3,000 in areas of higher density). | Heads of municipal units according to their charters are elected by voters or appropriate representative bodies. Local administrations are headed by heads of municipal units or by persons employed on a contractual basis and with account of the results of contests for filling the aforesaid positions | Law provides for the use of both majority and proportional electoral systems. In fact, majority electoral system prevails. | The number of members of representative bodies of settlements, including urban circuits, is determined by charters of municipal units and may not be less than: 7 for populations less than 1,000; 10 for populations over 1,000 and less than 10,000; 15 for populations of more than 10,000 and less than 30,000; 20 for populations more than 30,000 and less than 100,000; 25 for populations over 100,000 and less than 500,000; 35 for populations exceeding 500,000. The number of deputies of district representative bodies is determined by charters of municipal units, and may not be less than 15 The number of deputies of representative bodies of inner-city territories that are of federal significance are defined by charters of municipal units and may not be less than 10. | The terms of powers of local self-government bodies are defined by charters of municipalities |
| **Tajikistan** | Local self-government functions only at the lower level in small settlements. Local state representative bodies (councils of people's deputies) are formed in provinces and districts. | Heads of local state executive power are appointed by the President with consent of appropriate local councils of people's deputies. They also act as chairmen of these councils. | Majority electoral system is used. | | |
| **Turkmenistan** | System of local self-government is formed by directly elected local councils (Gengeshi) of settlements and territorial public self-government bodies. | Local state executive power is exercised by hakims appointed and removed from their posts by, and responsible to, the President. Local councils (Gengeshi) elect from their members chairmen (archyns). | | | Local councils (Gengeshi) are elected for 5-year terms. |

| State | Formation of local representative bodies | Local executive bodies | General features of electoral systems | Number of deputies (minimum and maximum) | Term of powers |
|---|---|---|---|---|---|
| Ukraine | There are two models of organization of local self-government. The first model at the level of villages, settlements and towns does not provide for local state administrations. The second model in Regions and districts provides for the mixed model, including establishment of district and Regional councils as organs of local self-government and Regional state administrations as local state organs. | The law provides for the election of heads of settlements, villages and towns (heads of territorial gromadas). Local councils form local executive bodies upon proposal of heads of settlements, villages and towns. Districts and provinces, Kiev and Sevastopol have local state administrations functioning as agents of the state and excluded from the system of local self-government. Heads of local state administrations are appointed and removed from their posts by the President upon proposal of the Cabinet of Ministers of Ukraine. | Majority electoral system is used for the elections of rural and settlement councils and heads of settlements, villages and towns. In other elections (city, district, Regional councils, Parliament of the Autonomous Republic of Crimea) proportional electoral system is applied |  | 4 years |
| Uzbekistan | Councils (Kengeshi) of people's deputies are representative bodies of local state government elected at the level of provinces, districts and cities. Local self-government bodies are formed at the level of settlements, villages, auls and in makhalya of cities. | Bodies of representative and executive power in provinces, districts and cities are headed by hokims of appropriate territorial units | Majority electoral system on multi-party basis is used in the elections of provincial, district and city councils of peoples deputies |  | The term of powers of councils of people's deputies and hokims is 5 years.<br><br>Chairmen (aksakaks) of councils and members of councils of local self-government are elected for term of 2 or 5 years. |

**Sources:** *UCLG Country Profiles (2007).*

## IV.1.  Local Government Bodies

All states of Eurasia have diversified models of local self-government organization. At the lowest (grass root) territorial level there are no permanent bodies. Local matters are resolved, as a rule, by means of direct democracy. Appropriate organs appear at higher levels of local self-government.

The organizational structure of higher municipal units in the Russian Federation, Armenia, Azerbaijan, Georgia and Moldova is composed of representative bodies, heads of municipal units, local administrations and other organs and elected officials of local self-government as stipulated by laws and charters of municipal units. The structure of local administrations is established by the representative bodies upon proposals of heads of local administrations.

As a rule, municipal units in the states of Eurasia do not have the rights of corporate persons. Nevertheless, they take part in civil law relations on an equal basis with other participants both physical and corporate (in particular, in Russia, Belarus, Kazakhstan, Tajikistan). The rights of corporate persons are granted to organs of municipal units acting on their behalf. They may obtain and exercise property and non-property rights and obligations and represent municipal units in courts. On the whole the status of corporate persons is held by local representative bodies and local administrations. In a number of municipal units (for instance, in Vologod oblast of the Russian Federation) this status is also granted to certain executive bodies or structural divisions of local administrations. Organs of local self-government as corporate persons are subject to obligatory state registration in the form of institutions.

Another model exists in Azerbaijan and Moldova. According to the Law of the Republic of Moldova "On Local Public Administration," administrative-territorial units have the rights of corporate persons in public law. They may obtain and dispose of property and enter contractual obligations through their own organs, acting within the powers as provided by normative acts and charters of municipal units.

The same powers are exercised by respective bodies of municipal units of Azerbaijan. Unlike similar bodies in other countries, such as Kyrgyz Republic, Ukraine and Uzbekistan, those in Azerbaijan do not have the rights of corporate persons.

## IV.2.  Local Political Systems

The role of political parties varies considerably according to the level of development and the extent of self-government.

***Role of political parties.*** Local representative bodies exist in all states of Eurasia. For instance, in Georgia there are 1,017 local councils (sakrebulo).

In Russia there are 252,000 elected members of local representative bodies; most members serve on a voluntary basis. Local councils are composed of not less than seven members for municipal units with populations above 1,000, and not less than 35 members for municipal units with population exceeding 500,000 persons.

Political parties in the countries in the region participate in local elections in different ways and to different degrees. In the countries with developed forms of local self-government, including Azerbaijan, Armenia, Georgia, Kyrgyz Republic, Russia and Ukraine, major political parties take part in all elections. In most of these countries, the creation of independent local parties is prohibited by law.

The main function of political parties is to support their own candidates (Belarus, Russia, Ukraine), or candidates who have proposed themselves (Armenia). For instance, in Russia 9% to 17% of candidates in municipal elections are put forward by political parties.

*In the countries where many elements of local self-government exist only at the lowest level of governance, the participation of political parties is less significant*

On the whole, local elections in these countries take place in a highly competitive atmosphere. Thus, in Azerbaijan candidates of 26 political parties took part in the municipal elections of 1999. In Georgia, 21 political parties and blocks took part in the elections of the Tbilisi municipal government held in 2002. In local elections in 2006, seven political parties participated; two of them presented joint lists of candidates. In Moldova, 22 political parties took part in the local elections of 2007.

In many municipalities in Russia, Armenia, Azerbaijan and Georgia, more than ten candidates compete for each vacant position.

In the countries where many elements of local self-government exist only at the lowest level of governance (Uzbekistan, Kyrgyz Republic and Tajikistan), the participation of political parties is less significant, though such participation is provided for by law. As a rule, elections for local government offices are non-partisan. Uzbekistan is an exception: five political parties recently participated in the elections of local representatives. Legislation in Kyrgyz Republic stipulates that candidates for elected municipal posts may be proposed by voters at their place of work, service or residence or education; by groups of voters at conferences of political parties; or by the candidates themselves.

In the states providing for separation of representative and executive branches (Armenia, Kyrgyz Republic, Moldova, Uzbekistan and Ukraine in district cities), candidates to the executive are directly elected by the population.

In Russia there are two procedures for electing local-level executive officials. Under the first procedure, the heads of the executive branch, who are also the heads of municipal administration, are chosen by direct popular election. Under the other procedure, they are appointed by council through a contract on the basis of a com-petitive examination. In the municipal elections of 2005, more than 30% of the heads of municipal entities were directly elected.

In Azerbaijan, each municipality has its own executive branch and executive staff, including the chairman of the municipality, heads of agencies and departments, specialists and other employees.

Representation of women is increasing in local governments in Russia, Belarus, Moldova, Ukraine and some other states. In the Russian Federation, women comprise about 30% of municipal leaders and 47% of local council members. In the local elections of 2007 in Belarus, women took 45.7% of the posts in representative bodies. In Ukraine, 40.2% of local council members are women. In Georgia's 2006 elections, women managed to take only 11.4% of local council seats, and in Kyrgyz Republic after the elections of 2004, representation of women in local councils was only 19.1%.

## IV.3. Electoral Systems

Election by majority vote is the rule for most local governments. In Ukraine, a proportional electoral system has been used broadly since 2004. In particular, this system is used for the election of deputies of city councils. At times it has caused excessive politicization of local government and inappropriate transfers to the local level of debates on regional, linguistic and foreign policy. It has also increased the number of inter-party clashes in some regions.

In Russia the law permits the use of both proportional and majority electoral systems for local elections. The system of choice is established by the charter of a municipal entity; most use the voter-majority system.

In Georgia's local elections of 2002 and 2006, a proportional electoral system was applied in Tbilisi. In other regions of that

*Representation of women is increasing in local governments in Russia, Belarus, Moldova, Ukraine and some other states*

country, a majority electoral system was used in 2002, and a mixed electoral system in 2006.

In Uzbekistan and Tajikistan, the majority electoral system is used for local elections.

## IV.4. Citizen Participation

Citizens demonstrate different attitudes toward local political life. As a rule, they still prefer to turn to the central state for resolution of their problems, although this is changing. In communities where local governments have sufficient resources, can decide local issues efficiently, and defend the interests of the local population, the authority and status of local government is high, sometimes rivaling state authorities. For instance, in Russia mayors of several cities are more popular than governors of the subjects of the Federation. In countries such as Armenia, Georgia and Moldova, where local resources are limited, the population typically regards local government as simply the lowest level of state power.

Overall, throughout the Eurasian region, voter participation in local elections is lower than the turnout for national elections.

In Russia, voter participation in elections for rural representative bodies and executive leaders was 56.43% and 54.81% respectively. In municipal districts, voter turnout for comparable elections was 50.46% for the representative body and again 54.81% for executive posts.

According to official data for the 2004 elections in Azerbaijan, 46% of registered voters took part in municipal elections there. In Belarus, local elections in 2003 saw 73% voter participation, and in Georgia the turnout for elections in 2005 was more than 40%.

In all countries of the region, legislation provides for different forms of direct democracy. In practice, these forms are employed with different levels of energy and consistency.

*Local referendums are only practised in Russia on the establishment or structure of local governments, although they are provided for all legislations. Forms of citizen participation at the sub-municipal level are still most popular*

In Russia, law establishes such procedures as local referendum, recall of local elected officials, voting on changes of the boundaries of municipal entities and on their reform, rulemaking initiatives, public hearings, meetings and conferences of citizens, and other civic activities. In 2004–2005, some 400 local referendums were held in 22 of the 89 subjects –districts– that comprise the Russian Federation; most of the referendums concerned the establishment or structure of local governments.

Belarus' Constitution and Electoral Code provides for local referendums and recalls of deputies of local soviets (councils) of deputies. However, there were no local referendums, and recalls of deputies were rare. At the same time, local meetings are broadly used in accordance with the Law of 2000.

In Ukraine, the law provides for elections, referendums, general meetings at the place of residence, local initiatives, public hearings, and recall of deputies and local elected officials. Forms most often used in practice include general meetings at the place of residence, local initiatives and public hearings on different issues, including taxation. Referendums are held only rarely.

Legislation of the countries of Central Asia does provide for elections and referendums. But in the main, only state-wide referendums are held. In Uzbekistan, local government takes the form of assemblies of citizens convened in settlements, villages, kishlaks, auls and makhalyas. Managing bodies of local government structures are elected by, and are responsible to voters residing in the respective territories.

The Constitution of Armenia establishes two main forms of direct democracy: elections and referendums. No referendum has yet been held.

In several countries, there are forms of democratic participation below the municipal level, including groups representing a neighborhood, part of a residential area or a common interest.

In Russia, this sub-municipal level may include groups speaking for an apartment building, part of an apartment building, a residential unit or a rural settlement. Public sentiments may be expressed in meetings and conferences of citizens, as well as by means of local elections. This civic sub-level is responsible for such issues as maintenance of residential buildings and adjacent territories and the resolution of local problems.

Azerbaijan enacted in 2001 the law "On the Model Rules of Block Committees of Municipalities," which serves as a basis for establishing new organizations to assist municipalities with governance at the sub-municipal level of apartment buildings and city blocks. Block committees composed of from five to 11 people are elected at civic meetings.

In Belarus, territorial government functions not only at the level of residential units – apartment complexes and city blocks – but also in settlements as well. In all, Belarus counts 43,758 such micro-units of governance.

In Uzbekistan, there are more than 10,000 local communities (makhalyas). Members of these communities are united by place of residence, traditions and customs, forms of communication, legal, economic and family relations. For centuries they served as a means for elaborating and regulating principles and rules of community life, for shaping ideological and philosophical views, forming morals, honoring traditions and expressing public opinion.

In Ukraine, citizens may on their own initiative create committees to represent apartment buildings, the residents on one street, block committees and other groups with the consent of appropriate local councils. Such self-organizing groups are more popular in some parts of the country than in others. For instance, in Faustov (population: 50,000) about 200 self-organized committees were created, yet in Kiev (population: 2,660,000) there are only 80.

Typically, citizens receive information about the activities of local committees and governments through traditional forms, such as mass media, posted announcements and word of mouth. But increasingly, electronic means of civic participation are being developed, especially in Russia and Ukraine. Electronic communication networks of local governments disseminate information to the public, albeit mostly official information and announcements. Information pertaining to citizen participation in local governmental affairs is still something of a rarity.

## IV.5. Central-Local Relationships

In all countries of the region, there is a system of state supervision over local agencies of state government as well as local self-governments. Such central supervision is exercised through executive powers, prosecution offices and courts. In several countries, these controlling agencies cooperate with each other; in other countries they function without noticeable coordination.

The President and the government of Russia and heads of subjects of the Federation may consider citizen grievances concerning the actions or inaction of municipal employees and officials. Federal ministries may also assist citizens seeking redress of grievances.

In Azerbaijan, supervision of local self-government is exercised by the Ministry of Justice. This ministry is not only responsible for ensuring that local governments act in a lawful manner, but also for controlling expenditure of public means and supervising observance of human rights. The Ministry of Justice provides an annual report on these issues. In 2005, some 240 local government actions were revoked and 70 acts of municipalities were amended.

*Typically, citizens receive information about the activities of local committees and governments through traditional forms, such as mass media, posted announcements and word of mouth. But increasingly, electronic means of civic participation are being developed, especially in Russia and Ukraine*

In the Russian Federation, the Ministry of Justice does not have such functions. Supervision of local self-government is exercised by prosecution units (prokuratura).

In Ukraine, control over local self-government is exercised by committees of the Parliament and by local offices of state administrations, and the prosecution office (prokuratura). Financial control is exercised by agencies such as the Accounting Chamber, State Control and Revision Service, or Fund of State Property.

*In all countries of the region, there is a system of state supervision over local agencies of state government as well as local self-governments. Such central supervision is exercised through executive powers, prosecution offices and courts*

Financial control, as a rule, is held by ministries of finance in Armenia, Belarus, Russia and Ukraine, and by the Ministries of Internal Revenue in Belarus. Branch oversight is carried out by appropriate departments of ministries and state agencies. Prosecution units (prokuratura) in all countries exercise control over strict and uniform execution of laws.

There are also forms of popular control over local self-government. In Russia, charters of municipal entities may provide for recall of local elected officials.

In Armenia, Russia and Ukraine, acts of local self-government entities may be quashed by courts or by the entity that issued the acts.

In other Eurasian countries, local acts may be revoked or suspended by the head of the state (Belarus), the supreme legislative body (Council of the Republic in Belarus, Parliament in Uzbekistan), or by offices of state power, which is the way in the countries of Central Asia.

The functions of bodies of local self-government may be terminated ahead of time on their own initiative (self-dissolution), by court decision (Armenia, Russia), or by decision of the Parliament (Kazakhstan, Kyrgyz Republic). In Azerbaijan, the dissolution of local self-government bodies is not provided for in law.

In the countries of Central Asia, the Russian Federation and Armenia appointed employees of local governing bodies may be dismissed by the higher officials who appointed them. Grounds for dismissal of municipal employees in Russia and Armenia often include: court decisions prohibiting the occupation of a particular position in municipal government bodies, expiration of contracts or reaching a specified age limit.

In the majority of the countries of Central Asia, there are systems of central-government executive branches that ensure the conduct of uniform state policy in appropriate spheres of activities. These central-government authorities cooperate with local governments on matters pertaining to execution of the functions of a local government, adopt within their competence normative legal acts and give instructions and recommendations on due exercise of powers on the local level. Ministries may exercise functions of coordination and control, with the exception of local organs of internal affairs (police), which have dual subordination, similar to the former soviet system of government.

In Armenia, Belarus, Russia and Ukraine, the impact of branch offices of executive power (central and regional) on the activities of local government and local self-government is demonstrated in the control over the execution of delegated state functions. In the event of violations, appropriate state officials may give in written form mandatory instructions for eliminating violations. In Russia, such instructions may be appealed in the courts.

In all countries of Eurasia, bodies of local self-government may sue a state authority or state officials for actions or decisions infringing local rights. Citizens also have the right to file a suit if they believe government at any level has violated their right to self-government. In several countries, conflicts between local self-government bodies and private (individual and corporate) persons may be resolved only in the courts, unless by mutual consent the dispute is relegated for resolution to some other body or procedure. In a number of countries as well, acts, local self-government bodies and officials can also be revoked by courts, as is the case in Armenia, Kazakhstan and Russia. According to legislation in Ukraine, implementation of local self-government actions may be suspended as provided by law with a simultaneous filing of a judicial suit. Disputes concerning local self-government in Ukraine are heard by administrative courts. At present, only the Supreme Administrative Court has been established. The functions of local administrative courts are still performed by courts of general jurisdiction. In several countries, including Russia and Ukraine, matters of local self-government are heard in economic courts ("arbitration courts"). These primarily consider disputes between local self-government bodies and citizens or corporate entities.

## IV.6. National Associations of Local Self-Government

In the countries of Eurasia with more developed forms of local self-government, there are national institutions representing interests of local self-government. In the countries of Central Asia there are as yet only plans to establish such institutions.

In a majority of countries, there are unions of municipal units. For example, the Russian Federation has the Congress of Municipal Units established by 46 associations and unions of municipal units, the Union of Russian Cities, and the Union of Small Cities of Russia, to name but a few. In Kyrgyz

Republic, local self-government is represented by the Association of Cities and Association of Local Self-government of Villages and Settlements. In Ukraine, there is a Congress of Local and Regional Governments. In Armenia, there are about 20 municipal associations and unions. Azerbaijan establishes regional associations of municipalities on the basis of the Law of May 3, 2005: "On Model Charter of Regional Associations of Municipalities." Several countries have associations of different groups of municipal units, such as rural and urban units. Many countries, including Kazakhstan and Russia, also have associations of different divisions or departments of local self-government.

Associations and unions of municipal units pursue the following goals: establishing and developing local self-government as a political institution and a basis for civil society, creating favorable conditions for complex social and economic development of municipal entities, coordinating cooperation of municipal entities and their associations with state authorities in the interests of local self-government and the development of inter-municipal cooperation.

Associations of councilors of representative bodies of local self-government are directed to increase the authority of the representative branches of local self-government, develop civic activity in the population, take part in campaigns before elections, and discuss with the central government draft laws on matters of local state government and local self-government, as well as any policy issue regarding local government. Their opinion is usually requested formally on the drafting of laws.

*In several countries, including Russia and Ukraine, matters of local self-government are heard in economic courts ("arbitration courts"). These primarily consider disputes between local self-government bodies and citizens or corporate entities*

## V. Conclusion

The countries of Eurasia have achieved different stages in the development of local self-government. But despite all differences, they share several general tendencies and features.

First, the legal framework of local self-government has been established in all the countries in this region. The constitutions of all states contain articles, sections and norms devoted to local self-government and guarantees of its realization. The constitutions proclaim that the rights of citizens to have local self-government may not be restricted. The constitutions of all countries except Kazakhstan, enshrine important powers of local authorities. Transfer of such powers to other persons or governing bodies is not permitted.

Beyond this fundamental and ubiquitous acceptance of the importance of local self-governance, broad themes of a common heritage give rise to a similarity in the problems that are being addressed throughout the region.

In all of these countries, there is an increasing aspiration among local communities to decide social issues locally and independently through their own representative bodies. This movement is, however, constrained by long-standing traditions; in some countries decentralization is prevented by unstable political and economic conditions. The general process of decentralization and reinforcement of local self-government is also hindered by the chronic shortage of resources, including those needed to exercise real power by local governments. In Kazakhstan and some other states, local self-government is only proclaimed by the Constitution. In practice, it is rare; in some states citizens are still wary of local power structures. It is possible to speak only of the gradual rapprochement of local communities and public institutions. In this regard, in all countries of the region a special role must be attributed to elections of representative bodies, provided their democratic fundamentals are constantly strengthened.

In all of these countries, the development of local self-government is undermined by a weak financial base. To remedy this it is necessary to reinforce local taxes, develop inter-budgetary relations and provide fair and objective procedures for raising and allocating local revenues and expenditures.

The development and strengthening of local self-government as a rule takes place within the framework of the larger, general administrative reform aiming to separate and distinguish clearly the powers of all levels of government, as well as workable principles of subsidiarity. Progress, however, is slow and some reforms are quite

fragile, in part due to complicated economic conditions in several countries and frequent political changes.

All Eurasian countries are strongly influenced in matters of local self-government and general democratic principles by the standards of the Council of Europe, especially those that are members of the Commonwealth of Independent States and the Eurasian Economic Community. Such shared influences permit the prediction of a high degree of accord in future legal regulation of local self-government.

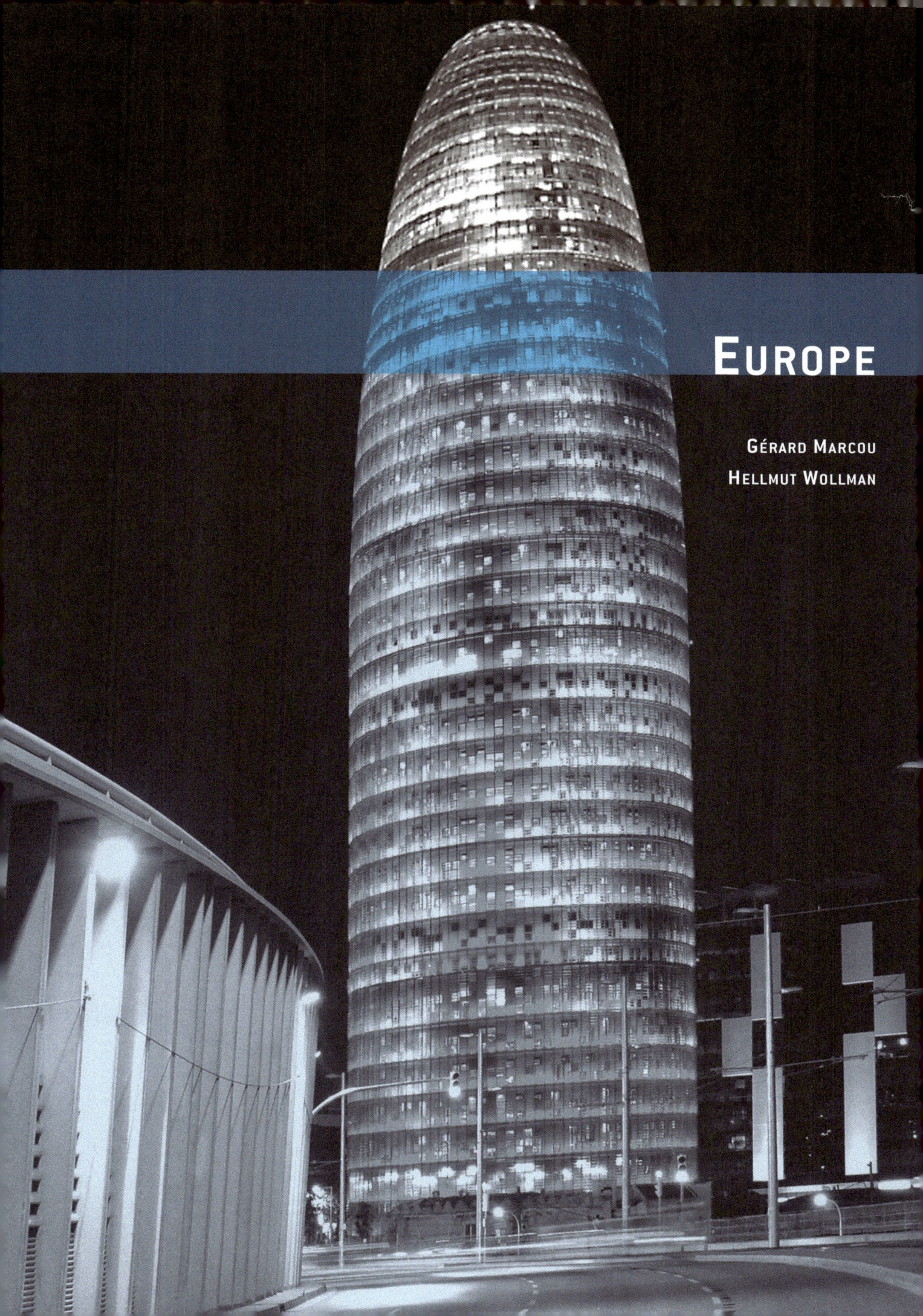

# EUROPE

Gérard Marcou
Hellmut Wollman

## I. Introduction

The Europe under study in this chapter covers more than the European Union (EU) and less than Europe the geographical entity because the area discussed here ends at the eastern border of the European Union. The states that make up this region (35) are more diverse than ever, yet they share two intrinsic characteristics that distinguish them from all other geo-political regions: 1) Every part of their territories is administered by a municipal government; 2) All of these states recognize a discrete set of fundamental principles on which local democracy is based. These principles, drawn up and implemented with the participation of local authorities and their organizations, were enshrined in the 1985 European Charter of Local Self-Government, which has since been ratified by several states outside the region defined here. Moreover, local self-government has been recognized as a governing principle by the EU.

However, behind this broad agreement on basic principles lies a striking variety of institutions and practices, and quite distinctive national exigencies. The traditional diversity typical of the western states has now been increased by the central and eastern new member states of the European Union, in which the principle of local self-government has only been translated since the 1990s into institution-building. Also joining in the process are other states in South-eastern Europe, where reforms are even more recent and fragile. Despite all this diversity, a number of major trends in common can be identified.

The first such trend concerns territorial organization. The European countries seem to be entering a new phase of territorial reform that is significantly different from those of the 1960s and 1970s. Not all states are similarly affected by this development; some in fact remain outside of it. In essence, the new territorial reforms are concerned with strengthening the municipal and inter-municipal frameworks, the

trend toward regionalization, and problems related to organizing urban areas.

The reforms of the 1960s and 1970s set the scene for two contrasting approaches to local government: the council as provider of public services (epitomized by the United Kingdom), and the council as public body based on a community of local people (epitomized by France). The countries that followed the second approach did not undergo territorial reforms at the time, but since the late 1990s these reforms are back on the agenda because of the now inescapable need to rationalize local government structures. Such reforms always aim at getting first-tier local governments[1] to take on greater responsibilities, directly or indirectly, by giving them adequate capacity to do so. What has sometimes worked against this approach, however, has been an avowed policy of bringing local government closer to local people; after regime changes in Eastern Europe, this localizing trend led to the break-up of many councils in the Czech Republic, Hungary, Slovak Republic, and the states that once comprised Yugoslavia, Serbia and Montenegro excepted for the moment.

The other important development in terms of territorial organization has been regionalization. Contrary to many assumptions, regionalization is much more a functional issue than an institutional one. Far more than a question of the number and character of institutions, regionalization concerns territorial policies adopted in response to problems that are neither strictly local nor national. Regionalization manifests itself very differently depending on the constitutional framework of each state, and on how it cuts across issues peculiar to that country. While it concerns urban organization in the Netherlands or institutional regionalism in Spain, regionalization takes many other forms as well. Sometimes it is a layer added to traditional intermediary authorities, without undermining them, as is the case with the French *département*. These examples also serve to draw attention to

*Every part of their territories is administered by a municipal government and all of these states recognize a discrete set of fundamental principles on which local democracy is based*

1. The "first-tier" or premier degré *is that of basic community-level local government, however they are defined within the national context.*

the potential impact of regionalization at the municipal level.

The organization of large urban areas, including their capital cities, is a key issue for all the European countries. Nor is this a particularly new issue. It has, however, come back under the spotlight in the past 10 years. The problem remains one of how to structure and connect the different levels of urban organization while allowing for functional needs as well as the demands of democracy. Responses have varied, such as between adapting common law and applying specific regulations, between integration within a metropolitan authority and focusing on the city as a centre.

*For all the European countries the organization of large urban areas, and capital cities, is a key issue*

The second major identifiable trend concerns the management of local authorities, and their powers and responsibilities. Summarized, the powers and responsibilities devolved to local authorities are increasing, though states are tending to strengthen their control over local finance. Combined with this general trend are a variety of issues specific to each state. The powers and responsibilities of local authorities have suffered from the establishment of regional autonomies[2], although some remedies have been put forward (e.g. the 2001 constitutional amendments in Italy and their implementation) or are being debated (e.g. the "local autonomy pacts" in Spain).The powers and responsibilities of local authorities have suffered from the establishment of regional forms of self-government. Some measures to remedy this, such as the 2001 constitutional review in Italy, have already been taken; others are being debated, including Spain's "local self-government pacts."

With regard to powers and responsibilities in a strictly technical sense, local authorities have been affected by sector-specific developments as well as more general ones. Under the latter category, it should be noted how the general competence clause on their powers and responsibilities has found widespread application despite

2.  *We distinguish between regional self-government and regional autonomy: the latter is a much stronger form, closer to federalism than to classical local self-government, and affecting the constitutional structure of the state.*

some resistance. The Charter's legal situation remains uncertain in Italy, Portugal, Spain and the United Kingdom, and there is an increasing tendency among local authorities to turn to the private sector to deliver public services; privatization has been less significant in countries with a long record of such outsourcing, including Belgium, France, Greece, Italy and Spain. Some countries have developed a system of delegated powers and responsibilities, in particular Austria, the Czech Republic, Germany, Hungary, Italy and Slovenia. This practice allows local councils to execute administrative tasks under state responsibility. Among the sector-specific developments, it is evident that local authorities are becoming increasingly involved in education as well as in public safety, though here central control is being reinforced in countries where the local councils and mayors already exercised broad powers.

Progress in public-sector management is evident throughout the European region, even in the newly democratized and decentralized countries that have benefited from various programs developed by international organizations, and through bilateral cooperation projects. The precepts of the "new public management" have been differently received among European countries, depending on individual public service traditions, but the increase in responsibilities and the accompanying rationing of resources intensified pressure on local authorities to find ways to rationalize their management in order to give themselves maneuvering room. "Performance culture" has advanced and spread, as has its peculiar lexicon: defining objectives, indicators for evaluating results and benchmarking tools.

Another major development affecting European local authorities concerns the dynamics of institutions and local democracy. Along with the steady progress made by local democracy, local government is further differentiating, regarding the relationship between an assembly and the executive body, between the design of the executive, the forms of election in use (e.g. increasing practice of direct election of mayors) and the place given to citizen participation. Despite the wide variety of processes and reforms involved, a common tendency can be identified: that of seeking to establish a political leadership that is clearly accountable to its citizens. Promoting local executive power, as distinct from the assembly, is widely regarded as a necessary means for strengthening political leadership and accountability, even where there is no direct election of a mayor, which is the case in the United Kingdom and the Netherlands.

A presentation of the condition of local democracy in Europe, however generalized, must account for both common tendencies and the diversity of institutions and practices. The split between shared and distinct elements underlies territorial organization, powers and responsibilities, management and finance and local democracy.

## II. Territorial Organization

The municipal level has to be distinguished from the intermediate levels, but we will focus here on the municipal level, including inter-municipal institutions. Any comparative presentation of the territorial structures of the European states must take into account all the reforms that have been carried out over the past thirty years, as well as their many structural offspring. Such a presentation presupposes defining the different levels of territorial organization.

### II.1. Definition of Jurisdictions and Government Levels

Traditional presentations are based on the idea that the local authorities within a state are usually organized into two levels –a local council and a higher level covering a more or less vast constituency. Powers and responsibilities are usually divided between these two levels according to functional criteria. (Marcou / Verebelyi:

1993; Norton: 1993). Even so, in the following countries certain councils can take on the powers and responsibilities of both government levels:

- Germany: municipality and district (*Kreis*), with larger urban municipalities having the status of a district and district-level concomitant powers and responsibilities. A similar system is now used in Hungary and Poland;

- England: district and county. Before the 1972 reforms, certain boroughs had the attributes of a county. Since the reforms of 1986 and 1996, some areas have only a single-tier local authority –the district in metropolitan areas, the unitary council in others;

- Belgium, France, Italy and Spain: the municipality and province, or *département*. This applied in Belgium, Italy and Spain before regions with constitutional status were set up[3].

This standard depiction more or less left out countries like Finland, Greece and Portugal, which traditionally had just one level of decentralization. Nor do these standard criteria take into account differences in size that can affect meaning at a higher level[4]. The traditional presentation also failed to account for administrative divisions existing exclusively to meet the needs of the central government, and excluded federal entities like those in Austria and Germany. Such shortcomings aside, the traditional form of presentation did offer a certain conceptual unity for the concept of local government based on one or two levels.

These days, the picture is far more complicated. For one thing, regions have been created in several countries but according to very different concepts that, moreover, have changed over time. Belgium became a federal state; in Italy and Spain, the development of regional autonomies put

3.  In Italy, the regions with ordinary status were not set up until 1970, although they were provided for under the 1947 Constitution.

4.  For example, the difference between the German *Kreis*, considered to be both a single local authority and a consortia of municipalities, and the British county, covering a much larger administrative division – the usual translation of *Kreis* with county blurred this significant difference.

an end to the unitary state. The United Kingdom has moved to an asymmetrical organization with regional autonomies for Scotland, and Northern Ireland, a unitary regime for England and to a lesser extent for Wales. (Wales has no proper legislative power after the Wales Act 2006). Meanwhile, in France the region is a third-tier local authority –a model that Poland has followed. Furthermore, those countries that did not undergo territorial reforms developed institutions for inter-municipal cooperation to take on the tasks that small local councils could not manage. This has resulted in further differentiation of the municipal level (the first tier). At the same time the new institutions have become closer to the second tier, and have begun to compete with traditional local authorities at that level. Analyzing authorities in terms of two-tier local government is thus no longer enough to give a proper account of the current reality. Asymmetric patterns are more frequent and the number and the nature of local governments may vary from one part of the country to another one. This new complexity means that we have to consider on the one hand, the different government levels of the territorial organization of the state as a whole and on the other the differences in the status of the institutions that we find at each of these levels.

In an effort to present territorial structures in simplified form while still accounting for the new complexity, the table below classifies states by the number of levels of territorial organization for which local governments have been established, and also according to whether they are unitary or composite states. Here the term composite states follows the definition provided by the Spanish Constitutional Court: federal states and states with regional self-government, which share the following features:

1) a plurality of legislative authority at the center, with the constituent mem-

*National capitals sometimes have a particular status positioning them in a direct relationship with their country's central authority*

bers as a major expression of their political autonomy;

2) the constitution sets out and guarantees the division of powers and responsibilities between the competence of the central authority and the competence of the constituent members.

By convention, two of the table's cells show those states that have an asymmetric structure; that is, regional autonomy in only part of the territory, or local councils not included in second-tier administrative divisions, or disappearance of the province when the region merges with its administrative area. Inter- or supra-municipal structures (including those of highly integrated inter-municipalities, such as in France or Hungary) will be treated as being part of the municipal level, as will infra-municipal bodies (e.g., the *freguesias* in Portugal or the "town councils" in Bulgaria).

Note that territorial reform is once again on the agenda, though this time based more on functional criteria[5]. Also, there is a general trend toward strengthening politically local governments at the basic level of the community as well as the guarantees for their self-governance; the intermediate levels typically show a tendency to regionalization, although only a minority of states is establishing strong political regions. Setting up such regions can have undermining effects on municipalities.

National capitals sometimes have a particular status positioning them in a direct relationship with their country's central authority (i.e., Berlin, Bucharest, Budapest, Paris, Prague and Vienna).

## II.2. Basic Community-Level Local Government (The Local Council)

In all countries, it is at the level of the local council that the issue of trying to balance political space with functional[6] space becomes particularly critical, especially in

5.  E.g., with the purpose to fulfil specific functions.

6.  This means that it aims at answering demands related to the implementation of competences.

| Table 1 | Levels of Local Governments by Country |
|---|---|

| Levels | Unitary states | Composite states |
|---|---|---|
| 3 levels: local council; département/ province/county/district; region or federal body | France, Poland | Belgium, Germany, Italy, Spain |
| 2 levels:<br>- 1) local council; province / département / county/district | 1) Croatia, Greece, Hungary, Ireland, Latvia, Netherlands, Norway, Poland (cities with district status), Romania | 1) none |
| - 2) local council, region or federal body | 2) Albania, Czech Republic, Denmark (at 01/01/2007), France (Paris), Serbia (Vojvodine), Slovak Republic, Sweden, United Kingdom (England, Wales) | 2) Austria, Belgium (Brussels-capital), Bosnia-Herzegovina, German Federation (kreisfreie Städte), Portugal (island regions), Spain (certain uni-provincial autonomous communities), Switzerland, United Kingdom (Scotland) |
| 1 level: local councils and consortia of local councils | 1) Bulgaria, Cyprus, Estonia, Finland, Iceland, Lithuania, Luxembourg, FYR Macedonia, Malta, Montenegro, Portugal (continental), Republika Srpska, Serbia, Slovenia, United Kingdom (England: unitary councils and metropolitan districts)<br><br>2) certain capitals: Bucharest, Budapest, Prague, Zagreb | Germany (city States: Berlin, Bremen, Hamburg); Austria (Vienna) |

the urban areas (Bennett:1989; Kersting / Vetter: 2003; Baldersheim / Illner / Wollmann: 2003).

Here it is useful to divide countries according to two criteria of the territorial pattern of municipalities:

• Countries with a highly fragmented municipal pattern (Austria, the Czech Republic, France, Hungary, Italy, Spain and Switzerland) compared with countries that have undergone municipal reorganization aimed at the establishment of larger units (Belgium, Eastern European countries from the 1950s to the 1970s, Germany, Greece, Lithuania today, Nordic countries and the United Kingdom);

• Countries with a uniform status of municipalities (Western and Northern Europe, except the United Kingdom), compared with countries operating a

distinct status for cities (Central and Eastern Europe, starting from Germany and the United Kingdom).

The growing pressures of increased urbanization explain this last distinction in the case of England long before the reforms of the 1970s; in the other countries, it is a consequence of social structures that for a long time made it difficult to expand municipal self-government in the countryside.

Today, territorial reform is back on the agenda in many countries, but from a different perspective. The reforms of the 1950s, 1960s and 1970s were aimed at establishing minimal or optimal sizes to match the powers and responsibilities to be exercised. The reforms of recent years have instead been driven more by functional concerns, and can therefore take more forms than the simple merging of municipalities; they also cover more of the civic and dem-

## Territorial Reform and Functional Reform

The great territorial reforms of the past did meet objectives of functional reform[7]. In Greece for example, the municipal reform of 1912 allowed for any built-up area with a population of more than 300 and a primary school to constitute itself as a municipality. In Sweden, the territorial reforms of 1952 and 1970 were devised mainly in order to help implement state education reforms at the municipal level. In Germany, the municipal reforms of 1965-1975 were based on the theory of central places, whereby a whole range of services and material resources would be provided from these for a given population. These reforms also aimed at giving municipalities a territorial basis for their powers and responsibilities to be expanded later through further functional reforms (Germany, Sweden). This has been the case over the last few years in Germany where the governments of certain *Länder* have transferred new responsibilities to the districts and cities with district status: Baden-Württemberg has undergone the most radical reform, as most tasks of the field services[8] of the *Land* government have been transferred to it.

The Greek reforms of 1997 illustrate the dramatic shift that took place. This was a radical reform, decreasing the numbers of municipalities (*demes* and rural councils) from nearly 6,000 to 1,033. But the real innovative aspect of the reform was that it was not just an amalgamation plan; it involved also a development and investment program, and the territorial reform was a necessary step to implement that program. The aim was to set up local authorities able to implement it, which meant equipping them with the necessary institutions, staff and financial resources. A five-year program (1997-2001) financed by the state was thus the support framework within which the new municipalities would operate and which would help finance a capital investment program. The five-year program was also aimed at facilitating the recruitment of managers for the new municipalities and to give them the necessary human resources for exercising a greater administrative and financial autonomy. Another innovative aspect of the reform was to keep a representation of the old local councils in the new local authorities, and secure their participation in the debates of the new municipal council, which doubtless helped to get the mergers accepted by the local communities.

In the new German *Länder* on the other hand, the transfer of the territorial reform realized in the west proved at first to be a half-failure. Regrouping smaller municipalities was seen as working against the aim of restoring democracy, and inter-municipal bodies (the *Verwaltungsgemeinschaft*) were set up in order to try and resolve this problem. However, the territorial reforms were successfully completed at the level of the districts. More recently, territorial reform has taken a new turn: the Brandenburg *Land* has removed many small municipalities by means of mergers, reducing at the same time the number of inter-municipal bodies, and the Mecklemburg-Vorpommern *Land* has carried out a radical reform of districts, bringing their average population to 350,000.

7. *Functional reforms: reforms concerning the attribution of certain powers and responsibilities and having the aim of improving the ways in which these are exercised.*

8. *Field services are administrative services with competence for a territorial jurisdiction that are subordinated to central government departments. In some countries they are referred to as "peripheral administrations".*

ocratic dimension of the municipal organization, rather than being concerned with just technical and management issues. Integrated forms of inter-municipal cooperation have then appeared as an alternative to amalgamation.

In the other countries of Central and Eastern Europe where post-war territorial reforms have endured, a form of representation for the old local authorities was maintained in the expanded local councils (Poland, Bulgaria). This was also the strategy adopted by Lithuania for its 1995 territorial reforms, which divided the country into only 60 district municipalities.

However, highly urbanized countries that underwent major amalgamation of municipalities are now seeking to re-establish local community institutions at the infra-community level (Sweden, United Kingdom). These various developments and experiences should serve to draw attention to the importance of "minor local entities," as these are termed under Spanish law (in *Castilla-La Mancha*), for giving voice to local democracy, and in particular to the experiences of countries like Portugal and Bulgaria, where large municipalities work by relying on strong infra-municipal institutions.

By contrast, the concentration of local governments that came into effect in Denmark on January 1, 2007, reduced the number of local councils from 271 to 98, and the number of "administrative municipalities" (counties) from 14 to 5 "regions." This effort was driven by a concern for economies of scale, taking into account the predictable rise in social expenditure, particularly for older people. While the local municipalities run nearly all the public services, it is planned to run the health service at the level of the expanded counties (regions). The counties will also take responsibility for public transportation,

regional development and planning, as well as some social services.

But in many other countries where municipal functions are certainly less extensive, it is mainly by developing a second level of municipal government that a solution has been sought for difficulties municipalities encounter in performing certain functions without undermining the pre-existing municipalities. France and Hungary provide illustrative examples of this approach, which encourages political vitality in local community institutions rather than working against them. But, the expansion of the functions performed at the inter-municipal level raises the problem of the democratic legitimacy of inter-municipal institutions, which are at present formed by the municipal councils.

It seems that instituting a second level of municipal government is probably a useful option in organizing large urban zones because urban development does not follow municipal and administrative boundaries (Hoffmann-Martinot: 1999; Hoffmann-Martinot / Sellers: 2005; Le Galès: 2002). In this respect, French law provides for the status of "urban community" for the biggest metropolitan areas (excepting Paris); fourteen have been created. The law also provides for the status of "agglomeration community" for smaller urban areas (164 established to date). In the Netherlands, a "cooperative framework" approach has been adopted following the failure of an attempt through a 1994 law to create urban regions for the seven biggest metropolitan areas of the country. The "cooperative framework" is based on an inter-municipal public corporation –though without own taxing powers. This formula has been revised by the law of December 2005 (law known as "Regio Plus") with the purpose of extending it to other urban areas. In Germany, *Länder* laws have on occasion instituted similar types of urban area bodies, for example for Frankfurt, Munich and Stuttgart. In the case of Italy however, the *Città Metropolitana*, introduced by the law no. 142 of 1990, has still failed to materialize properly, even though it was enshrined in the Con-

*Highly urbanized countries that underwent major amalgamation of municipalities are now seeking to re-establish local community institutions at the infra-community level*

**Territorial Reform through Cooperation**

In France, a country of 36,000 municipalities, cooperation has long been the means to run the public services that single municipalities on their own cannot provide. But since the introduction of a law in 1999, supported by a strong commitment from the central government and financial incentives, inter-municipal public corporations with own tax powers have developed rapidly. These inter-municipal corporations are vested by the law with various strategic functions (e.g. planning, economic development, major capital investments etc.) and have own tax powers independent of those of member municipalities. At the beginning of 2007, 33,414 municipalities and 54.2 million people had been reorganized under 2,588 *intercommunalités* (inter-municipalities), as they have been called.

In Hungary, a law from November 2004 provided for the development of inter-municipal cooperation within 166 micro-regions in order to meet local development objectives, the main one of which was to ensure that the management of public schools would be taken on by these inter-municipal corporations. At the beginning of 2006, such consortia had been set up in 118 micro-regions, and in 90 of these, all municipalities have joined the consortium.

This was also the approach followed by Italy, with its unions of municipalities, and in Spain, with the bill on local government reform following the 2005 White Paper, which aims at encouraging inter-municipal cooperation[9].

However, the French *intercommunalités* will keep the distinction of having their own tax-levying powers and a wide range of functions provided for by law.

stitution by amendment (new article 114) in 2001. Only three perimeters have been drawn up (Bologna, Genoa and Venice), but these only constitute rather loose frameworks for voluntary cooperation. In some regions, including Campania and Piedmont, the provinces of the regional capitals would like to turn themselves into *Città Metropolitana*, but it seems uncertain that this will actually happen. Consequences on local democracy are not one-sided; they depend on the selected institutional setting.

In the United Kingdom, first- and second-tier reforms are linked. The White Paper published in October 2006 (Strong and Prosperous Communities, Cm 6939) provides for a further round of unitary council formation in those regions where there is still a two-tier system. The government announced on the 25th July 2007 the formation of nine new unitary councils, and the Law of 30th October 2007 created the legal conditions for the realization and the continuation of the process (Local Government and Public Involvement in Health Act 2007, c.28).

## II.3. Intermediate Levels

It is at the intermediate level that the most important changes in the territorial organization of states have taken place over the past two or three decades. Moreover, these changes have been both institutional and functional (Marcou: 2000 and 2002).

Historically, the intermediate level is closely linked to the creation and augmentation of the state. More specifically, it is essential for what has been called

9. *Whitebook for the reform of Local Governments, Madrid, Ministry for Public Administration.*

"territorial penetration," the political and institutional process by which centralized powers were able to establish authority over all of their territory and the people within it. This has been illustrated in very different ways by France, Prussia and the United Kingdom. Not all the European countries brought this process to completion; sometimes it was completed very late or challenged by later transformations of the political scene. Moreover, national boundaries have shifted considerably, even in the past century. Some once-powerful European nation-states have disappeared altogether, including Austria-Hungary, the Habsburg Empire, Prussia, and Yugoslavia. But territorial penetration proved decisive in the formation of certain enduring territorial frameworks, including the *département* in France and the provinces of neighboring countries on which the Napoleonic model left its mark. Also it was decisive in forming the county in England and Sweden; the district (*Kreis, powiat, okres*) in most Central European countries; and the "government district" or primary division of a *Land –Regierungsbezirk–* in Germany. Similarly, this organizational process affected such typical institutions as the *préfet* or regional governor; in Germany it was the *Landrat*. This functionary, who came to be known by several different titles, was appointed a senior civil servant in 1872 by the King of Prussia. At about this time, the *Kreis* acquired the characteristics of a local self-government –even as it continued to serve as the framework for an administrative authority of the state. Thus, the original role of the intermediate tier was to represent and relay the authority of the central power, either reliant on local aristocracy, as in England, Hungary and Germany, or against them, as in France.

Since the end of the 19th Century, however, under the influence of liberalism and democracy, the intermediate tier evolved. Partly to accommodate the social and economic tasks that the modern state was increasingly responsible for, the intermediate tier underwent two forms of institutional and functional development. They were, broadly speaking: 1) the establishment of a local authority evolving to become more like a municipality, both as an institution and in terms of the services it performed; 2) the differentiation and reduction of the administrative tasks of the state. Since the end of the 20th Century, regionalization has been making its mark as a practical response to new socio-economic and political developments. The transformation sometimes manifests itself in the emergence of new territorial frameworks and institutions, but it is also apparent in changes and reforms within existing institutions.

Gradually the original consolidating and centralizing mission of the intermediate tier of government gave way to incipient democratization. The election of a representative assembly gradually became the rule in all the countries. Election of provincial councils in Belgium was based on the 1831 Constitution; that same year France introduced elections for the *departement*; the Netherlands followed in 1853 with elections in provincial states; Prussia saw district elections in 1872; and in 1888 Great Britain allowed elections for county councils. The intermediate level local authority institutions later became more like municipal institutions, particularly in the election of executive officers. The exceptions are Belgium and the Netherlands where these offices remain appointed posts at both the municipal and second-tier level, despite the law having been able to introduce an elective element. (see section III). These local authorities progressively took on tasks designated by law to address experimentally two needs: 1) providing primary or supplemental services in sectors, such as health, roads and schools, which did not normally come within the remit of municipal services; 2) promoting community solidarity and equalization of social services and support for small municipalities.

*Gradually the original consolidating and centralizing mission of the intermediate tier of government gave way to incipient democratization*

Today these kinds of tasks are carried out by second-tier local authorities in Central and Eastern Europe, particularly in Croatia (*Županije*), Hungary (*megyiei*), Poland (*powiat*) and Romania (*judet*). They are also part of the responsibilities delegated to the Czech and Slovak "regions" (*kraj*).

Three factors differentiate these second-tier local authorities: size, urban administration system, and the presence or absence of competing sector-specific authorities.

In countries that were significantly affected by the late arrival of local self-government in rural areas, or were heavily influenced by Germany or Austria, second-tier local authorities are apt to be small (German *Kreis* and Polish *powiat* in particular). Other countries have larger authorities, including France with its *département*, England and Sweden with counties, and Hungary with its *megyei*. This applies as well to provinces in Belgium, Italy, the Netherlands and Spain, *nomos* in Greece, and Czech and Slovak "regions." Except for the Czech Republic and Slovak Republic, these territorial divisions have ancient origins and are connected to the administrative divisions of the state authorities that preceded the creation of local authorities. But differences in size do not necessarily correspond to differences in responsibilities. The responsibilities delegated to this tier of governance depend more on the extent and nature of powers and responsibilities exercised at the municipal level, the role of state authorities, and the presence of sector-specific authorities.

Cities in several countries are not included in the territorial framework of second-tier authorities, though they may have similar responsibilities. This corresponds to an institutional differentiation between city and countryside with respect to the local authority system, the significance of which has been emphasised. In countries where cities assume much se-

cond-tier responsibility, they benefit from a reinforced status within the administrative system. This was the situation in the United Kingdom between 1888 and 1972 (the borough-counties), and again after the removal in 1986 of county councils in metropolitan areas. A decade later the United Kingdom saw the constitution of unitary councils. A similar ascendancy of the city occurs in Hungary where 22 towns have the status of *megyei*, in Germany with 116 *kreisfreie Städte*, and in Poland which accords to 65 towns the status of *powiat*. A similar system existed in Denmark before that country's 1970 territorial reforms.

The presence of specialized sector-specific authorities, such as hospitals, affects the powers and responsibilities at the intermediate level. Public hospitals are incorporated at the intermediate level local government in Denmark, Sweden and Hungary, whereas they are part of a national organization in the United Kingdom (the National Health Service), in France with the regional hospital care agencies (though hospitals have kept their legal status as local public corporations) and in Italy though the regions finance "local health units." Similar arrangements also characterize the education sector in many countries.

In federal states and states with regional autonomies, it is the federated states or autonomous regions which have taken on responsibility for these services, directly or indirectly. In Germany, the *Länder* are responsible for education and for the statutory regulation of hospitals, and also for investment in public hospitals. However, management in these areas is devolved to the districts. In Spain, public hospitals were transferred to the autonomous communities in 2002. In the United Kingdom, the national health system is under the supervisory control of regional authorities in Scotland and Wales, but is nonetheless organized according to sector-based principles[10]. In Belgium, health and education are

10. *The management of the health system is not part of the local governments' functions.*

designated as "personalizable" areas pertaining to the powers and responsibilities of the *communautés*[11].

The preceding examples indicate, that the organization of the intermediate levels now tends to be associated with developments towards regionalization. In functional terms, it is a response to the new importance given to territories with respect to economic development. In institutional terms, it is a formal recognition of the changes in responsibilities at the intermediate levels. However, regionalization manifests itself in states whose size, constitutions and territorial institutions are extremely varied, and which fulfil other tasks than those connected to regional development. If we also take into account the political factors, then the very great institutional diversity through which regionalization can manifest itself is hardly surprising. In many countries, it is limited to an administrative regionalization, i.e. it is based on institutions subordinated to the central authorities (e.g. England –as opposed to other parts of the UK–, Greece, continental Portugal, Bulgaria and Hungary). By contrast, it gave rise to autonomous regions in some countries (e.g. Italy, Spain, the status of Scotland). In many countries, regionalization is reflected in the kind of powers and responsibilities devolved to the local authorities or to the institutions which depend on them (e.g. Finland, Ireland, Netherlands and Romania). Finally, other countries have simply extended their system of local self-government to the regional level or have invested their intermediate level authorities with functions of regional scope, without impinging on the unitary nature of the State (Denmark since 1 January 2007, France, Poland, Czech Republic, Slovak Republic).

## III. Powers and Responsibilities, Management and Finances

Local governments operate within a system that requires interaction with the state, and more generally with higher authorities. Managing such a system has become an ever more complex business, as the powers and responsibilities of local authorities have expanded to cover tasks important enough to merit regional or national legislation and policies. The challenges to be met include how to apportion and share powers and responsibilities, how to finance local budgets and how to decide what administrative capacities local authorities should and can have.

In theory, it is the powers and responsibilities to be exercised which determine the level of resources necessary to cover the corresponding costs. The European Charter of Local Self-Government puts it this way: The financial resources of local authorities should be commensurate with the powers and responsibilities they must exercise as provided for by the law, and these resources must be sufficiently diversified and progressive to allow them to keep pace with the real changes in costs (Art. 9, paras. 2 and 4). In practice, local finances are the product of each nation's complex history of public finance, as well as its particular administrative history. More than any others, these factors explain the various characteristics of local finance, as well as the size, in budgetary terms, of local powers and responsibilities. These same factors pertain to countries that only recently introduced local self-government institutions, or are in the process of doing so. Setting up an efficient tax system and reorganizing financial networks takes more time than changing the law does. Therefore, consider the financial systems of local government before moving on to comparisons of powers, responsibilities and administrative capacities.

### III.1. Finances

Financial autonomy is the basis of local self-government, as stated in Article 9 of the European Charter of Local Self-Government, and it has three dimensions:

11. These are constituent members of the Belgium federal system, nowadays run by institutions shared, or largely shared, with those of the region.

*In most European countries local public expenditure varies in reality between 6 % and 13 % of GDP*

resources must be in line with the costs associated with the duties conferred upon local authorities by law; the authorities must be able to dispose freely of the resources allocated to them; and they must have certain powers to determine the level of their own resources.

However, despite the abundance of national and international sources, carrying out an international comparison of local government financial systems presents real difficulties of methodology and interpretation, even in Europe. In the following study, regional autonomies have been treated as similar to federal entities and have therefore not been considered as local authorities, contrary to how certain international sources erroneously represent them.

Analysis of major trends concerning expenditure and resources reveals the growing role of local authorities in Europe (Dafflon: 2002; Travers: 2005). However, this increase in importance is often accompanied by a reduction in financial autonomy.

### III.1.1.  Local authority expenditure

The following chart shows the proportion of each nation's GDP that is allotted to local public expenditure, based on figures published by Eurostat. The term local public expenditure refers to the expenditure of local public authorities; that is, intra-national authorities with the exception of federal entities and regional autonomies[12]. Note that although Spain is treated as a federal state, Italy is not, despite high levels of powers and responsibilities for public spending, as well as legislation devolved to the Italian regions. The same applies to the United Kingdom with respect to Scotland and Northern Ireland. Wales could also reasonably be included in the matter of public finances because of the volume of expenditure devolved to it. Although the European states usually have one or two tiers of local authority, the table slightly overestimates in comparative terms local public expenditure for countries

with three tiers of local authorities (France, Poland). Despite these approximations, the chart reveals three fairly distinct national groups:

- Three Nordic countries (Denmark, Finland, Sweden) and Switzerland, whose local public expenditure is greater than 20% of their GDP;

- a large group of countries whose local public expenditure varies in reality between 6% and 13% of GDP: in fact in Italy, the expenditure of local councils and of their consortia, and of the provinces, was around 6.3% of GDP in 2003; in the same year such expenditure in the Netherlands was 8.5%;

- a small group of countries in which local public expenditure is less than 5% of GDP: Greece, Cyprus, Former Yugoslav Republic of Macedonia and Malta.

In the median group, there is a continuum in which it is nearly impossible to place a threshold. But below 8% or 8.5% of GDP, we find only fairly small countries maintaining a certain financial centralization, along with the federal states and states with autonomous regions (insofar as part of the expenditure borne by the local authorities in the unitary states is paid for out of regional budgets.)

However, the amount of expenditure alone is not enough to characterize financial autonomy. Functional independence also depends on how much discretion a local authority has to allocate and commit its expenditures, and to manage its resources.

Figure 2 shows local authority capital expenditure as a percentage of GDP. This indicator helps show the role played by local authorities with respect to the flow of capital investment. It relates only to the Europe of the 25, as there is insufficient data for the other countries. In the

12. *See above : footnote 2.*

same year, public sector investment in the Europe of the 25 was 2.4% of GDP, with figures ranging from 1.1% for Austria to 5% for the Czech Republic.

What emerges from the chart is that local authorities represent the greatest share of public-sector investment, except in 10 countries: Austria, Cyprus, Czech Republic, Estonia, Greece, Hungary, Lithuania, Luxembourg, Malta and Slovak Republic. The chart takes into account only local authority investments, and not those of federal entities. It does however take into account the capital expenditure of the autonomous regions in countries that have such entities, leading to the aforementioned overestimate of local authority investment. The same applies to France with respect to the first and second levels, because the regions, being local authorities, have a much greater investment capacity; they currently account for about

**Figure 1**  Local Public Expenditure as % of GDP

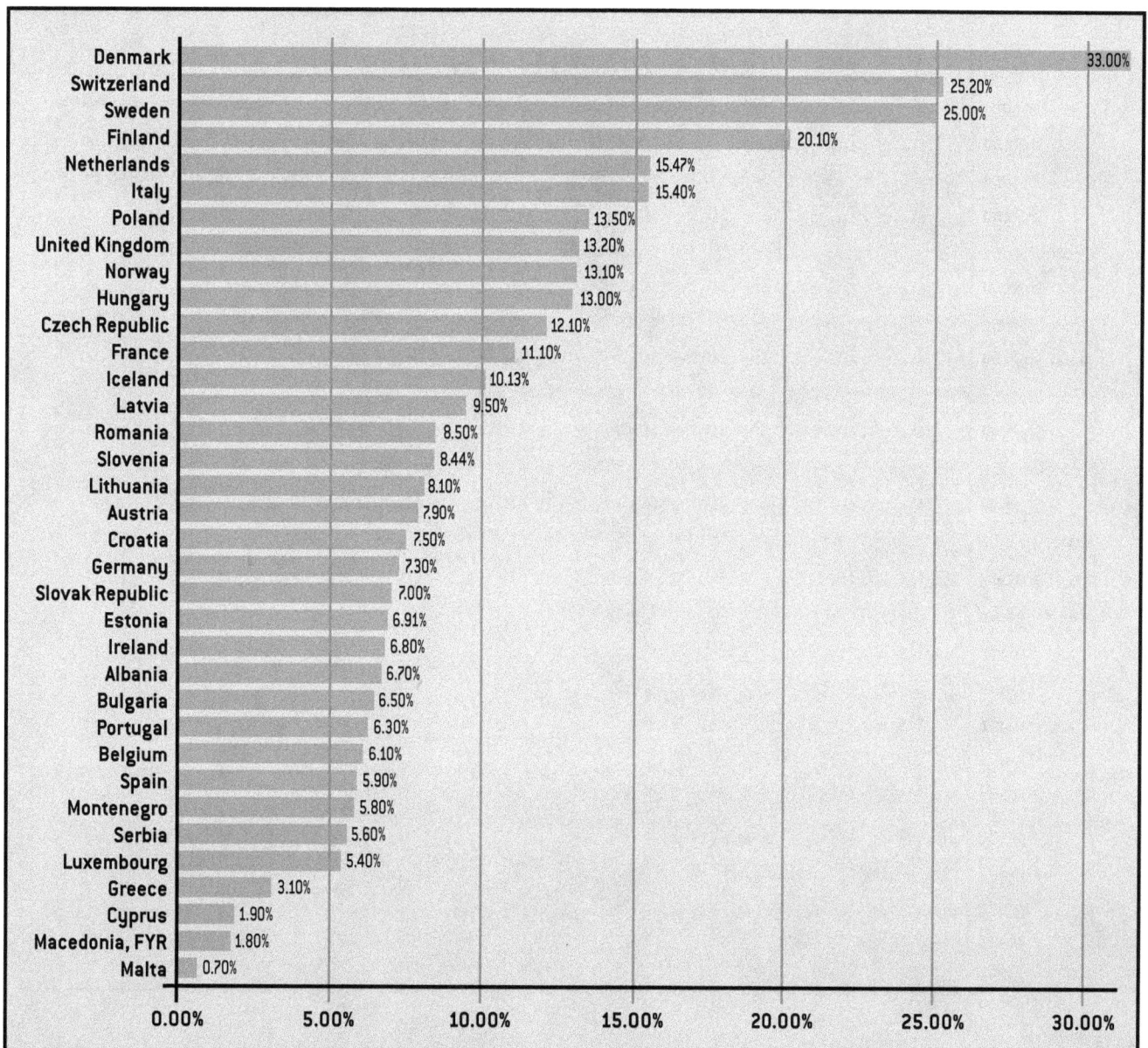

| Country | % of GDP |
|---|---|
| Denmark | 33.00% |
| Switzerland | 25.20% |
| Sweden | 25.00% |
| Finland | 20.10% |
| Netherlands | 15.47% |
| Italy | 15.40% |
| Poland | 13.50% |
| United Kingdom | 13.20% |
| Norway | 13.10% |
| Hungary | 13.00% |
| Czech Republic | 12.10% |
| France | 11.10% |
| Iceland | 10.13% |
| Latvia | 9.50% |
| Romania | 8.50% |
| Slovenia | 8.44% |
| Lithuania | 8.10% |
| Austria | 7.90% |
| Croatia | 7.50% |
| Germany | 7.30% |
| Slovak Republic | 7.00% |
| Estonia | 6.91% |
| Ireland | 6.80% |
| Albania | 6.70% |
| Bulgaria | 6.50% |
| Portugal | 6.30% |
| Belgium | 6.10% |
| Spain | 5.90% |
| Montenegro | 5.80% |
| Serbia | 5.60% |
| Luxembourg | 5.40% |
| Greece | 3.10% |
| Cyprus | 1.90% |
| Macedonia, FYR | 1.80% |
| Malta | 0.70% |

**Source:** *Eurostat, 2005.*

10% of the real capital expenditure of local governments and their public institutions.

Here analysis must be put in context to take into account the wider economic climate and the stage of development for each situation. Macro-economic policies can have a heavy impact on local authority investments, as is the case for Austria and Germany. Over several years, capital expenditure can show greater fluctuations than running costs. Although there has been dynamic growth over the past few years in local authority investment across the European Union as a whole, it has been greater in the new member states; this reflects the need for new infrastructure in these more recently admitted countries. Between 2000 and 2005, the average growth in local authority investment across the Europe of the 15 was 2.9% a year. At the same time it was 4.9% in the new

**Figure 2** Local Public Capital Expenditure as % of GDP

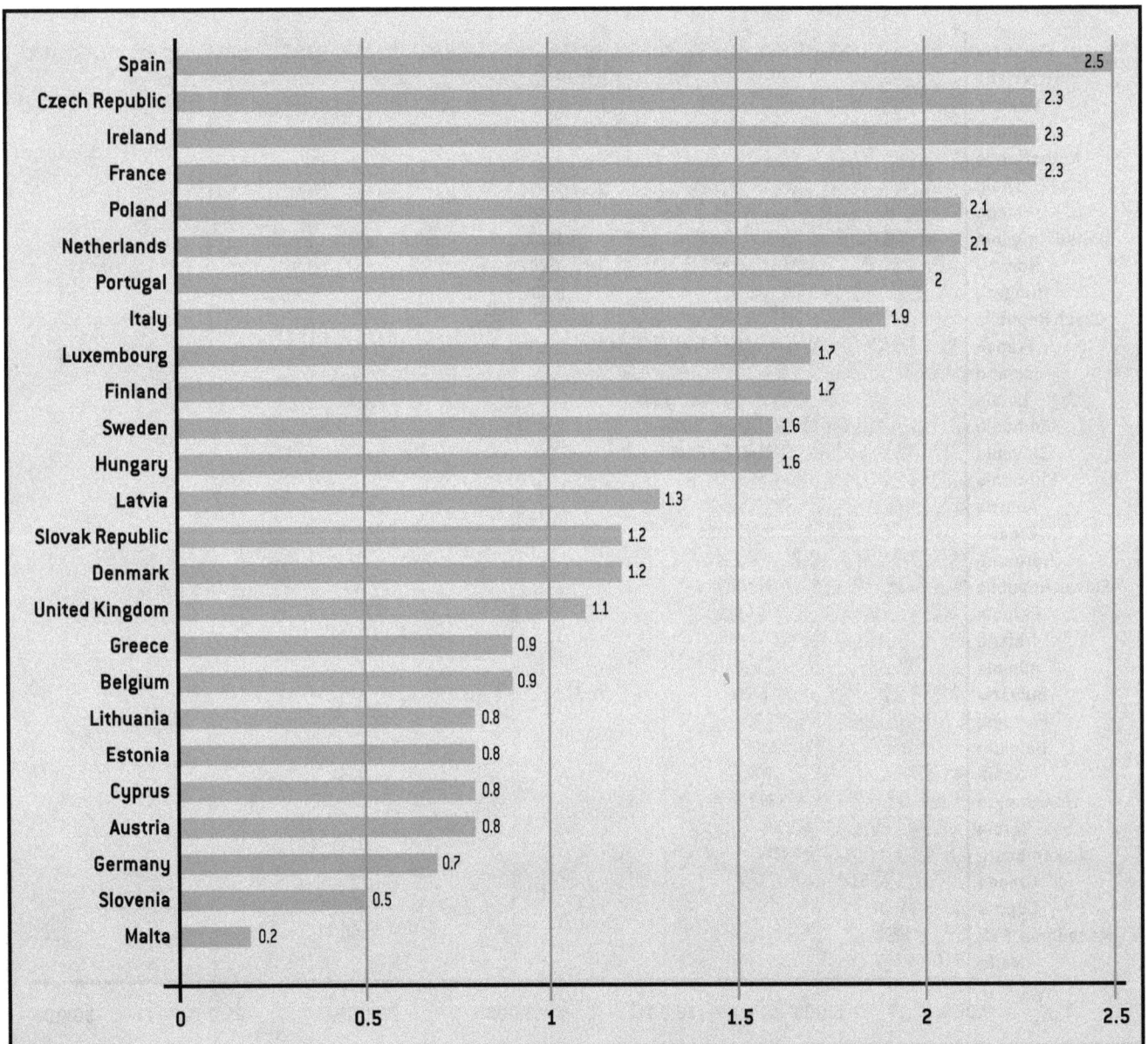

|  |  |
|---|---|
| Spain | 2.5 |
| Czech Republic | 2.3 |
| Ireland | 2.3 |
| France | 2.3 |
| Poland | 2.1 |
| Netherlands | 2.1 |
| Portugal | 2 |
| Italy | 1.9 |
| Luxembourg | 1.7 |
| Finland | 1.7 |
| Sweden | 1.6 |
| Hungary | 1.6 |
| Latvia | 1.3 |
| Slovak Republic | 1.2 |
| Denmark | 1.2 |
| United Kingdom | 1.1 |
| Greece | 0.9 |
| Belgium | 0.9 |
| Lithuania | 0.8 |
| Estonia | 0.8 |
| Cyprus | 0.8 |
| Austria | 0.8 |
| Germany | 0.7 |
| Slovenia | 0.5 |
| Malta | 0.2 |

**Source:** *Dexia, 2006.*

member states, and there was negative growth in Austria and Germany[13].

In the countries of the former Yugoslavia, as well as Albania, Bulgaria and Romania, central authorities at first kept control of investment funds, including those for local public investments. This started to change in 2004. There has been easier access to loans in Bosnia Herzegovina, Croatia, and the FYR Macedonia and Serbia. In Albania, a call-for-tenders procedure was introduced to select local projects receiving state funding. In Bulgaria and Romania, the role of local authorities regarding investment in economic or social infrastructure has been growing thanks to access to European funds[14].

### III.1.2. Local government resources

Two questions arise concerning resources: the level of resources with respect to costs, and the degree of control the authorities have over their capacity to increase their resources.

The European Charter of Local Self-Government stipulates that local authorities must have "adequate financial resources of their own, of which they may dispose freely within the framework of their powers," and that the financial resources of local authorities must be "commensurate with the responsibilities provided for by the constitution and the law" (art. 9, paras. 1 and 2). The first provision is a condition for local freedom; the second is a guarantee for local authorities that they should be given the necessary resources to finance the tasks devolved to them by law.

The requirement that legally prescribed functions (duties) should correlate with the resources allocated –known as the principle of connexity– is the most difficult one to satisfy because it depends on how costs are calculated. This calculation in turn depends on the level of services deemed sufficient and practicable for the population. This requirement is at the heart of

the requests made by local authorities to the higher authorities that their resources depend on. Increasingly, legislation is providing that any transfer of powers and responsibilities prescribed by law must be accompanied by an adequate transfer of resources. In France, this principle was first stipulated by a 1982 law, and later enshrined in the Constitution in 2003 (art. 72-2, para. 4). In Germany, the constitutional review of August 28, 2006, provided the occasion for enshrining in the Basic Law (the Constitution) a ban on using federal law to devolve material responsibilities to municipal councils and their consortia (new art. 84, para. 1). This was intended to put an end to the practice whereby the federal legislator created new costs for local authorities without providing the concomitant resources. By contrast, within *Länder*, constitutional courts of *Länder* ensure that the principle of connexity is respected.

However, financial autonomy depends on the resource system and structure. It is here that the development of local finances is now showing signs adverse to local self-government.

### a) *The structure of resources*

In most of the European states, the tax revenues of local authorities consist for the most part of shared taxes, for which the central authorities hold the tax-setting powers. But the only ordinary revenue over which local authorities have sufficient powers, allowing them to vary the amount of resources through their own direct decision-making, is own tax revenue and income from fee-based local public services. As income obtained from these local public services depends heavily on how the services are managed –directly by the authority, or by a utility receiving direct payment from the users– the most significant variable with respect to the local authorities' ability to determine the development of their resources through their own decision-making is local own tax revenue. Conversely, their part of shared taxes, from the

13. Dexia, *Finances publiques territoriales dans l'Union européenne. Evolutions 2000-2005*, November 2006 [*Territorial public finances in the European Union. Trends for 2000-2005*, November 2006].

14. Ken Davey (2007), *Fiscal Decentralization in South-Eastern Europe*, in: Council of Europe, "*Effective democratic governance at local and regional level*", Budapest, OSI, Skopje conference papers, 8-9 Nov. 2006.

economic as well as the political point of view, is equivalent to receiving grants (transfers). The only difference is that the local authority's allocation is sometimes calculated on the basis of local tax revenue. For example, in Germany, the municipal share of income tax is related to the local yield of the income tax; the idea here is that the taxpayer is supposed to be pleased knowing that part of their tax is helping finance local public services. Even so, their

elected representatives have no say in setting the tax rates and there is no connection between the rate of taxation and the number and quality of services provided.

The differences among the various European local government finance systems stem from their different sources of local budget resources. All draw in particular on own tax revenue, on various kinds of grants, on shared taxes and on revenue

**Figure 3    Structure of Local Budget Resources: Own Tax Revenue and Grants or Shared Taxes**

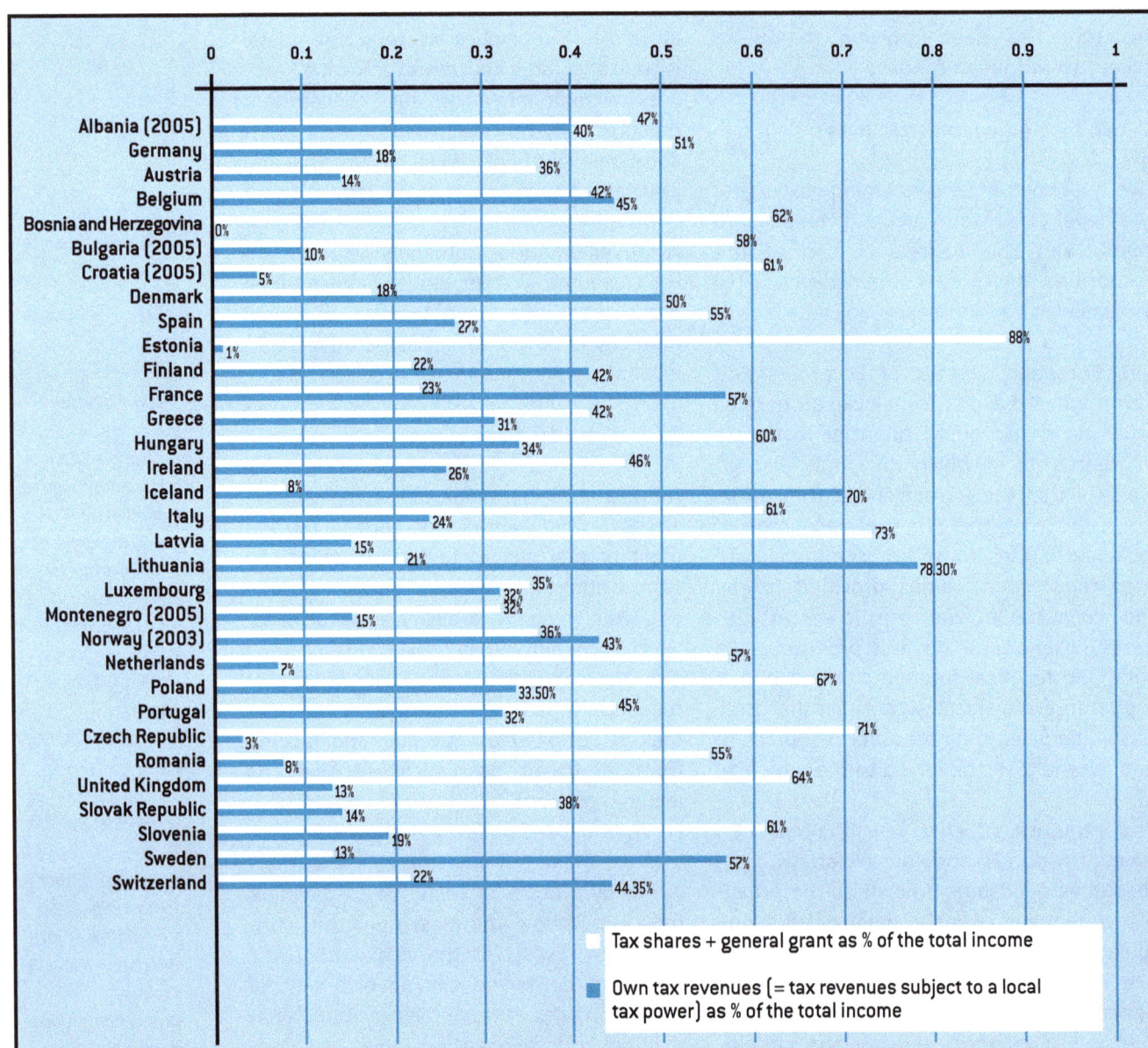

Source: *DEXIA 2002, Council of Europe, 2003 or 2005.*

from service delivery. However, they diverge in the different weighting given to their income sources, and in the characteristics of the most important ones. We can for example distinguish local finance systems according to whether the resource structure is governed by own tax revenue or instead by grants, including allocations carved from national tax revenues. Figure No. 3 compares these two types of resources against the total resources of local authorities in the majority of European countries. As in previous charts, this one takes into account only the local level, usually one or two tiers, but three in France and Poland and not the federal entities and autonomous regions. This chart also includes data available on Albania and some states from the former Yugoslavia.

The chart shows clearly that own tax revenue is greater than the total revenue from national tax shares and grants in only eight countries[15] –Belgium, Denmark, Finland, France, Iceland, Norway, Sweden and Switzerland. In all these countries, the income from own tax revenues comprises more than 40% of the total for local budget resources. In the other countries, own tax revenue falls below 35% as a proportion of total resources, except in Albania where it reached 40% after reforms took effect in 2005. It rises above 30% only in Greece, Hungary, Luxembourg, Poland and Portugal. But even in these countries the proportion of grants and national tax shares represents a much higher percentage of resources (except in Luxembourg).

Analysis suggests that there are indeed differences among the various local finance systems that operate with between 30% and 40% of resources coming from own tax revenues. Such resources are greater than those from grants and shared taxes. When these two conditions are met, it can be said that the resource system is governed by local taxation. Grants then have the role of providing a basic source of funds or of fund equalization, or of offsetting costs prescribed by the law. The own tax revenue is

enough to allow local authorities to establish their own fiscal policies. Conversely, in the countries where own tax revenue is considerably lower than income from grants or tax shares, and is considerably lower than 30% of total resources, it can be said that such resource systems are governed by grants. In this case, own tax revenue theoretically helps fund non-mandatory expenditures, such as those for discretionary tasks, or helps pay for costs that are insufficiently covered by grants and tax-share revenues. But the lower own tax revenue is as a proportion of total resources, the more difficult it is in political terms to raise extra resources because a significant increase in resources necessarily implies a significant increase in tax rates. This political aspect may change where the central government puts pressure on local authorities to raise local taxes or cut expenditure by rationing budgetary transfers and national tax shares. However, connection charges and user fees paid locally for services can provide alternative non-tax resources, especially at the local council level. Increases in local service charges and ancillary fees are apt to be accepted more easily than higher taxes. A final point on this matter: in the central and eastern European countries, property revenues (income from alienation or licensing) can continue to play an important role and to increase the proportion of local resources kept under the control of local authorities; this is only a transitional situation, but it is just what is needed to facilitate transition.

b) Own local tax revenue

As far as the structure of own taxation is concerned, there are several observations worth consideration. All countries except Sweden collect property tax, and this tax is generally held to be the most appropriate one for local taxation because of the localization of the tax base. This view is shared by most governments throughout the world. But this tax is dependent on the existence of a fully-functioning land register. As yet no such system functions properly in the Cen-

*In only eight countries is own revenue greater than the total revenue from national tax shares and grants, and is in excess of 40% of the total revenue*

15. Lithuania is not included as there are clearly errors in the statistical classification of their resources: in 2002, the local tax revenue of local authorities did not exceed 8.4% of the total of their resources (G. Marcou, Les structures régionales dans les pays candidats et leur compatibilité avec les fonds structurels (Europe centrale et orientale) [Regional structures in applicant countries and their compatibility with the structural funds (central and eastern Europe)], Luxembourg, Parlement européen STOA 105 FR, 2002, [Part B: country files]).

tral and Eastern European countries, some of which have no register at all. Local taxation of households is rarely based on a local income tax, though it is the practice in the Nordic countries and in Switzerland; these countries also have the highest levels of local governmental expenditure. In many other countries income tax is a shared tax whose yield is partly or wholly allocated to local budgets. For example, shared income taxes account for part of the local allocations in Austria, Germany, Hungary and Poland; all income tax revenue is used to fund local budgets in Bulgaria, Croatia and Romania. In some countries, local governments can vote for an additional income tax, calculated on top of the state tax (Switzerland) or based on the income tax revenue leveled locally (Croatia). One advantage of channeling income tax revenue to the local level is the taxpayers' increased perception of a direct connection between taxes paid and services used. In Greece, local taxation mainly comprises taxes that represent funding for public services, and not taxes in the strict sense. This was also the case in France with the *taxe d'habitation* (community charge), that is now a direct tax; there is also the same process with the tax for household refuse collection that has in recent years been used as an adjustment variable by many local and intercommunity councils voting rates higher than needed by the service costs.

*The general tendency has been to squeeze own tax revenues, and to prioritize securing revenues over financial responsibility*

By contrast, fewer than half of the European Union countries have a local tax specifically levied on economic activity: Austria, Cyprus, Denmark, France, Germany, Hungary, Ireland, Luxembourg, Portugal and Spain. The tax base for economic activity is variable, but considering local tax revenues and budget levels as a whole, this tax is only a significant resource in France, Germany, Hungary, Ireland, Luxembourg and Spain. Moreover, it is vulnerable to economic policy measures aimed at reducing the burden of businesses; such measures have reduced this tax base in recent years, particularly in France, Germany and Spain.

Overall, the general tendency has been to squeeze own tax revenues as a proportion of the total resources of local authorities, to benefit resources whose variations are controlled by the central authorities. In France as in Germany, the tax base for the business tax has been reduced. In France, the business tax rate was capped at 3.5% of value added, a move that affects nearly half of those qualifying to pay the tax. In the Netherlands in 2006, local property taxes were abolished for tenants and capped for landlords, resulting in a reduction in financial autonomy. Sweden and Italy, each within very different contexts, have proved to be remarkable exceptions to this general tendency to shrink own tax revenues. The same has been true since 2005 in Slovak Republic where new local taxes have replaced the allocation of grants. In Sweden, own revenues still provide more than 70% of the resources of local authorities. Italy, since 1992, has continued the process of restoring own taxation, which was virtually abolished in 1971 in an effort to promote equalization. All this means that in most countries, securing resources is prioritized over financial responsibility. The rules used for calculating shared tax allocations, insofar as these are relatively stable or negotiated (as in Austria or Germany) and the guarantees pertaining to changes in grants (as in a "stability pact") ensure that there is a certain balance between resources and costs – within the limits allowed by the economic situation.

## c) Other funding techniques

Among the alternatives to public budget funding that have emerged and developed in recent years to fund investments are the various forms of public-private partnerships (PPPs) inspired by the British Private Finance Initiative (PFI) of 1992. Since the end of the 1990s, many countries have adopted legislation on PPPs which, under the various legal formats in different countries, nonetheless follows the same basic process: the public authority entrusts a company or a consortium with an overall mission of designing, realizing, financing and operating or maintaining a public works on the local government's behalf. This widens the possibilities traditionally offered with the system of concession. The real reason for the development of PPPs is a budgetary one.

Results have been mixed. Even in the United Kingdom, PPPs do not account for more than 11% of public investment. This limited success can be explained by the fact that conditions for local authorities' access to credit were very restrictive until the Local Government Act of 2003, so that the PFI represented the possibility of accessing extra resources.

Although PPPs often help speed funding for certain operations, they also have certain disadvantages. One is that capital raised by the contract partner on the market will be obtained under less favourable terms than those usually given to public authorities. Additionally, the fees payable by the public authority have to cover all costs, including the financial ones, so that the PPP in effect turns the debt into operating costs, though this does not in itself assure an overall saving. Another point of concern is the private companies' push for higher profit margins for additional risks they pretend to bear, and it is difficult for public authorities to control these margins[16]. In the other countries, the share of PPPs in public investment continues to be fairly modest, even if governments sometimes set ambitious targets, as for example in France where the avowed goal is 10% by 2010.

Such limitations of the PPP as a tool for funding may explain the re-emergence of funding bodies aimed solely at local authorities. Founded on a cooperative basis, they are modeled on *Kommuninvest*, a cooperative body founded in Sweden in 1986 to provide funding to local authorities[17]. Until it was absorbed in a 1996 merger, Belgium's *Crédit Communal* was similar.

## III.2.  Powers and Responsibilities

It is necessary to make clear the status of the different categories of powers and responsibilities, before reviewing the functions (Committee of Regions: 2002; Marcou, 2007).

### III.2.1.  Categories of powers and responsibilities

The first thing is to note how the general clause on the scope of local self-government as provided under article 4.2 of the European Charter of Local Self-Government has found widespread application, at least at the level of municipal authorities. This clause is not concerned with the division of powers and responsibilities. Rather, it defines a principle of freedom. This principle is of paramount importance, even if the activities it sanctions remain modest in budgetary terms. Most of the European states at the Council of Europe level now recognize the principle of the general clause as applying to local councils, through their constitutions or laws. A few countries, including Portugal, the United Kingdom and some Central and Eastern European nations, are exceptions; Spain and Italy raise questions of interpretation.

The fact remains that most of the powers and responsibilities exercised by local authorities are established by law. There is a noticeable general inclination to extend the scope of local authority, sometimes in the form of "powers and responsibilities for specific purposes" (as stated in art. 4 of the Charter) exercised in the name of the state and under its direction. This is particularly the case in Germany, Austria, Italy, the Czech Republic, Hungary and Slovenia. It leads to local councils exercising administrative tasks traditionally performed by the state. This does contribute to the overall empowerment of local government, but the real reach of this type of extension of powers and responsibilities depends on the control exercised in practice by the state.

In the Central and Eastern European states, the range of material tasks for which local authorities are responsible is vast, especially where they are the heirs to

16. *Numerous inquiries reported by the Committee of Public Accounts of the House of Commons suggest cautiousness regarding benefits that can be expected by public authorities from PFI (for example HC 567, 16 July 2003 ; HC 446, 31 March 2005 ; HC 553, 14 June 2005 ; HC 694, 3 May 2006).*

17. *Kommuninvest consists of 196 municipalities and 7 county councils.*

local bodies formerly controlled directly by the central state. Exceptions are countries where a separate state administration has been re-established or maintained in some domains at the local level. The "powers and responsibilities for specific purposes" are then predominant in the mission of local government, and can effectively keep local authorities in the position of being agents of the state. This is the case, for example, at the regional level in the Czech Republic. Because the resources provided to local authorities are hardly enough to finance the tasks delegated to them by the state, there is little time or occasion for local bodies to exercise their autonomy.

A more detailed study of the system governing local powers and responsibilities also raises the question of how relevant some commonly held distinctions are. Basic powers and responsibilities are always regulated by law wherever they affect domains or tasks that have a national dimension (and are therefore mandatory). What then determines the degree of local autonomy are the fine details and the scope of the pertinent legal regulations. In extreme cases the regulations can make the system governing such functions almost indistinguishable from the system governing delegated tasks. Such a situation led to reforms undertaken in the Nordic countries in the 1980s. These reforms were often grouped under the term of "free municipality," and their aim was reducing the heavy burden of national regulations and financial controls on local governments. In some countries the courts occasionally can ensure that regulations respect the rights of self-government by censuring provisions deemed to exceed the stated aims of the regulations, as in Germany, but such judicial intercession is unusual.

### III.2.2. Functions

Regarding functions effectively exercised in application of the law, we will limit our study to the level of municipalities and their consortia. A detailed comparison reveals that certain tasks are carried out by local councils or their consortia in virtually all European countries. Providing a slight variation, Portugal delegates these tasks to sub-divisions of the local councils. These local tasks typically include: town planning (urban planning, planning permission, development projects), the allocation of social benefits and the management of social institutions for certain categories of the population, particularly for the elderly. They also include roads and public transport, water distribution (with the notable exception of England), accommodation and housing (with the notable exception of the Netherlands, Italy and Switzerland), and the construction and maintenance of school buildings. These days we can add to this list education support in all countries, along with actions for economic development, that can be carried out also through powers that are not specifically deemed to this function, when they are not listed by the law. Together, these tasks can be considered the common substance of local powers and responsibilities in Europe.

The most important variations relating to powers and responsibilities occur in the fields of education, health, and social security or benefits. Broadly, local governments by national law are responsible for such services in the Nordic countries and to a large extent in the United Kingdom. As of this year, regional authorities in Denmark have overall management of healthcare and the health insurance system, which had previously been run to a great extent by the counties. In Sweden, social security is managed at the national level, but the counties run the hospitals and the healthcare system. In Germany, France, Italy and Spain, on the other hand, local governments exercise only partial or marginal powers and responsibilities in these areas. The same applies to education: the recruitment and management of staff is generally the task of state or regional authorities. This is a duty of German and Austrian *Länder*, of the autonomous communities of Spain and in Belgian *communautés*. In the

*The most important variations relating to powers and responsibilities occur in the fields of education, health, and social security or benefits*

Nordic countries it is the responsibility of municipalities, as it is still to a large extent in the United Kingdom. In Italy, education is outside the domain of regional authorities.

Public safety responsibilities are also devolved to local governments in many, though not all, European countries. In Belgium, the Netherlands and the United Kingdom public safety by tradition is an important responsibility of the mayor or other local authorities. By contrast, in Germany, Hungary and Sweden, public security hardly appears at all in the remit of local governments.

In the Eastern European countries, responsibility for education and health varies considerably, even within individual nations over time. In Bulgaria for example, management of the health system and the schools was first assigned to municipalities, but was returned to the state level in 2003. In Albania, these tasks have been financed out of the state budget since 2003, even though the local councils administer the staff payroll. In Hungary, Lithuania, Poland and Romania, the management of schools and education staff is decentralized. In Estonia, Latvia, the Czech Republic, Slovak Republic and Slovenia, on the other hand, it is divided between the state and local governments, the state retaining responsibility for staff management.

Movement toward centralization can be seen in several countries in the areas of education (United Kingdom), health (Norway) and public safety (Belgium, Netherlands). However, in many other countries local councils are getting more involved in education, as well as public safety. Previously, local councils in these countries had had only limited administrative responsibilities in these areas. A third approach is favoured in the Netherlands, Sweden and the United Kingdom: enlisting the private sector. In these three countries, management reforms focused on attracting the private sector have reduced the remit of local governments.

## III.3.  Administrative Capacity

Administrative capacity depends on the human resources and style of management, both of which have undergone important changes in the past few years.

### III.3.1.  Human resources

There are substantial differences in the staffing levels of local governments. Unsurprisingly, these differences reflect those already noted for the powers and responsibilities: countries in which local government and particularly municipalities manage both essential public services and the human resources they require, are the countries with the highest staff levels. In the Nordic countries, Switzerland and the United Kingdom, local government staff represent about 80% of the total for public sector employees (63% in Norway). These employees for the most part work in education and the health services. Despite an extensive range of functions, local governments in Eastern Europe have far lower staffing levels (around 40%), except in Hungary (69%) and Slovak Republic (90%) (CNFPT: 2005; Pollitt / Boukaert: 2004).

The political structure of a state hardly impinges on these staffing issues. In fact it tends to be in unitary states that we find the proportionally highest levels of staff employed by local governments. For the most part, levels of employment for local governments are similar: for example they are 28% in Germany, 31% in France, 24% in Spain, 34% in Belgium, 19% in Italy and 18% in Portugal. Federal states and states with autonomous regions, for their part, are distinguished by the lower staffing levels of their central civil service. Local staffing is also comparatively low because the bulk of their human resources are employed at the regional level[18]. The lower staffing levels of local governments in Greece and Ireland also reflect their limited powers and responsibilities.

In recent years, local governments of many countries have had to cut staff levels be-

18. *Pollitt / Bouckaert (2004), p.44 et seq.*

cause of budgetary constraints and the outsourcing of many activities. Outsourcing increased markedly after the implementation of strategies inspired by the "New Public Management" philosophy, and measures aimed at improving performance.

Staff skills and qualifications are also important factors affecting the quality of local public service. Best practices include recruitment based on merit so the impartiality of the public service is protected. A reasonable level of personnel mobility among local governments makes it easier for small and medium-size governments to attract qualified staff. There are many ways of achieving these objectives, but equally, authorities can fail to achieve them because of an inappropriate employment system.

In the employment structures of local governments, as is the case for public administration in general, we can identify two types of system:

- A career employment structure governed by public law, essentially characterized by a system of appointment and job security;

- A contract-based employment structure with private law as the reference, and no guarantee of job security.

But the employment systems in the European countries vary widely, and often include a mix of methods. Moreover, certain situations can be misleading, and public law structure and career employment structure do not always come to the same thing in practice. In the Netherlands for example, a contract employment system prevails within a public law structure, while in Italy and the Czech Republic, local authority employees have access to a career path within an employment structure determined by collective agreements.

Although local government employment systems have been developing in the direction of increased flexibility of employ-

ment conditions and incentive-based remuneration, thus taking their inspiraton from the message of "New Public Management", they continue to take different forms depending on specific national traditions. While some countries have gone more determinedly down the path of contract-based employment, others have maintained the professional career structure as their main system. In many cases, the outcome has been hybridization, mixing features from both models.

The countries that have gone furthest in aligning the status and conditions of local government staff with those of the private sector under labor laws include the United Kingdom (where there is no history of a legal distinction between public and private sector employment) and a group of countries that have almost entirely abandoned their old career employment structures in favor of a contract-based system. These countries are Sweden (1974), Denmark (1969) and Italy (1993). In most countries, the contract-based system has been partially introduced while maintaining a career employment structure for managerial posts. Such "mixed" systems, with their strong element of career employment structure, are particularly common in Germany, Finland and Switzerland. In Germany, this system has long been a feature of local governments, the great majority of staff being employed on fixed-term contracts; but the two systems have ended up converging: after 15 years of fixed-term work, staff are given a permanent post.

In the post-communist countries of Central and Eastern Europe, building employment systems for local government was an uncertain process throughout the 1990s. The form of local employment system that each country chose, often after going through various changes, depended on specific national traditions, different reactions to the post-communism transformation, and efforts focused on training qualified staff and preventing corruption. In addition,

*The countries that have gone furthest in aligning the status and conditions of local government staff with those of the private sector under labor laws include the United Kingdom , and a group of countries that have almost entirely abandoned their old career employment structures in favor of a contract-based system*

| Table 2 | Typology of European Countries According to the Employment System of Local Governments |

| Public or private law career structure for executive and managerial posts | Public law career structure applied generally | [Contract-based] private or public law employment |
| --- | --- | --- |
| Albania | Belgium | Bulgaria |
| Austria | Cyprus | Denmark |
| Bosnia and Herzegovina | France | Macedonia, FYR |
| Croatia | Greece | Netherlands |
| Czech Republic | Hungary | Norway |
| Estonia | Ireland | Poland |
| Finland | Latvia | Slovak Republic |
| Germany | Lithuania | Sweden |
| Italy | Luxembourg | United Kingdom |
| Serbia | Malta | |
| Switzerland | Montenegro | |
| | Portugal | |
| | Romania | |
| | Slovenia | |
| | Spain | |

countries preparing for accession to the European Union made changes to accommodate the process of accession itself. The combination of all these factors yielded different results in different countries. Thus, some systems lean more toward contract-based employment, particularly in Bulgaria, Poland and Slovak Republic, while the career employment structure predominates in Hungary, Latvia, Lithuania, Romania and Slovenia.

The fact remains that overall, the career employment structure governed by public law is still predominant. Applying labor law to public service presupposes that there is a system of strict collective agreements in place, which cannot exist without powerful local authority associations and equally powerful trades unions. However, this is the case in only a handful of countries. We should not be misled by the coexistence of two employment systems, because when this is the case, the public law career structure does in fact apply to the executive and managerial positions, even if staff on fixed-term contracts are sometimes employed in such posts. It has kept therefore a decisive place in the system of human resources

management and a key role in the relations between managers and the political staff. Furthermore, in many other countries, we find the vast majority of staff employed under a public law career structure. These observations can be summarised as in Table 2 according to the dominant feature of the employment system.

A major criticism of public administrations based on the career employment structure is lack of recognition for good performance by the remuneration system. Another is that promotion tends to be heavily based on length of service and seniority. The aim of policies to move from career employment structures to a contract-based system was made in order to introduce elements of internal competition and a system of incentive-based remuneration. Systems with the strongest focus on incentives seem to be those introduced in the United Kingdom, Sweden and Italy. However, a move towards incentive-based remuneration can be noted within career employment structures as well.

In countries where employment systems continue to be dominated by public-law career structures, the move toward more

*The career system tends nevertheless to prevail, in particular for executive and managerial positions*

flexible payment and promotion systems has been slower and less marked. Nonetheless, they are now making demonstrable headway in Germany and France.

### III.4.1. Management Reforms

From the beginning of the 1980s, the process of modernization has been driven by New Public Management (NPM) ideas, though the vogue for these seems to be diminishing (Pollit / Boukaert: 2004; Kersting / Vetter: 2003).

The key idea of NPM was to overturn the inflexibility and inefficiency traditionally attributed to public administration ("let managers manage") and to replace its system of hierarchical control with management based on indicators, feedback and follow-up.

*European Community law has a decisive influence on how the management of public services evolves and develops*

In the United Kingdom after 1979, the reforms forced local authorities to accommodate in their organizational structure for services a separation between the roles of buyer and supplier, and to open their services to competition by soliciting outside suppliers (competitive tendering). In 2000, these principles came under review upon the arrival of a new program dubbed "Best Value Authorities," which puts a greater stress on performance over costs. The separation of the roles of buyer and supplier was also introduced for local authorities in Sweden. In Germany, this trend took the form of a "new management model" (*Neues Steuerungsmodell*), which challenged the traditional primacy of legality and hierarchical control. In France, the 1983 elections led to the election of mayors claiming to be inspired by a new concept of municipal management, whereby a town was to be governed like a commercial company. However results of municipal elections have indicated that this model has lost its attraction. Even so, they have not signaled a move away from modern management techniques. At present, the extension to local budgets of the principles of the state budget reform (organic law on budget laws

of 2001: management based on programs and directed to results) is discussed.

In the Central and Eastern European countries, the traditional model was first used to set up the new administrative structures, so the managerial model has been slower to filter through.

In the debate on modernizing the public sector, two arguments were advanced to promote privatization and the market (Lorrain / Stoker: 1996).

First, turning to privatization was advocated as a means of reducing the weight of the central functions of the "welfare state" by letting market forces take over. The idea of the "lean state" (*Etat modeste, schlanker Staat...*) has been widely promoted since the 1980s at both national and international levels.

Moreover, turning to the market for the supply of services was advocated on the grounds that public authorities should be restricted to an enabling function. Actual performance of public services should be contracted out to private companies on a competitive basis. The European Commission also argued for this approach with the aim of promoting the single market.

These tenets had perhaps their greatest impact in Sweden and the United Kingdom, because it was there that the local public sector monopoly was most extensive. But in Sweden, only about 15% of municipal services have been effectively contracted out. In the Central and Eastern European countries, where social services were wholly delivered by the state or by public bodies under the communist system, there have been fundamental changes in the management and range of services offered. The private sector now plays an increasing role in their delivery. In Germany however, where most social services have traditionally been delivered by private non-profit bodies (*freie Wohlfahrtsverbände*), the local authorities concentrate on organizing and monitoring tasks. The impact of NPM was thus rather limited, though it did later lead to a diversification of "suppliers." In countries like France and Spain, with a long tradition of devolving the operation of local public services to the private sector, the NPM principles did not seem of much relevance, although new tools to facilitate recourse to the private sector have more recently been created. But the focus on performance as the driving force has gained a lot of ground, both through state interventions (for example, reforms in France of local accounts models) and through initiatives taken by the local authorities themselves.

European Community law has a decisive influence on how the management of public services evolves and develops. This is because all services that can be classified as services of general economic interest –as defined under article 86.2 of the Treaty on the European Community– are subject to the rules on competition, unless these rules impede the realization of their mission in conditions compatible with the viability of the enterprise. According to the Court of Justice, if a local authority decides to devolve the operation of a public service to a private company, that local authority must use a competitive [tendering] procedure. This applies even if the authority itself has created a local enterprise specifically to deliver the service in question, unless it can establish that it exercises the same control over this enterprise as it does over any of its administrative services (known as the "in-house" exception). For the Court, it suffices that the company has external shareholders, even if only minority ones, to invalidate this latter condition. The result is that integration through the market, as interpreted by the Court of Justice, means that the freedom of local authorities to choose how to manage the public services they are responsible for is restricted. This applies even though this freedom has long been considered an important part of local self-government in many countries, including France, Germany and Spain. Of course,

other countries have sought to restrict the freedom of local authorities in this respect, in the name of opening up the market (Italy and the United Kingdom, in particular). In the same way, the new regulation 1370/2007 (23rd October 2007) concerning public rail and road transport puts an end to the exception that preserves urban and regional public transport from open competition. However, competent local authorities still have the possibility to provide public transport services directly or through a separate entity over which they exercise a similar control as for their own services and to which they may assign the service directly. The urban transport systems of numerous large European cities will necessarily be reviewed when the new regulation comes into force (3 December 2009). The free choice of local authorities regarding the operational system will therefore be limited. By contrast, most Services of General Interest (SGI) should not be affected by the application of the so-called "Services" directive of 12 December 2006.

## IV.  Local Democracy

The main trends we can identify can be presented by distinguishing among local political systems, supervisory structures, the impact of decentralization on national policies, and the role of the associations of local councilors and mayors, and of local governments.

### IV.1.  The Local Political System

The election of municipal councils, or more generally of community-level local governments, by direct, free and secret universal vote is today a reality in all the countries of the Council of Europe. A look back over even recent history is enough to show what important gains have been made. As far as intermediate-level local governments are concerned, the situation is a little more complex: In some cases, indirect elections seem to be a better option for linking intermediate-level tasks

*The election of municipal councils or local governments, by direct, free and secret universal vote is today a reality in all the countries of the Council of Europe*

with local-level responsibilities. This is desirable to prevent legitimate interests at the middle level from competing and conflicting with those of local councils, and also to protect the independence of the latter, as exemplified by regional authorities in Ireland, regional councils in Finland and Romania, and provincial delegations (*deputación provincial*) in Spain. The provincial delegations in Spain are considered part of the local level and are meant to serve the local councils. However, it was decided in Norway and Hungary not to use indirect elections for the county-level councils.

*The most significant developments have taken place in the executive ranks of community-level local governments, namely for a certain personalization of the executive role and for direct elections*

The most significant developments have taken place in the executive ranks of community-level local governments, namely for a certain personalization of the executive role and for direct elections (Bäck / Heanelt / Magnier: 2006; Szücs / Strömberg: 2006). The most typical changes here occurred in Italy, Germany and the United Kingdom. In Germany, the former variety among municipal institutions has given way to a unique model, broadly speaking characterized by the election of mayors by direct universal vote, and the possibility of removing them from office. Italy has introduced the direct election of mayors, provincial presidents, and regional presidents. In the United Kingdom, following the election of a mayor of London by direct vote, the law has also provided for other cities to adopt a similar model, along two variant forms. In Central and Eastern Europe, mayors are elected by direct vote, except in the Baltic States, Poland, the Czech Republic and Croatia. The question is being debated in Belgium and the Netherlands. In the Netherlands, a draft bill to amend the Constitution to allow the election of burgomasters failed in 2005, so these officials continue to be appointed by central government on the basis of nominations from the municipal councils, but with the nominations being open to citizen consultations. Mayors continue to be appointed in Belgium and Luxembourg, but, as in the Netherlands, the

executive body is a collegiate executive body whose other members are elected by the council.

In the United Kingdom, the Local Government Act 2000 led local authorities to abandon the traditional system of council committees exercising executive tasks, to differentiate the executive and non-executive roles and, in some circumstances, to submit to referendum proposals for a local constitution that could include direct election of a mayor. But these reforms did not receive the expected support. Among the 386 local authorities potentially qualifying for an elected mayor, referendums had been held by only 31 local authorities by the end of 2006. The results favored the direct election of a mayor in only 12 referendums. However, a feature of these reforms is that local residents can take the initiative to hold a referendum on the role of mayor by submitting a petition, signed by 5% of registered voters, to their local authority. A less well-known aspect of the reforms, but one with perhaps a greater impact over the long term, is the differentiation of the executive and non-executive roles. This should lead to an enhanced role for local councils in providing policy guidance, and also supervision with respect to the executive bodies. The October 2006 White Paper has resumed revitalizing institutional reforms by reinforcing political leadership in the local authorities. "The Local Government and Public Involvement in Health Act 2007 (c.28) makes possible the election of the council in one ballot and requires the choice between two alternative executive formulas: a leader elected by the council or a directly elected mayor, who, in either case, then forms his cabinet by appointing at least two members of the council".

Useful parallels emerge here with the Netherlands reforms known as "dualization" (*dualisering*), introduced by the laws of March 7, 2002, governing municipalities and January 16, 2003 governing provinces (amending the law of September 10, 1972), providing for a separation of the executive branch from the assembly. Henceforth, the aldermen (at the province level, the deputies) can no longer be members of the council, and nearly all administrative powers are concentrated in the executive body. To balance this, the legislators wanted to reinforce the assembly's role of policy guidance and supervision. The split timing of the different mandate terms also contributes to this dualization: four years for the council and aldermen, six years for the mayor (the Queen's commissioner).

Behind all these developments and reforms, apparently very different in spirit, lies the same key goal: restoring or reinforcing political leadership in local governments, and above all at the municipal level. Of course this has not been an issue in countries like France or with the *Länder* in the south of Germany. In both places, the figure of a strong mayor is deeply rooted in history. But it should be noted that all of the Western European countries mentioned here have either traditionally had a collegiate local executive body, or have not had an executive body that was distinct from the council. In most countries in Eastern Europe, it was the desire for democracy that drove the introduction of directly-elected mayors. However, it is clear that the various countries have very different approaches to this issue. In most cases, direct election of mayors has seemed the best way to guarantee political accountability, to the extent that their mandate is renewable. But in the Netherlands and probably in the United Kingdom, the preferred approach to reinforcing political leadership is to focus on strengthening the political role of the councils. This ambition was also in the background of the so-called "free community" reforms in the Nordic countries in the 1980s, which gave municipal councils the freedom to determine the internal organization of local government. Previously, the executive committees had been determined by law. The reforms (see in particular the Swedish law of 1991 on local administra-

tion) meant that the councils could have their own choices on their administrative organization in relation to their functions; they have also reinforced the executive council's management lead role in the various specialized sectors.

For local assemblies, the changes are less clear. There appears to be a definite tendency toward what is called "parliamentarization." This condition is characterized by a reinforcement of the rights of councilors, and the possibility of calling the executive branch to account politically. This is particularly evident in Spain in the devolving of powers and responsibilities from the council to the mayor. One avowed aim of this reform is strengthening the executive branch's capacity for action, particularly in the major cities (laws of 1999 and 2003). Calling the mayor to account can in some countries require a procedure for recall by the citizens. This kind of procedure is seen in most of the German *Länder* as well as some Central European countries, including Poland, where several such cases have occurred. In a more general form, we are seeing political groups gaining official recognition in local assemblies of the larger local governments. As in France, these political factions have certain rights recognized by the law in larger councils. This is a form of legal acknowledgment of the role of political parties in the running of local institutions.

*In all of these countries, there is a clear trend toward professionalizing the status of local executive officers, and toward strengthening the professional safeguards necessary for the exercise of their mandate*

The increasing responsibilities of local governments have inevitably affected the status of elected officials (Guérin-Lavignotte / Kerrouche: 2006). In all of these countries, there is a clear trend toward professionalizing the status of local executive officers, and toward strengthening the professional safeguards necessary for the exercise of their mandate. This tendency to professionalize manifests itself also in the move away from a system of remunerative allowances to one of real salaries, complete with social security and pension rights. In tandem with this, there is a move toward preventing officials from assuming several executive roles. In Eastern Europe, the former classification of local executive officers as civil servants has acquired a particular relevance in the new institutional context. In Germany, a full-time mayor is classified as a public-sector employee for the duration of his mandate; in most of the other countries, such status is only partial.

On the other hand, the situation for ordinary councilors –the members of the deliberating assemblies– is generally speaking less satisfactory. The system of leave of absence, paid leave and compensation for loss of income that are thought necessary for exercising their mandate often provides insufficient protection. The training of elected officers is poorly organized, and the system for defining ineligibility and inappropriate practices, aimed at preventing conflicts of interest and improper use of certain positions, falls short of acceptable standards in many countries.

Despite all these reforms, one troublesome fact continues to haunt the modern electoral process: low voter turnout for local elections (Gabriel / Hoffmann-Martinot: 1999). Declining voter participation and stagnation in voter numbers reflect a worrying disaffection with politics at large. This new iteration of a kind of voter torpor appears to be more a response to high-level politics at national level and perhaps the international levels, rather than a widespread unhappiness with local authorities. An exception may be found in Eastern Europe where local elections provoke dramatically lower participation than national elections, perhaps reflecting a general feeling that local authorities don't have much of a role to play. Only three countries are bucking the trend: Hungary, Ireland and Switzerland. The United Kingdom is also seeing a rise in voter participation, albeit from a very low benchmark. In Spain the trend in voter participation simply is not clear enough to characterize.

*In Eastern Europe local elections provoke dramatically lower participation than national elections, perhaps reflecting a general feeling that local authorities don't have much of a role to play*

## IV.2. Citizen Participation

These developments have been accompanied by another notable change, increased citizen participation that alters traditional political dynamics. The most obvious form is the referendum, particularly the citizens' referendums initiated by popular demand. This is being increasingly provided for by the law, though actual use of referendums is still rare, except in Switzerland and to some extent in Germany where they are a traditional institution.

This should be contrasted with the increasing importance given to infra-municipal entities, which allow a representation and a participation of citizens at the closest possible level to where they live. These entities are essentially to be found in countries with large municipalities. They are traditional in Bulgaria, and in Portugal their role appears to be growing, which in turn is giving rise to criticism from council management viewpoint. They can be found in countries that have undergone territorial reforms, but without a role in local administration; in such instances they are intended more to maintain a representation to legitimize the amalgamations, such as parishes in England, communities in Wales and villages in Poland, Greece and Lithuania. These can be compared to the neighborhood institutions in Spain. In the Nordic countries, management tasks are devolved upon infra-municipal institutions with corresponding forms of sector-based citizen participation. In other countries, neighborhood councils have been set up, representing local residents; in France they are mandatory for cities with a population of more than 80,000, and are optional for smaller municipalities. In Italy, neighborhood councils had some popularity in the 1970s, but have since declined.

In fact, it has often been thanks to sector-based procedures that progress has been made in citizen participation, particularly in the fields of urban planning, environmental protection and quality-of-life protection. Here local government has sometimes usefully turned to international instruments and used them to raise public awareness and mobilize campaigns. This happened with the Aarhus Convention, and more recently with the environmental impact study plans and programs following the European Community Directive of 2001. The real impact of these procedures on public participatory processes is difficult to assess. Particularly in light of the circumstances and situations where non-compliance of procedures leads to the annulment of the decisions already taken, thus providing citizens with a more realistic appreciation of the room for participatory maneuver and its subsequent bearing on the decision-making process.

Progress in the area of citizens' right to information should not be forgotten either. This does not just concern the publication of local public records. It also speaks to the right of access to administrative documents, which is an essential condition for transparency in local government. Europe has Sweden to thank for the widespread recognition of this principle. Although it has not been implemented in the systematic way seen in Sweden, improved access to local government data does give citizens, associations and the media a more complete picture of the workings of their administration. This is, of course, a prerequisite for effective participation and supervision by civil society. Over the past few years, several Central and Eastern European countries have passed legislation to improve public access to administrative documents, most recently and particularly the Czech Republic and Slovak Republic. The United Kingdom also recently adopted such a law, The Freedom of Information Act.

One related development is the advent of electronic administration in all the European countries. This trend is not restricted to local authorities, and has several aspects[19]. The most important relates to the authorities' intention to simplify administrative procedures. The de-materialization of the public markets illustrates the potential information technology has for improving administrative procedures. One factor inhibiting more computerization of procedures is the need for increased computer security to protect personal data. In many cases this need for confidentiality prevents electronic production and distribution of official notices and certificates. With respect to local democracy, the Internet serves an educational function by multiplying the sources of information that citizens can consult. Of course, it does not guarantee that relevant information will be made available to them for assessing local management or policies. That would require regulations governing what information should be made available to citizens, as is the case in the United Kingdom for performance indicators.

Restrictions, active and passive, still exist in some countries on the voting rights of part of the population. For example, Latvia, Estonia and Lithuania restrict voting by their Russian-speaking citizens. Such voter exclusion is difficult to square with the European Convention on Human Rights. Conversely, the Netherlands and Sweden are extending voting rights to foreign residents (non-European Union nationals), under certain conditions.

## IV.3. Supervision

The supervision of local governments is usually exercised by the state, though in federal states this is usually done by the federal members and in self-governing regions supervision is at least partially devolved to the regions.

With regard to administrative controls, there is a general tendency to limit these to legal checks on the lawfulness of actions and procedures, at least as far as the own (or basic) powers and responsibilities of local authorities are concerned. However, one recourse is the "jurisdictionalization" of supervision. This trend is beneficial for local self-government. However, a closer consideration does reveal that in most of the

*With regard to administrative controls, there is a general tendency to limit these to legal checks on the lawfulness of actions and procedures, at least as far as the own powers and responsibilities of local authorities are concerned*

19. Chatillon, G. / Du Marais, B. (dir.) (2003), Electronic administration at the service of citizens, Bruxelles, Bruylant.

states, the administrative authorities have the power to first censure the act under dispute, after which the local authority may submit the case to the courts. The administrative authority also has the power to suspend any act it submits to the courts. Few countries limit the power of the supervisory authority to the submission of cases to the courts. In France, Hungary and Spain, the act under dispute remains enforceable –subject to a few exceptions. In Italy however, the 2001 constitutional review led to the total removal of the legal checks that had previously been carried out at the regional level, though not by the region. There remains a power of substitution (stepping in for the lower authority) that the government can exercise in cases where Italy's international and European Community obligations in particular are at stake. The government also has the possibility of appointing an "extraordinary commissioner" to resolve a problem on behalf of a local authority that has proved unable to do so. This procedure has been used to resolve problems related to water supply and refuse disposal services in a few cities in the south.

Regional authorities can also exercise certain controls, as is the case for urban planning and development in Italy and Spain, where they have the power of prior approval of local council plans and can stipulate certain amendments as a condition for approval.

In some countries, the power of higher authorities to dismiss or dissolve local bodies is only very rarely regulated by the law, and could lead to abuses. Such cases are steadily decreasing under the influence of the Council of Europe and through monitoring of the implementation of the European Charter of Local Self-Government.

Controls on financial management can affect local self-government. While there has been a tendency to decrease the traditional audits for checking the lawfulness of accounts, the development of new management tech-

*Increasingly worthy of note are the widespread forms of cooperation among various levels of government based on contractual arrangements*

niques based on the accountability of staff and officials, and on performance evaluation can translate into heavier controls. These controls can be an even more sensitive issue given that the performance indicators and objectives will have been defined in greater detail. When such controls are carried out by a higher authority, they are by their nature potentially harmful to local self-government, no matter that the official aim is to improve effectiveness.

The case of the United Kingdom (England) is exemplary on this. Recent developments there have led to a reinforcement of the inspections carried out on local authorities, either directly through the audits effected by the Audit Commission for Local Authorities, which can submit cases to the courts, or indirectly through procedures aimed at promoting better public sector management (Best Value Inspection, with the mission of inspecting all services on this basis). If local authorities, bound by the Local Government Act 1999 to constantly improve their results, improve their performance and obtain the qualification of "best value authority," they are rewarded with a greater freedom of action, particularly in what use they can make of the grants they receive. The Best Value Performance indicators are set by the various ministries when these are preparing the annual budget. The Audit Commission (pursuant to the Audit Commission Act 1998) must publish to that purpose a report on its evaluation of the performances of local authorities, and classify these according to their performances into different categories defined by the Secretary of State for Communities and Local Government (pursuant to the Local Government Act 2003, in particular sections 99 and 100). The October 2006 White Paper provides for reducing the number of indicators used in the evaluations from 1,200 down to 200.

Increasingly worthy of note are the widespread forms of cooperation among various levels of government based on contractual arrangements. Such agreements are used under many different conditions for a variety of purposes. These arrangements are found in the various areas of shared powers and responsibilities, where cooperation creates interdependence. They are used in Belgium, France, Germany, Italy, the Netherlands, Portugal, and Poland (see in particular the 1999 law on territorial development). They even appear in Ukraine (see the adoption in 2005 of the law on regional development and the adoption in 2006 of its implementing provisions).  In England the regional offices of the government have since 2004 been negotiating "Local Area Agreements" with the local authorities in order to implement some 40 programs set by ten ministries. The October 2006 White Paper provides for this to apply to all authorities, setting out a legal framework for these agreements that would make them mandatory across the country. This approach has raised considerable interest, which is understandable because it sets an official framework for negotiations, and facilitates the monitoring of how the mutual undertakings are honored. Developing cooperation between the various levels of government represents a step beyond the notion of local self-government as something defined in opposition to the state. Instead, it redefines it positively along the lines of a general participation by local authorities in the different collective responsibilities that the public system must carry out. This highlights how relative the idea of local self-government is in modern states.

## IV.4. The Impact of Decentralization and Local Democracy on National Policies

It is paradoxical that apathy toward local institutions, as reflected in the increasingly low voter participation in local elections, is manifesting itself at a time when the powers, tasks and independent decision-making of local authorities have markedly increased in most countries. Again, evidence suggests that generally speaking this development cannot be blamed on the local institutions themselves.

There is also the phenomenon, well noted for a long time now, by which the more national policies depend for their implementation on local authorities, the more these are in a position to influence *de facto* the national policies. Or they may cause distortions at the local level, forcing the national government to anticipate things by, at least partly, taking into account the demands of the local authorities. This phenomenon has often been studied, and was illustrated a few years ago in France by a report of the *Cour des Comptes* (national audit office) on the "city contracts." The report showed how the contents of the contracts and their implementation strayed from the priorities initially set out by the government (*Cour des Comptes*, 1992).

However, we should not extrapolate too much from this analysis, which only applies to countries where the local authorities, and in particular the mayors, have acquired sufficient political weight to reduce the scope of the methods of control available to the government. In particular, there are no indications that similar observations could be made about the local authorities of Eastern Europe, despite the progress made there.

Connections between national and local politics should not be overlooked. An extreme case of intermingling is France, where the practice of politicians being elected to several mandates exists. This has allowed some local issues to permeate debates in the national parliament, but has also slowed the renewal of the political scene by allowing elected officials to keep at least one mandate if defeated in election for another. This practice makes it difficult to introduce global reforms that would challenge the collective interests of local representatives. The extensive reach of this system stands in contrast to the countries where radical reforms have been carried out, such as the United Kingdom (particularly the reforms of 1972 and 1996). The British system is famous for the separation it maintains

*There is also the phenomenon, well noted for a long time now, by which the more national policies depend for their implementation on local authorities, the more these are in a position to influence de facto the national policies*

between national and local institutions, and between politicians of both levels.

In the other countries, although multiple mandates are usually excluded, at least at the level of executive roles, the practice nonetheless appears in several countries in diluted or indirect forms. In Germany for example, municipal or district councillors may also be elected as members of the regional parliaments (*Landtag*); the regional parliaments do in fact play an important role in local administration and finances.

*Local government associations are playing a greater role in Europe, in particular with respect to the EU. Four main functions may be distinguished in their activities, none of them being exclusive*

The growing influence of national political parties in local elections –at least in countries with a system of political parties with well-established local presence– works both ways, but more in favor of centralization. Political loyalties do lead to a certain homogeneity in the playing out of issues, even if local candidates for office try to put forward issues specific to their constituency or area. This has long been observed in the United Kingdom, especially since the Labour party established itself at the local level. But for the same reasons, local elections are often considered as a test for the government in power, which means that national issues tend to predominate over local ones.

It is harder to assess the role local politics play in the careers of politicians. Even in France these days, national political careers are more frequently consolidated by a local mandate, a likelier option than getting into parliament after having become known as a mayor. In the other countries, there are few examples of local political leaders who went on to the national level. At most, this applies to the mayors of a few large cities.

### IV.5.  The Role of Local Government Associations

It can safely be stated that local government associations are playing a greater role in Europe, even though their importance varies from country to country. One of the goals of local self-government building in Central and Eastern Europe was to establish associations of local governments capable of representing their collective interests to central government. These associations in the Western European countries provided crucial support for their establishment.

The role of these associations in the European countries can be evaluated by their status and by the work they carry out.

With respect to their status, legally they are always associations governed by private law. Even so, they are increasingly being given official recognition, to a greater or lesser degree. In most countries there is just one organization representing the local councils, or respectively the intermediate level local governments. This is the situation in Belgium, Denmark, Italy, the Netherlands, Spain and Sweden where, since 2005, only one association has represented the local and county councils. In Austria and Germany, certain differences between cities and municipalities are reflected in the two different associations they have. Added to this is the association representing the districts (*Landkreis*). Austria for its part is the only country where the role of the associations has been enshrined in the constitution: article 115.3 stipulates that the Austrian Federation of Local Councils and the Austrian Federation of Towns are bound to represent the interests of the local councils. A few other constitutions enshrine the right of local councils to form associations to represent their interests (Bulgaria, Estonia and Hungary). In France and Hungary there has been a definite increase in associations forming along sectorial or partisan lines.

From the functional perspective, four categories of associations can be distinguished by what they do in practice. None of these activities is exclusive; on the contrary, most associations take over several jointly. However, the weight taken by one function compared with others allows distinctions

to be made among four categories of associations. The first is that of the associations whose activities are essentially to represent the collective interests of local governments to the central government, or to the regional authorities. These are found particularly in Austria, Belgium, France, Germany, Greece, Italy and Spain, as well as most associations from the eastern countries. The second category is associations that have developed a role of representing the local authorities as employers, and thus play a part in labour relations with the local government's staff; it is these associations that sign the collective agreements legally required for fixing the employment terms of local personnel. This concerns the countries where the employment of local government staff is governed by private law, in particular Denmark, Norway, Sweden, the United Kingdom, and more recently, Italy. This does not mean that the other associations are not interested in such matters; they just do not have any legal responsibilities for the staff. Third, some associations have developed a role as agents for consultancy and other services to the local govern-

*Today, the Council of European Municipalities and Regions (CEMR) is a non-governmental umbrella organization for the national associations of local and regional authorities of 35 European States*

ments; these are often the same ones that appear in the second category, though with the addition of associations in Austria, Germany, the Netherlands, Ireland, Finland, and most of the Central and Eastern European countries. In the latter countries the associations receive support for this from their counterparts in the Western European countries. The fourth category is characterized by the difficulty of distinguishing the associations that represent specific interests from those that are legal tools for facilitating cooperation between separate local councils in jointly carrying out shared work on specific tasks (Bulgaria, Estonia, Lithuania). This last category reflects some confusion, at the same time obscuring distinctions that absolutely must be clear if inter-municipal cooperation is to develop on a stable foundation.

We can expect that the growing interdependence of different tiers of government –financial as well as functional– will lead to the development of the role of local government associations in all the countries.

Moreover, local government associations have been developing cooperation at the European level since the 1950s. Today, the Council of European Municipalities and Regions (CEMR) is a non-governmental umbrella organization for the national associations of local and regional authorities of 35 European States. The mission of the CEMR is to promote a European Union founded on local self-government, and it lobbies to be permitted input on European Community legislation and EU policies. It regularly publishes documents describing its position on EU initiatives or projects in progress, for example on the Commission's Green Paper on energy efficiency (February 15, 2006), on the urban contribution to growth and jobs in the regions (March 10, 2006), on the proposal for a regulation of the European Parliament on public passenger transport services by rail and by road (April 2, 2006), on the role of local and regional governments in relation to migration (October 23, 2006), and on the directive proposal establishing a framework for the protection of soil (April 14, 2007). The CEMR is also the European branch of United Cities and Local Governments. There are other European-level local authority associations, in particular Eurocities, a network of 130 big European cities in 30 countries that has existed since 1986, and whose aims and forms of action are similar, though more from the point of view of the big cities. These organizations can find a support and a relay for their proposals in the Committee of the Regions of the European Union, though this institution is not their only channel for making representations.

## V. Conclusion

This panoramic presentation of decentralization and local democracy in the European countries has shown how local self-government has become the general rule, whatever the diversity of institutions through which it manifests itself. In this respect, there are greater similarities between states at the local government level than at the regional level, which does not exist in all countries in institutional form and displays a great variety where it does.

However, similarities can be observed at the level of values and tendencies, rather than between systems. The principles of local self-government at present in Europe form a corpus to which all states adhere. One seeks to rationalize territorial divisions and their scale to make them adequate to their functions. Local government responsibilities can no longer be devised with regard to a local public interest, but more and more to their participation in

functions of overall national interest in a framework established by the law. The distance that existed formerly between European countries, in broad terms between Northern and Southern Europe, is shrinking. This convergence can be found also in the spreading of contractual relationships between government levels. The role of local government has increased considerably, from the economic point of view, in the performance of major collective functions, as well as their autonomy in it. But own resources tend to decrease, although some countries are excepted, if under these terms are meant the resources of which local governments are entitled to vary the yield, at least within some limits. From the institutional point of view, the tendency to stronger political leadership and the development of participation procedures can be observed everywhere. In sum, Eastern and Western Europe are becoming closer.

The major ground for these convergences has to be found, without any doubt, in the growing integration and interdependence between the various government levels,

whatever the differences in legal status. This is the consequence of the extension of local government functions and of correlative increase of their budgets. Local self-government is not the Asterix' village; this is a relative notion that has to be built through a network of relations, resulting itself from the functions and powers assigned by the law.

By contrast, local government systems are not converging. They further differentiate regarding the forms of regionalization and the role of the intermediate level of local government. Countries with large municipal units further contrast with countries with small municipal units. The understanding of central-local relationships is still marked by historical factors, reflected in local government functions. Only history can explain that in some countries a function is considered local whereas in others it is considered as national. Local finance systems are marked by the structure of national tax systems; it derives from this that the financing of local government budgets be led by transfers and tax shares or by own tax revenues. Local institutions further differentiate markedly between countries with traditions of representative democracy and countries with participative traditions. In Central and Eastern Europe, and even more in South-East Europe, the burden of the transition is still there; local government is indeed only one piece in the state-building process. Nevertheless, differences do not impede cooperation or exchanges of experience.

Lastly, if decentralization contributes to the development of political democracy, it would be an illusion to think that the confidence crisis reflected in the lower rates of participation in local elections be solved by decentralizing more. Local government is part of a whole. Local government may suffer a loss of sense of politics at the national level that cannot be ascribed to it. But it can demonstrate that it can contribute to give it sense again.

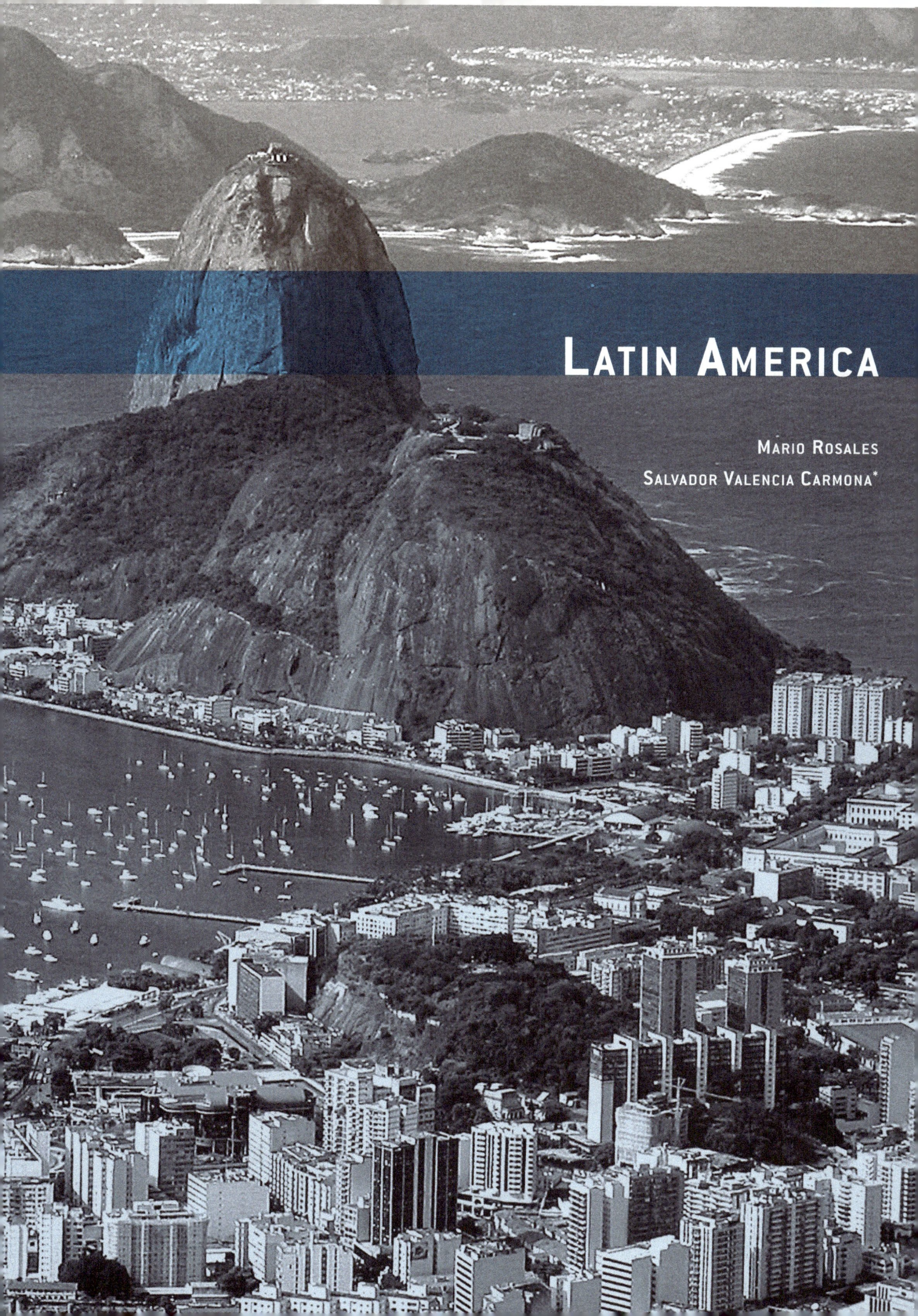

# Latin America

Mario Rosales
Salvador Valencia Carmona*

*   In developing this study, the support, information and suggestions kindly
    provided by Edgardo Bilsky of CGLU, Iván Finot of CEPAL and Néstor Vega of
    FLACMA have been extremely important. The authors wish to acknowledge
    their contribution and express their gratitude. Nevertheless, the authors are
    entirely responsible for all statements and data.

# I. Introduction

Latin America is made up of a large group of countries located in the territory extending from Mexico's Río Bravo in the north to Tierra del Fuego at the southernmost tip of South America. Latin America for the purposes of this report is divided into four subregions: Mesoamerica, including Mexico and the Central American nations of Belize, Costa Rica, Guatemala, Honduras, Nicaragua, Panama and El Salvador; the Antilles with Cuba and the Dominican Republic[1]; South America, which comprises the Andean countries of Bolivia, Colombia, Ecuador, Peru, and República Bolivariana de Venezuela; and the Southern Cone, which encompasses Argentina, Brazil, Chile, Paraguay and Uruguay.

An estimated 540 million people live in Latin America. Predominant cultures include those embodied by descendants of Native Americans, Spanish and Portuguese colonizers, African slaves and successive waves of European immigrants during the past two centuries. It is the most urbanized of the developing regions. Although levels of urbanization vary between 93% in República Bolivariana de Venezuela and 42% in Haiti (see Table 1), an estimated 77.8% of all Latin Americans live in cities.

Latin American countries present very different degrees of development. While the average regional GDP is $4,044 (CEPAL, 2005), it is a continent with great inequality in the distribution of wealth. Almost 40% of the population lives below the poverty line. The inequality has an unfavorable impact on the advance of democracy and full exercise of citizenship (Human Development Report, UNDP, 2005).

The forms of states are diverse as would be expected in a vast area containing 100 states or provinces in federal countries, 250 regions or departments, and more than 16,000 local governments —municipalities, districts or cantons— across the subcontinent. Several countries, including Brazil, Mexico, Argentina and República Bolivariana de Venezuela, have adopted a federal system with at least two levels of sub-national government. The other countries have unitary state systems.

In Latin America, the presidential regime is the most prevalent form of governance, with a clear predominance of the national executive over other state powers. From 1980 onward, the authoritarian regimes that dominated the area for generations have slowly given way to democratic governments that foster popular election of local authorities.

A few Latin American countries did have democratically elected local governments before 1980, and now all of the nations have municipal governments elected by universal suffrage (see Table 2). The majority of the countries are democratizing and reforming their states through institutional, political and legal transformations, of which decentralization[2] and strengthening of sub-national governments are part[3].

*In Latin America, the presidential regime is the most prevalent form of governance, with a clear predominance of the national executive over other state powers*

---

1. The English-speaking countries (Antigua, Barbados, Granada, Jamaica, Saint Lucia, Trinidad and Tobago) are not included in this study. Nor is Puerto Rico or the overseas territories of France, the United Kingdom and the Netherlands. Only brief mention will be made of Haiti.
2. The notion of decentralization is broadly understood as the process of transfer of power and functions from the central state to the intermediate and local levels of government and administration. We make a distinction between political decentralization or devolution —with the transfer of responsibilities and resources in the framework of local autonomy— and administrative decentralization or "deconcentration," which refers only to the transfer of functions and resources without autonomy. Both processes are accompanied by varying degrees of fiscal decentralization, i.e., the capacity to establish, collect and administer financial resources, to fulfill functions and provide services. Complex forms arise from the various combinations of these three processes.
3. Valadés, Diego and Serna, José María, 2000; Carbonell, Miguel 2004; Fix, Héctor and Valencia, Salvador, 2005.

| Table 1 | Development Indicators in Latin America |

| Country | Type of state | GDP per inhabitant in $ US | GDP per inhabitant PPP in $ US | IHD ranking 2006 * | % population below poverty line | % urban population 2005 |
|---|---|---|---|---|---|---|
| Argentina | Federal | 4.747 | 13.298 | 36 | 26.0 | 91,8 |
| Bolivia | Unitary | 990 | 2.720 | 115 | 63,9 | 64,2 |
| Brazil | Federal | 4.250 | 8.195 | 69 | 36,3 | 83,4 |
| Chile | Unitary | 7.085 | 10.874 | 38 | 18,7 | 86,6 |
| Colombia | Unitary | 2.663 | 7.256 | 70 | 46,8 | 76,6 |
| Costa Rica | Unitary | 4.632 | 9.481 | 48 | 21,1 | 62,6 |
| Cuba | Unitary | 2.797 | ------ | 50 | --- | 76,1 |
| Ecuador | Unitary | 2.761 | 3.963 | 83 | 48,3 | 62,8 |
| El Salvador | Unitary | 2.469 | 5.041 | 101 | 47,5 | 57,8 |
| Guatemala | Unitary | 2.492 | 4.313 | 118 | 60,2 | 50,0 |
| Haití | Unitary | 454 | 1.892 | 154 | --- | 41,8 |
| Honduras | Unitary | 1.139 | 2.876 | 117 | 74,8 | 47,9 |
| Mexico | Federal | 7.239 | 9.803 | 53 | 35,5 | 76,5 |
| Nicaragua | Unitary | 896 | 3.634 | 112 | 69,3 | 56,9 |
| Panama | Unitary | 4.797 | 7.278 | 58 | 33.0 | 65,8 |
| Paraguay | Unitary | 1.201 | 4.813 | 91 | 60,5 | 58,4 |
| Peru | Unitary | 2.841 | 5.678 | 82 | 51,1 | 72,6 |
| Dominican Rep. | Unitary | 3.815 | 7.449 | 94 | 47,5 | 65,6 |
| Uruguay | Unitary | 4.860 | 9.421 | 43 | 18,8 | 91,9 |
| Venezuela, R. B. | Federal | 5.275 | 6.043 | 72 | 37,1 | 92,8 |
| **Latin America** | | 4.471 | | | 39,8 | 77,8 |

**Source:** *CEPAL, 2006; United Nations Development Report, 2006.*
*\* Index of Human Development: High is from 1 to 63; Medium is from 64 to 146; Low is from 147 to 177.*

Nevertheless, the depth of the reforms and their impact differ from one country to another. Argentina, Brazil and Mexico —the three biggest nations in the region— have chosen federalism; in the unitary countries, the role of the municipalities has been expanded, and intermediate governments have been organized in the regions and comparable departments.

Argentina, Bolivia, Brazil, Chile, Colombia and Ecuador have redistributed functions and resources in favor of sub-national governments.[4] In Peru, the process of decentralization that began in the 1980s was reversed in the 1990s, and restarted after 2000. In República Bolivariana de Venezuela, the decentralization of the 1990s has, in recent years, been muddled by contradictory reforms that could affect the nature of local institutions. In Uruguay and Paraguay, decentralization is still in the early stages.

Mexico has moved forward with a "new federalism," through the opening of the political system and democratic alternation. Legal and financial reforms favor sub-national governments; progress is slower at the municipal level.

The Central American countries are evolving to a lesser extent. Guatemala and Nicaragua are passing decentralization laws. Honduras and El Salvador are increasing the amount of money transferred to the municipalities. Costa Rica and Panama are progressing comparatively slowly: in Costa Rica, the popular election of mayors was introduced only in 2002; in Panama, decentralization is being raised to a constitutional level.

For the past ten years, decentralization in the Dominican Republic has been on the public agenda, and there has been a gradual increase of municipal resources as well as enactment of new legislation favoring the municipal regime. Cuba remains centralized, and Haiti, though still facing severe problems at all levels of government, recently held its first local elections in several years.

## II. Evolution of Local Governments

Tension between centralization and decentralization existed in the region long before the emergence of the nation states. The colonial era saw only the centralism of the Spanish and Portuguese Crowns. Decentralization first appeared during the wars for independence and in the time of the *Cabildos Abiertos* (People's Councils). Struggles to preserve the colonial system or to discard it have flared periodically throughout the region ever since.

During the 19th Century, wars and conflicts took place in the nascent Latin American nations setting federal tendencies against unitary ones. Throughout the 20th Century, many emerging nations opted for political and economic centralization, to the detriment of the intermediate and municipal organizations. After the Second World War, national planning and new policies to replace imports coveted by the pro-development sectors, reinforced centralizing tendencies. The tide of centralization began to change in the 1970s as a consequence of successive economic and political crises.

### II.1. Decentralization Cycles

During the 1980s and 1990s, the democratic transition saw state reforms and decentralization. The centralist model was deemed outmoded and inefficient as a way to liberalize economies and reduce state costs. It is customary to distinguish between two decentralizing cycles: one more economic and neo-liberal, the other with greater emphasis on social and democratic aspects[5].

The first decentralizing cycle developed from the 1980s in a context of debt crisis and high inflation. One of its avowed goals was to reduce the size of the central administration in order to eliminate the fiscal deficit and drive the market. The economies made strong structural adjustments, delivery of services was transferred to the sub-national

*During the 19th Century, wars and conflicts took place in the nascent Latin American nations setting federal tendencies against unitary ones*

4. The concept of sub-national governments refers both to state or intermediate governments and municipalities, also known as local governments.

5. Finot, Ivan, 2001 and Wiesner, Eduardo 2003.

governments or privatized by passing responsibility to privately held or state companies. Results were mixed at best. Although this first policy cycle did not produce the hoped-for results, it did cause serious social, economic and political problems.

The second decentralization cycle took place at the end of the 1990s, in the midst of the financial and social crises that affected countries such as Argentina, Bolivia, Brazil, Ecuador, Mexico, Peru and República Bolivariana de Venezuela. It involved strategies to correct the neo-liberal paradigm with more democratic and social policies. The decentralization movement was stimulated by the progress of municipal management of the region.[6]

Predictably, these great cycles translate differently in each sub-region of Latin

6. New paradigms for local government management come to light, as in the cases of Curitiba or Porto Alegre, in Brazil; Villa El Salvador, in Peru; Bogota, in Colombia; Cotacachi and Guayaquil, in Ecuador; Santiago de Chile; Mérida, San Pedro Garza García or San Nicolás de los Garza, in México; Rafaela in Argentina; or La Paz in Bolivia, among many others.

7. Sub-national expenditures used as indicators for decentralization are limited in nature, given that they usually aggregate municipal and federal level expenditures. For example, a higher level of expenditure in the provinces in Argentina does not represent more municipal expenditure.

| Figure 1 | 1980-2005: Evolution of Decentralization in Latin America[7] |
|---|---|

**Percentage of the Expenditure of Sub-national Governments in Total Governmental Expenditure**

| Country | Year | Value | | Country | Year | Value |
|---|---|---|---|---|---|---|
| | | | | Brazil | 2002 | 42.1 |
| Brazil | 1980 | 32.4 | | Argentina | 2004 | 41.6 |
| Colombia | 1982 | 26.3 | | Mexico | 2000 | 31.9 |
| Argentina | 1980 | 22.2 | | Colombia | 2005 | 29.8 |
| Mexico | 1980 | 22.0 | | Bolivia | 2005 | 29.5 |
| Ecuador | 1980 | 18.3 | | Peru | 2005 | 26.8 |
| Bolivia | 1986 | 14.8 | | Ecuador | 2004 | 22.1 |
| Latin American average | | 11.6 | | Latin American average | | 18.8 |
| Peru | 1990 | 9.1 | | Chile | 2005 | 15.0 |
| Uruguay | 1980 | 8.6 | | Uruguay | 2005 | 13.2 |
| El Salvador | 1978 | 5.8 | | Guatemala | 1997 | 13.0 |
| Paraguay | 1980 | 5.5 | | El Salvador | 2005 | 8.7 |
| Guatemala | 1980 | 4.5 | | Paraguay | 2005 | 7.0 |
| Costa Rica | 1980 | 4.0 | | Dominican Rep | 2004 | 7.0 |
| Chile | 1980 | 3.7 | | Costa Rica | 2005 | 6.0 |
| Dominican Rep. | 1980 | 3.5 | | Nicaragua | 2002 | 3.8 |
| Nicaragua | 1988 | 3.4 | | Panama | 2002 | 3.8 |
| Panama | 1980 | 2.0 | | | | |

**Source:** *UCLG Country Profiles (2007), National Files.*
*Drawn up by: Mero.*

America (see figure 1). The federal countries mainly strengthened the intermediate levels of government and, after these, the municipalities.

Brazil is one of the most decentralized countries in the region[8]. It is based on a federal tradition that goes back to the birth of the republic at the end of the 19th century. The main attempts to reduce federalism to the advantage of the central state occurred under the presidency of Getúlio Vargas (1937-1945) and during the military governments (1964-1985). With the end of this last authoritarian period, decentralization was pushed forward in order to resolve the state crisis. Thus, the 1988 Constitution defined Brazil as an "indissoluble union of states and municipalities and the federal district." Autonomies were strengthened and local responsibilities and powers were increased. The municipalities received federal entity status and were granted full autonomy by the Federal Constitution. In 1993, hyper-inflation and state indebtedness pushed the national government to fiscal recentralization, and to reorganizing and privatizing the states' banks and public services. In 2003, the government of Luiz Inácio Lula da Silva promoted greater dialog and coordination between the federal level and the municipalities through the Secretariat for Federal Matters. The Ministry for Cities was also created to establish a national urban development policy that would guarantee the "right to the city," relying on the municipalities to carry out policies to redistribute income and social programmes like "Zero Hunger." In March 2003, during the VI March in Defence of the Municipalities, the federal government and municipal entities signed a protocol for the creation of the Committee of Federal Articulation —CAF. This committee became the main instrument for negotiations between the Federal Union and the municipalities, helping to further advance municipal interests in Brazil in matters such as teacher salaries, school transport, and fiscal and pension reform.

In Argentina, there was an historical and troubled relationship between the federal government and the provinces. The Constitution of 1853 attempted to regulate this relationship by transferring support for the municipal government to the provinces. After the military governments (1976-1983), the already centralized division of powers and resources was reviewed. In the ensuing decade, the national government and the provinces redefined the rules of financing through co-participation which increased transfers in exchange for a decrease in local tax revenues and the privatization of services. The constitutional reform of 1994 took up essential aspects of fiscal co-participation between the central government and the provinces. Thus, municipal autonomy was recognized and the city of Buenos Aires, capital of the country, was granted an autonomous local government. However, it was still within the provinces' power to define the municipal regime, allowing great diversity among them.[9]

Mexico, throughout the 20th Century, lived through a process of expansion and enlargement at the central level, in accord with provisions of the 1917 Constitution. The national government absorbed local responsibilities and their sources of income, to the detriment of the sub-national governments. As recently as 1977, 1983 and 1999, constitutional reforms favored municipalities, particularly in order to introduce party pluralism into the councils, and to strengthen the treasury and local public services. During the 1990s, the national government undertook policies to favor sub-national bodies through a "new federalism." In turn, pluralism and political alternation facilitated local reactivation. In 1994, the statute of the Government of the Federal District of Mexico City was approved, and three years later its Head of Government was elected by popular vote. Mexican municipalities were organized by the states, but continued to depend on the national government. However, innovative changes were taking place in many munic-

*Brazil is one of the most decentralized countries in the region. It is based on a federal tradition that goes back to the birth of the republic at the end of the 19th century*

8. With over 40% of public expenditure delegated to states and municipalities, Brazil has the most equitable distribution of resources between the two levels of the state in the region.

9. Many provinces usually restrict the local autonomy of small municipalities. For example, in the province of Santiago del Estero only five out of 126 municipalities enjoy full autonomy.

ipalities, which were demonstrating modernization in local management.

Although República Bolivariana de Venezuela officially has a federal system, it is a strongly centralized country, heightened by the model of sustained development in financing public expenditure through the distribution of oil income. In 1989, the *Ley Orgánica de Descentralización, Delimitación y Transferencias del Poder Público* (Decentralization, Delimitation and Transfers of Public Power Act) drove the decentralization process, of which the first achievement was the direct election of mayors and governors. The process ground to a halt in the second half of the decade. In 1999 the Bolivarian Constitution seemed to re-launch the process, but subordinated municipal autonomy to the *Ley Orgánica del Poder Público Municipal* (Organic Law of Municipal Public Power) and its fiscal responsibilities to a *Ley Nacional* (National Law) in 2005. The tension between centralism and local autonomy increased with the *Ley de los Consejos Comunales* (Community Councils Act of 2006), which set up a network of local organizations directly connected to the presidency in order to channel local financing. At the start of 2007, the *Ley de Habilitación Legislativa* (Enabling Act) was passed, authorizing the national government to regulate the provincial states and municipalities.

In the unitary countries, the debate about decentralization focused on the relationship between the national government and the municipalities. The process advanced more slowly at the intermediate level which, in fact, worked in tandem with the national level. In the majority of South American and Central American countries, intermediate administrations depend on the central power and are the responsibility of an official appointed by the latter. Despite this, there is a growing tendency toward the popular election of intermediate authorities, as already occurs in Colombia, Peru, Ecuador, Bolivia and Paraguay.

*Decentralization in the Andean countries has taken place through far-reaching constitutional and legislative reforms, in a relatively brief time*

Decentralization in the Andean countries has taken place through far-reaching constitutional and legislative reforms, in a relatively brief time.

In Colombia, after the extreme centralization of the 1960s and 1970s, and the political crisis expressed in the civil strikes of the 1970s and early 1980s, a clear decentralizing process began in the middle of the 1990s. The 1991 Constitution laid the bases for a unitary and decentralized territorial government, with autonomy of the territorial bodies: departments, municipalities and districts. Moreover, indigenous territories, regions and provinces were created to regroup bordering departments and municipalities. Direct election of mayors (1986) and of departmental governors was thus established by 1992. Throughout the 1990s, abundant legislation was passed regulating different aspects of local management, such as the mechanisms of transfer and participation, distribution of responsibilities and territorial organization. By the end of the 1990s, problems of indebtedness and the economic crisis made it necessary to review the transfer system and impose a regime of austerity on sub-national government spending, along with a redistribution of competences.

Bolivia implemented an original decentralizing process that recognized its multi-ethnic and multicultural character by strengthening two levels of sub-national government: the municipalities and the departments. After many election-free decades, in 1987 municipal elections were held. In 1994, the *Ley de Participación Popular* (Popular Participation Act) was passed, strengthening the municipalities politically and financially and strongly promoting the participation of grassroots communities. In 1995, the *Ley de Descentralización Administrativa* (Administrative Decentralization Act) benefited the departments at the intermediate level, granting them elected assemblies. In 1999, the new *Ley de Municipalidades* (Municipalities Act) was passed. The departmental prefect was initially appointed by the national government, but in 2006 he was elected by popular vote. In that year, after a prolonged social and political crisis, Evo Morales' government took power and convoked a new Constituent Assembly, in which questions pertaining to the regions, municipalities and indigenous communities took priority. The richest departments, in particular those in the east, demanded greater autonomy.

In Ecuador, mired in a deep political and social crisis that led to the fall of various presidents and the dollarization of the economy, the 1998 Constitution ratified the decentralization, deconcentration and participation prescribed by previous laws. *La Ley de Juntas Parroquiales* (Parish Councils Act) of year 2000, the Decentralization Plan and the regulation of the *Ley de Descentralización y Participación Social de 1997* (Decentralization and Social Participation Act of 1997) in 2001, as well as the reforms to the *Ley del Régimen Municipal* (Municipal Government Act) of 2004 further mandated improvements in services and the obligation to transfer responsibilities. Two main levels of autonomous government were recognized: provinces and cantons (municipalities). However, the provincial level was limited by its scanty responsibilities and resources, and by the coexistence of two authorities: a popularly elected Prefect and a governor appointed by the central government. In small municipalities, mayors and council presidents had been elected since 1935; since 1988 all mayors have been democratically elected.

In Peru, the Constitutional Reform of March 2002 placed emphasis on the creation of regional governments, effectively restarting decentralization plans that had been blocked under the authoritarian government of Alberto Fujimori. That same year the *Ley de Bases de la Descentralización* (Bases for Decentralization Act) was passed, followed in the period from 2002 to 2005 by various rulings, including the *Ley de Gobiernos Regionales* (Regional Governments Act), a new *Ley Orgánica de Municipalidades* (Municipalities Act), the

*Ley de Descentralización Fiscal* (Fiscal Decentralization Act) and the *Ley Marco de Presupuestos Participativos* (Framework for Participatory Budgets Act). In November 2006, regional governors were elected for the first time by popular vote. Peru now has several levels of government: national, regional, as well as distinct levels for both provincial municipalities (cities) and district municipalities.

The unitary states of the Southern Cone –Chile, Uruguay and Paraguay– have also carried out reforms shaped by their respective characteristics.

Chile has been a centralized country since the middle of the 19th Century. However, in 1891 following a brief civil war, the *Ley de la Comuna Autónoma* (Autonomous Community Act) was passed, and it was very advanced for the time. Nevertheless, the ruling did not work and the Constitution of 1925 recentralized the country. During the 1980s, the military regime applied an administrative decentralization that handed over to the municipalities the administration of primary health care, primary and secondary education, and the management of social funds. With the return of democracy in 1990, the country moved toward a more political decentralization with the direct election of mayors and town councillors in 1992. In 1993, 13 regional governments were created, although *intendentes* (mayors) were appointed by the national government. In later years, new responsibilities, tasks and resources were allocated to the municipalities by reforms to the *Ley Orgánica Municipal* (Organic Municipal Law) of 1999-2000.

In Uruguay, local government is identified at the departmental level, which includes various centers of population, and possesses an extension and population far above the average for Latin American municipalities (table 2). After the return to democracy in 1985, the constitutional reform of 1996 for the first time confirmed the obligation of the state to formulate

*The unitary states of the Southern Cone –Chile, Uruguay and Paraguay– have also carried out reforms shaped by their respective characteristics*

decentralizing policies in order to "promote regional development and social well being." It was set down that departmental elections should be held on a different date from the national elections. Now the tendency is to dissociate the local level –*Juntas locales* (Local Councils)– from the departmental, although no legislation has been passed to this effect. The 19 departmental *intendentes* (chief executives) have been directly elected since 1966[10].

In Paraguay, after 35 years of dictatorship (1954-1989), the first elections for municipal *intendentes* were held in 1991, and the first elections of departmental governors and councils in 1992. The constitution of 1992 recognized the political autonomy of municipalities in handling their affairs, collecting taxes and managing their expenditure. The autonomy of the departments was far more limited. In 2000, the National Council for Decentralization of the State was set up. However, despite the new constitutional framework for democratization, the municipal code has not yet been reformed, and national officials in concert with the legislature continue to exercise strong control over the municipalities.

The Central American countries have passed decentralizing laws, and their main challenge now is to implement them. Above all, they need to broaden the scant financial capability of the municipalities.

In Costa Rica, the reform of the Municipal Code (1998) allowed direct election of mayors for the first time in 2002. It also approved, through the constitutional reform of 2001, a gradual increase in responsibilities and transfers to the municipalities, rising to 10% of the national budget. However, strong resistance has arisen and there is not yet any legislation to achieve its implementation.

El Salvador made a concerted effort to draw up its National Strategy for Local Development, with strategic guidelines for decentralization to be implemented during the period 1999-2004. A law was passed in 1998 to increase financial transfers to the municipalities (revised in 2005), and recent reforms have been made to the Municipal Code (2005). A new General Decentralization Act is now in discussion in the Parliament and a Civil Service law was approved.

In Guatemala, the *Ley General de Descentralización* (General Decentralization Act) was enacted through Decree 14-2002. In 2002, the new Municipal Code and *Ley de Consejos de Desarrollo Urbano y Rural* (Councils for Urban and Rural Development Act) also came into force in 2002; the *Ley del Catastro* (Land Registry Act) (2005) was enacted; the *Política Nacional de Descentralización del Organismo Ejecutivo* (National Policy of Decentralization of the Executive Organism) was passed in 2005.

In Honduras, the National Plan for Decentralization and Municipal Development was passed in 1994, the Executive Commission for Decentralization was established and the Plan of Action 1995-1998 was drawn up, though it was not put into effect. The topic was taken up again in 2000 and linked to the eradication of poverty. In 2003, a new *Ley de Ordenamiento Territorial* (Decentralized Spatial Planning Act) was issued. Then in 2004 the *Ley de Descentralización del Servicio de Agua* (Decentralization of the Water Service Act) was issued. Other reforms to the *Ley de Municipalidades* (Municipalities Act) are underway.

In Nicaragua, the constitutional reforms of the beginning of the 1990s strengthened the power and self-financing of the municipalities, and reaffirmed the autonomy of the two regions created in 1987 along Nicaragua's Atlantic Coast. In 2003, a decentralization policy was defined as the crux of the *Estrategia Reforzada de Combate y Eradicación de la Pobreza* (ERCERP) (Reinforced Strategy to Combat and Eradicate Poverty). Between 2002 and 2004, the *Ley de Régimen de Presupuesto Mu-*

10. The term intendente *was coined during the colonial reforms of the 17th Century. Such officials displaced the greater mayors. In Uruguay the* intendentes *are in charge of the departments, assisted by a council of aldermen, to the detriment of local bodies.*

*nicipal* (Municipal Budget Regime Act), the *Ley de Participación Ciudadana* (Civic Participation Act) and the *Leyes de Transferencias Financieras y de Solvencia Fiscal Municipal* (Financial Transfers and Municipal Fiscal Solvency Acts) were passed.

In Panama, decentralization of the state was included in the constitution through the constitutional reform of 2004 and a new legal framework was developed for provinces, town councils and *corregimientos* (mayoral jurisdictions)[11].

In the Spanish-speaking Caribbean, authorities at the provincial level in the Dominican Republic are appointed by the central government. The town council is the only elected level of local government. Among recent reforms, mention should be made of the division of the National District into various municipalities in 2001, and the law of 2003 that made it possible to increase transfers to the municipalities. The convocation of a Constituent Assembly in 2007 is being contemplated; among its prerogatives would be the deepening of the decentralization process. The new Law of the Participatory Budget has been enacted and a Municipal Bill is under debate.

In Cuba, the Constitution in force since the mid 1970s recognizes the legal status of 14 provinces and 169 municipalities. They are administered as representative institutions whose leaders are elected in the Popular Power Assemblies with their own electoral division. These are governed according to the principles of "socialist democracy," have very limited autonomy, and generally defer to higher levels of government.

## II.2. Municipalities, Cities and Metropolitan Areas

The sub-national administrations and governments of Latin America are extremely heterogeneous. Among the intermediate levels of government —states, provinces or departments —some, such as São Paulo and Buenos Aires, possess populations and productive capacities surpassing those of many nations; many others are small and have quite limited resources.

Nearly 90% of the 16,000 Latin American municipalities have fewer than 50,000 inhabitants. Some administer broad territories, some are meager in size. The majority have to deal with considerable financial difficulties, and restrictions on human technical resources.

Where local autonomy is a goal, legislation in many countries sets minimum requirements for a municipality: population and territory of reasonable size, and sufficient economic, social and political capacities to ensure adequate institutional consistency. As a practical matter, many municipalities are nevertheless established without these minimum requirements, giving rise to what is often referred to as municipal fragmentation. Such inconsistencies often generate problems in the delivery of municipal services and in coordination between the intermediate and national governmental authorities.

Sometimes called the "atomization" of municipalities, fragmentation is to some degree endemic throughout Latin America. Consider: In Brazil, out of a total of 5,562 municipalities, 1,485 were created between 1990 and 2001. This gave rise to a constitutional amendment –the 15/96– to specify the requisites for creating municipal corporations. Mexico now has 2,438 municipalities, and it may cause little surprise that in many of its states municipal fragmentation is the norm[12].

Fragmentation has also been observed in some unitary countries, especially those with numerous municipalities. Colombia, for example has 1,099 municipalities, Peru more than 2,000 provincial and district municipalities. In Bolivia, the 1994 Law of Popular Participation created 198 new municipalities, bringing the total to 327.

11. The corregimientos are elected sub-municipal entities. In effect, the Panamanian Constitution decrees that there must be a municipal council in every district, and this council must include representatives of the corregimiento who have been elected in this electoral division.

12. In Oaxaca there are 570 municipalities; 217 in Puebla; 212 in Veracruz and 124 in the State of Mexico.

| Table 2 | Number of Sub-National Governments and Population |

| Country | Population | | Federal countries | | Unitary countries | | Democratic |
| | (milions) | Average population per municipality | States | Municipalities | Departments | Municipalities | municipal elections following authoritarian rule |
|---|---|---|---|---|---|---|---|
| Brazil | 190.127 | 34.183 | 26 | 5.562 | | | 1986 |
| Mexico | 107.537 | 44.091 | 32 | 2.439 | | | 1977 |
| Colombia | 47.078 | 42.837 | | | 32 | 1.099 | 1986 |
| Argentina | 38.971 | 17.531 | 23 | 2.223 | | | 1983 |
| Peru | 28.349 | 13.695 | | | 25 | 2.070 | 1981 |
| Venezuela, R. B. | 27.031 | 80.690 | 24 | 335 | | | 1992 |
| Chile | 16.436 | 47.641 | | | 15 | 345 | 1992 |
| Ecuador | 13.408 | 61.224 | | | 22 | 219 | 1935 |
| Guatemala | 13.018 | 39.211 | | | 22 | 332 | 1986 |
| Cuba | 11.400 | 67.456 | | | 14 | 169 | ---- |
| Bolivia | 9.627 | 29.440 | | | 9 | 327 | 1987 |
| Dominican Rep. | 9.240 | 60.789 | | | 32 | 152 | 1978 |
| Honduras | 7.518 | 25.228 | | | 18 | 298 | 1982 |
| El Salvador | 6.991 | 26.683 | | | 14 | 262 | 1984 |
| Paraguay | 6.365 | 27.554 | | | 17 | 231 | 1991 |
| Nicaragua | 5.594 | 36.803 | | | 15 + 2 regional autonomies | 152 | 1990 |
| Costa Rica | 4.399 | 54.309 | | | 7 | 81 | 1948 |
| Panama | 3.284 | 43.787 | | | 9 | 75 | 1996 |
| Uruguay | 3.478 | 183.053 | | | | 19 | 1985 |
| Total | 549.851 | 33.548 | 105 | 10.559 | 251 | 5.831 | |

**Sources:** *CEPAL 2005. UCLG Country Profiles (2007). Drawn up by authors.*

More than half of the population of Latin America dwells in cities with more than a million inhabitants. No fewer than 50 Latin American cities have populations of a million or more; of these, four rank among the ten largest cities on earth: São Paulo (17.8 million), Mexico City (16.7 million), Buenos Aires (12.6 million) and Rio de Janeiro (10.6 million). Three other cities, Bogotá, Lima and Santiago de Chile, have populations in

excess of 5 million; the 3 million mark has been surpassed in Brazil by Belo Horizonte, Salvador de Bahía, Fortaleza, Porto Alegre and Recife; Caracas in República Bolivariana de Venezuela, Santo Domingo in the Dominican Republic, and Monterrey and Guadalajara in Mexico also have passed this population milestone. Many more cities in Latin America are of intermediate size –between 100,000 and one million inhabitants– and generate significant demographic and economic dynamism.

The great size of most big cities in Latin America and the Caribbean means that they typically encompass many municipal territories and, in some cases, an entire state or province. Mexico City and its Metropolitan Area, as defined in 1995, envelops more than 41 municipalities in two states, as well as the Federal District. Buenos Aires covers the territory of the autonomous City of Buenos Aires plus that of 32 municipalities in the province of Buenos Aires; *Gran Santiago* (Greater Santiago, Chile) takes in 52 municipalities, and São Paulo in Brazil has 39 *prefeituras* (prefectures).

Territorial administration and management of the big cities poses a major problem. While various Latin American capital cities have special regimes, such as Bogotá, Buenos Aires, Caracas, Lima, Mexico City and Quito, few have a metropolitan government that allows them to manage the urban territory in an integrated manner. Among this latter type are the Metropolitan Municipality of Lima[13], with a special regime that grants it the faculties and functions of Regional Government within the jurisdiction of the Province of Lima;  the Metropolitan District of Quito, created by law in 1993, and the Metropolitan District of Caracas, created in 2000[14]. In Montevideo, the national government has recently created a Metropolitan Consortium, which encompasses the municipal councils of the departments of Canelones, Montevideo and San José, with, altogether, 2,000,000 inhabitants. In most metropolitan areas only mechanisms for sectoral coordination of limited scope are in operation[15].

In Central America, some coordinating institutions also function: the Corporation of the Metropolitan Area of San Salvador (COAMSS) and in Costa Rica the Metropolitan Federation of Municipalities of San José (FEMETROM) whose aims are limited to spatial planning and land use-management.

Given the level of urban and territorial complexity, various countries are trying policies to realign land use. Others, such as Argentina, Bolivia, Brazil, Colombia, Ecuador and a few other Central American countries, are promoting the creation of *mancomunidades* (associated municipalities) and other associative forms to help solve the problem of the small size of many municipalities, which is limiting their capacity to respond effectively to the demands of their communities and citizens.

More than 70 municipal *mancomunidades* have been set up to develop and provide services in Bolivia. In Argentina, there are 72 inter-municipal bodies which group 770 local governments of 22

*While various Latin American capital cities have special regimes, such as Bogotá, Buenos Aires, Caracas, Lima, Mexico City and Quito, few have a metropolitan government that allows them to manage the urban territory in an integrated manner*

---

13. *The Metropolitan Region of Lima is created by Article 33 of Law Nº 27783, on Bases for Decentralization. Article 65 and following of Organic Law Nº 27867, on Regional Governments (modified by Law Nº 27902). Article 151 of Organic Law Nº 27972, on Municipality. The Mayor of Metropolitan Lima carries out the functions of Regional President, as executive organ; the Metropolitan Council of Lima, exercises functions of Regional Council, as normative organ and inspector; the Metropolitan Assembly of Lima, made up of the metropolitan mayor, the district mayors and representatives of civil society and base organizations of the province of Lima, exercises competencies and functions of the Council of Regional Coordination, as consultative and coordinating organ.*
14. *Quito has a relatively decentralized configuration, endowed with a council and a metropolitan mayor with responsibility over most of the territory. Caracas has a system of municipal government on two levels with a metropolitan mayor and a legislatively elected council, covering the zones of Libertador (the federal district of Caracas has been eliminated) and the municipalities of the neighboring state of Miranda.*
15. *See the Comité Ejecutor del Plan de Gestión Ambiental y Manejo de la Cuenca Hídrica Matanza-Riachuelo (Committee to carry out the Plan for Environmental Management and Handling of the Matanza-Riachuelo River Basin) in Buenos Aires. Or else partial and incipient experiments in inter-institutional cooperation, such as the ABC Chamber of São Paulo (with Santo André, São Bernardo and São Cayetano).*

Argentinian provinces, aimed mainly at the promotion of micro-regional economic development, tourism development and the preservation of the environment. In Ecuador, there are more than 20 *mancomunidades*, bringing together more than 100 municipalities[16], with a similar number of associative arrangements between provincial, regional and micro-regional entities to promote development. There are more than 60 regional, sub-regional and sectoral local government associations operating in Chile; and in Colombia there are over 44 local government associations representing 454 municipalities that work jointly for the provision of public services, public works and/or carry out administrative functions that are delegated to the municipal associations.

## III. Finances, Responsibilities and Management Capacities

### III.1. Progress in Decentralization and Financing Capabilities

The progress in financing sub-national governments may be seen as a whole in Table 3, though the figures used —based on data from the IMF and World Bank, national accounts and others— are not always homogeneous and must be considered with caution. Nevertheless, the positive impact which decentralization has had on all of the countries is obvious. The simple average decentralized expenditure in Latin America went up from 11.6% of total governmental spending around 1980, to 18.8% between 2002 and 2005.

Drawing from the information for aggregated expenditure in the table below (see column 2 in Table 3), the following classification can be made:

- The first group of countries with sub-national public expenditure greater than 20% includes federal countries –Argentina, Brazil and Mexico– and the unitary countries, Colombia, Peru, Bolivia and Ecuador. However, in federal countries, the states and provinces take up the largest share of expenditure, while local government expenditure is lower than 20% in Brazil and less than 10% in Argentina and Mexico[17].

- A second group of nations –with an intermediate degree of centralization– with sub-national public spending between 10% and 20% includes República Bolivariana de Venezuela, Chile, Uruguay and Guatemala.

- A third group of countries has only incipient decentralization, with public expenditure less than 10%. These are Costa Rica, the Dominican Republic, Nicaragua, Panama, Paraguay and El Salvador.

All the same, the indicator for municipal expenditure shows (Table 3: column 3) that only three countries exceed 15% of general government expenditure: Ecuador, Colombia and Brazil. They are followed by Chile, Guatemala and Uruguay at 13% (in Uruguay, the Departments, given their size, are closer to the intermediate rather than municipal level). Next come Argentina, Bolivia, Peru and El Salvador with between 7% and 9% of general government expenditure. The remaining countries range between 3.8% and 7% of this indicator.

Brazil stands out in the first group of countries mentioned above; not only is it the country with the greatest degree of fiscal decentralization, but it is also the country that demonstrates the greatest balance in expenditure (vertical equity) between the three levels of the state.

Argentina, Brazil and Colombia have had to overcome critical processes arising out of the excessive indebtedness of their sub-national and central governments. This has made it necessary to make severe adjustments, especially in Colombia. Even so, in Colombia the fiscal balances in territorial governments have shown important improvements. At the

16. *Example in Ecuador: the* Mancomunidad *of Municipalities for the Rehabilitation of the Ecuadorian Railway, created through an agreement signed in June 2005 by 33 municipalities.*

17. *One criticism of this classification is that in federal countries the index for sub-national expenditures usually conceals the level of centralization by state agencies.*

| Table 3 | Evolution and Distribution of Expenditure by National, Intermediate and Local Governments in Latin America |

| Countries | 1. Non-financial public expenditure (% GDP) | 2. Evolution of expenditure by sub-national governments (% expenditure of central government) | Distribution of total governmental expenditure between national government, intermediate governments, and local governments, 2002-2005 | | | |
|---|---|---|---|---|---|---|
| | | | 3. Local government | 4. Intermediate government | 5. National government | 6. General government |
| Argentina | 25.2 | 41.6 | 7.8 | 33.0 | 59.1 | 100.0 |
| Bolivia | 30.0 | 29.5 | 8.5 | 21.0 | 70.5 | 100.0 |
| Brazil | 24.6 (CG) | 42.1 | 16.6 | 25.5 | 57.8 | 100.0 |
| Chile | 34.2 | 15.0 | 13.2 | 1.8 | 85.0 | 100.0 |
| Colombia | 35.2 | 29.8 | 17.0 | 12.8 | 70.2 | 100.0 |
| Costa Rica | 25.5 | 6.0 | 6.0 | ---- | 94.0 | 100.0 |
| Dominican Rep. | 19.3 (CG) | 7.0 | 7.0 | ---- | 93.0 | 100.0 |
| Ecuador | 24.5 | 22.1 | 17.2 | 4.9 | 77.8 | 100.0 |
| El Salvador | 17.5 | 8.7 | 8.7 | ---- | 91.3 | 100.0 |
| Guatemala | 11.7 (CG) | 13.0 | 13.0 | ---- | 87.0 | 100.0 |
| Honduras | 34.1 | 5.6 | 5.6 | ---- | 94.4 | 100.0 |
| Mexico | 23.3 | 31.9 | 4.3 | 27.5 | 68.1 | 100.0 |
| Nicaragua | 30.3 | 3.8 | 3.8 | ---- | 96.2 | 100.0 |
| Panama | 24.8 | 3.8 | 3.8 | ---- | 96.2 | 100.0 |
| Paraguay | 33.3 | 7.0 | 5.2 | 1.8 | 93.0 | 100.0 |
| Peru | 19.2 (GG) | 26.8 | 8.5 | 18.3 | 73.2 | 100.0 |
| Uruguay | 29.6 | 13.2 | 13.2 | ---- | 86.8 | 100.0 |
| Venezuela, R. B. | 32.2 | ---- | ---- | ---- | ---- | ---- |

**Sources:** *IMF Finance Yearbook 2002 to 2006; World Bank; Central Bank of Colombia; General Audit Office of Chile; "Descentralización Fiscal en C. América", G. Espitia. CONFEDELCA, GTZ, 2004. "Descentralización en Ecuador", CONAM; Ministry of Economy of Ecuador; State Bank of Ecuador, 2006. Country Profiles. GC = Gobierno Central. GG = General Government. Drawn up by: MERO.*

end of 2004, the sector of regions and local governments presented a high surplus of 1.1%, and repeated that mark in 2005 and 2006.

In the unitary states, the weight of the intermediate bodies is less. This is the case because they usually depend wholly or in part on the central government budget, and because frequently their self-administered revenue is not significant. In general, in these countries progress toward decentralization is subject to the rhythm of the municipalities or local governments.

Overall, the nations that have carried out more decisive decentralizing processes have

*In the unitary countries that have intermediate entities, only a few types of tax revenue are allocated to the middle level*

visibly improved the situation of infrastructure, services and degrees of participation in the poorer, more remote and rural areas. Bolivia provides a notable example: there has been a substantial increase in the resources which reach the outlying territories, as well as in the degree of organization and participation of rural communities.

In the countries with a medium degree of decentralization there are contradictory situations, as in Chile. While there are notable advances in the democratization of the municipalities, the intermediate level continues to depend to a great extent on the central government. Curiously, Chilean legislation uses the term "regional governments" to refer to the de-concentrated intermediate level, and the expression "local administration" to refer to the municipalities, even if they possess autonomy and their own resources, and deliver a wide range of services.

### III.2. Income and Taxation Capacity of Intermediate and Municipal Bodies

In essence, the political autonomy of any sub-national government depends largely on its financial strength. Self-administered revenue comes primarily from local taxes, over which autonomous local governments exercise direct control. But in Latin America, restrictions on local taxation powers are one of the main limitations of decentralization processes. In most countries, the municipalities do not have the power to impose duties and local taxes. Rather they have a high level of dependence on central funds transfers, and although the degree of dependence varies from one country to another, the overall trend appears to be moving toward increasing dependency.

In the federal countries, most local income is derived from fiscal co-participation, although important revenues are sometimes set aside at the intermediate level.

- In Argentina, the provinces receive taxes on income, property, fiscal stamps and

18. In Colombia, in 2000 the tax income from the departments corresponded to 10% of the national total, 1.8% of the GDP, while that of the municipalities rose to 15%, 2.7% of the GDP. (Jaime Bonet, *Descentralización fiscal y Disparidades en Ingreso Regional*, Banco de la República, CEER, Nov. 2004).

vehicles (64%, 14.5%, 7% and 6%, respectively, in 2004).

- Brazil has allowed the states to receive the sales tax (Circulation of Goods and Services Tax - ICMS), which represents 26% of the national revenue.

- In Mexico, some states receive taxes on personal income and from the acquisition of used cars. Since 2005, local taxes on professional services, transfers, and temporary usufruct of property or business activities have been permitted.

- República Bolivariana de Venezuela grants to the states only the tax revenue from stamps and salt mines.

In the unitary countries that have intermediate entities, only a few types of tax revenue are allocated to the middle level. For example, in Colombia intermediate entities receive revenue from the sale of alcoholic beverages, tobacco and lottery tickets, plus vehicle registration fees[18]; road, highway and harbor taxes in Chile, in Bolivia, departments receive royalties for exploitation of hydrocarbons. In Bolivia, the amount of the income and the system of compensation to departments that do not produce hydrocarbons explains the relative importance of the intermediate-level expenditure.

Most countries do not grant municipalities the right to determine taxation. Usually, the intermediate governments in the federal countries, or the national governments and parliaments in the unitary countries retain the right to approve the respective values for municipal income laws.

With some exceptions, taxation powers are similar in federal and unitary country municipalities. The most common taxes are those on property, vehicle circulation and economic activities, including licenses for businesses and industries or income from industry and commerce. Throughout the region, the most important source of municipal revenue is the tax on property. The exceptions are Argentina, where it is a provincial tax; El Salvador, where it is the responsibility of central government; and the Dominican Republic, which does not have property taxes. As far as the tax on vehicle circulation is concerned, Argentina and Brazil are also exceptions; in those countries it is managed by the intermediate government. Mexico allocates it to the national government.

In general, taxation pressure in Latin America is low (16.9% of the GDP, CEPAL[19]), and this is especially critical at the local level where the capacity to collect taxes is weak. What is collected generally represents a limited percentage of the local budget. Because of the heterogeneity of the territories, population and wealth of the municipalities, the yield of taxes and duties is extremely unequal. The most developed urban municipalities have access to significant resources of their own, but this is certainly not the case in poor or rural municipalities.

In Brazil, self-administered fiscal resources represented almost 32% of the budget in municipalities with more than 500,000 inhabitants in 2000, but only reached 5% of the budget in municipalities with fewer than 20,000 inhabitants, yet the latter comprise 72% of all the nation's municipalities. In República Bolivariana de Venezuela, 50% of the municipalities with fewer than 50,000 inhabitants depend on 80% of the national transfers, while 2% of the municipalities with a greater number of inhabitants have 90% of the self-administered resources. In Argentina, local tax collection amounted to 48% of revenue in the year 2000, although in some provinces it did not reach 10%[20]. In Colombia, taxes collected by Bogotá represented 40% of total municipal revenue in 2000. Something similar occurred with the metropolises of the Central American countries.

This inequality in taxation capacity translates, in many countries, into a tendency toward stagnation in the collection of municipal taxes and local duties. This typically leads to an increase in transfers, as in Bolivia, Colombia[21], Ecuador, El Salvador, Guatemala, Mexico, Nicaragua and República Bolivariana de Venezuela. In Mexico, self-administered municipal taxes did not increase from 1994 to 2004, but transfers increased three times[22] during those years.

However, there are some clear indications that decentralization does not necessarily induce fiscal laziness. Territorial revenues in Colombia have grown steadily over the past decade, and as regards revenue behavior patterns, the municipalities have done better than the departments[23]. Increases in territorial entities' share of national income have often been accompanied by an increase in regional tax collection efforts. Between 1996 and 2004, the great majority of municipalities enjoyed a real increase in tax revenues. There is no evidence, given the experience of the municipalities over the

---

19. Cited by Oscar Cetrángolo, "Descentralización y Federalismo Fiscal: aspectos teóricos y práctica en América Latina," Seminario internacional, Arequipa, 30 and 31 October 2006. The country with the highest fiscal pressure is Brazil (35.9%) and the lowest is Guatemala (10.6%).

20. The main sources of resources are the taxes for services of lighting, sweeping and cleaning, environment and health regulations for companies and industries, road maintenance and improvement of infrastructures.

21. The percentage of self-administered taxes collected from the Colombian municipalities went from 76% in 1984 to 44% in 2000 and that of the departments from 97% to 45% over the same period.

22. Peru is in a similar case: local collection increased at a rate less than the transfers (21% and 82% respectively between 2003 and 2006), which is due to the acceleration of the process of transferring responsibilities and resources since 2002, National Decentralization Council, Report 2005.

23. In real terms, municipal revenues increased by 28% between 1996 and 2004, compared with 20% at the department level. Source: la Comptroller General's Office of the Republic: "Informe social. Evaluación a las transferencias intergubernamentales 1994-2005" and Boletín de Coyuntura Fiscal 3 CONFIS, Ministry of Finance and Public Credit, Colombia.

*The collection of property tax is far from efficient because of outdated property registers and real estate evaluations, excessive exemptions, and a culture rife among municipalities and citizens of tolerance for not collecting or paying taxes*

past years, to support the hypothesis that an increase in transfers causes a reduction in local tax collection[24].

Frequently, the municipalities do not have the mechanisms needed to increase collection, either because they are not the ones who do the collecting or because they do not have the authority to set levels of taxation. In particular, the collection of property tax is far from efficient because of outdated property registers and real estate evaluations, excessive exemptions, and a culture rife among municipalities and citizens of tolerance for not collecting or paying taxes. This matter should be a priority and is a key issue in decentralization[25]. However, the situation varies from country to country, and among municipalities. In Costa Rica, for example, when the municipalities assumed cadastral management, their revenues increased considerably; however, the central government changed the rules of the game, to the detriment of the municipalities that are making a greater fiscal effort[26]. The law in Ecuador imposes a bi-annual review of the cadastral evaluations, from a minimum 2/1000 up to 5/1000.

Local taxation structures –often archaic and inefficient– also have much to do with the low level of tax collection. For example, in the Dominican Republic, the local tax structure includes 70 taxes, but the municipalities only bring in 30% of these monies. In Central American municipalities, tax revenue represents, on average, 0.58% of GDP. The municipal contribution to the GDP is what is reflected in minimum local taxation. In El Salvador, Guatemala and Nicaragua, the municipalities depend to a large extent

on central transfers. In Nicaragua, local taxation had great importance in the last decade, thanks to the Municipal Sales Tax (ISV), but this decreased from 5% to 1% of gross sales.

In Costa Rica and Panama, the weakness of the transfers, and above all the reduced municipal responsibilities and levels of spending mean that local revenue –local taxes and duties– represents between 96% and 75% of municipal income. Something similar occurs with Paraguay in the Southern Cone where transfers represent just 11% of municipal budgets. But in this group, local budgets are mostly low. All the same, within this group of countries, good levels of income are not synonymous with greater autonomy; rather, it points to a lack of interest and efficiency in the central governments' systems for redistribution of revenue to less favored territories. In this sense, the high percentage of own-source revenues stands out against the limited budget and responsibilities for local governments.

### III.3.  Transfers and Compensatory Financing

Transfers from central governments –or intermediate governments in the federal countries– to local governments have increased in recent years. These may be free of use or directed and tend to include compensation mechanisms to limit regional imbalances. Free transfers support autonomous sub-national decisions and are financed through tax revenue co-participation systems. Directed transfers address the operational costs of national policies, such as those for health and education

---

24. *Different studies show that there is not sufficient evidence to support the existence of fiscal laziness. rather, it has been proven that in regions with greater economic activity, the decentralization process tends to revitalize the tax collection process.*

25. *Nickson, Andrew, 2006. Certain cities make an effort to improve the outdated register of the commercial values of properties (Bogotá, La Paz, Quito, Nicaraguan municipalities). Among the measures are: restructuring the legal framework, modernizing collection, computerized systems and self evaluation.*

26. *Information provided by the National Union of Local Governments in Costa Rica, UNGL.*

| Box 1 | Transfer Systems in Latin America |

- **Argentina.** The Regime of Federal Co-participation with the provinces contributes 57% of the collection of taxes on income, wealth and sales[27]. The provinces transfer part of these funds to the municipalities, to which they add two transfers: a) maintenance of schools, hospitals and specific projects, and b) discretional resources. Together it adds up to more than 50% of municipal revenue.

- **Brazil.** The two main sources are the Municipalities Participation Fund (FPM) and the States and Federal District Participation Fund (FFE); both are fed by national taxes[28]. Furthermore, the municipalities receive transfers from the states (25% tax on the circulation of goods and services, 50% tax on vehicles and the exportation of goods). Some municipalities receive royalties for the exploitation of natural resources. Transfers over the municipal budget have increased in the past decade, reaching 90% of the budget for the smallest municipalities.

- **Mexico.** Allocates participations and contributions to draw on federal income. The former are transferred to the states and municipalities through the Municipal Promotion Fund. The latter are for restricted use by the states and municipalities[29]. Other transfers exist through oil and export revenue in certain states. Transfers go from 52% of municipal resources in 1990 to 90% in 2005, in particular thanks to "branch 33."

- **Venezuela, R. B.** Municipal dependency on transfers rose from 35% in 1986 to 48% in 1998. It is based on the Treasury Fund (20% of tax income) and extraordinary contributions (Inter governmental Decentralization Fund, with resources from VAT and the Law of Special Economic Assignations, with oil resources).

- **Colombia.** The General Participations System (articles 356 and 357 of the Constitution) provides the resources transferred by the state to territorial entities (departments, municipalities and districts, and indigenous reserves) to finance the services that are their responsibility. The resources are divided into: sector allocations for education (58%), health (24.5%), drinking water and basic sanitation (17%), and special allocations (4%). The distribution of resources is based on population, attended population, population to be attended, equity, fiscal efficiency, administrative efficiency and relative poverty.

- **Bolivia.** Tax co-participation transfers to the municipalities amount to 20% of the national taxes, less the Special Hydrocarbon Tax. To this are added resources from debt cancellation (HIPC I y II) for education, health and investment in infrastructure and the Fund for Productive and Social Investment (FPS). The transfers contribute two thirds of the municipal budgets; 85% is used for investment.

- **Ecuador.** The transfers derive from the Sectorial Development Fund (FODESEC) and the distribution of 15% of current income from the central government budget. Both sources allocate 80% and 70% respectively of their funds to the municipalities and 20% and 30% to the provincial councils. The transfers represent between 47% and 74% of the municipal budgets (1998-2000), and are generally conditional —they are usually earmarked for public investment, not for current expenditure.

- **Chile.** The Common Municipal Fund redistributes 30% of municipal taxes (zoning tax, commercial patents, vehicle tax) with the role of addressing imbalances between rich and poor municipalities. The Ministries of Health and Education allocate transfers to finance the corresponding responsibilities. The National Fund for Regional Development, FNDR, and the National Fund for Social Investment, FOSIS, deliver resources to projects for social investment and to reduce poverty. Various other sectorial funds exist. The transfers constitute half of the total municipal resources.

- **Peru.** Free availability transfers more than doubled between 2003 and 2006 and the municipalities were the main beneficiaries. Of these transfers, 36% come from the Municipal Compensation Fund based on the national taxes collected, 16% of the *Canon* (levy) and royalties for exploiting natural resources, and 2% for participation on Customs Duty. The regional governments receive 2% from FONCOR, 4% from the *Canon* and 1% from Customs Duty. In addition there are transfers of funds from sectorial programs and projects (FONCODES, PRONAA, PROVIAS, etc.)

- **Uruguay.** Transfers account for between 33% and 16% of departmental budgets.

- **Paraguay.** Limited transfers derive from royalties from bi-national hydroelectric companies.

- **Central America.** The legislation allocates a growing percentage of the national budgets to the municipalities: 10% in Guatemala, 7% in El Salvador, 6% in Nicaragua (it will reach 10% in 2010)[30], 5% in Honduras, although the government failed to meet the targets. In Costa Rica the constitutional mandate (2001), which allocated 10% of the national budget to the municipalities, has not yet been implemented. In Panama there is no norm for transfer to the municipalities.

- **Dominican Republic.** Although Law 166 (2003) raises transfers to the municipalities from 6% to 10% of the national budget, only 8% had been transferred (2005). Even so, resources have more than doubled in two years. The Dominican Municipal League, in charge of the transfers, fulfils a controlling and inspecting role over the town councils. Transfers represent 90% of the local budget in most municipalities.

27. *Moreover, through fiduciary funds for provincial development, the provinces receive resources for debt reduction programmes, in exchange for greater fiscal control.*

28. *They receive 22% of income tax, 21.5% on industrial products, 50% of the rural property tax and 30% of the tax on financial operations. In addition, the Compensation Fund for the Exportation of Industrial Products (FPEX), the Fund for the Maintenance and Functioning of Teaching (FUNDEP) and the Rural Property Tax (ITR).*

29. *Branch 33 of the budget includes 7 funds for municipal activities: primary and normal education; health; social infrastructure; strengthening of municipalities and delegations of the Federal District; multiple contributions; technological and adult education; public safety. To these are added specific funds from branches 25 and 39, such as resources for state infrastructures and for natural disasters.*

30. *The Law of Financial Transfers of 2004 stipulates that, beginning with 4% of the current revenue of the state, transfers to the municipalities must increase annually to 10% of the budget in 2010. The municipalities also receive resources for investment from the FISE and the Institute of Rural Development (IDR).*

services. These services are delivered by sub-national governments with transfers carried out through difficult systems of monitoring, control and evaluation.

In Latin America, different transfer systems are used –over fiscal income or the national budget– with varying fixed or variable percentages, distribution criteria by levels of government and other conditions (see box)[31]. Distribution criteria for transfers involve different factors –population, levels of poverty, access to services, economic potential, efficiency in management– but they have limited impact on limiting regional gaps.

Directed transfers encompass a wide range of objectives that respond to national policies, and only collaterally to the strengthening of democracy and local governance. The majority of countries have sectorial funds for carrying out projects, which in federal countries may be administered by the intermediate governments[32]. In the unitary countries they are usually administered by autonomous institutions that manage resources from the central government and international financing in a centralized way[33]. For example, the Fund for Productive and Social Investment (FPS) in Bolivia co-finances the provision of infrastructure and equipment for educational establishments.

In Central America, the funds were created through peace agreements to deal with emergency situations or reconstruction, or as social compensation for national macro-economic adjustments. However, they have become permanent and now channel investment into infrastructure, basic services or the promotion of productive development. Frequently, they handle resources that surpass those of the municipalities without being subject to the democratic and civic control of the latter[34].

The excessive proliferation of bidding funds for projects has a negative impact on intermediate and small municipalities. Smaller cities often can not partake of such funds because the terms are too complex, and the local staff lacks the ability to draw up sufficient projects. In Chile, it is calculated that there are some 200 funds and sectorial programs related to municipal management.

Recently, systems of direct transfer from the national government to poor families and people are taking on greater importance. Some of them bypass sub-national bodies, or tolerate little intervention.[35] In Mexico these transfers give rise to the "Opportunities" program; in Argentina to the "Heads of Household" program; in Brazil the "Family Grant"; in República Bolivariana de Venezuela it gave rise to "Different Missions"; and in Colombia to "Families in Action." In Chile a new National System of

31.  Martín, Juan and Martner, Ricardo, 2004 pp. 77 and following; Finot, Iván, 2001, pp. 87 and following.

32.  This is what occurs with the National Funds for Housing, Provincial Roads and Rural Electrification in Argentina, the transfers from the Single Health System and the Social Contribution to the Education Salary in Brazil, and the Funds for Contributing to Primary and Normal Education and the Health Services in Mexico.

33.  Fund for Productive and Social Investment (FPS), Bolivia; Fund for Compensation and Social Development in Peru; National Fund for Regional Development, FNDR and Fund for Solidarity and Social Investment, FOSIS, in Chile; Fund for Social Investment (FIS) and Solidarity Fund for Community Development (FDSC), in Guatemala; FISDL, in El Salvador; FHIS, in Honduras; FISE in Nicaragua; Fund for Indigenous Guatemalan Development, and Fund for Agricultural Development and Guatemalan Housing Fund.

34.  The Fund for Social and Economic Investment (FISE) in Nicaragua is another example: an autonomous organization which depends on the Presidency of the Republic, with funding from the central government, bilateral donations from foreign governments and loans from the Inter-American Development Bank and the World Bank. Something similar occurs with the Social Investment Fund for Local Development (FISDL) in El Salvador, which finances strategies for the eradication of poverty and local economic development, along with the Honduran Fund for Social Investment (FHIS).

35.  On occasion they are even manipulated for election purposes.

Social Protection was organized for the unification and better coordination of the different social subsidies granted to poor families through the municipalities.

## III.4.  Control Systems and Difficulties of Indebtedness

The expenditure of Latin American municipalities is subject to internal and external controls. For internal control, the bigger municipalities establish a municipal accounts office or audit unit –organs granted a certain technical autonomy. In municipalities with a weak structure, this task is entrusted to the municipal treasurer or the person in charge of finance.

There are different models of external control. In some countries there is still a control of the budget by national institutes whose function is to support, control and inspect. This is the case with the Dominican Municipal League, but also with the Institutes for Municipal Promotion or the Comptrollers Offices in some Central American countries. In Costa Rica, for example, municipal budgets have to be approved by the controlaría before they can be allocated.

In many unitary states, the external control over the intermediate-level local government bodies is exercised by the Controlaria. Bolivia, Chile, Costa Rica, Ecuador, Guatemala, Nicaragua, Paraguay and República Bolivariana de Venezuela still maintain this form of external control. In El Salvador and Honduras, control is exercised by the audit board or the superior auditor body.

In the federal countries, external control is more complex, since both international and national entities intervene. Thus, in Argentina and Brazil external scrutiny of the mayor —*intendente* or *prefeito*— is conducted by the Deliberating Council or Town Council with the assistance of the provincial or State Court of Auditors or the Municipal Court of Auditors, created by the provincial or state government. Should the federation have transferred resources to the municipalities, the audit would be carried out by the Court of Auditors of the Union. The state legislatures are the organs of oversight of the municipalities, although control of federal resources is exercised by the Superior Auditor of the Federation's Office, which in turn depends on the Union Congress.

In recent years, the problem of debt has been a priority. Different countries face fiscal problems through the indebtedness of the sub-national entities. Although in most countries sub-national government borrowing must be approved by national government, this does not guarantee discipline; some countries are trying more innovative solutions to avoid excessive borrowing[36].

In 1997, Colombia established a 'traffic light' system for regulating sub-national borrowing relative to the level of debt incurred by the regional entity. The law establishes the basis for territorial fiscal adjustment through borrowing performance agreements that are controlled at national level. These not only limit the debt capacity, but also manage the repayment of loans, essentially duplicating the IMF system internally. Other laws have complemented this policy with good results.

## III.5.  Public Services

The financial capacity of the municipalities is closely connected to the delivery of public services. In the second half of the 20th Century, national and intermediate governments absorbed public services which, according to the principle of subsidiarity, are most effectively provided by the municipalities. New support for decentralization has begun to reverse the old approach[37].

The public services generally attributed to municipalities include the provision of: urban cleanliness, refuse collection and treatment, drinking water, drainage and sewers, public lighting, town planning, parks, gardens and spaces for sport, markets, cemeteries and slaughterhouses,

36. *Law of fiscal responsibility in Brazil (2000), the "semaphore system" in Colombia – by Law 358 of 1997, in Ecuador, the Law of Responsibility, Stabilization and Fiscal Transparency of 2002.*

37. *Martín, Juan and Martner, Ricardo (coordinators), "Estado de las finanzas públicas: América Latina y El Caribe", cit. pp. 62 and ff, see table 9 on revenues and total expenditure at government level.*

traffic regulation, roads and civic safety, public shows and culture (see table 4).

Bolivia, Brazil, Chile, Colombia and Mexico have transferred to intermediate and local levels responsibility for managing health care, primary and secondary education, and social assistance[38] .

Latin American municipalities also share the management of public services with the intermediate entities and the national government. The specific services differ in each country, but among the most common are planning, education, health, civil protection, environmental protection, sport and culture. When these are shared by different levels of government, each level takes responsibility for certain components of the policy. However, problems of coordination as well as ambiguities with respect to management responsibility are fairly common at each level.

Under the influence of neo-liberalism in the 1990s, many countries opted for the concession or privatization of local services. In Argentina all of the local public services in the metropolitan area of Buenos Aires and the provinces in the interior were granted in concession: mainly water, sanitation and energy services. In Chile, the basic services of water, sewers, electricity, gas and telephone systems were privatized and taken over by regional and national companies. In Bolivia and Ecuador, the management of drinking water and sewers has been privatized, granted in concession or delegated to

private sector operators[39] in the major municipalities of La Paz, Cochabamba and Guayaquil. Nevertheless, the management of some services is returning to public authorities at the local (as is the case in Bolivia and shortly in Guayaquil) and national (Buenos Aires) levels.

In Brazil, there is some overlap of responsibilities between levels of government in some regions; others have some inadequate services or lack certain services entirely. While responsibility for education and health is transferred to the intermediate governments and municipalities with sufficient administrative capacity, small municipalities give up part of their responsibilities, such as construction and maintenance of roads, in exchange for a portion of the fuel tax. The division of responsibilities usually follows sectorial logic (water and sanitation and education are dealt with by the states; the financing of health, housing and sanitation is done by the federal government).

In Argentina in the 1990s, while services managed by the national Government and provinces were privatized, the municipalities held onto the services for which they were responsible. Furthermore, those with greater capacity[40] took on new responsibilities[41]. In addition, through delegation of the upper levels of the government, some municipalities administer social policies and temporary work programs, programs offering assistance to micro-companies, and small and medium companies, and the development of sanitation.

---

38. *There are important differences among countries. In Chile, the municipalities administer integrally primary health care, and primary and secondary education. In Bolivia, they are only responsible for the administration and maintenance of infrastructure and equipment of the establishments. In Argentina, the municipalities carry out complementary actions for infrastructure maintenance, and in the health sector they share primary health care.*

39. *The concept of "privatization" is generally avoided as it tends to generate strong resistance. Bolivia, for example, opted for "capitalization" where private firms bring capital to public enterprizes, taking over their control.*

40. *The municipality of Rio Cuarto, in the province of Cordoba took on the water supply company —first national, then provincial; through excellent management of the water service, self-financing has been achieved for the first time in years.*

41. *Among the new responsibilities: environment, civic safety, economic promotion, access to justice and resolution of conflicts between family members and neighbors without recourse to the law; social promotion (young people, senior citizens, gender equality, disability), health, promotion of culture and sport; and education insofar as it complements the efforts of other levels of government.*

## Table 4 — Municipal Responsibilities in Latin America

| Country | Basic services | | | | | | Food distribution | | Urban planning | | | | Social services | | | | | | Economic development | | | City safety | | | |
|---|---|---|---|---|---|---|---|---|---|---|---|---|---|---|---|---|---|---|---|---|---|---|---|---|---|
| | UO | W | DW | SS | SL | Cem | M | B | P | RI | TRNS | T | PS | PHC | H | SS | C | S/L | ED | J | Tourism | CS | FB | RP | E |
| Argentina | X | X | S | S | X | X | X | | X | X | S | X | | S | S | S | X | X | S | S | S | | | X | X |
| Bolivia | X | X | X | X | X | X | X | X | X | S | X | X | S | S | S | S | S | X | S | S | S | X | X | X | X |
| Brazil | X | X | X | X | X | X | X | | X | S | X | S | X | X | X | X | X | X | S | S | S | S | S | S | S |
| Chile | X | X | X | X | X | X | X | X | X | S | X | X | S | S | S | S | S | X | S | S | S | S | S | S | S |
| Colombia | X | X | S | X | X | X | | X | X | X | X | S | S | S | S | S | X | X | S | X | | S | S | S | S |
| Costa Rica | X | X | * | X | X | X | | X | X | X | X | | S | | | | | | | | | X | S | S | X |
| Dominican Rep. | X | X | X | X | X | X | | X | O | X | X | | | | | | | O | | | | | | O | |
| Ecuador | X | X | X | X | X | X | | | X | X | X | X | Conv | Conv | | | | | X | | | X | | | |
| El Salvador | X | X | Pil exp | X | X | X | X | | X | X | C | | S | | | | | | | | | | | | |
| Guatemala | X | X | X | X | X | X | X | X | X | X | X | | S | | | | X | | | | | X | X | | |
| Honduras | X | X | X | X | X | X | X | X | X | X | X | | | | | | X | X | | | | X | X | | X |
| Mexico | X | X | X | X | X | X | X | X | X | X | X | X | | | S | X | X | X | X | | X | X | X | X | X |
| Nicaragua | X | X | S | S | X | X | | | X | X | X | | | | S | X | X | X | X | | X | | X | S | X |
| Panama | X | X | X | X | X | X | X | | X | X | | | | | | | X | | | | | | | | |
| Paraguay | X | X | S | S | X | X | X | | X | S | S | | | | X | | | | | X | | | | | |
| Peru | X | X | X | X | X | X | X | X | X | X | X | | S | S | S | S | S | X | S | | S | X | | | S |
| Uruguay | X | X | X | X | X | X | X | | X | X | X | | S | X | X | X | X | X | X | X | X | | | | |
| Venezuela, R.B. | X | X | X | X | X | X | X | | X | X | X | X | S | X | X | X | X | X | X | | X | X | X | X | X |

**S:** Shared; **O:** Optional; **Pil exp:** Pilot experiencies; **Conv:** Convention; **UO:** Urban ownership ; **W:** Waste; **DW:** Drinking water; **SS:** Sewer system; **SL:** Street light; **Cem:** Cemetery; **M:** Market;
**B:** Butchery, slaughterhouse; **P:** Urban planning - land regulation and territorial planning; **RI:** Road infrastructure; **TRNS:** Transport; **T:** Traffic; **PS:** Primary school; **PHC:** Primary health care;
**H:** Housing; **SS:** Social services; **C:** Culture; **S/L:** Sport and leisure; **FB:** Fire brigades; **RP:** Risk prevention; **E:** Environment.
**ED:** Economic development; **J:** Job offer; **Tourism:** Tourism; **CS:** City safety;
* In rural areas.

In Mexico, the state institutions and occasionally federal ones intervene in the delivery of local services. Responsibility for drinking water, the management of town planning, roads and the collection of taxes has often been taken over by the states. The participation of local governments in administering education is limited to the maintenance of certain infrastructures. By contrast, since 1997 the financing of social programs has been decentralized. The granting of services to the private sector is less common than in other Latin American countries.

In Bolivia, a uniform strategy of decentralization has been applied to all public services, including health, education, roadways and micro–irrigation. Most are now allocated to the municipalities. Since 2001, the decentralization policy in Ecuador has opted for voluntary transfers of responsibilities through the signing of individual agreements between the central government and the municipalities involved. New responsibilities of special interest to local governments are: the environment, tourism, social welfare and, to a lesser extent, education, housing and health[42].

In Paraguay, the municipalities provide a limited number of basic services[43]. The central government assures the provision of most of the services, in particular drinking water, education and public transport[44]. In Uruguay, these services are delivered at the departmental level, including more and more social services (primary health care), environmental protection and cultural development.

In Central America, with the exception of Guatemala, the majority of local governments take on the basic services with difficulty and, in many cases, in precarious conditions. The activities that involve greater responsibility and require greater investment –education, health, social well being, housing, aqueducts and sewers– are delivered at the national level, in the majority of cases.

The municipalities frequently take on responsibilities not anticipated in the legislation. The municipality of San Pedro Sula in Honduras allocates resources for the maintenance of the hospital and payment of salaries to doctors, nurses and skilled workers, in addition to providing refuse collection services to the hospitals free of charge. In several countries, the municipalities take part in the construction and maintenance of the basic infrastructures of education and health. In Honduras, water management, previously in the hands of a state company, was decentralized in 2003[45].

Regrettably, there are few studies that make it possible to measure the impact of all these processes of transfer on access to, or quality of basic services. Nevertheless, the existing data is promising: in Ecuador, for example, it is calculated that since the beginning of decentralization the

42. Fernando Carrión, "El proceso de descentralización en Ecuador," July 2006. Interest in new responsibilities for local governments is centered on three topics: environment 31.5%, tourism 24.6% and social well being 23.3%. To a lesser extent, education at 7%, and housing and health at 4%.
43. Hygiene, waste management, public lighting, slaughterhouses, markets, cemeteries, transport terminals.
44. At the end of the 1990s, agreements were made between the Ministry of Health, the departments and the municipalities to create departmental and local health councils with limited responsibilities in planning and management. In 2005, only 25% of the municipalities had signed agreements with the Ministry of Health. In 1996, the Department of Itapúa created a Rotating Fund for Medication for Social Pharmacies, which administers 70 social pharmacies in 30 municipalities (2002). Paraguay File.
45. In El Salvador, around 15 pilot projects have been set up transferring the management of water to mancomunidades or local companies. In Nicaragua, there are municipal companies or franchises at the municipal or regional level. Also in El Salvador and Nicaragua, in the social areas, a limited direct de-concentration is taking shape, aimed at the community and designed centrally (Ministries of Education, Health, Public Works). Ex: EDUCO program –Education with Community Participation"– in rural zones of El Salvador, and Co-management of Education and Health in Nicaragua.

percentage of houses connected to the public sewer system has risen from 39.5% in 1990 to 48.5% in 2001; homes with electricity went from 78% to 91%; domiciliary connection to the drinking water supply rose by 10%; and refuse collection went up 20% at national level[46].

In Chile, the favorable impact of local management is expressed in the positive evolution of the main indicators of social and human development (education, basic sanitation, health). For its part, the system of directed subsidies, applied from the municipalities, has contributed decisively to reducing poverty from 38% in 1989 to 18% in 2002[47].

National Planning observed that in Colombia decentralization has improved the rates of educational provision, literacy and coverage of health services. Nevertheless, according to the same source, progress is insufficient in basic social infrastructures and provision of services, and regional disparities have increased. Improvements in management have been significant, but are still not adequate, although pre-existing imbalances have influenced this factor, as have the difficulties related to the armed conflict and lack of governance of certain territories.

### III.6.  Local Government Personnel and Civil Service Career

For the intermediate sub-national entities and municipalities, the absence of a civil service career is a serious failing. In the majority of countries the predominant system in sub-national government is the spoils system which gives rise to a large scale rotation of staff, in particular at the upper and intermediate levels, every time there are political changes that affect the administration.

The best performing countries in terms of development and institutions at the state level are Chile, Brazil and Costa Rica.

Another group of countries –República Bolivariana de Venezuela, Mexico, Uruguay, Colombia and Argentina– present civil service systems that are not particularly well organized. The situation is more critical in the remaining Central American countries and particularly in Bolivia, Peru, Paraguay and Ecuador, where the degree of politicization is higher[48]. This situation is worse at the level of sub-national governments.

In the best-qualified countries –Brazil, Chile, Costa Rica– local officials have generally become integrated into national career systems that are now being matched by systems at the municipal level. In Brazil, the 1988 Constitution allowed local governments to define their own statute for their three million employees, but application of this is limited.

In Chile, the 185,000 municipal employees (54% of public personnel, including teachers and health workers) are mostly integrated into different national personnel evaluation systems and career services statutes[49].

Costa Rica had 10,755 municipal workers in 2004 (4.7% of public personnel), of whom 25% worked in San José[50]. In 1998 a municipal administrative career path was established, but it has not yet been implemented to any effect. Similarly, in 2004 Nicaragua adopted the *Ley de Carrera Administrativa Municipal* (Municipal Administrative Career Act).

Ecuador and Colombia have a legal framework concerning the career civil service for the public sector as a whole. In Colombia, it is calculated that in the 1990s municipal staff accounted for less than 10% of public personnel. In Mexico it was 5%.

In some provinces of Argentina, the regime of employees is uniform between the provincial and the municipal level; in others, local governments have their own regime, although mixed situations are the most common.

46. Ponce, Juan. La vivienda y la infraestructura básica en el Ecuador: 1990-2001. SIISE. Cited by F. Carrión, el proceso de descentralización en Ecuador, July 2006.

47. Ministry for National Planning in Chile (MIDEPLAN).

48. See the Report on the Civil Service in Latin America, AIDB, 2006.

49. Department of Studies of the Chilean Association of Municipalities (Asociación Chilena de Municipalidades – ACHM).

50. Ministère des Affaires Etrangères-DGCID, Bilan des politiques de Décentralisation en Amérique Latine, décembre 2005.

In most countries, public employees are subject to national workers legislation and a special employment status for public or municipal employees, although these practices are rarely applied in practice. Unfortunately, the majority of these countries does not possess precise statistical data on public employees.

In theory, in the majority of countries, subnational government officials and employees are covered by the national work law and by statute as public or municipal employees. However, in practice this is rarely fulfilled. Regrettably, most countries lack precise statistics about personnel in the intermediate governments and municipalities[51].

## IV.  Local Democracy

### IV.1.  Local Electoral Regimes

With regard to municipal government, the terms *cabildo*, town council, council or municipal corporation are used, with different national nuances. In most cases the municipal institution is made up of: the mayor, *intendente*, *síndico* (trustee), municipal president or *prefeito* (prefect), who presides over it, represents it and is in charge of the administration. The *concejales*, *regidores* or *vereadores* (town councilors) act as a legislative body, although at times they receive specific commissions.

Direct election of mayors predominates in the region, generally through a majority system, on different dates from those designated for the national elections (Chile, Ecuador, Argentina, Uruguay, Brazil, Peru, Dominican Republic, El Salvador, Nicaragua). In the federal countries, local elections tend to coincide with the provincial or state elections (Argentina, Brazil, Mexico). In Bolivia, the mayor is elected indirectly from among the members of the Municipal Council who are elected by direct universal suffrage. Recently, the method of election has changed from indirect to direct in Chile (2001), Costa Rica (2002), Nicaragua (1995), and República Bolivariana de Venezuela (1989). For the town councilors, proportional representation or the

mixed systems are regularly established (example: single names and lists in República Bolivariana de Venezuela). The specifics observed in different countries are influenced by respective norms and traditional customs.

The duration of the mandate of mayors and representative councilors varies from country to country. The majority tend to have mandates of four years (Central American countries, Argentina, Brazil, Chile, Colombia, Dominican Republic, República Bolivariana de Venezuela), but there are also some with three-year terms (Mexico), two and a half (Cuba), and five-year terms (Bolivia, Peru, Uruguay, Paraguay and Panama). Re-election of the mayor and councilors is usually allowed, except in Mexico and Colombia where re-election to office is prohibited.

The municipalities of each nation possess their own territorial division, with sub-municipal entities with different names. Such entities are beginning to be granted greater participation, and direct election of municipal authorities is now taking place in various countries. Promising results have been observed in the *corregimientos* of Panama; in the Neighborhood Associations' legal status and election through direct suffrage in Chile; with the *Juntas Vecinales* (neighborhood associations) in Bolivia; the *Juntas Parroquiales electas* (elected parish associations) in Ecuador, which were briefly interrupted in 1980; the elected auxiliary presidencies of Tlaxcala and the municipal communities of Tabasco, in Mexico.

In recent years, the great Latin American metropolises have driven processes of partial decentralization (18 community centres in Montevideo and 15 communes in Buenos Aires) or deconcentration into delegations, sub-mayoral areas or sub-prefectures (16 in Mexico City, 31 in São Paulo). In Mexico City, the delegation chiefs are elected by direct vote; in Buenos Aires community councilors are to be elected for the first time in 2007.

In the unitary countries, the process of electing intermediate government authorities has been slow. In 2004, only half of the de-

51. *In Paraguay there are 13,250 municipal employees (7.7% of the public workforce), half concentrated in the city of Asunción (6,500 employees). In Nicaragua, the number of municipal employees rose to 8,648 in 2000; 31% of them work in Managua.*

partments or regions held elections (Colombia, Bolivia, Ecuador, Peru and Paraguay). In the federal countries, the duration of government terms of office does not always coincide with those of the municipal authorities. In Mexico, for example, the governors have a mandate of six years, as opposed to three years for the mayors.

As for women's participation in local government in Latin America, recent studies show that women's political representation remains very low. Between 1999 and 2002, there were 838 women mayors serving in 16 Latin American countries, representing only 5.3% of the total (Table 5). The ratio of women to men councilors is slightly higher.

There is open public debate in all the countries throughout the region on the under-representation of women at local levels, and measures have been taken to improve the proportion of democratically elected women officials in local government. The quota system is the most common mechanism used to improve women's political participation[52].

| Table 5 | Women Mayors in Latin America (between 1999 and 2002) | |
|---|---|---|

| Country | Number | Percentage |
|---|---|---|
| 1. Panama 1999 | 11 | 14.8 |
| 2. Costa Rica 1998 | 10 | 12.3 |
| 3. Chile 2000 | 39 | 11.4 |
| 4. Honduras 2002 | 29 | 9.7 |
| 5. El Salvador 2000 | 22 | 8.3 |
| 6. Nicaragua 2000 | 11 | 7.2 |
| 7. Colombia 2002 | 76 | 7.0 |
| 8. Argentina 1999 | 136 | 6.4 |
| 9. Bolivia 2002 | 19 | 6.0 |
| 10. Brazil 2000 | 317 | 5.7 |
| 11. Paraguay 2002 | 12 | 5.6 |
| 12. Venezuela, R. B. 2000 | 16 | 4.7 |
| 13. Mexico 2002 | 80 | 3.3 |
| 14. Peru 2002 | 52 | 2.6 |
| 15. Ecuador 2000 | 5 | 2.3 |
| 16. Guatemala 1999 | 3 | 0.9 |
| Latin America | 832 | 5.3 |

**Source**: "Participar es llegar", Alejandra Massolo, INSTRAW. United Nations. Dominican Republic, 2006.

52. In Argentina, for example, the law provides that women candidates must be positioned in proportions sufficient to get elected; in Bolivia, a minimum of one in three candidates has to be a woman; and in Paraguay, one in five candidates has to be a woman; by law in Mexico no more than 70% of the candidates can be of the same gender; and in Peru, at least 25% of the candidates must be women. There are electoral gender quotas also in Ecuador and Dominican Republic.

### IV.2.  Civic Participation

Latin American democracy has made progress. According to the Index of Electoral Democracy (IED) –whose values vary between 0 and 1– the region goes from 0.28 in 1977 to 0.93 in 2002. Moreover, 89.3% of the potential voters are registered on the electoral rolls, 62.7% actually vote and 56.1% cast a valid vote. These percentages for participation in elections are below those of European countries, but are superior to those recorded in the United States[53]. But significant progress is still needed in many respects: transparency in the financing of parties, the struggle against corruption, and in overcoming clientism.

At the local level, participation in elections is high, although in some countries it is tending to decrease. In Argentina, Brazil and Uruguay, where participation exceeds 80%, voting is mandatory.

In Bolivia, participation in local elections has oscillated between 59% and 63% from the mid-1990s to the present. In Paraguay, participation declined from 80% between 1991 and 1996, the first period of democratically elected local authorities, to 50% between 2001 and 2006. In the local elections of 2005 in República Bolivariana de Venezuela, up to 69% of the voters abstained, because of the political situation and the call by opposition sectors to abstain from voting. However, historically the level of participation in municipal elections in Venezuela has been quite low.

In Central America, general average participation is near 50% of the population of voting age, except for Nicaragua where participation exceeds 70%. In Guatemala in the election of 2003, 58% of registered voters voted in the municipal and general elections. In Costa Rica, in the first local elections for mayor in 2002, abstentionism reached 48% of the electorate in some municipal cantons.

Political pluralism has taken root throughout the region, except in Cuba. In Mexico, for example, at the local level a genuine politi-

cal competition has emerged, and in just a few years it has overtaken the institutional quasi-monopoly exercised by a single party, contributing to the democratization of national political life. New local and regional parties, supporting new leaders, have also emerged.

In Peru, the new *Ley de Partidos Políticos* (Political Parties Act) allows the appearance of regional political groupings and the formation of provincial and district political committees that obligate the national political parties to review their structures and renew their leaders. In Colombia and other countries, national political figures are starting to emerge from the local level.

Multiple procedures for citizen participation have been formally introduced into almost all the countries, although these are not always effective or really used. The constitutions and legal reforms define a broad range of forms of participation.

In Brazil, the Constitution of 1988 mentions the plebiscite, referendum, popular tribune, popular councils, and the right to popular initiative with the support of 5% of the voters. But it is the participatory budget that has achieved world recognition as the expression of direct democracy whereby the community becomes involved in formulating the plan for municipal investment. This procedure has been applied in Porto Alegre since 1989, and is used in more than 100 Brazilian cities. It has also been extended to some municipalities in Argentina, Ecuador, Colombia, Uruguay, the Dominican Republic, Paraguay and Chile, albeit in simplified form. In the Dominican Republic, in 2006, more than 110 municipalities (two thirds of the country) were applying the participatory budget.

In Bolivia, the *Ley de Participación Popular* (Law of Popular Participation) of 1994 has generated new participatory practices in the municipalities through the Territorial Base Organizations (OTBs). Through these, the communities take part in the municipal development and annual operating plans that are required in order to access co-par-

*Multiple procedures for citizen participation have been formally introduced into almost all the countries, although these are not always effective or really used*

53.  La democracia en América Latina PNUD, 2004, pp. 77 and following.

ticipation funds. The oversight committee elected by the OTB monitors the implementation of development plans, along with the sub-mayors and social syndicates. The result has been encouraging in most municipalities, above all in the regions of Chapare and Santa Cruz. But in many cases, legal requirements have given rise to bureaucratic practices that get in the way of genuine participation, reinforcing clientism and corruption.

In República Bolivariana de Venezuela, the Constitution and the law are fairly careful in setting up mechanisms for civic participation, but do not clearly define the ways to make them operational. The recently passed *Ley de los Consejos Comunales* (Community Councils Act) of April 2006 creates a new framework for participation through the Community Councils responsible for bringing together different community organizations, social groups and citizens for the direct management of public policies at local level. This initiative does however present the risk of displacement to these Community Councils, which are highly dependent on presidential authority, of programs and resources that should be channeled through the municipalities, as the primary political unit of the national organization and democratic participation.

In Ecuador, in a context in which national institutions have lost their legitimacy, citizen participation has been channeled toward local governments through strategic planning in formulating provincial plans (18), municipal plans (more than 100) and participatory budgets, and through local sectorial committees for public works and service provision; one outstanding example is the participatory experience in the municipality of Cotacachi[54].

Also in Peru, recent legislation has promoted the creation of Councils for Regional and Local Coordination as spaces in which to participate, and Development Plans and Participatory Budgets in the different levels of government (districts, provincial municipalities and regional governments).
In the majority of countries, incentives are offered for organizing the population through Neighborhood Associations, commissions or neighborhood councils and other forms of association (Argentina, Chile, Paraguay, Ecuador, República Bolivariana de Venezuela, Colombia, Uruguay). In Chile, more than 65,000 local organizations linked to the municipalities manage requests and projects. Regrettably, the level of participation in neighborhood elections and in the life of the organizations is tending to decrease[55].

In Uruguay, the neighborhood councils in Montevideo are elected and have a consultative role. Moreover, "defenders of the people" (ombudsmen), have been created; this post is also included in the Argentine constitutional reform of 1994.

Popular initiatives and consultation are provided for by law in various Latin American countries, including Chile and Uruguay. For its part, the *cabildo abierto* –open session of the Municipal Council– with a broader participation by the community, serves to sound out the community with respect to certain impending decisions. This last modality has spread particularly in Central America (Costa Rica, Nicaragua and El Salvador), and since 2004 Guatemala has instituted popular consultation with neighbors and indigenous peoples. Such processes are, however, still in the earliest developmental stages[56].

Procedures for the recall of municipal elected officials also exist. In Colombia, the programmatic vote is taken into account: the mayor submits his program and if he does not carry it out, revocation may take place. In República Bolivariana de Venezuela, the legislation allows for a revocatory referendum for the mayors. In other countries, revocation is allowed for cases of corruption or non-fulfillment of the municipal development plan (Ecuador, Costa Rica). In Bolivia, the mayor is removed from office by the constructive censure vote of 60% of the councilors, who then choose from among themselves the person who will replace him. It is often used in

54. See "La Asamblea Cantonal de Cotacachi" - International Experiences www.municipium.cl
55. UNDP: Social capital Map of Chile.
56. Procedures of social participation have also been instituted in local planning: community development councils, COCODES, and municipal development councils, COMUDES, in Guatemala; Councils for Municipal Development, CODEM, in Honduras, etc.

response to party political issues rather than questions of bad management.

In the interests of greater transparency in management, Brazil and other countries have legislated to oblige local governments to publish their public accounts, and are exploring other mechanisms for the diffusion of public information.

In Cuba, "socialist democracy" establishes the principle of presenting accounts once a year, and revoking the mandate of the delegates elected to the Popular Power Assembly.

### IV.3. Minority Rights

*The rights of indigenous peoples and of other minorities are moving forward through different options, although the process is still incipient and does not apply in all countries*

Native peoples are an important part of the population in numerous Latin American countries. In Bolivia, Ecuador, Guatemala, Peru and some regions of Mexico, they make up between 12% and 70% of the population. Significant minorities constituting 10% or more of the population live in specific regions of Belize, Chile, Paraguay, El Salvador, Honduras, Nicaragua and Panama. The rights of indigenous peoples and of other minorities are moving forward through different options, although the process is still incipient and does not apply in all countries.

- In Bolivia, the *Ley de Agrupaciones Ciudadanas y Grupos Indígenas* (Civic Associations and Indigenous Groups Act) of 2004 gives electoral guarantees, the right to present candidates, and recognition of the traditional authorities. The practice of old forms of direct democracy inherited from the *ayllus*, agricultural syndicates, neighborhood associations, and other forms of community participation is very common in local life.

- Brazil recognizes indigenous rights in the constitution.

- In Colombia, indigenous territorial entities may be formed with their Council, and a special circumscription is anticipated for ethnic groups, political minori-

ties and Colombian nationals abroad, with five representatives in Congress.

- Guatemala recognizes the multi-ethnic and multicultural character of the municipalities, as well as the indigenous mayoralties, councils of Mayan Advisers and the law of national languages.

- As a result of the Chiapas uprising, in Mexico indigenous rights are included in the Constitution. Among state legislatures, Oaxaca stands out with 480 municipalities electing their authorities by use and custom.

- Nicaragua grants constitutional autonomy to two regions on its Atlantic Coast by means of a Statute of Autonomy and each region's own *Ley de Propiedad* (Property Law). In this way, native indigenous peoples live alongside Afro-descendants and other social groups.

- In Panama, the *Comarca de San Blas* (Indigenous Community of San Blas) has constitutional autonomy because that is where the Kuna people live, having been granted their own charter. Their highest authority is the Congress of Kuna Culture. They are entitled to two legislators in the parliament.

- In República Bolivariana de Venezuela, the law recognizes that in the municipalities where there are indigenous communities, their values, ethnic identity and traditions must be respected. The figure of the indigenous municipality is established, and through it the indigenous peoples and communities define, execute, control and evaluate public management.

### IV.4. Municipal Associativism and Defence of Municipal Autonomy

The transformations in local governments caused by decentralization processes permit the creation and strengthening of national and regional associations of local

| Table 6 | Associations of Municipalities in Latin America | | |
|---|---|---|---|
| Country / Region | Name of the association | Acronym | Year founded |
| | Regional Associations | | |
| Latin America | Latin American Federation Cities, Municipalities and Local Government Associations | FLACMA | 2003 |
| | Sub-regional Associations | | |
| Central America | Federation of Municipalities of the Central American Isthmus | FEMICA | 1991 |
| Mercosur | Mercocities | | 1995 |
| | National Associations | | |
| Argentina | Argentine Federation of Municipalities | FAM | 1997 |
| Bolivia | Federation of Municipal Associations of Bolivia | FAM | 1999 |
| Brazil | Brazilian Association of Municipalities | ABM | 1946 |
| | National Confederation of Municipalities | CNM | 1980 |
| | National Front of Prefects | FNP | 2001 |
| Colombia | Colombian Federation of Municipalities | FCM | 1989 |
| Costa Rica | National Union of Local Governments | UNGL | 1977 |
| Chile | Chilean Association of Municipalities | ACHM | 1993 |
| Ecuador | Association of Ecuadorian Municipalities | AME | 1940 |
| El Salvador | Municipal Corporation of the Republic of El Salvador | COMURES | 1941 |
| Guatemala | National Association of Municipalities of Guatemala | ANAM | 1960 |
| Honduras | Association of Municipalities of Honduras | AMHON | 1962 |
| Mexico | Association of Local Authorities of Mexico | AALMAC | 1997 |
| | Mexican Association of Municipalities | AMMAC | 1994 |
| | National Federation of Municipalities of Mexico | FENAMM | 1997 |
| Nicaragua | Association of Municipalities of Nicaragua | AMUNIC | 1993 |
| Panama | Association of Municipalities of Panama | AMUPA | 1995 |
| Paraguay | Paraguayan Organization of Inter-municipal Cooperation | OPACI | 1964 |
| Peru | Association of Municipalities of Peru | AMPE | 1982 |
| | National Association of District Mayors | ANADIS | 2003 |
| | Network of Rural Municipalities of Peru | REMURPE | 1997 |
| Dominican Rep. | Dominican Federation of Municipalities | FEDOMU | 2001 |
| Uruguay | National Congress of Intendentes | CNI | 1959 |
| Venezuela, R. B. | Association of Venezuelan Mayors | ADAVE | 1996 |
| | Association of Bolivarian Mayors | ADABOVE | |

authorities. With the exception of Brazil, Ecuador and various Central American countries, the majority of regional and national associations of municipalities in Latin America were established between 1980 and 2000 (see table 6).

In some countries, the associations enjoy a legal status recognized by national legislation (Argentina, Bolivia, Ecuador, Colombia, Paraguay, Uruguay). However, their representative and institutional capacities are uneven. In general they offer advisory services, information and training, maintain contact with the governments and channel resources from international cooperation. Many of them have incipient institutional structures.

*In some countries, the associations enjoy a legal status recognized by national legislation. The majority of countries also have sub-national associations of regional municipalities*

The Latin American Federation of Cities, Municipalities and Local Government Associations (FLACMA), whose roots date back to 1981, brings together the majority of national associations in the region. In addition, two sub-regional organizations operate: FEMICA with the six national associations of Central America (AMHON, AMUNIC, AMUPA, ANAM, COMURES, UNGL) and the Mercocities Network with 181 associated cities in Argentina, Brazil, Paraguay, Uruguay, República Bolivariana de Venezuela, Chile and Bolivia. Recently, a network of Andean cities has been set up, and COSUDAM, another organization made up of local government associations, was established.

The majority of countries also have sub-national associations of regional municipalities. Bolivia's FAM is, in fact, a federation of departmental associations of municipalities. There also exist associations of indigenous mayors (AGAAI in Guatemala, Coordinator of Alternative Local Governments in Ecuador) and associative

structures of aldermen or town councillors (Colombia, Paraguay, Uruguay).

The governors of provinces and states, and more recently of regions or departments, create their own organizations, such as CONAGO in Mexico, and the National Conference of Governors in Colombia. At the end of 2004, the Latin American Organization of Intermediate Governments, OLAGI, was set up, bringing together governors, *intendentes*, prefects and regional presidents from 14 Latin American countries that administer intermediate governments.

A number of local-government women's organizations have been formed in Latin America, including: the Association of Women Councilors of Bolivia (ACOBOL); the National Association of Women Councilors and Mayors of El Salvador (ANDRYSAS); the Ecuadorian Association of Female Municipal Employees (AMUME); and the Paraguayan Network of Women in Municipal Government (RMMP). In other countries, there are organizations operating at sub-regional levels, such as the Network of Women Councilors of Ayacucho in Peru. Additionally, a bi-annual Congress of women mayors and councilors is held within the organizational framework of the Chilean Association of Municipalities. In 1998, the Latin American and Caribbean Federation of Women in Local Government (FEMUM-ALC) was set up; the organization is linked to FLACMA.

## V. Achievements, Limitations and Perspectives on Decentralization

Although progressive and sometimes contradictory, the decentralization and strengthening of the municipalities and intermediate governments of Latin America is a reality. In just over two decades, there have been important achievements.

- Election by the people of local authorities has become common, changing the way that parties operate, bringing about renewal of leadership and transforming the municipality into a space in which leaders are formed, from which various Presidents of the Republic have already emerged;

- Multiple constitutional and legal reforms have transformed the states, with competencies and resources being transferred to sub-national governments, although not always with clear strategies and methods;

- Sub-national resources have increased significantly, although unevenly, and the average decentralized continental expenditure has risen from 11.6% in 1980 to 18.8% of total government expenditure between 2002 and 2005;

- The new responsibilities of the local governments translate into progressive institutional development – though uneven – where some municipalities stand out because of their capacity for initiatives and innovation, while others still cling to their traditional structures and practices;

- The local spaces for civic democracy have given rise to new experiences of participation by citizens, such as the strategic participation plan and participatory budgets;

- Experiences in municipal de-concentration or decentralization have also been developed to share management with the communities and open spaces to groups that were previously marginalized (indigenous populations below the poverty line);

- The new responsibilities of the local governments and the transformation of relations with the national governments are expressed in the creation and strengthening of the national and regional associations of local authorities;

- In various countries, such as Bolivia, Brazil, Chile, Colombia and Ecuador, the positive results attained through decentralization are reflected in the increases of local investment, extension of basic services, improvement in human development indicators, decrease in poverty and broadened citizen participation.

However, the decentralizing process shows gaps and faces obstacles, such as:

- Unequal relations and frequent subordination of the intermediate entities and municipalities to the central governments, heightened by the increase in fragmentation and municipal heterogeneity;

- Gaps between the proliferation of legislation and weakness in its application, which may be attributed largely to prevailing political and institutional cultures;

- Limited financial capacity of local governments, because of central resistance to handing over resources in a context of macro-economic instability, lack of financing policies and adequate credit, citizens not used to paying for subsidized services, but also because of the lack of political will to strengthen the local capacity to collect taxes;

- Low efficiency of many local administrations in delivering services, because of the absence of human resource policies and bad handling of personnel (rotation, lack of career paths), resulting in a low level of efficiency and professionalism in local personnel;

- Limitations in civic participation in development management due to a lack of adequate financial and local human resources, poor adaptation of central laws and policies, and difficulties in organizing and mobilizing the actual communities.

*A bi-annual Congress of women mayors and councilors is held within the organizational framework of the Chilean Association of Municipalities*

The decentralizing process in Latin America has shown diverse and contradictory signs, and is passing through a moment of uncertainty. In big countries like Brazil, there is a need to review the federal pact and transfer policies in order to deal with the growing cost of the new responsibilities of education and health.

In Argentina, party political centralism continues to be a limiting factor for local autonomy, particularly at the provincial level. In República Bolivariana de Venezuela, it is feared that the government will intervene increasingly in the provincial states and municipalities, cutting down their autonomy.

In Mexico, where democratization of national and local political life has made significant advances, strong pressure persists on the federal government to move forward with questions of federalism and decentralization.

In some unitary states, this process has been slowing down. In Colombia, local government spending is controlled in order to reduce the fiscal deficit of the central government. During the last years, decentralization has not been intensifying. In Colombia, sub-national expenditure is controlled to alleviate the deficit of central government, and the decentralization process has not deepened over the last years. In Ecuador, the transfer of competencies is at a standstill; local authorities are asking the government to undertake concrete measures to re-launch the process. In Peru, local authorities have shown concern about recent unwelcome measures taken by the national government[57].

In Bolivia, where local governments now administer half of the national public investment, the rigidity of the transfer system and the overlap of responsibilities at the local, regional and state levels, generate tensions between the municipal and departmental levels. In the framework of the current Constituent Assembly, the topic of decentralization and regionalization is at the heart of the national political debate.

However, in Peru, Ecuador and the Dominican Republic, intended constitutional reforms have positive implications for local governments. In the Dominican Republic, a new Law of *Presupuesto Participativo* or Participatory Budget has been passed, and a new Municipal Law is expected.

Meanwhile, in Chile the national government and the Chilean Association of Municipalities are negotiating a new Municipal Reform to increase the responsibilities and resources of the municipalities with the hope of stimulating local development and reducing social and territorial inequalities.

In those countries with more incipient processes, the situation seems stable. In Paraguay, control from central government continues to be decisive in the action of the sub-national governments, although the Paraguayan Organization of Inter-municipal Cooperation, OPACI, has presented a project to the national government to pass a law reforming municipal legislation.

In Uruguay, various *"Intendencias Departamentales"* (department executives) insist that the Local Commissions or *Juntas* be further strengthened, and propose new mechanisms of citizen participation. There is a new bill in parliament for Local Decentralization, which intends by 2010 to bring the public administration closer to the people through the municipal authorities in towns or villages with more than 2,500 inhabitants.

57. Centralized establishment of remunerations by local authorities, cutting of transfers and centralization of decisions to finance projects.

*Despite advances in decentralization, Latin America is still a continent with a high degree of political, territorial and economic centralization, exacerbated by concentration in the metropolises and immense social and territorial disparities*

## VI.  Conclusion

Despite advances in decentralization, Latin America is still a continent with a high degree of political, territorial and economic centralization, exacerbated by concentration in the metropolises and immense social and territorial disparities.

In the near future, new debates are envisaged. New centralizing trends have emerged that are curtailing local self-government, such as the accreditation of local capacities needed in Costa Rica to qualify for the transfer of responsibilities and resources. Public purchase[58], information and monitoring systems –through administrative mechanisms–

control, condition and restrict municipal autonomy.

The decentralizing experiences have reignited the debate about the importance of local development for sustainable and socially equitable development at the national level. The issue of good local governance is emphasized and understood as a form of territorial self-government based on participatory networks of local actors, public-private alliances and the mobilization of own territorial resources to activate the endogenous processes of development.

58.  *In Chile, Chile Compras, as the only public sector purchasing website, is presented as an example of procedural transparency and rationalization of public purchasing for central government and municipalities. Yet it is not very practical for local governments, as it displaces local providers, favors national companies and slows down the administrative process, to the detriment of municipal responsiveness to the demands of the community.*

# MIDDLE EAST / WESTERN ASIA

MUSTAPHA ADIB

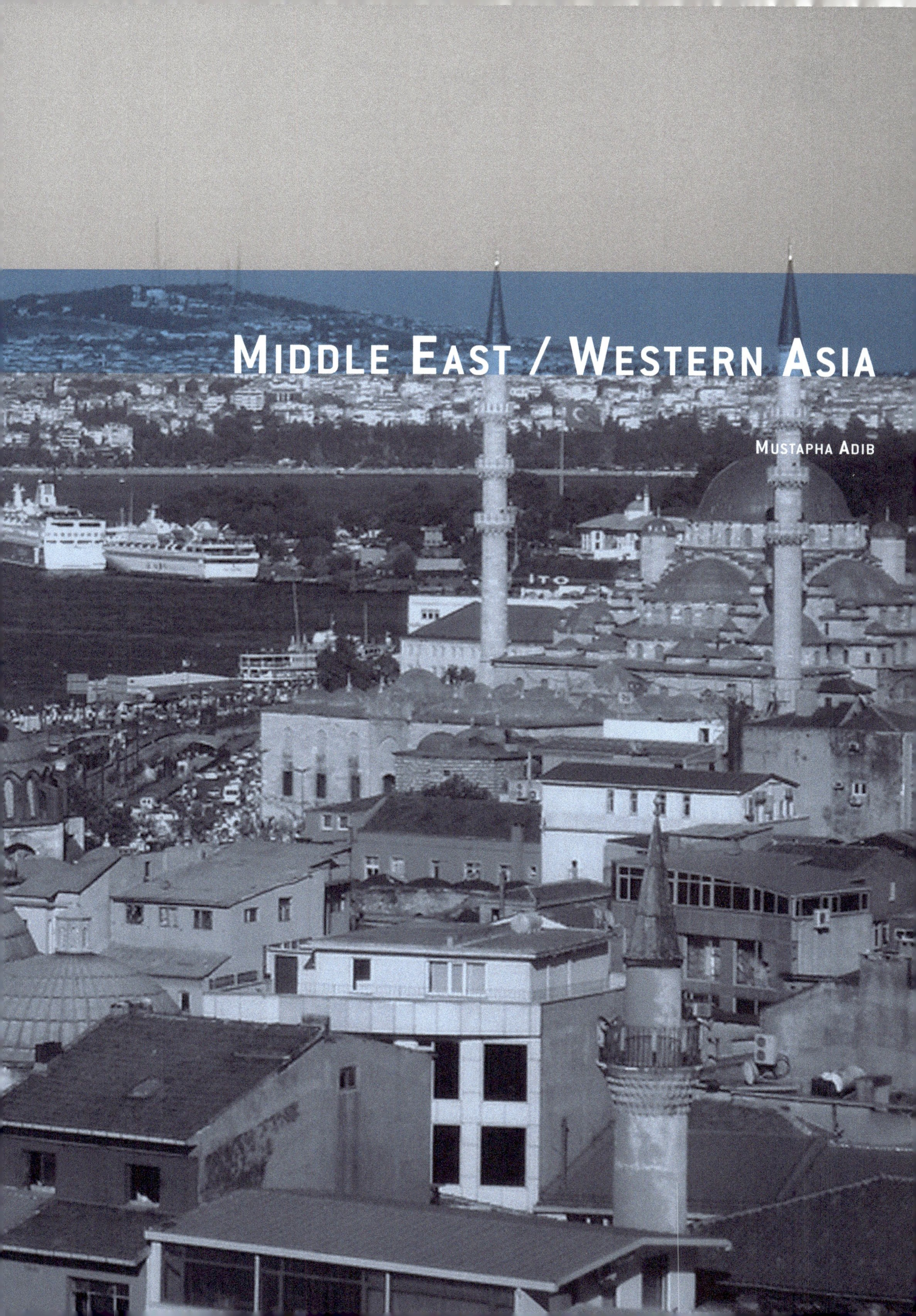

## I. Introduction

The geographical region of Western Asia/the Middle East encompasses Turkey, the Near East[1] –with the exception of Israel–, the Arabian Peninsula, and Western Asia, including Islamic Republic of Iran. The region has, for many decades, undergone political, military, ethnic, and religious tensions that have affected its stability. Of the countries that we will be examining, seven are monarchies (Bahrain, Jordan, Kuwait, Oman, Qatar, Saudi Arabia and United Arab Emirates), six are republics (Islamic Republic of Iran, Iraq, Lebanon, Syria, Turkey and Yemen) and the autonomous territory of Palestine, which has not yet all the attributes of a state. Indeed Turkey is the only country that has enjoyed stability, for several decades, based on secular and democratic institutions. The religious factor is also important and omnipresent throughout the region, in the constitution and across private and political spheres.

This grouping of over 260 million inhabitants is dominated from the demographic standpoint by Turkey (74.7 million inhabitants) and Islamic Republic of Iran (69.5 million). The population is now predominantly urban (Syria 50.1%, Islamic Republic of Iran 67%, Iraq 67.2%, Turkey 67.3%, Oman 77.6%, Jordan 79%, Lebanon 87.5%, Kuwait 96.3%), with the exception of Yemen (25.6%). But the existence of a few industrialized economies and the wealth generated by oil revenues must not lead one to overlook either the huge differences that exist between the countries of the region, or their sometimes mediocre performances in terms of education, governance, and freedom –performances which were highlighted by the 2004 UNDP report.

Nevertheless, in spite of the ceaseless political, military, and religious tensions, wars and other perennial obstacles to the regions' stability as a whole, and certainly to the development of local autonomy and decentralization, some advances deserve recognition: the first local elections in Saudi Arabia, the holding of democratic local elections in

the West Bank and Gaza, the restoration of mayoral elections by universal suffrage in Jordan, and the 2002 constitutional reforms in Bahrain. Under pressure from elite segments of their populations, Islamic Republic of Iran and Kuwait have also begun tentative changes in this direction. Turkey, which has had a modern municipal system since 1930 and whose citizens as a whole support decentralization as one of the criteria for membership of the European Union, is something of an exception to this description; three new laws favorable to decentralization were adopted in Turkey in 2004-2005.

These changes, however, cannot conceal a broader trend throughout the region –Turkey excepted– toward the gradual confiscation of local authority by central governments. In certain cases, even the tasks of providing street cleaning, sewer maintenance, and public health measures, are being taken away from local governments. The most extreme case is Jordan where the provision of 13 different types of service has been taken back by the state. This form of centralized control typically involves privatization, under the pretext of improving efficiency and overall services.

Decentralization only appears in the constitutions of Lebanon, Syria, Islamic Republic of Iran, and Turkey. Turkey has a middle-level local government, but in the other three countries decentralization applies to only the lowest tier, municipalities.

Apart from the Sultanate of Oman, Saudi Arabia, and Bahrain, where the roles of the municipal councils have been defined from the start as purely and openly consultative, legislation in other countries in this region – especially Kuwait and Turkey – does grant certain powers to local authorities.

Nevertheless, the existing laws rarely present a precise list of local powers, such specifics being the province of future implementation orders promised but never published. The vagueness of such laws

*The religious factor is omnipresent throughout the region, in the constitution and across private and political spheres*

1. Insofar as there does not exist any generally accepted definition of the terms 'Near East' and 'Middle East,' we shall refer to the former Levant, (Lebanon, Syria, the West Bank and Gaza, and Jordan) as the 'Near East,' and the countries of the Arabian Peninsula, Iraq, and Islamic Republic of Iran, as the 'Middle East.' Turkey for our purposes here is considered part of Western Asia.

*With the exception of Turkey, local authorities' limited financial independence is coupled with a priori administrative control of local council proceedings, as well as a posteriori control of all work by local authorities*

creates overlapping areas of responsibility in practically all fields. The central government uses this vagueness to retain most of the powers, leaving municipal authorities with only derisory duties.

Reliance on conveniently vague laws typically results in a paucity of financial resources for local authorities, and the concomitant restriction of the services local governments can realistically provide. Apart from Turkey, the only economy in which local authorities have decent (although not large) resources at their disposal is the West Bank and Gaza, where they keep up to 90% of the taxes they collect plus income provided by non-government organizations (NGOs). In the majority of nations in the region, obtaining money for operations and services requires unceasing appeals to the central government, or to the organizations that manage national finances. One result: increasing levels of debt.

A single figure is enough to describe the scale of the problem. Whereas the local government share of public expenditure represents 20% of the gross domestic product (GDP) in OECD countries, money for local government averages only about 5% of GDP in the Arab countries.

Furthermore, with the exception of Turkey, local authorities' limited financial independence is coupled with *a priori* administrative control of local council proceedings, as well as *a posteriori* control of all work by local authorities. Together, these two measures ensure complete control of local powers by central government.

By contrast with Turkey, there is, in Islamic Republic of Iran and Syria, 'cascading' supervision of lower councils by higher councils. In the West Bank and Gaza repeated outbreaks of violence often make it impossible to submit matters to the central power, leaving local authorities with *de facto* autonomy.

Local governance is underpinned by local democracy, which is itself boosted and

supported by civil society. Within the region, the voice of civil society is sometimes hesitant to make its opinions heard, and this in turn has repercussions for decentralization and local government.

This trend toward centralization has experienced an unprecedented intensification since the first Gulf War. In fact, because of a particularly unstable geo-strategic situation due to the upsurge of armed conflicts, the heightening of community and sectarian tensions and the interplay of international pressure, the governments of the region are haunted by the fear of the break-up of national entities. This is particularly the case where the ethnic or religious groups in power are a minority, or comprise a very slight majority. In Islamic Republic of Iran, which is a mosaic of 80 communities, 51% of the population is Persian; in Lebanon, 18 communities, each with a different religion, live together; Jordan has a very strong Palestinian minority; and several countries in the region have a large Kurdish community.

## II. Evolution of Local Government Structures

The following table presents local government organization in the region.

Before going further with an analysis of the region's governmental structures and their recent evolution, it is necessary to emphasize that Turkey is unique in this part of the world. Turkey is included in this study of the Near East and Middle East because of its geographical location at the gates of the Levant, and its majority Muslim religion. However, as Yves Lacoste has stressed, "The North-South model experiences a stumbling block in the very exceptional case of Turkey"[2]. Turkey is a secular state adjacent to Europe, but most of its residents are Islamic. Turkey is geographically part of the Middle East; its topography affects many Middle Eastern states, and has done so for countless millennia. Within the framework of a secular state, Turkey is relatively cen-

2. Yves Lacoste, *Géopolitique*, Larousse, 2006, p. 227.

| Table 1 | | Administrative Organization | | | |
|---|---|---|---|---|---|
| Country/ territory | Population / land area | Political regime | Federal entities or autonomous regions | Second tier | Local level |
| Bahrain | 0.727 m   690 km² GDP (per capita): 14,370 USD* | Constitutional monarchy | | | Municipality (12) |
| Iran , Isl. Rep. | 67.7 m   1,648,200 km² GDP (per capita): 2,770 USD | Islamic republic | | Province (28) Department (314) | City/town (931) Small town Village |
| Iraq | 26.5 m **   438,320 km² GDP (per capita): 928 USD*** | Parliamentary republic | Kurdistan | Region Governorate District | Municipality |
| Jordan | 5.4 m   88,800 km² GDP (per capita): 2,500 USD | Constitutional monarchy | | Governorate (12) | Municipality (99) |
| Kuwait | 2.5 m   17,818 km² GDP (per capita): 24,040 USD* | Absolute monarchy (Emirate) | | Governorate (5) | Municipality |
| Lebanon | 3.6 m   10,452 km² GDP (per capita): 6,180 USD | Parliamentary republic | | Region (6)  (Mohafazah) Department (Caza) | Municipality (930) |
| Oman | 2.6 m   309,500 km² GDP (per capita): 9,070 USD* | Absolute monarchy (Sultanate) | | | Municipality (43) |
| Qatar | 0.813 m   11,000 km² GDP (per capita): 28,833 USD*** | Absolute monarchy (Emirate) | | | Municipality (10) |
| Saudi Arabia | 24.6 m   2,149,700 km² GDP (per capita):11,770 USD | Absolute monarchy | | Province (13) Governorate Center (A or B) | Regional council (7) Principal council (5) Council (107) Group of villages (64) |
| Syria | 19 m   185,180 km² GDP (per capita): 1,380 USD | Authoritarian presidential republic | | Department (14) | Town (107) Small town (248) Village (207) Rural unit |
| Turkey | 72.6 m   783,820 km² GDP (per capita): 4,710 USD | Parliamentary republic | | Special departmental administration (81) | Municipality (3,519)[3] 16 Metropolitan Municipalities Village (35,000) |
| United Arab Emirates | 4.5 m   83,600 km² GDP (per capita): 23,770 USD* | Federation of absolute monarchies (Emirates) | Emirates (7) | | Municipality |
| West Bank and Gaza | 3.5 m 5,842 km² (The West Bank) +365 km² (Gaza Strip) | 'Palestinian Authority' | | Governorate (14) (9 in the West Bank 5 in the Gaza Strip) | Municipality (74) (63 in the West Bank 11 in the Gaza Strip) |
| Yemen | 21 m   527.970 km² GDP (per capita):  600 USD | Authoritarian presidential republic | | Governorates | Municipality (326) Provincial municipality (20) District municipality (326) |

**Source:**   World Bank 2005, except:  * Source: World Bank 2004.  ** Source: World Bank 2003.  *** Source: World Bank 2002

3.  Beside these ordinary municipalities, the metropolitan municipalities provide urban services at the metropolitan level to ensure greater efficiency, as well as harmonization and coordination between municipal districts. The metropolitan municipalities supervise and provide assistance for district municipalities.

tralized, but its local government system is subject to a constitutional jurisprudence that is extraordinary in the region.

Turkey is the only pluralist secular democracy, and has always attached great importance to developing its relations with European countries. Historically, Turkish culture has had a profound impact over much of Eastern and Southern Europe. After the First World War and the proclamation of the Turkish Republic in 1923, the Kemalism, to which the present Turkish state is heir, deliberately distinguished its political and social system from that of the Arab countries. This was particularly emphasized by the abolition of the Caliphate and the adoption of the Latin alphabet, modified only slightly[4]. Turkey's modern democratic conception and acceptably functional institutions present more contrast than similarity to other Middle Eastern nations. This contrast is no less apparent in regard to decentralization.

### II.1.  The Objectives of Decentralization

By means of constitutional and legislative reforms during the past ten years, all the countries in the region have embarked upon a change of direction toward increased administrative decentralization. However, far from being uniform, the underlying motives and results are quite different and wide-ranging.

### a)  External factors

*Membership of the European Union.* As a country where decentralizing reforms are increasing in scale, Turkey has been motivated by its desire to gain membership of the European Union, whose criteria for membership include respect for human rights. It is therefore within the framework of the European Charter of Local Self-Government, signed in 1988 and ratified in 1992, that this wide-ranging renovation of state structures – including new local government laws and constitutional changes – is taking place.

*U.S.A. policy in the region.* The United States maintains a military presence in the region, particularly in Iraq. The promotion of the principles of « good governance » and democracy have become the declared US policy in the region. With the on-going support of different countries, the United States sustains its regional policy through direct and indirect means.

*Economic pressures.* Along with political pressures and within a context of neoconservative globalization, the non-petroleum-producing countries – Lebanon, Jordan, and Palestine – face demands from international backers for the restructuring, not only of their weak economies, but also of their societies. The strengthening or the establishment of local government is one of the pillars of these reforms in that it constitutes the first step in applying the principles of good governance.

### b)  Internal factors

*Internal population pressure.* Although civilian society is not accustomed to making its voice heard, there has recently been an increasing demand for local democracy by two groups whose interests converge only in this single area. Both appear to see in moves toward democracy the means of bringing victory to their overall concept of the state. One group, often referred to as radicals, wants a more rigid system of government. The other group, the intellectual elite, wants to establish real democracy. An example of this urging toward democracy is the 100 Saudi intellectuals who in January 2003 presented the Crown Prince with a petition requesting changes; similar pressure led the Jordanian government to restore the election of mayors by universal suffrage.

*Coming to terms with demands for autonomy.* In the specific case of Iraq, where internal pressures are nationalist in nature, decentralization has enabled the granting of extensive autonomy, including legislative powers, to Kurdistan. However, these powers do not grant or imply independence for that region.

4.  *These reforms also fell within the framework of the 'Six Arrows' as Ataturk's general nationalist policy aimed to ensure the modernization of Turkey.*

*The need for economic restructuring.* With the exceptions of Turkey, Lebanon, Jordan, and Yemen, the economies of the region are based on oil; only Syria and Turkey can be considered industrialized countries.

Yet the exhaustion of oil reserves in the near future appears likely[5]. The governments of oil-producing nations are therefore trying to anticipate a profound structural change in their economies to facilitate rapid expansion of private initiative. This concerns Syria in particular. Dubai, which does not have any oil, but which benefits from oil revenues through the federation of the Emirates, represents a striking example of success in this type of restructuring.

*Restoring impetus to governance in general.* After almost 30 years of systematic destruction of Palestinian state structures by Israel, the Palestinians, according to the 1993 Oslo Accords, wanted to set their state structures back on their feet in order to construct a state. However, as it is impossible to establish a real central government inasmuch as there is no territorial continuity between the West Bank and the Gaza Strip, the only way of providing services to the people and to enable them to take effective action regarding the affairs which concern them is through the local governments. This removal of central authority has greatly increased public confidence and trust in local Palestinian government, the institution closest to its citizens.

It is surprising that providing better public services is mentioned as a concern only in Turkey. One explanation may be that, for this purpose, administrative decentralization (*déconcentration*) in Saudi Arabia, and a rather authoritarian management are perceived as quite effective. In fact, the management of the city of Dubai, which is a resounding success in terms of town planning, infrastructure, economic development, and service provision, results solely from the will of the Emir.

## II.2. Encouraging Progress

In Turkey, where the decentralization process is most advanced, three new reforms[6] were passed in 2004-2005. Furthermore, the 2005 union of municipalities' law[7] will finally make the villages a real tier of decentralization. It is now possible for the local authorities, on their own initiative, to organize referendums on specific local issues —an interesting system of direct democracy.

Likewise, Iraq's 2004 constitution establishes decentralization as a priority, (Iraq's 1990 constitution did not) devoting an entire chapter to "regions, governorates, and municipalities." This document sanctions the autonomy of Kurdistan, which becomes a "region" with a regional government, parliament, and judicial authority. Moreover, it encourages the creation of regions by the grouping together of governorates. In addition, and in contrast to other countries of the region, except Turkey, where administrative decentralization (*déconcentration*) and delegation prevail, Iraq's new constitution organizes decentralization on the basis of the administrative and financial autonomy of local authorities, including regional and municipal councils[8].

Following this same trend, in 1999 Islamic Republic of Iran finally achieved a long-standing reform: the elections of councils. This reform was first presented as far back as the 1907 Constitutional Revolution, and was again championed after the revolution of 1979. Some 92 years after it was first proposed, this change took effect under the presidency of the reformer Khatami.

Another important reform is currently in progress in Jordan, a country whose king has made good governance principles one of the national objectives. This reform aims to divide the country into three regions, each of which will have its own regional parliament as well as local management of its own affairs.

5. On this subject, it is interesting to compare the official figures provided by the governments and the large oil companies with those provided by ASPO.

6. On the municipalities (no. 5393 of 3 July 2005), on the metropolitan municipalities (no. 5216 of 10 July 2004) and on the special administration of the department (law no. 5302 of 22 February 2005).

7. Law no. 5355 of 26 May 2005.

8. In actual fact, this is only really applied in the north, in Kurdistan. Elsewhere, the local authorities only enjoy a weak level of autonomy, and it is not uncommon to find that municipal councilors and mayors are appointed directly.

Lebanon used to have properly functioning municipal governance, but this lost all substance during the 1975-1990 war, as security concerns led to the centralizing of all services within the different ministries. Executive power was concentrated[9] in the office of a President of the Republic, who was always a Maronite Christian. However, at the end of the war, the Taëf Pact, a constitutionally valid document signed to put an end to the war, made more room for all communities. In the first place, executive power passed to the Council of Ministers, whose members represent different faiths in proportion to their demographic importance. The document also mentions administrative decentralization as one of the main areas for reform, thereby distinguishing itself from the constitution, which does not mention it at all. The new accord directs that "a more extensive decentralization be adopted at the level of the smallest administrative units"[10] and that "the municipalities, agglomerations, and unions of municipalities see their resources strengthened by the provision of the necessary financial resources"[11]. Within this framework, it became far easier for local communities to voice their demands for a greater degree of self-government; the creation of 25 municipalities since 2004 testifies to the acceptance of this reform at high levels of the Lebanese state.

In a similar case, the Palestinian Authority, which was formed as a result of the Oslo Accords, was especially keen to proceed with the strengthening of local government. The population naturally made these bodies its favorite forum for public expression of demands, including practical requests regarding services. All this was in a situation where the increasingly weak states, or the mokhtars[12], who had lost the confidence of the population because of their suspect role during the occupation, were not in a position to ensure the provision of services. As viable power centers, these municipalities are becoming increasingly autonomous.

Two other cases also deserve mention. In Bahrain the new constitution, promulgated

in 2002, states that[13] the law "will do so as to ensure the independence of local authorities under the supervision and direction of the State," and "will do so as to ensure that the local authorities are able to manage and supervise local affairs." In Saudi Arabia, the first election of half the municipal councilors was organized in 2005.

Yet in Turkey the reform of the executive committees (encümen) –the entities responsible for municipal management– still raises concerns. In fact, each tier of decentralization –Special Provincial Administrations (SPA), ordinary and metropolitan municipality and village– has a deliberative body called a council, which is elected by universal suffrage. At the municipal and village level, the executive officer (the mayor or the Muhtar respectively) is also elected by universal suffrage. On the other hand, at the top provincial level is a governor appointed by the state. Moreover, each council works in conjunction with an executive body called the 'executive committee.' Before the reform, this executive committee was fully appointed in the metropolitan municipalities, fully elected in the SPA and half was elected and half was appointed in the ordinary municipalities. The new legislation directs that, without exception, half of all executive committees must be elected and half must be appointed. Although this measure is based on a managerial vision of local government management, the presence on an executive committee of members appointed by the mayor or the governor runs counter to the full exercise of local democracy and decentralization. It is, moreover, the interpretation that the Turkish Constitutional Court gave of it[14] in 1988: all deliberative bodies must be elected. It is therefore not impossible that these texts will be amended in the near future.

Likewise, according to the new law[15], the SPA council now elects a chairman from among its own members. Although this chairman is responsible for the council agenda, it is the governor who stays at the

9,  Lebanese
    constitution, art. 17.
10. Taëf Pact [III : A,
    art. 3].
11. Id. Art. 4
12. Maire de quartier.
    This institution
    exists in many Arab
    countries, including
    Lebanon.
13. Art. 50.
14. Notice no. 1988/23
    of 22 June 1988 and
    decision no.
    1988/19 of 13 June
    1988.
15. Law no. 5302 of 4
    March 2005, art. 11.

head of the executive committee and who represents the SPA[16].

In Islamic Republic of Iran, the new law regarding councils, which was adopted at its first reading by the Islamic Consultative Assembly, also seems intended to restrict the councils' room to maneuver.

## II.3. The Persistence of the Centralized Model

### a) Central state supervision

These advances toward further decentralization are quite significant, even though, for the most part, they are still reforms on paper or are restricted to administrative decentralization only.  Most such reforms still await the fiscal and economic decentralization that is essential for their implementation. Consequently, the standard system of government in the region remains strongly centralized. Moreover, it bears mentioning that some countries, such as Oman and Qatar, do not even mention local powers in their constitution. In Saudi Arabia, provisions for local governance are also absent from the constitution; instead, they are specified in a separate text, the 1992 'law on the provinces.' Even this document does not deal with municipalities. Rather it addresses only provinces, all of which are controlled by princes of the royal family.

Independent decision-making by local authorities is allowed in Turkey, the West Bank and Gaza, and Iraq, but in other countries in the region, real decisions are made only by higher authorities, either a single designated official or some lesser officials holding power through a complex of arcane laws. Where there is a clear, single channel of authority, municipalities are subject *de facto* and *de jure* to government authority through their relevant ministry. This is the case in Saudi Arabia, where local authorities are dependent on the Ministry of Rural and Municipal Affairs. In Jordan, little can be done without the backing of the territory's

governor; in Bahrain, Oman, and Lebanon up to 80% of the decisions must be checked by the Ministry of the Interior, or by a governor with regional executive powers.

Other governments practice a more insidious form of control. Under the guise of a nominal freedom to make decisions, an arsenal of measures appreciably limit the decision-making powers of local authorities.

*'Cascading supervision.'* In Syria and Islamic Republic of Iran, there is 'cascading supervision' of lower-tier councils by higher-tier councils. In Islamic Republic of Iran, the constitution specifies, moreover, that "the provincial governors and the mayors [...] must apply, within their jurisdiction, the decisions of the Higher Provincial Council"[17], a fact that clearly calls into question public professions of a desire for decentralization.

*The executive committees.* Two countries have, in addition to local councils, municipal legislative bodies vested with executive powers; these are called executive committees in Turkey, executive *bureaux* in Syria. While the members of local councils are elected by the people, the members of executive committees or the executive *bureaux*, are appointed by more or less direct procedures[18]. In Turkey, the constitution[19] defines local authorities as bodies that have a legal personality, and whose legislative bodies are elected. This, in fact, opens the way to the election of all or part of the members of the executive committees, as much at the Special Provincial Administration level as at the municipality level[20].

Syria's case is slightly different. There a third of the members of the executive body can be recruited from outside the municipal council –on the basis of criteria which are far from clear.

*The ambivalent role of popular councils.* In addition to the municipal councils, the *mahalle muhtarligi* (neighborhood councils) chaired by a *muhtar* have existed in

16. *Id. Art. 25 et 29.*
17. *Art. 103 'Of the power [of the Higher Provincial Council] on local government.'*
18. *In Turkey, the appointed half of the executive council is selected by the mayor from among the municipality's chief officers, within the framework of the 'strong mayor system.'*
19. *Art. 127.*
20. *The Turkish Constitutional Court has ruled that the executive councils are governing bodies and that their members must be elected.*

Turkey since the Ottoman Empire. They are very similar to the Lebanese *mokhtar*. The role of these local community leaders was made official by Article 9 of the new municipal law.[21] This law gives them official functions, notably in the field of the registration of births, marriages, and deaths, and in tax collection. In addition, they ensure contact with the municipality and represent their local community area on the 'town councils' by passing on the requests and comments of the people from their administrative area. Introduced by the new municipal law, the "city council" –*kent konseyi*– is a consultative institution, an outcome brought by the success of the Turkey Local Agenda 21 Program. This constitutes a unique mechanism of governance in Turkey that brings together the central government, local government and civil society within a framework of partnership. In general, this participatory mechanism encompasses a broad spectrum of local stakeholders, representatives of working groups, neighborhood committees, women and youth councils.

In other countries, however, authorities working in parallel with the municipal council can represent an important opposition force in the hands of the central government, particularly when they have the potential to report on and perhaps slow down the work of the municipal councils. It is this second situation which applies for the Syrian 'popular organizations,' which represent various socio-professional categories, such as manual workers, farmers, and women, and which must make up at least 60% of local councils. Furthermore, their elected representatives, even those not on the municipal council, have the right to monitor their activities.

### b) The weight of the political and social system

The report of the United Nations Development Programme (UNDP) indicates that "the progress in the field of decentralization in the Arab countries has been very slow, particularly because of the uneven level of involvement in decentralizing reforms."[22] In fact, it is difficult not to see in the persistent strong centralization a reluctance on the part of the governments of the region to accept local governance and the independence inherent therein.

*The refusal of a loss of sovereignty.* The main reason for government distrust of local governance is fear of a loss of sovereignty. Excluding Turkey, where power belongs to the institutions, governing tradition is based on the personal exercise of power, with the government, on its own initiative, delegating a part to people of its own choice. Given this context, to put in place real decentralization would require a complete overhaul of state structures, beginning in some cases with a separation of powers and election of legislative bodies by universal suffrage.

In the particular case of Lebanon, which nevertheless satisfies these conditions, the only area of agreement of the traditional community leaders is their wish to put a brake on the resumption of municipal governance. In fact, they consider local municipal authorities to be usurping some of their prerogatives. They seem to believe that municipal authorities are only intended to provide services for their supporters in exchange for their votes. This vicious circle keeps the local councils in a state of lethargy. Members of parliament, who are themselves traditional leaders or who owe allegiance to them, use their legislative position to gradually weaken the power of the municipalities.

This analysis is equally valid for those states where members of the ruling families, or those of a political party, or of a dominant movement have all the power.

*The security factor.* The other factor which hinders the decentralization of the states is security. Some large fault-lines cross the region, the main one being the community organization. In fact, the risk of subversion is

21. Law no. 5393.

22. ELISSAR SARROUH, *Decentralized Governance for Development in the Arab States*, report presented during the forum on governance in the Arab states, Sana'a, 6-9 September 2003.

far from negligible in those states with a large Shiite community, as in Saudi Arabia, Iraq, and Bahrain. Neither are Islamic Republic of Iran, Lebanon, and Iraq safe from implosion.

*The inertia of civilian society.* Again excepting Turkey, those in power are not alone in their indifference to decentralization. In the general population, it is mostly identifiable groups who desire increased decentralization. Such groups include the cultured urban elite, extremist parties, and those who see it as a means to autonomy or even sovereign independence.

Civilian society reduced to its most simple expression is typically comprised to a greater or lesser degree of client networks, which are perceived as being more efficient and more reliable than the state, sharp divisions among different cultural and religious communities, and a widespread tradition of submission to central authority. Indeed, in this region the desire for freedom is embodied far more in religion than in politics, suggesting that the larger citizenry plays an insignificant role as a driving force for change. Evidence for this is the absence of political parties in six of the 14 countries studied (Saudi Arabia, Bahrain, the United Arab Emirates, Kuwait, Oman and Qatar). In Jordan, political parties were not legalized until 1992. Further support for the weakness of political systems for expressions of popular will can also be seen in the rapid expansion of radical religious movements. It is through religious organizations that we receive calls for reform, the popular expression of demands that can not be voiced successfully by political means.

*The influence of the religious factor.* Most of the countries in the region base their legislation on the *Sharia*. This is the case of Saudi Arabia, (Const. art. 1), Bahrain (Art. 2), Islamic Republic of Iran (Art. 2), Jordan (Art. 2), Kuwait (Art. 2), Oman (Art. 2), Qatar (Art. 2), and Yemen (Art. 3). The Syrian Constitution establishes a slight nuance by indicating that "Islamic

jurisprudence will be one of the main sources of legislation." The exceptions are Turkey and Iraq, which are secular states, and Lebanon, where a hybrid system entrusts private legal matters to the religious tribunals of each religious community, Christian or Muslim, but takes as its basis secular business and public law.

The original feature of Islam in comparison with other religions is that it provides guidance not only on private life, but also on the system of government. This, however, does not mean that its interpretation is totally unequivocal, and the two famous *ayets* —"Consult them in the affairs which concern them"[23] and "Let them consult each other"[24]— gives rise to a wide range of interpretations. It is on the narrowest of these interpretations that Saudi Arabia, Bahrain, and Oman have based their decision to replace the legislative bodies with a consultative assembly, the *Majlis-al-Shura*; the same *ayets* have, on the other hand, given rise to the election of councils in Islamic Republic of Iran and Jordan.

*The perception of a supranational identity.* With the exception of Oman and Turkey, all the countries of the region claim in their constitutions to be an "Arab nation," (Bahrain, Jordan, Lebanon, Kuwait, Qatar, Syria, and Yemen), or an "Islamic nation" (Islamic Republic of Iran); both in the case of Saudi Arabia. This is seen as the ultimate goal toward which the national structure would be a stage. It is a question of the translation into political terms of the sense of belonging to the Umma (the community of Islamic believers). This mythic identity would in no case succeed in resulting in a federal reality, but it tells us a good deal about religious aspirations and about the dominance of the group over the individual, and of global over local policy.

*Between necessary change and an inward-looking identity:* Most of the countries of the region are recent in origin, and are currently grappling with two major trends: the wish for change and modernization,

23. *Koran, [3:159].*
24. *Koran, [42:38].*

and the influence of Islamic movements. Caught in the crossfire between globalization and an inward-looking identity, and faced with real threats of destabilization, a number of leaders prefer to play the stability card to the detriment of structural reforms – all the more so because such reforms are sometimes perceived as being encouraged by the West.

## II.4.  Specific Structures for the Organization of the Metropolitan Cities

The region of Western Asia/Middle East encompasses 28 big cities of more than a million people[25]. In 2006 these cities together had 77.14 million people which represents 37% of the whole population of the region[26].The metropolis experienced a very fast growth: 10.6% between 2005 and 2006 compared to only 2.56% experienced by the population of the whole region.

Only Turkey in 1984 granted its major cities the special status of 'metropolitan municipalities,' a status that was reformed in 2004[27]. Turkey's 16 metropolitan municipalities have a total population of 25.9 million inhabitants –38% of the country's total population.

This special political status enables Turkish cities to be run with comparative efficiency. Big cities are divided into two levels: the proper metropolitan municipality, and the ordinary first-tier municipalities. The metropolitan municipality is responsible for urban services: urban planning, large parks and green areas, collection and disposal of household and industrial wastes, water, sewerage, natural gas and public transportation, establishing and operating marketplaces for wholesalers and slaughterhouses, sports, leisure and large recreation areas.

Nevertheless, the latest reform was keen to encourage coordination and cooperation between the two levels, as well as among the different municipal councils that make up the metropolitan municipality. If this reform has indeed successfully strengthened the metropolitan municipalities' range of activities, some balance remains. On one side, a mayor elected by direct universal suffrage; on the other, the presence of members of the first-tier ordinary municipality councils within his council.

In other countries, there is no special status for big cities, although this has been discussed, but never undertaken in Jordan.

Only Amman, Beirut, and Damascus have special status, and this only in matters of security. Their municipal councils are essentially deliberative bodies with no real power.

Regarding the organization of metropolises, some are based on a hierarchical model, e.g. a central municipality vested with the executive authority and lower level municipalities the functions of which are mainly licenses (such as delivering building permits) and administrative work. This is the case, for example, in Amman. Others follow a "horizontal" model, with equal status, as for example Mashad in Saudi Arabia.

However, in most cases there are big cities with a municipal council vested with executive and legislative functions; there exist sometimes inner city district municipalities, whose status goes from pure executive bodies (Tehran) to consultative bodies (Baghdad). In this case, surrounding municipalities located in the metropolitan area are subject to the regional authority (region or governorate).

The case of Dubai is exceptional. The management of the city has been devised as for an enterprise, the head of which is a general director.

It is clear that, apart from the exceptions of Turkey and some cities elsewhere, such as Amman and Dubai, the exponential deve-

25. In decreasing order of their population in 2006: Tehran, Istanbul, Baghdad, Riyadh, Ankara, Ispahan, Jeddah, Amman, Izmir, Alep, Mashed, Damas, Kuwait, Beirut, Sana, Mosul, La Mecca, Damn, Dubai, Tabriz, Bursa, Gaza, Basra, Shiraz, Andana, Gaziantep. Qom and Ahvaz.

26. In Yemen 8% of the population, in Syria and in Islamic Republic of Iran 25%, in the Emirates 30%, in Iraq 37%, in West Bank and Gaza 38%, in Saudi Arabia 43%, in Jordan 46%, in Lebanon 55% and in Kuwait 72%. Bahrain, Oman and Qatar don't have any city of more than one million inhabitants.

27. Law no. 5216 of 10 July 2004.

lopment of metropolises has taken authorities by surprise. Most have to establish an urban planning considering all aspects of this expansion, in particular socio-economic aspects.

## III. Responsibilities, Management and Finances

### III.1. Local Authority Finances

*The lack of reliable data and the issue of transparency.* First, it must be acknowledged that obtaining reliable up-to-date data on the finances of local authorities in this region is a formidable challenge. Several factors limit accessibility to pertinent data:

**Practical obstacles to data collection:**
- The lack of reliable data compiled in accord with international standards; international organisations have not been able to publish comparative data on public finance in relation to the countries examined in this report.
- Lack of training for municipal employees in the principles of accountancy and in the exacting standards of accurate book-keeping.
- Lack of computerization of data, although some countries are on the right track.
- In the case of the West Bank and Gaza, the destruction of the archives by Israel.

**Informal obstacles:**
- A tradition of secrecy that pervades the entire region.
- Lack of cooperation from some municipal officers.

Few national governments in this region have demonstrated sufficient concern about accounting practices to cause a discernable decline in the widespread public perception of corruption. However, some progress is apparent in a few countries. In Lebanon, Prime Minister Fouad Sanioura introduced an annual independent audit of all the ministries, along with the computerization of

accounting data. Jordan has become a member of the International Monetary Fund's Government Data Dissemination System and has started to communicate verifiable data. Saudi Arabia and Oman have also started to publish their accounting data, and Turkey has achieved remarkable transparency, partly due to government efforts and partly because of a citizens' initiative called 'Society Follows the Budget.'

*The weakness of local taxation.* In Turkey, local expenditure amounts to 4% of the Gross Domestic Product (GDP), 75% of this share goes to the municipalities and 25% to the SPAs. This is the highest share of GDP in the region, except Jordan (which is 6% according to UN-POGAR).

In Turkey, the Constitution and the laws require the national government to contribute to the financing of local functions. State funding covers little more than 50% of municipal budgets; 55% of these state funds represent a 6% share of national taxes, redistributed to the municipalities in proportion to their population. Moreover, the metropolitan municipalities receive a share of 4.1% of the taxes collected in the region, revenues which in turn are redistributed to the metropolitan municipality itself (55%) and to the municipalities (35%). A further 10% is allocated to water and sanitation. In addition, 15% of the municipal budget is paid as subsidies from the various ministries. National government subsidies and transfers assure a more balanced distribution of financial resources among local governments throughout the country.

The share of local taxes, those collected within the municipalities' own financial resource base, remains rather small, reaching only 12.4%. To that are added various taxes paid directly by the municipalities, including taxes on property ownership, gambling, public shows and activities, as well as on electricity and gas consumption. Although small, this local share of tax revenue collected locally has been increasing since 1988.

The system's stumbling block is that local authorities have no taxing rights, with the exception of the tax on property ownership, because they are members of the committee that fixes the tax base. All the rates, including those for the property ownership tax, are fixed by the central government, in accordance with article 73 par. 3 of the constitution, which states that "All types of taxes and rights are to be established by the law," and that the Council of Ministers can be empowered by law, and within the limits laid down by law, to fix the exemptions, reductions and rates. Between 1980 and 1990, the Constitutional Court delivered several rulings which interpreted these constitutional provisions as meaning the termination of any local authority taxing right.

A bill currently under consideration predicts an increase in municipal and SPA revenues as well as a real equalization; however, it stops short of granting taxing rights to these bodies.

In Lebanon, own taxation only reaches 30% at best. However, the legislation since 1992 has gone in the direction of reducing this type of taxation, and replacing it with taxes collected by central government –a good example of the political desire to weaken the municipalities. In Syria, local finances can hardly be said to exist, as all public expenditure is included in the national budget. Local governments receive funding from central government for running expenses, to which unspent balances are eventually returned (POGAR).

*Insufficient and haphazard resources.* One of the recurring problems of the region's municipalities is the lack of resources, which prevents them from successfully carrying out their functions. In Syria, Lebanon, Jordan, the West Bank and Gaza, and Yemen, the municipalities are poor, or even very poor. In Jordan the total budgets of 99 municipalities increased, in 2006, to 161 million dollars.

As we mentioned earlier, this is partly due to weak or non-existent local taxing powers. The second problem is the low level of state subsidies, which are haphazard and arbitrary. Most of the time, state funding barely covers operating expenses – sometimes not even that – in economies such as Jordan, Lebanon, and the West Bank and Gaza. This does not leave much leeway for investment potential or the financing of cultural and social activities. For that the municipalities have to rely on the good will of wealthy locals ("evergets") or people living abroad. There are even local authorities that are so deprived of decent resources that the mayors are paid by central government, and all the services are provided by other bodies.

Moreover, the financing of local authorities is under no circumstances considered to be a priority; services such as health, education, civil engineering, and water and power supply, are run either by the ministries or by centralized sector-based bodies. In Islamic Republic of Iran, the present law on municipalities does not even mention finances. For that, the earlier law of 1982 must be consulted. It is also perhaps interesting to note that in Bahrain's annual budget for 2006[28], the items 'Municipalities' and 'Agriculture' appear under the heading of 'Miscellaneous,' along with the upkeep of the royal stud farms.

In the West Bank and Gaza, there was a slight improvement in 2002, since the mayors then obtained the right to collect directly taxes on fuels and road traffic, in addition to an education tax, the only tax they were allowed to collect directly until then. The Palestinian Authority is supposed to pay back to the municipalities 90% of these local taxes, but it does not do so. Result: the municipalities are becoming increasingly poor. Furthermore, Palestinian cities are not able to collect taxes in the surrounding areas. Realistically, tax revenues can be collected only in villages, to which many people who now live abroad send money, or towns with longstanding strong

28. *Figures provided by the Bahrain Finance Ministry.*

commercial activities. Until recently, 90% of local investment expenditure was funded by the Palestinian Authority, thanks to funding from outside organizations, such as the World Bank, the European Union for the urban areas, and the UNPD for the rural areas, as well as bilateral technical aid from the G8 countries. However, unhappy about the recent takeover by Hamas, most sources of outside funding have stopped all aid, and there is now a movement toward a fragmentation of services.

Similarly, in Lebanon municipalities are supposed to receive a percentage of revenues collected by the electricity, telephone, and water services. This percentage is supposed to be redistributed to them by the relevant ministries in proportion to the amount collected in each geographical area. In reality, these ministerial organizations return the money only in dribs and drabs.

In theory, a significant part of the municipalities' revenues comes from a percentage of tax revenues allocated to the state where they are managed by an organization called the 'Independent Municipal Fund'[29]. However, this fund has never materialized so revenues payable to municipalities go directly into the national treasury. By some estimates, in 2002 this represented 0.75% of Lebanon's GDP and 2% of the general budget[30]. Despite the modest percentages, the money takes years to be paid, and typically flows only after intervention by a local leader. The situation is improving, but the state, bankrupt and heavily in debt, is still two years behind in its payments.

Those municipalities with a theoretical right to collect local taxes often encounter reluctance among citizens to pay the levy, however legal the tax may be. Particularly in Lebanon, Jordan, and the West Bank and Gaza, most local authorities lack the means of compelling payment. For a variety of practical, social, or security-linked reasons, tax collection is at best uncertain.

*The high level of municipal debt.* Borrowing is standard practice for a modern local authority, especially for infrastructure. Bahrain[31] and Kuwait[32] have included in their constitutions provisions for municipalities to "take out, agree to, or secure a loan". Such borrowing power is also possible for the executive body of municipal administration in Islamic Republic of Iran, though not for the municipal councils.

But such measures in municipal funding can lead to disaster, particularly when they are used to compensate for a lack of operating revenue, when they are not used for investments, and when local authorities do not have the means to repay the loans. This is the case in Jordan and the West Bank and Gaza, and both economies are incurring increasingly high levels of debt. Following the Hamas election victory, the withdrawal of international donors from the West Bank and Gaza, as providers of direct financial assistance to local governments, led to the rapid deterioration of the municipalities. In Lebanon, due to scarcity of fiscal resources, some municipal governments have to resort to advance payments from the Independent Joint Municipal Fund, which are disbursed at high interest rates.

In Jordan, new measures address this borrowing crisis. Where municipalities have borrowed to cover operational costs, especially salaries, and are overwhelmed by interest and service fees, the state has paid off the loans. Thanks to a reduction of about 20% in its general administrative expenses, the government has wiped the slate clean for third- and fourth-class municipalities (the smallest), and has committed itself to do the same for the remaining 27 municipalities by 2011.

The increase in the need for public services in Turkish metropolitan municipalities has led to an increasing level of debt. In 2002, this debt was the equivalent of 4% of the GDP –a full year's revenue for the municipalities. However, there is no legal requirement that municipalities balance

29. Established by decree no. 1917 of 6 April 1979.
30. Al-Dawlyia lal Maalumet (International Journal of Information).
31. Art. 108, 'On public lending.'
32. Const. Art. 136 and 137. 'On public lending' and 'On local authority lending.'

their budgets, and the state has always made up the shortfall with agreeably flexible loans from the Bank of the Provinces.

*State supervision of local authority finances.* State monitoring of local authority finances is a normal, necessary and healthy measure as it ensures that finances are managed not only efficiently, but also with integrity. However, this monitoring should not immobilize the decision-making process. In Lebanon, for example, three separate entities monitor public municipal finances: the comptroller general, the auditor-general, and the State Audit Office. The State Audit Office carries out *a priori* and *a posteriori* inspections of local authority finances, focusing particularly on municipal property management above a specified threshold, the signing of public contracts, public works, and service provision. In effect, such oversight power negates local governmental autonomy for municipalities. Jordan, Saudi Arabia, and Bahrain have similar systems; budgets are proposed by municipal councils, but the councils can not vote to approve their budgets.

With the aim of reconciling decentralization and the careful management of municipal finances, Turkey has set up a supervision system based on internal bodies called audit committees. These consist of from three to five council members who must be elected annually by their respective municipal councils in towns with more than 10,000 inhabitants, and the SPAs. Their role is to provide a check on the income and expenditure of local authorities. As such, they make up a form of democratic counterweight to the established authority, particularly in those places where the mayor is both the municipality's highest authority and the official with the power to authorize expenditure.

*A posteriori* checks are carried out, as in any modern country, by the State Audit Office.

This lack of resources, combined with their incapacity to implement the areas of

responsibility that they have been allocated, makes local authorities dependent on the state, transforming them into central government go-betweens. The central government also manages in an authoritarian and arbitrary way the money that is actually distributed to local treasuries. Unequal distribution is often the rule rather than the exception. For example, the money allocated for street cleaning in just the city of Amman amounts to a third of the entire budget for all Jordanian municipalities. In a similar case, over the past few years the Lebanese government has withdrawn huge amounts of money from the Independent Municipal Fund to pay for street cleaning in metropolitan Beirut. In the same way equalization is nonexistent in numerous countries, such as Jordan and Lebanon.

## III.2. Responsibilities

### III.2.1. Extensive theoretical areas of responsibility

In most countries in this region, municipalities have official responsibility for a wide range of tasks, including infrastructure and many human services. On paper, municipalities are responsible for highways, public buildings and drains, outdoor lighting, and waste collection, and also health, education, culture, sports, and social services. Lebanon's law on municipalities[33] gives municipal councils extensive prerogatives in all these areas, including the support of destitute and disabled people. Similarly, the Palestinian and Jordanian municipalities[34] are supposed to have, respectively, 27 and 39 different areas of responsibility.

### III.2.2. A reality often out of step with the legislation

However, in many countries, there is a gap between legislation and its implementation. Many factors prevent municipalities from meeting their official responsibilities.

*The overlapping of areas of responsibility with central government.* In Saudi Arabia,

33. Art. 47 and following.
34. The law of September 1997 gives them a discretionary power in many sectors.

the Ministry of Rural and Municipal Affairs has drawn up a very precise list of municipalities' areas of responsibility[35]. In Oman, the Ministry of Regional Municipalities, Water, and the Environment has done the same. But several national constitutions remain vague on the subject, mentioning only the major sectors of planning, health, and education: or nothing at all. Where they exist, ordinary laws and statutory instruments for their implementation retain this legal vagueness. The predictable result is overlapping of areas of responsibility, which is highly prejudicial to the efficiency of local government work.

Again, Turkey provides the exception. There a *modus vivendi* seems to have been established between the municipalities and the Special Provincial Administrations (SPAs), with each providing services according to its ability. Such is the case for environmental concerns shared by municipalities and the National Administration for the Protection of the Environment, and also for collective housing issues addressed jointly by local authorities and the National Administration for Collective Housing. The distribution of responsibilities is also organized on a territorial basis. In territories where there is a metropolitan municipality, the municipality is responsible for most services; this accounts for the present explosion in expenditure. This also occurs within the administrative area of a normal municipality; in areas not dependent on either, the SPAs are responsible for providing services. The recently legislated reorganization of responsabilities has also contributed to this development.

Unlike Lebanon and Jordan, Turkey does not have a general competence clause of municipalities. At the present time, the main responsibilities of local bodies, particularly the municipalities, are urban planning, public transport and communications, water supply, sanitation, and the treatment of solid waste. Law no. 5302 added economic action, although what exactly this covers is less clear for municipalities than for SPAs. The law also

confirmed the pre-existing situation of the involvement of the municipalities in the maintenance of school buildings and the provision of the necessary supplies. However, the provision permitting municipalities to open preschool establishments was suspended by the Constitutional Court[36] on the grounds that this runs counter to the spirit of the constitution, for which education is strictly a state prerogative.

Everywhere else, almost all the responsibilities are carried out by the central government through its ministries, leaving the municipalities only planning tasks and basic functions such as lighting, drainage, highway maintenance, and waste collection. Of course, there are exceptions, most notably Jordan where 13 essential service responsibilities were taken away from the municipalities by the law of 1995. Beirut, Lebanon, is also a special case. There the provincial governor has executive power, the municipal council being a deliberative body. Also in Lebanon, the *mokhtar* has supplanted most municipal authorities in the registration of births, marriages, and deaths. It should be noted that this is the *mokhtar*'s only real responsibility, though in theory their remit[37] covers public order, health, and education.

In Jordan, some of the responsibilities that have been taken away from the municipalities have been taken over by private national and foreign companies.   Similarly, in Lebanon the state has begun to sign contracts directly, not only without the consent of the municipalities, but sometimes without even informing them. Such was the case with contracts for street cleaning, public lighting, and street paving in Beirut and Mount Lebanon. The money for these contracts is directly withdrawn by the state from the funds of the theoretical Independent Municipal Fund. Hope for more profitable public services induced Palestinian central government to enlist the private sector to manage services that require a high level of investment for infrastructure construction and maintenance —water, electricity, and sanitation.

35. For the precise list, see the 'Saudi Commerce and Economic Review', November 2004. It can nevertheless be noted that street cleaning, public health, town planning, (vice-minister of town planning) and the maintenance of public buildings, public transport, and traffic management (Department of Transport and Traffic Planning) all come under the authority of the Ministry of Rural and Municipal Affairs, with water distribution infrastructures and the building of sewers being administered by a special service that has seven regional branches.

36. Notice no. 2005/14.

37. Art. 25 and following of the law on the mokhtar.

*Administrative checking and central government supervision.* In a decentralized country, the state exercises three checks on local decisions: legal, financial and administrative. When this type of checking is carried out *a posteriori* it is the sign of a state that is concerned about good local management. On the other hand, checks conducted *a priori* entail the infringement on local autonomy; this is so, even when some local authorities – particularly those in Lebanon – who are faced with depleted resources, interpret it as a sign of protection and guarantee.

Taking a broader perspective, two fairly distinct systems emerge in the region. In Saudi Arabia, Kuwait, and Oman, municipalities are branches of their controlling ministry, though they occasionally function as go-betweens. Elsewhere in the region, laws and regulations delineate a minimal, quasi-autonomous status for local authorities, albeit with significant political and financial constraints.

We have seen how much *a priori* financial monitoring weighs heavily on the autonomy of municipalities, preventing them from performing their functions. Similarly, with the exception of Turkey, municipal council discussions are also subject to *a priori* monitoring by the central government or by one of its representatives, such as the provincial governor in both Lebanon and Jordan. Technically, this monitoring of virtually all discussions may even be illegal in some countries where it occurs routinely. Indeed, in Jordan and Lebanon, the constitutions state in almost identical terms that all local affairs must be managed by the municipal councils. Yet in Lebanon, on average only 20% of municipal council decisions are immediately enforceable, 33% require the prior approval of the provincial or regional governor, and 47% need approval from the Ministry of the Interior and the Municipalities[38].

In a similar way, local councils in Islamic Republic of Iran rely on the Higher Provincial Council, an assembly of all the local repre-

sentatives, to convey concerns to national authorities. The Higher Provisional Council is responsible for the monitoring and coordination of the lesser councils. It also drafts bills that concern local authorities, and presents the bills to the National Assembly.

In Turkey, on the other hand, central government supervision has been reduced by the latest reforms, with the provincial governor no longer having direct control over council proceedings or their finances. His powers are now restricted to submitting a case to the administrative tribunal when there is a suspicion of malpractice. In addition, within the framework of a new managerial vision of municipal management, the new laws emphasize the importance of a performance audit based on modern audit methods, rather than on a legality oversight.

The comparative administrative autonomy of local governments in the West Bank and Gaza is offset by significant fiscal control by the central government. Communication difficulties make centralized administrative control impractical, but most financial resources flow downward from the central authorities.

In Syria, Islamic Republic of Iran and Saudi Arabia, there is an additional administrative check in the form of an electoral system requiring that candidates for local posts be approved by an *ad hoc* electoral committee; this could be called an 'absolute *a priori* check' since it takes place prior to the discussions themselves.

*The security factor.* The Palestinian Authority's exclusive powers apply only to 20% of its territory (the category A areas, which are mainly urban), the rest being run jointly with Israel or by Israel alone. As a result, the municipalities only rarely see their decisions, whether about urban planning or tax collection, applied in their area. The use of law enforcement personified by the Palestinian Police is subject to the prior authorization of Israel, which retains control of the vast majority of the rural areas. In addition, everything to do with heavy infrastructures

38. ABDELGHENI IMAD, Municipal elections, Jarrous Press, p. 20.

and land use planning is dependent on an outside body: the State of Israel.

On the whole, local authorities throughout the region have only nominal, if not fake, autonomy. At best, national leaders either retain a traditional concept of the role of local authorities, or consider them unable to deliver higher-quality services; at worst, they do not want them to gain increased importance. As usual, the exception is Turkey, where a certain number of responsibilities are actually carried out – some since the latest law – by decentralized local authorities.

### III.2.3. External solutions to the municipal framework

The myriad formal and informal arrangements that prevent local governments in the region from representing their citizens in a meaningful way, lead with little surprise to increasing interest in alternative means of civic participation.

*Unions of municipalities.* Some municipalities in the West Bank and Gaza and Lebanon have sought a solution in the pooling of their resources. In the West Bank and Gaza, for example, 'Joint Service Councils' have been set up by the Ministry of Local Government to construct and run communal infrastructures. This has obvious appeal to the mayors of small local communities, but worries city authorities. The higher municipal authorities understandably fear the loss of their prerogatives, and would rather bring pooling activities to a halt. In Lebanon, on the other hand, it is the lack of resources which prevents the communities of municipalities from functioning, as state subsidies are never fully paid out.

In Turkey, where the municipalities work well, inter-municipal cooperation occurs primarily in rural areas where there is a marked shortage of skilled administrative personnel. The 2005 reform[39] reorganized inter-municipal organizations, making them a new tier of decentralization, with the responsibilities recently granted to the Special Provincial Administrations and with a proper budget. This

reform should lead to an improvement and increased local management of services in the rural areas. Thanks to these, all Turkish villages should benefit, before the end of 2007, from water supply, drainage, and access roads. There are two types of cooperative structures: unions of municipalities and unions for irrigation.

*Neighborhood committees.* During the Israeli occupation in the West Bank and Gaza, Palestinian neighborhood committees were gradually created to deal with those services that would ordinarily be provided by municipalities. They still continue to provide some services, such as waste collection, in the Al Mahâta area of Khan Younès in the Gaza Strip, for example. This system exists also in Iraq, where in the city of Basra 170 local informal committees sustain the municipal council not elected to be distributed food and fuel.

In Turkey, on the other hand, the neighborhood committee consists of a traditional structure organized by the latest law as a direct link between the inhabitants and the municipality.

*Private benefactors.* Despite the informal and seemingly haphazard nature of private aid, private benefactors ("evergets") have always played an important role in Middle Eastern municipal life, Turkey again excepted. At times private funds make up for state inadequacies, but more often private benefactors provide cultural and social services. Primarily in the West Bank and Gaza and Lebanon, though sporadically throughout the Middle East, most municipalities are reduced to relying on private benefactors for grants for schools, health centers and some hospitals, free meals, and cultural centers. During the July 2006 war in Lebanon, traditional leaders and businessmen took responsibility for financing the reconstruction of bridges.

### III.3. Administrative Capacities

After finances, recruitment methods and training for local government employees is the least transparent administrative element. It is

*39. Law no. 5355 of 26 May 2005.*

difficult, if not impossible, to obtain precise, reliable figures on the people employed by local authorities. A tradition of patronage makes such information especially difficult to obtain. However, certain major trends are becoming apparent.

*Central government supervision.* In Lebanon, only lesser municipalities are permitted to draw up their own organization charts[40]. Government employees in provincial capitals and in important towns are public servants dependent upon the National Council of the Public Service, which answers directly to the Prime Minister. In Jordan the recruitment of public sector employees, for which the Civil Service Office is responsible, has been decentralized, to each governorate, by the creation of councils run by the governor.

In the countries where some or all municipal councillors are appointed by the central government, they are public servants in the service of the central government; municipal employees who report to them cannot therefore be considered local government personnel. This has been the case in Saudi Arabia, Jordan, and Kuwait since the last elections in those countries.

*The issue of the training of local government staff.* The lack of training for most local authority employees is a serious impediment to efficiency. Aware of this, several countries of the region, with the encouragement of the UNPD, have launched extensive training programs for local government personnel.

In Saudi Arabia, the 'Municipal Chairmen's Performance Improvement Service,' a special department of the Ministry of Rural and Municipal Affairs, has created a program to improve the skills of municipal personnel, and to encourage their geographical mobility. This is taking place within the framework of a long-standing training program for public servants. The number of those who have received training has risen from 12,649 in 1989 to 23,056 in 2004, and nearly doubled to 43,132 in 2005.

In Turkey, a new municipal law sets deadlines for payment of salaries, and fixes a ceiling for staff expenditure, making it the personal responsibility of the mayor if these limits are exceeded. At the same time, municipalities have been given more flexibility in their staffing structure.

Jordan too launched a series of training programs after an assessment showed that lack of skills and low productivity among municipal employees was slowing the general restructuring of the municipalities.

By contrast, Lebanon has effectively imposed a freeze on municipal hiring since 1975. True, a 1977 law on the municipalities directed the Minister of the Interior to organize training seminars for local employees, but it also seems that nothing substantive has been done since. An indicator of decline in the public sector is the average age of local municipal employees: 55 years. As a result, the number of local government employees is insufficient, as it also is in all branches of the civil service.

In Syria, as in most countries in the region, skilled people are moving out of local authority jobs, and into the private sector where pay and career prospects are much better.

*Malfunctioning recruitment methods.* Many local authorities actively circumvent arcane official hiring regulations. Instead, they hire increasing numbers of local people on short-term contracts. In principle, this strategy allows the municipalities to have more local management of their affairs.

Practices in Turkey are illustrative. Although recruitment of public servants has a high priority in the national legislature, and a competitive examination has been established for government employment, the number of official public servants has remained more or less stable. At the same

40. Law on the
    municipalities in
    Lebanon, art. 88.

time, the number of temporary workers, most of whom are not well-qualified, and are employed for an average of one year, is steadily increasing. From 1995 to 2003, the percentage of temporary municipal employees increased from 21.4% to 35%. These temporary workers can be far more easily taken on and dismissed.

Throughout the region, the recruitment of municipal employees is not done on the basis of their skills and experience, but rather through patronage based on political or community factors.

This practice results in an excess of staff, many of whom are poorly qualified or unqualified. Officials simply award jobs in local government as a means of establishing their personal influence. Though to some degree ubiquitous, this practice is especially common in Lebanon and Jordan.

*Inefficiency is by no means the only harmful effect of pervasive nepotism and patronage.* Such practices perpetuate a system of corruption whereby the person who provided the job expects favors in return. The perception of corruption is strong in the region. When citizens in a 2002 Turkish survey assessed their confidence in local authorities at only 5.2 out of 10, the national government was moved to create a special ethics committee to investigate corruption, and three new laws[41] were passed to address the situation. But this requires a strong political will. It should also be noted that the countries that obtain the best scores regarding corruption are also those, such as Dubai, with the most visibly proactive state policies.

## IV.  Local Democracy

### IV.1.  A Changing Local Democracy

Table 2 summarizes significant advances in local democracy in the Middle East region. Note that if the local elections in some countries are based on specially devised election law, they are still in the process of development.

In Saudi Arabia, Prince Mansour Bin Mitab, a firm supporter and the main organizer of municipal elections, did not hesitate to describe them as the first stage, emphasizing that improvements are still needed, including women having the right to vote. As evidence of the newness of the election, the electoral districts themselves had to be drawn up after the registration of voters on electoral lists.

Jordan, since the first local elections in 1999, has been going backward and forward. The government went back on the nomination of mayors in 2003, but promised to hold new elections on the basis of universal suffrage before the beginning of 2007 – except in the city of Amman, which has special status. There were until now 360 appointed council members compared with 920 who are elected. The number of municipalities has been reduced from more than 300 to 99. With the new municipal law of 2007, all council members are elected, except in Amman. Indeed, the municipal elections took place on the 31st of July 2007; about 2,300 candidates ran for 1,022 seats.

In Lebanon, the election by universal suffrage of mayors and their senior deputies was abolished just before the 1998 elections by an amendment *in extremis* of election law. Mayors are now elected by the municipal council.

In the West Bank and Gaza, the voting method is not fixed. Since 2005, when municipal elections were conducted in five successive stages, there have been changes to the procedure, passing from voting for a single candidate to proportional representation. Moreover, the right to vote is not the same throughout the Palestinian territories. In the Gaza Strip, all refugees can vote, regardless of their place of residence; in the West Bank, refugees who live in the towns take part in the voting, but those who still live in the refugee camps indicate their wish to return to their homeland by unanimously keeping well away from local political life.

41. Law no. 3628 of 4 May 1990 amended by law no. 5020 of 26 December 2003, law no. 5237 of 26 September 2004 of the penal code.

| Table 2 | The Lack of a Democratic Tradition |
| --- | --- |

| Country/ territory | Date of the last local council elections | Date of the first election of a municipal council | Political parties |
| --- | --- | --- | --- |
| Saudi Arabia | 2005 | 1963 in Riyadh – but no elections between 1963 and 2005 (First election on a national scale) | No |
| Bahrain | 2006 | 1921 in some towns – but no elections between 1921 and 2002 (First election on a national scale) | No |
| United Arab Emirates | No elections | No elections | No |
| Iraq | 2004 (Dhi Qar province) 2000 & 2001 (Kurdistan)* 1999 (Rest of Iraq) | 1869 – but no elections between 1957 and 1999* | Yes |
| Iran Islamic Rep. | 2006 | 1999 | Yes |
| Jordan | 2003 | 1878[42] – but no elections between 1957 and 1989 | Yes (since 1992) |
| Kuwait | 2006 (partial) | 1932 | No |
| Lebanon | 2004 | 1878 – but no elections between 1963** and 1998 (2001 for the villages in the south) | Yes |
| Oman | No elections | No municipalities | No |
| Qatar | 2003 | 1999 | No |
| Syria | 2003*** | 1878 – but no free elections between 1972 and 2007*** | Yes |
| Turkey | 2004 | 1856 (for Istanbul); 1878 (for Ottoman Empire); 1930 (for the Republic of Turkey) | Yes |
| West Bank and Gaza | 2005 | 1927 No elections between 1934 (Gaza Strip) or 1976 (West Bank) and 2005 | Yes |
| Yemen | 2006 | 2001 | Yes |

42. This refers to municipal elections held in certain municipalities of the Ottoman Empire in 1878 in accordance with the Law on Municipalities in the Provinces of 18 May 1877.

\* February 2000 for the areas dominated by the Kurdish Patriotic Union and May 2001 for those areas under the control of the Kurdish Democratic Party.
\*\* First significant municipal elections carried out on a national scale.
\*\*\* That is to say without a closed list.

Syria, where the municipal councillors have long been elected by universal suffrage, now wants to move toward real pluralist local democracy. The 2007 reform law stipulates that people may elect the candidates of their choice, and not, as has been the case so far, just one from a list drawn up by the National Progressive Front –a coalition led by the Baath party currently in power.

## IV.2. Partially Kept Promises: The Central State and Local Politics

The only two states in the region where there is absolute centralization are the United Arab Emirates and Oman. There are no elections in these two states, though the possibility of introducing elections is being considered on an official level.

Municipal elections have been established in all the other countries. For all that, secular traditions, which are more based on the voluntary 'consultation' by the sovereign than on the sovereignty of the people, are not easy to circumvent. The electoral process in many places is still marked by central government intervention.

### a) *A priori* state intervention

*Nominations.* The clearest and most official type of intervention is, of course, the nomination of all or part of a municipal council, including mayors. This is presently the case in Saudi Arabia, Jordan, Bahrain, and Kuwait.

In Syria, as we have seen, it is the existence of an 'executive council' or 'executive bureau' parallel to the municipal council which embodies this central control.

*Prior examination of the candidates.* Another form of interference is the prior examination of the candidates by the central power. This permits the central government to effectively steer the election in a particular direction. It is this process that caused the extraordinary length (from February to mid-December) of the 2005 elections in Saudi Arabia. In Islamic

Republic of Iran, candidates are accepted only after an examination validates the intensity of their faith, or their belief in the authority of a jurisconsult, the *Velâyat-é-Faghih* – a situation which continues to arouse strong suspicion. In Syria, according to the present law, the party in power compiles the list of candidates.

*Election into office.* This type of election limits the number of candidates to the number of vacant posts, ensuring that all candidates will attain public office. Seen as a cost-saving measure, it is reserved for unusual circumstances. When, on the other hand, it is the result of pre-electoral bargaining, it can be detrimental to the exercise of socially aware democratic principles.

Pre-election arrangements influenced Lebanon's most recent elections; 121 municipal councils and 400 *mokhtar* were elected into office following an alliance between the political parties and traditional leaders; in effect, the two factions merged. In Jordan, a similar approach was observed in 17 municipalities.

### b) *A posteriori* intervention

*The modification of municipal councils.* In Jordan in 1999, the king changed the composition of municipal councils to include a woman in each of them – a rather positive action. By contrast, in Kuwait in 1986, the Emir simply dissolved all the municipal councils.

In Syria, once the local councils are elected, they in their turn elect an executive bureau; a third of the executive bureau candidates can be recruited from the local councils themselves. Furthermore, after an election, certain specific public service-related issues can be placed in the hands of permanent or temporary committees that include people from outside the municipal government.

*Intervention in the election of the mayor.* This form of tutelage of the State is harmful to democracy and to good governance. In Lebanon, the abandonment of direct elections has contributed to this tutelage.

### IV.3. The People's Participation

The 2005 Palestinian elections were the first in 71 years in the Gaza Strip, and the first elections in 29 years in the West Bank. Voter turnout was extraordinary: average turnout was 82% and rose to 98% in certain areas. The elections were widely perceived as the restoration of the right of the Palestinian people to self-determination after years of the systematic destruction of their state structures.

In Turkey also, the turnout percentage is generally quite strong, proof of the population's involvement in local life. In 2004, average voter turnout reached 72.3%.

In the rest of the region, voter turnout is much lower. There are two main reasons for this. The first is the widespread perception that the game is corrupt. The second, which must not be underestimated, is public disappointment with most of its elected officials. When dishonesty is expected, whether by pre-election selection of candidates with reserved seats — the case in Saudi Arabia and Syria — or by manipulation of election results or even election law, turnout is apt to decline. Allegations of corruption were particularly strident in Yemen after the last election there; the Shiites of Saudi Arabia, and most Lebanese elected officials are widely suspected of cheating. In Lebanon, however, low overall turnout figures (33.3%) can mask wide disparities in local turnout, depending upon what is at stake or the extent of candidates' mobilization. Thus, the low figure of a 21.4% turnout in Beirut contrasts starkly with the 70% turnout in the Bekaa, and the 65% turnout in Nabatiah; in both high-turnout areas, the main beneficiary of the surge in participation was Hezbollah. The second reason, voter

disappointment with the outcome of previous ballots, or the subsequent ineffectiveness of elected officials, does take a toll. Disillusionment with elected officials and the process by which they come to power has been noted especially in Jordan and Islamic Republic of Iran.

However, voter disinterest can vanish when the vote is perceived as an expression of popular demand or a form of approbation. The 2006 municipal elections in Bahrain thus had a turnout — a clear increase — of 72% because of the involvement of the Shiites. Similar elections in Islamic Republic of Iran saw a 60% turnout because of immense discontent with the policies of President Ahmadinejad.

### IV.4.  A Specific Problem:
### The Representation of Women

*A low representation.* Unsurprisingly, in its 2005 report Transparency International severely criticizes the Middle East as being the region of the world where the political representation and participation of women is the lowest[43].

Turkish women were given the right to vote in 1930, and since 1934 the right to be elected[44]. Saudi women, on the other hand, will only be given the right to vote in 2009, whereas nothing of the kind is planned in the Emirates. Kuwaiti women obtained the right to vote in 2005.

Elsewhere, their representation figures are derisory, hardly reaching 2% of the municipal councils in Lebanon, 1.53% in Islamic Republic of Iran, 3.4% in Qatar, 6.6 % in Syria, and an unabashed 0% in Bahrain.

In most of these countries, entering the political arena requires strong-willed women at a time when merely working outside the home is still discouraged. Women who want to take part in politics often face extremely difficult social factors, such as family opposition and public disapproval. Some allege that women also must over-

43. www.transparency.org.
44. The right to vote was given to women in 1948 in Syria, in 1952 in Lebanon, in 1963 in Islamic Republic of Iran, in 1967 in Yemen, in 1973 in Bahrain, in 1974 in Jordan, and in 1980 in Iraq.

come the reluctance of party managers to accept women, but in all fairness, such male intransigence is hardly unique to the Middle East.

*Steps towards the participation of women.* Faced with a glaring lack of female representation in local and national political life, several strategies have been put in place. The quota system, which is applied in Palestine, reserves a minimum of two seats per council for women[45]. Jordan and Kuwait have chosen the direct nomination of one woman per council. At the same time, important campaigns in favor of women have been launched in Jordan and Syria.

Thus, municipal councils throughout the region face enormous difficulties, leading, in some instances, to their resignation, as in Jordan; in other countries, an even larger number of councils have renounced any form of concrete action.

## IV.5. Local Elections as an Ideological and Community Platform

If it is necessary and healthy that a country's political life should rest on nationally constituted parties, it is not desirable that national issues override local concerns. Municipal elections are, after all, intended to create an efficient local authority management.

Lebanon provides an illustrative example. Although the number of national parties is negligible, elections are well and truly fought on religious community issues which are national in scope.

A curious development is the way in which local elections can become a forum for banned national parties or factions. Because local elections are considered less of a threat to the central government, they may not be as tightly controlled as national elections. Local elections therefore present an opportunity for disapproved or illegal parties and

ideologies to appear on the ballot, overwhelming local issues with far more potent national matters. Such was the case in the West Bank and Gaza when Hamas triumphed, and in Saudi Arabia when Shiites of the Eastern Province boasted of having won the election in their regional stronghold. Similarly, the victory of Hezbollah in South Lebanon used local elections to effect a national change, and in Islamic Republic of Iran the 2003 municipal elections in Tehran led to the return of the conservatives, and particularly of President Ahmadinejad, the city's mayor. Ironically, the 2006 municipal elections rejected his policies throughout the country, with the population going to the polls on a massive scale in order to vote for the opposition. This was also the situation in Bahrain, which was the scene of a very strong Shiite upsurge in November 2006.

## IV.6. The Role of the Security Factor and the Delicate Situation of the Governments

*The religious community issue.* Many countries are currently the scene of deep-seated tensions, some attributable to the merging of religion and politics, others to centuries-old feuds between Islam's Shiite and Sunni communities. The latter is especially important where the Sunni have held power for a long time in spite of the presence of a strong Shiite minority, or indeed a majority, as in Lebanon, Iraq, and Bahrain. Saudi Arabia's government contends with a Shiite community that could deliver a 20% turnout – not the 5-15% which is generally reported. The central government there exercised strong control during the election in the Eastern Province where the Shiites are a clear majority, and where, it is useful to note, there are important oil-fields. Likewise, the King of Bahrain faces the risk of destabilization by the Shiite majority there, as the results of the recent parliamentary elections showed.

45. There are 15 seats in the cities, 13 in medium-sized towns and 8 in small towns according to the electoral law of 1996, amended in 2005.

The risk of destabilization is real. This is why the Lebanese and Iranian governments (the Persians in Islamic Republic of Iran are only in a majority of 51%) exercise such strong control over local governance.

*Kurdish nationalism.* The recognition of Kurdistan by the transitional Iraqi government, and the granting of extensive autonomy which even includes legislation, gave hope to the Kurdish communities in neighboring Syria and Turkey. It is clear that municipal elections provide a convenient means for Kurdish people in those two countries to agitate for a degree of autonomy comparable to that granted in Iraq.

*Religious extremism.* The other factor which must not be neglected is the rise of hard-line religious extremism. Such religious fanaticism characterizes several factions of fundamentalist Islam. Their avowed goal is to establish regimes based on a particularly narrow reading of religious texts. These groups are not only opposed to secular governments, but also to those that, like Saudi Arabia and Jordan, are already governed by the Sharia. Even these officially Islamic states are perceived by fundamentalists as being too inclined toward westernization. Some fundamentalists in Saudi Arabia refuse to vote in legislative elections because, they say, "God is the only dispenser of law."

# V. Conclusion

What emerges from this study is that decentralization, understood as the devolution of responsibilities, and financial and decision-making self-government, is not yet completely operational in the countries of the region, with the exception of Turkey. Currently, the majority of municipalities have little room for maneuver, subject as they are to a twofold dependency – formal and informal - on the State and traditional leaders.

At the same time, one should take into account the social organization and security environment of the region. Limited progress in the processes of decentralization should be considered in the overall context of tensions and conflicts, in the relations between traditional leaders, either tribal or religious-based, as well as in relation to the population at large.

All these factors help explain UNDP-POGAR's[46] more prudent approach to change that advocates a gradual pace of reform as part of a comprehensive strategy of restructuring of the State, beginning with the strengthening of national legislatures. Broad awareness campaigns on local governance and effective institutions are also key.

Problems in service delivery and weak local management functions in general need to be addressed, as underlined by UNDP POGAR, through the development and strengthening of local capacities as well as of transparency.

The success of decentralization efforts depends on the selection and training of municipal civil servants and employees. That requires special focus and attention.

Local governments should be equipped with the adequate means to carry out their tasks i.e. the necessary fiscal and budgetary resources accompanied by the transfer of independent decision-making authority.

Finally, although many countries in the region are on the right track towards decentralization, it will take some time before these processes become fully operational.

46. See:
www.pogar.org/
governance/
localgov.asp.

| Annex 1 | Great Metropolises of the Region |
|---------|----------------------------------|

| Country/ territory | Number of large cities (more than 1 M. inhabitants) | Total population of the three largest cities, 2006 (in M. inhabitants) | % population of the country in 2006 | % population of the country in 2005 (1) | Increase of total country population 2005-2006 (in %) | Existence of a municipal specific structure in the three largest cities | Municipal organization |
|---|---|---|---|---|---|---|---|
| Iraq | 3 | 10,83 | 37% | N/A | 2,8% | No | One single municipality and councils as advisors in Baghdad and Basra districts |
| Iran, Islamic Rep. | 7 | 17,27 | 25% | 23% | 0,0% | No | One single municipality with a main municipality and many councils and district municipalities under the first level |
| Jordan | 1 | 1,9 | 34% | 24% | 1,8% | No, but possible reform for the large cities | Amman has a metropolitan structure |
| Kuwait | 1 | 2,02 | 72% | 71% | 3,7% | No | Only one municipal council |
| Lebanon | 1 | 1,97 | 55% | 50% | 0,8% | No | One single municipality, but for security reasons the 'Prefect' has the power |
| Saudi Arabia | 4 | 10,86 | 43% | 36% | 2,4% | No | a) One municipality which supervises many municipalities of district on administrative matters only (Riyadh and Jeddah) b) one single municipality (Mecca and Damman) |
| Syria | 2 | 4,87 | 25% | 25% | 2,6% | No | One single municipality with the administration in the districts |
| Turkey | 6 | 22,01 | 30% | 26% | 1,4% | Yes | Metropolitan municipalities and others of first level |
| United Arab Emirates | 1 | 1,42 | 30% | 29% | 4,4% | No | Unique structure : Dubai is managed as an enterprise under a 'General Director' |
| West Bank and Gaza | 1 | 1,43 | 38% | 25% | 5,6% | No | One single municipality |
| Yemen | 1 | 1,92 | 9% | 9% | 2,9% | No | Special status for the Sana governorate |
| Total | 28 | 77,14 | 37 % | 10,6% | 2,56% | | |

*Source:* World Bank Indicators.

## Annex 2 — Local Democracy

| Country/ territory | Municipal councils | | | | Executive local authority | | | | | |
|---|---|---|---|---|---|---|---|---|---|---|
| | Form of scrutiny (proportional/ majority) | One or several electoral districts | Number of periods and duration of the terms | Participation estimates | Mayor elected by vote | Mayor elected by the municipal council | Mayor appointed by a superior authority | Power in hands of the Mayor or in a collegiate body | Number of periods and duration of the terms | Indictment by the citizens or by the municipal council |
| **Bahrain** | Majority | Several | 4 years | 72% for 2006 (increasing) 51,3% for 2002 | No | No | Yes (Ministry MHHE) [3] | Ministry MHME | 4 years | No |
| **Iraq** [5] | Variable | Var. | Var. | 79% in Kurdistan in 2001 | Var. | Var. | Var. | Var. | Var. | Var. |
| **Iran, Islamic Rep.** | Relative majority | Unique | 4 years | 60% 2006 (increasing) 49.96% 2003 | No | Yes [6] | No | Mayor | 4 years | Yes by the Municipal Council [7] |
| **Jordan** | Majority | Several | 4 years | 58% in 2003 (decreasing) | No | No | Yes [8] | Municipal council | 4 years | No |
| **Kuwait** [9] | Majority | Several | 4 years | 50% (decreasing) | No | No | No | Mayor | 4 years | No |
| **Lebanon** | Majority | Unique | 6 years (unlimited) | 33,3% in 2004 (decreasing) | No | Yes | No | Mayor (in Beirut the governor) | 6 years unlimited [10] | Yes, by the Municipal Council after 3 years |
| **Oman** | NA | NA | NA | NA | NA | NA | NA | NA | NA | NA |
| **Qatar** [14] | Majority (at first round) | Several | 4 years | 30% in 2003 (decreasing) | No | Yes | No | MMAA | 4 years | No [15] |
| **Saudi Arabia** | Majority | Several | 4 years [1] | 40% in 2005 [2] | No | No | Yes (The King) | Mayor | 4 years | No |
| **Syria** [16] | (List of candidates with fixed seats) | Unique except Damasc and Alep | 4 years | 29,3% in 2003 (decreasing) [17] | No | No [18] | Yes, Ministry of Municipal Affairs | Municipal Council [19] | 4 years | No |
| **Turkey** | Proportional | Unique | 5 years | 71,75 % mayors 69.97% metropolitan mayors (65% in 2004) | Yes (relative majority, one round) | No | No [20] | Mayor | 5 years | Evaluation every year by less than 3/4 of councils or motion of indictment by 3/4 |
| **United Arab Emirates** | . | . | . | . | . | [4] | . | . | . | . |
| **West Bank and Gaza** | Proportional [11] | Several | 5 years | 82 % in 2005 | No | Yes | No [12] | Yes | 5 years | Yes by the Municipal Council (by offence) [13] |
| **Yemen** | Majority | Unique | 5 years | 65% | No | No | Yes by Ministry of local administration [21] | Mayor | 5 years | No |

NOTES

1. Only half of the councils are elected, the rest are appointed.
2. About 18% of the potential voters, one third of them is registered in the electoral lists.
3. Ministry of Housing, Municipalities and Environment. General Director.
4. A Sharjah only, but the Municipal Council itself is not elected.
5. There are several situations: Municipal Councils chosen among the Ministry of Municipalities and Public Works employees (MMPW) Basra; elected by universal vote, Baghdad; chosen by a group of important citizens, Mosul.
6. Accumulation of jobs is forbidden for Minister, Vice minister, Congress Deputy and Director of Bank or Director of other public entity.
7. Article 73 of the Municipal Council Law. The Council can accuse the Mayor who has to present his arguments in 10 days. The Council then decides if he is removed or not.
8. Ministry of Municipal, Rural and Environment Affairs.
9. In each Council 10 members are elected and 6 are appointed.
10. The election of the Mayor and that of the Mokhars take place together.
11. The number 5 Law of 1996 for the councils' election was amended in 2004 and twice in 2005. From majority, the scrutiny became proportional.
12. From 1976 to 1993 a great proportion of the Mayors were appointed by Israel.
13. But the destitution has to be approved by the local Interior Ministry.
14. There is only one Municipal Council for all the country
15. Only by decision of the Minister of Municipal and Rural Affairs.
16. But a new more liberal law will be passed in 2007.
17. 21% in cities, 34% in small towns and 33% in very small villages, while 66% in 1999.
18. It should be done according to the new law
19. It is in fact a council of the city.
20. But the Executive Council has elected and appointed members.
21. The government has to approve it.

# North America
## (Canada and the United States)

Jefferey Sellers

# I.  Introduction

This chapter compares local government and decentralization in Canada and the United States. These two North American countries share important, parallel inheritances. Both are settler societies that emerged out of British colonialization. The similarities in their local government systems have frequently led to their classification together (Hesse and Sharpe 1991; Sellers 2006, 2007), and with other countries with similar legacies such as Australia and New Zealand.

Both countries are established constitutional democracies with federal structures of government. Both possess highly developed economies and have in common legal, institutional and cultural legacies from British colonization from the seventeenth to the nineteenth centuries. Other colonial and pre-colonial legacies also mark the practice of local government in certain areas of each country. Most notably, French influences have been strong in the Canadian province of Québec, and have also affected aspects of institutional practice in Louisiana in the U.S. In parts of each country, indigenous traditions remain important to local government practice.

Local government in both countries was established in the original British colonies prior to the creation of a national government. The arrangements for local government in what would become New England in the United States grew directly from those in early colonial settlements. In Canada, provincial acts of the 1840s and 1850s established the framework of local government prior to the Constitution Act of 1867.

Although present-day local government in these countries can possess considerable powers, it lacks either national constitutional protections or a legislated grant of autonomy. What powers local governments have received have come from either national legislation or measures taken by individual states or provinces. In both federal countries local government is a creature of federal states, provinces, or territories. In Canada and a number of U.S. states, state legislatures determine the content and powers of local government. The main exceptions are provisions in some U.S. state constitutions for local government powers. In the United States, approximately half of these documents specify some general power for local governments.

Institutional practice in these countries also reflects the legacies of the British ultra vires principal that limits the general purpose authority of local governments. The "Dillon Rule" in the United States –the principle that local governments cannot claim powers beyond those specifically granted by the state legislatures—provides a good example. Thirty-one of the fifty U.S. states continue to apply Dillon's Rule to all municipalities, and eight further states apply it to some but not all types of municipalities (Richardson, Gough and Puentes 2003: 17). Increasingly, however, exceptions to this principle have been introduced. Beginning in the nineteenth century, U.S. states legislated guarantees of general local government authority in "home rule" legislation as well as in state constitutions. This trend continued up to the 1990s. As a result, local government in all but three states has some degree of home-rule powers, and 28 U.S. states have broad powers that in some cases amount to grants of full local autonomy to treat local affairs (USACIR 1993). In Canada, in 1994 in Alberta, in 1999 in British Columbia and, since 2000 in Ontario and Québec have also given broader powers to localities, even as larger cities continue to call for additional institutionalized local powers.

These variations reflect another way that local government in the United States, and to a lesser degree Canada, differs from that of many other countries. Because dif-

*Institutional practice in these countries also reflects the legacies of the British ultra vires principal that limits the general purpose authority of local governments*

ferent U.S. states have established a variety of legislative frameworks, there are some fifty American local government systems. Even within states, the diversity of local arrangements has produced more heterogeneous systems of local institutions than elsewhere. Most of the largest cities in the United States, as well as Montreal, Winnipeg, Vancouver and Saint John in Canada, have individual charters from their respective state or provincial governments.

*The evolution of local government structures in Canada and the United States needs to be understood in relation to the distinctive model of local decentralization that has long prevailed in these countries*

Expansion of local powers has been only one of several local government reforms. Along with enhanced local powers, legislation in both countries has articulated local responsibilities in greater detail, and has specified mechanisms for accountability in a variety of specific functional domains, such as local educational services, environmental regulation, and planning. In the United States but much less frequently in Canada, privatization has emerged as a more recurrent strategy in service delivery. In various ways, local governments have also evolved practices to address the growing horizontal interconnectedness of localities and regions. In Canada these reforms have often taken the form of inter-governmental consolidation or metropolitan governance; in the United States, informal inter-local cooperation and special district governance have proliferated.

In both countries, state or provincial governments as well as local governments themselves, have been the sources of reforms. The extent of recent reform generally has fallen short of the comprehensive reforms passed in New Zealand or parallel reforms in Australia. But local governments in Canada and the United States already possessed many of the powers recently given to local governments in the two Australasian nations.

## II. Local Government Structures and Their Evolution

The evolution of local government structures in Canada and the United States needs to be understood in relation to the distinctive model of local decentralization that has long prevailed in these countries. On the one hand, the national and other higher level governments have generally granted local governments limited legal authority compared with that permitted in continental European countries, and less financial support from above. On the other hand, local governments are also less subject to the direct local supervision of territorial field offices or prefectures, and enjoy high levels of local fiscal autonomy compared with counterparts in Europe and Asia (Sellers 2006; Sellers and Lidström 2007). In recent years, the elaboration of policymaking in North America, both at local and higher levels, has changed this model in several functional areas. Higher level governments have introduced new responsibilities in many of these areas. Although this trend can be seen as a move toward centralization in one sense, new activities and often new powers and fiscal resources for local governments have often accompanied it.

Local government takes a variety of forms, with a different nomenclature in each country (Table 1). In the United States, local government in many states has at least two traditional tiers of government: counties and towns. Counties play an important role in every state outside of New England as major providers of general services like courts, jails, land records, welfare, health, and roads. A number of eastern and Midwestern U.S. states have also maintained an intermediate level of town or township governments between counties and municipalities. The legal status of the town level varies considerably according to state laws. In Canada counties and their equivalents generally have less power and are only present in some provinces, but the types of municipalities

| Table 1 | Governmental and Country Characteristics |
|---------|-------------------------------------------|

| Name | Canada | United States |
|------|--------|---------------|
| Inhabitants (thousands) | 31,362 | 288,205 |
| Area (km2) | 9,984,670 | 9,631,420 |
| Inhabitants/km2 | 3 | 30 |
| GDP/capita | € 35,758 | € 42,623 |
| National | Federal Government | Federal Government |
| Intermediate | Provinces (10), Territories (3) | States (50) |
| Local: | | |
| Upper Tier: | Counties, Regions, Districts (199) | Counties (3,034), consolidated Cities |
| Lower Tier: | Cities, Towns, Villages, Townships (3731) | Townships/towns (some states) (16,504) Municipalities (Cities, Boroughs, Villages) (19,429) Special Districts (48,558) |

**Note:** *Population and GDP data for 2002; Area (land and water) for 2006; Canada (Upper tier), United States), 2006 (Canada (lower tier).*

**Sources:** *(area) CIA World Factbook (retrieved December 10, 2006 at https://www.cia.gov/cia/publications/factbook/geos/us.html); (population and GDP) OECD Statistics Portal (retrieved December 10, 2006 at http://www.oecd.org/statsportal/0,2639,en_2825_293564_1_1_1_1_1,00.html); (governments) Rivard and Collin 2006, p. 5; Commonwealth Local Government Forum 2002a, p. 2; Commonwealth Local Government Forum 2002b, p. 3; U.S. Census Bureau (2002), p. 3.*

vary widely. Single-tier local governments predominate in all but three provinces of Canada, Ontario, Québec, and British Columbia.

**Local government consolidation and inter-local governance.** Recent trends toward new regional arrangements or local government consolidation in much of Europe have had mixed resonance in North America. Part of the reason for this may be the roles that established governmental units –Canadian provinces and territories, U.S. states, and U.S. counties and town-

ships– have played in providing regional and inter-local governance. Especially in the United States, informal and specialized inter-governmental arrangements have often taken the place of formal and general-purpose institutions.

In Canada, consolidation of local government units took place in Québec, Nova Scotia, Ontario and a number of metropolitan regions since 2000 (Rivard and Collin 2006). More recent initiatives have rolled back some of these reforms in Québec and elsewhere. In the United States, the degree of consolidation has always varied widely by regions. In recent decades consolidation and annexation of territory by local governments have been commonplace in faster growing areas of the South and West, but have remained more limited or exceptional in the Northeast and other areas of older settlement. On the whole, recent counter-trends toward creation of new municipalities have offset counter-trends toward consolidation. From 1992 to 2002, the number of municipal governments increased by 150 to 16,504 (U.S. Bureau of the Census 1992, 2002).

*Much more than in Canada and other countries, inter-local governance in the United States has taken place through separate, special-purpose district governments that are independent of local governments*

Local government consolidation has been only one of several types of arrangements that could foster inter-local governance within metropolitan regions. An upper tier of local government or a new form of functional cooperation among municipalities may also provide mechanisms for this task. Practical moves in this direction over the past decade have taken a variety of forms.

Canadian provinces and municipalities have undertaken some of the most far-reaching reforms in metropolitan governance. Mainly in eastern Canada, reorganizations in most metropolitan areas have produced more encompassing metropolitan units of governance. Alongside the consolidations of municipalities, regional bodies have been formed in three provinces, and metropolitan planning initiatives have taken place in a number of the largest metropolitan areas (Rivard and Collin).

Such a move is less apparent in the United States. Only a few of the large metropolitan areas, such as Portland, Oregon, and Minneapolis-St. Paul in Minnesota, have

developed distinct metropolitan institutions. County governments like King County in metropolitan Seattle, Washington, and Pima County in metropolitan Phoenix, Arizona, have encompassed large portions of the metropolitan area, and have often addressed issues on a metropolitan scale. In a few small-to-mid-sized metropolitan areas, such as Jacksonville, Florida, and Sacramento, California, consolidation of city government into county government has created what amounts to a metropolitan government (Leland and Thurmaier 2004). Advisory regional councils of governments, a legacy of federal requirements for transportation planning, frequently provide a basis for coordination of planning issues. Most states also authorize cooperation among local governments (Richardson, Gough and Puentes 2003).

Much more than in Canada and other countries, inter-local governance in the United States has taken place through separate, special-purpose district governments that are independent of local governments. The largest number of these (13,506 in 2002) administered separate public school systems across the country. Others deal with water and sewers, hospital services or transportation. Although the total number of these districts (48,588), as counted by the U.S. Census of Governments, exceeds the number of traditional local governments (35,933), the actual number of specialty, inter-local districts is probably higher. The number of school districts declined slightly (900) from 1992 to 2002, typically due to consolidation among municipalities within metropolitan areas. But the number of other special districts increased by 3,500 over the same period. In Canada too, most primary and secondary education is administered by school boards independent of local government, and a number of agencies, boards, and commissions see to special functions jointly shared among municipalities. Unlike their U.S. counterparts, however, these boards do not have independent powers of taxation.

Decentralization has attracted the most critical attention in the United States where both local government powers and local geo-political fragmentation have remained extensive. Patterns of local governance there have been found to exacerbate inequalities among de facto segregated groups by means of inequalities in local services (Joassert-Marcelli, Musso and Wolch 2001; Blakely 2000). In particular, inequalities in educational opportunities in the United States have generated widespread debate and many reform initiatives.

The wider effects of regional integration between North American countries for local governance are difficult to discern, and less pronounced than the consequences of cross-border integration across Europe. The most notable impact has occurred in the cross-border regions of Cascadia in the Pacific Northwest mainly between the provincial and state governments (e.g., Blatter 2001).

## III. Functions, Management and Finance

### III.1. Finance

In terms of its place in public expenditures, public finance and functions, local government in Canada and the U.S., occupies an average place within the spectrum of developed countries. In the

---

**Table 2**  Financial Management

|  | Australia | Canada | New Zealand | United States |
|---|---|---|---|---|
| Total Public Expenditure (% of GDP) | 37% | 42% | 42% | 35% |
| (per capita) (Euros) | € 11,486.56 | € 13,717.90 | € 9,692.57 | € 14,507.04 |
| Local Public Expenditure (% of GDP) | 2.4% | 7.5% | 3.9% | 9.6% |
| (per capita) (Euros) | € 275.68 | € 1,031.16 | € 380.50 | € 1,386.30 |
| Local/Total Public Expenditure (%) | 6.6% | 17.8% | 9.4% | 27.4% |
| Local/Total Public Investment (%) | 6% | NA | 16% | 8% |
| Local Revenues: | | | | |
| Local taxes (% of local revenues) | 38% | 41% | 58% | 38% |
| Property tax (% of local taxes) | 100% | 92% | 91% | 72% |
| Local tax autonomy (0 (high) - 2 (low)) | 0.34 | 0.12 | 0.43 | 0.82 |
| Grants (% of local revenues) | 16% | 40% | 10% | 39% |

**Sources:** *(Public expenditure) OECD in Figures 2005; (Local expenditure) IMF Government Finance Statistics (Australia, Canada, US: 2001, New Zealand: 2003); (Local Revenues, Taxes and Grants) IMF Government Finance Statistics (Australia, Canada: 2001; US: 2000; New Zealand: 2003): (Local tax autonomy, Supervision of borrowing) Sellers and Lidström 2007, Table 4; (public investment) U.S. Bureau of the Census, 2005 Statistical Abstract of U.S. Section 9; Compendium of Government Finances: 2002 Table 1; (Australia and New Zealand) Brilliantes et al. 2007, Table 4.*

United States, the role of local government has generally been more pronounced, but in Canada that role still exceeds local government powers in other countries with similar British colonial legacies, including Australia and New Zealand. The relative discretion that North American local governments exercise over their own finances, and the modest supervision by higher government officials also set local government in both countries apart from most of their counterparts worldwide, including in Europe and East Asia.

*In both countries local governments have in recent years found themselves less reliant on grants from higher level governments for local revenues*

**Expenditures.** Overall, the proportion of Gross Domestic Product (GDP) devoted to governmental expenditure in Canada and the U.S., remains somewhat lower than the average for the OECD (Table 2). The local government portion of this expenditure, though it varies considerably, also remains below levels reported for Northern Europe. In Canada and the United States, 18% and 27%, respectively, of public expenditure was distributed to local governments. The bulk of these distributions is spent on education. Education consumes 57% of all local expenditure in the United States, and 40% in Canada. Security services such as police and fire represent about eight percent of local expenditures in the United States, nine percent in Canada. In both countries, local public expenditures as a percentage of the total public expenditure have also crept upward slightly in recent years.

**Revenues.** Locally raised revenue pays for most educational and security expenditures. As in other former British colonies, such as Australia and New Zealand, the property tax remains by far the most important source of local government revenue. In Canada, it has generated 80% to 90% of all local tax revenues. In the United States, partly in the wake of tax-

payer resistance in some states, other local taxes, such as sales taxes, income taxes and user fees grew from 22% of local tax revenues in 1975 to 28% in 1999. Even so, the property tax has continued to supply 72% of local tax revenues (OECD 2001).

A distinguishing feature of the property taxes, as well as most other local taxes in these countries is the comparatively large degree of discretion local authorities possess in setting rates and in assessing property. Ratings of local tax autonomy consistently show this discretion to be high compared with that seen in other countries. In the United States, the laws of some individual states restrict local initiatives to raise taxes or change assessments by requiring prior approval by local voters. In Canada, setting these rates is almost always left to the discretion of local government but subject to control by the provinces.

In both countries local governments have in recent years found themselves less reliant on grants from higher level governments for local revenues. In the United States and Canada, state or provincial grants for education and other services remain considerable but modest by comparison with many other OECD countries. The current 39 percent of total revenues in the U.S. represents a decline from levels of up to 45 percent in the late 1970s, but has fluctuated over the 1990s and early 2000s. The current 40 percent in Canada represents a decline from levels as high as 50 percent in the late 1970s, down 2 or 3% from levels in the 1980s (OECD 2001).

**Revenues in relation to tasks.** Despite dwindling access to funds from above, as well as local opposition to tax increases, local governments in Canada and the United States have assumed more responsibilities. Additional areas of responsibility that are increasingly being delegated to local governments include: environmental regulation, planning, transportation, public health, immigration, education, emergency preparedness and security. Even so, the fiscal autonomy of local government in these countries makes local governments especially vulnerable to unfunded mandates. Higher-level governments sometimes contribute funds for these added tasks through legislation and new policies. But higher-ups can impose such tasks without contributing funds, leaving local governments to cope as best they can.

In Canada, the Federation of Canadian Municipalities has noted an increase in the delegation of responsibilities to municipalities. Although the local government portion of expenditures remained stable relative to the provincial level from 1990 to 2000 – increasing in some provinces but declining in others (Diaz 2003) – local revenues as a percentage of the whole have decreased. In the United States, despite the federal Unfunded Mandates Act of 1995, the federal government has imposed such measures as the No Child Left Behind Act of 2002, which gave state governments incentives to administer regular tests as measures of performance for public schools. The resulting programs in many states gave rise to accusations that the Act really just forced school districts to abandon more worthwhile

programs in order to provide resources for the new standardized tests.

**Local government borrowing.** In the face of such pressures, there have been shifts in restrictions on local borrowing. This practice has been most widespread in the United States (Sbragia 1988). Although often conditioned upon local voter approval, borrowing by local governments is subject to approval by a higher level government in only one state. In Canada, local borrowing sometimes generally requires approval by a provincial board, and has been more limited. In both North American countries, local governments have also turned to user fees and other charges to supplement revenues.

### III.2. Functions

The limited role of local government in the overall public expenditure and revenue of these countries reflects limits in the functions that local government has assumed. With the exceptions of local education and public safety, local governments continue to play a subsidiary role to central and intermediate level governments in the broad run of public policies (Table 3). In recent

| Table 3 | Local Government Functions |

| Functions | Australia | Canada | New Zealand | United States |
|---|---|---|---|---|
| **Planning** | | | | |
| Housing | State, Local | Province, Local (DS) | Central, Territorial (DS) | Federal, Local (DS) |
| Town planning | Local | Province (DS), Local | Regional | Local |
| Agriculture land planning | State | Province, Local (DS) | Local | State (DS), Local (DS) |
| Regional planning | Local | | Regional | State (DS), Local (DS) |
| **Education** | | | | |
| Pre-school | State | Province | Central | Local (DS) |
| Primary | State | Province | Central | Local |
| Secondary | State | Province | Central | Local |
| Vocational and technical | State | Province | Central | State, Local |
| Higher education | Federal, State | Federal | Central | State |

| Table 3 | Local Government Functions (Continued) |
| --- | --- |

| | | | | |
| --- | --- | --- | --- | --- |
| Adult education | State | Province | Central | State, Local |
| Other | State | | Central | |
| **Provision of social services** | | | | |
| Kindergarten and nursery | State | Province | Central | State, Local (DS) |
| Family welfare services | State | Province | Central | Federal, State, Local |
| Welfare homes | State, Local (DS) | Province, Local (DS) | Central | |
| Social security | Federal | Province | Central | Federal |
| Others | | | Territorial (DS) | |
| **Provision of health services** | | | | |
| Primary care | Federal | Province | Central | (Private) |
| Hospital | State | Province | Central | Federal, Local (DS) |
| Health protection | Federal, State, Local | Federal, Province | Central, Territorial | Federal, State, Local (DS) |
| Mental hospital | State | Province | Central | State |
| **Water supply** | | | | |
| Water and sanitation | State, Local | Local | Territorial | Local (DS) |
| Water supply | State, Local (DS) | Province, Local | Territorial | Local (DS) |
| **Energy supply** | | | | |
| Gas services | State | Province | Central, Regional | Local (DS) |
| Electricity | State | Province | Territorial (DS) | Local (DS) |
| **Public transport** | | | | |
| Roads | State | Local | Central, Territorial | Federal |
| Transport | State | Local | Central, Regional, Territorial | State, Local |
| Urban roads | State, Local | Local | Territorial | State, Local |
| Urban public transport | Local | Local | Territorial | State, Local (DS) |
| Ports | State | Federal, Province, Local | Territorial (DS) | Local (DS) |
| Airports | State | Federal, Province, Local | Central(DS), Territorial(DS) | Federal, Local (DS) |
| Other transportation | | | | Federal, Local (DS) |
| **Business development support** | | | | |
| Agriculture, forests, and fisheries | Federal, Province, Local (DS) | Federal, Province | Central, Territorial (DS) | Federal, State |
| Economic promotion | Federal, Province, Local (DS) | Province, Local | Central(DS), Territorial(DS) | State, Local (DS) |
| Trade and industry | Federal, Province, Local (DS) | Federal, Province | Central (DS) | Federal, State, Local (DS) |
| Tourism | Federal, Province, Local (DS) | Federal, Province, Local | Cen(DS), Reg(DS), Terr(DS) | State, Local (DS) |
| Other economic services | Federal, Province, Local (DS) | | Central(DS), Territorial(DS) | Local (DS) |
| **Security** | | | | |
| Police | State | Local (generally) | Central, Regional | Local |
| Fire | State | Province, Local | Regional, Local | Local |

**DS:**  *Discretionary Services by the local authority. For Australia, provinces includes territories.*

**Sources:**  *Commonwealth Local Government Forum (2002a, 2002b, 2002c); Stephens and Wikstrom. 2000, p. 156; supplemented by author's research on government websites.*

years, however, local governments have become more active in a wide range of policy domains in both countries, mirroring certain global trends. The most widespread trend has been toward the growth of multilevel governance as both local governments and higher-level governments assume new roles in areas where they were less active before.

**Local government functions.** Local governments in Canada and the United States take on certain functions that are unusual in most established democracies. The greater local expenditure in the North American nations stems largely from local government responsibilities in education and public safety. In the United States, individual states assign to local governments responsibility for primary, secondary and pre-school education, as well as for police and public safety. These traditional areas of local responsibility have become more complex in recent years, but have remained comparatively stable in recent decades.

Canadian provinces and U.S. states vary widely in their responses to other functions relegated to local government. Several provinces and states, for instance, have their own policies for land use and agricultural planning; others have set down specific mandates for local planners to follow. In most states and provinces, however, planning remains predominantly a local function. Provision of health and social services also varies. Some states and provinces have enacted legislation that gives localities more responsibility for welfare services, hospitals and other matters. Ontario, for instance, assigns localities authority for administering social security and kindergartens; other provinces do not.

Environmental services, planning, building permits, land use, sanitation, and refuse collection usually require some local responsibility, as they do in many countries. Even road maintenance may require some local government participation,

especially in urban areas in Canada. In both countries, cultural services, such as museums, may also fall to local government along with some responsibility for local infrastructure, and fire protection or health services.

Over the past four decades, there has been a gradual expansion in the number and types of responsibilities local governments have taken on. However, most have involved some sharing of responsibilities with higher government tiers.  In several domains where local governments have become more active, such as environmental policy, waste management, public health, and transportation, authorities at the national, provincial or state level may play as decisive a role as local authorities.

**Shifts in local service provision.** One of the most far-reaching recent transformations in provision of local services has been the shift toward privatization. Contracting for services with private businesses or non-profit organizations has become a common practice among local governments in the United States. For the most part, this has come about without the legal mandates that have spurred privatization in New Zealand or Europe. In the U.S., privatization is now well-established as a pragmatic alternative when other resource channels will not serve. In surveys, two thirds or more of local managers report that privatization has been considered and approved as an alternative to public provision (ICMA 2003). After a surge in the 1990s, it seems safe to say that privatization has been a staple of  local government since 2000. Although privatization has been on the agenda in Canada as well, it has not been pursued as aggressively as it has in the United States. Even so, in neither country has the shift to privatization been as dramatic as it has been in Australia, New Zealand, and some European countries.

Local entrepreneurship, in the sense of local ownership of utilities, transport authorities, and facilities, is more limited than it is in parts

*The greater local expenditure in the North American nations stems largely from local government responsibilities in education and public safety*

*The overwhelming proportion of the additional local personnel in the United States works in the localized education system, and in both North American countries public safety officials also make up much of local government staff*

of Europe. However, it is common to find local governments generating revenue through administration of airports, ports and other commercial operations. In the United States, special authorities controlled by local governments typically take on these administrative roles. The city of Los Angeles, for instance, derives a large portion of its revenue from Los Angeles International Airport and the Port of Los Angeles.

### III.3. Administrative Capacity

The size of local government staffs varies widely. This has not prevented implementation of largely parallel practices designed to secure integrity in local government, to carry out management reforms, to introduce at least limited elements of e-government, and to pursue policies supporting gender equality.

**Personnel.** Far more people work in local government than might be expected in light of the comparatively modest expenditures at the local government level (Table 4; compare with Table 2 infra). In the

United States more than 60% of all government employees work in local government. This rate approaches that of the Nordic democracies or Japan, where much of the welfare state is administered locally. In Canada the proportion is lower but still considerable at 35%.

These contrasts owe largely to the differences in the functions local government has assumed. Although local government in Canada and the United States is not responsible for large public health sectors and social benefits as in the Nordic countries, it retains responsibility for some of the most labor-intensive public social services. The overwhelming proportion of the additional local personnel in the United States works in the localized education system, and in both North American countries public safety officials also make up much of local government staff. The additional sectors of social service, health, infrastructure and educational provision in Canada also employ personnel who work at provincial or national levels in Australia and New Zealand. The low staffing levels in these countries

| Table 4 | Government Personnel, by Level of Government |

| Name | Australia | Canada | New Zealand | United States |
|---|---|---|---|---|
| Total | 1,485,800 | 2,552,613 | 227,220 | 19,869,558 |
| National | 248,500 | 357,308 | 205,540 | 2,878,819 |
| Federal units | 1,090,600 | 1,313,379 | | 4,370,562 |
| Local | 146,700 | 881,926 | 21,680 | 12,620,177 |
| Percentages | | | | |
| National | 17% | 14% | 90% | 14% |
| Federal units | 73% | 51% | | 22% |
| Local | 10% | 35% | 10% | 64% |

**Years:**    2000 (United States), 2001 (Australia, Canada, New Zealand).
**Source:**    OECD 2002.

also reflect the consequences of systematic policies that have contracted out more of infrastructure and local services.

The growth of local government in the United States has outstripped that at other levels. While the federal government has declined as a proportion of all government personnel, and the state governments have maintained essentially the same proportion, local governments now hire four percent more government employees than in the 1980s (U.S. Department of Commerce 2006). In Canada, local government employment declined along with public employment over the course of the 1990s. It has been rising again since 2002 (Statistics Canada 2006: pp. 6-7), roughly in tandem with growth in provincial government employment.

**Public service rules and guarantees for employees.** A distinguishing characteristic of local government in both countries is the absence of a national civil service for local government. In most other developed countries, either a national civil service or a national local civil service dominates local government staffing. But in North America, municipal hiring is by individual, private law contract. Although there are civil service systems in many local governments, the character of these varies widely (e.g., Freyss 1995). Partly as a consequence, many local government employees are recruited locally. Within specific domains of local government activity, professional credentialing and certification often provide a partial substitute for civil service standards. This is notably true in the United States, where public school teachers, police officers, firefighters and financial officials must have professional accreditation and associated training.

Mechanisms for enforcement of public integrity are present in each country. Most U.S. states and Canadian provinces have enacted codes of conduct for public ethics that include openness and proper resolution of conflicts of interest. Often provi-sions for ethics in local government are part of a more general system of norms applied to all public employees within a state or province. Measures of this kind have helped to assure comparatively high standing for public officials in these countries (World Bank 2006).

*A distinguishing characteristic of local government in both countries is the absence of a national civil service for local government*

**Reforms and management initiatives.** Efforts to improve quality and efficiency have proceeded steadily at the local level in the United States and Canada, though it is difficult to assess how much difference these efforts have made. Professional organizations like the International City/County Managers Association have sought to provide benchmarking studies and best practices guidelines for these local efforts.

**E-government.** A growing majority of local governments in both countries have adopted "e-government" practices. Most local governments now have websites; larger municipalities use these to distribute increasing volumes of public information. Local e-government varies widely in scope and amount. Studies in the United States show that it is most extensive and widespread among wealthier communities where residents can easily afford computers, and are apt to be highly educated (Reece 2006). Several municipalities and some state and provincial governments have moved beyond passive online content. In Canada, Nunavet and Yukon have "introduced legislation which allows council and committee meetings to be held electronically." (UNESCAP 2005).

**Gender equality policies.** In both countries, an array of general workplace guarantees of civil rights extend protections on gender equality to local governments.

## IV.  Local Democracy

In the workings of democracy at the municipal and other local levels, Canadian and
U.S. local governments maintain some of
their most distinctive practices. Non-partisan elections, single-member electoral districts, frequent elections, direct democracy,
and greater local choice of institutions set
local institutions in these countries apart. A
number of these practices mark clear divergences from inherited British traditions,
as well as from the institutions in comparable
countries like Australia and New Zealand.

### IV.1.  Parties and Partisanship

In Canada and the United States the overwhelming proportion of local elections are
non partisan. Canadian candidates tend to
be listed either as independents, or to be
affiliated with local, rather than national
parties (UNESCAP 2005b). Even when
national politicians run for local office, the
links between local elections and national
party organizations remain loose. In the
U.S., most states, particularly those in the
"reform" areas of the South and West,
require elections to be non-partisan. In
larger cities, partisan affiliations are often
well known even in formally non-partisan
elections and can play an important role.

### IV.2.  Elected Executives

Although a variety of arrangements characterize local elections, several broad institutional patterns have predominated
(Table 5). In the United States some 38%
of municipal governments feature a
mayor-council system, with an elected
mayor who often exercises considerable
independent authority (MacManus & Bullock, 2003 pg. 3). This arrangement is
most common in larger cities. A growing
majority of U.S. cities – a 2001 survey estimated the proportion at 53% – have
adopted instead a council manager system. In this system the mayor is elected
by the council from among its members
and usually has few powers. In Canada,

*Voters in the United States and Canada often have the opportunity to vote more frequently for local officeholders than do their counterparts in other countries*

mayors of lower-tier authorities are generally elected. But in rural authorities, the
mayors, reeves and wardens who exercise
executive authority are generally
appointed by councils.

### IV.3.  Council Voting Systems

Council voting systems vary, but display
some overarching commonalities. Although
the single-member district method of election is part of the British local government
tradition, in the United States at-large elections have grown to predominate. In a 2001
city council survey 45% of councilors in
cities with populations over 25,000 reported
this form of elections, compared to 28%
with ward elections and 26% with a mixture
(Svara 2003; p. 13). Among cities over
200,000, however, ward elections remain
most frequent. In Canada as well, the type
of representation varies among and within
provinces. There the ward system with first
past-the-post voting generally predominates.

### IV.4.  Citizen Participation

One of the distinguishing features of local
government in Canada and the United
States has been the greater extent of participatory opportunities for local citizens.
Electoral terms are short, elected offices
often more numerous, direct democratic
procedures like recall and referenda more
widespread, and citizen commissions have
long been a regular feature of local government.

Voters in the United States and Canada
often have the opportunity to vote more
frequently for local officeholders than do
their counterparts in other countries. The
three years that correspond to the average
term in U.S. cities for elected executives
and councilors, and corresponding practices
in Canada, represent only one dimension
of this additional opportunity. Even for
councils with four-year terms, the terms
are often staggered so as to schedule an
election for part of the council every two

years. In the U.S. there are often multiple local electoral offices, including boards, local administrative officials and sometimes local judges. Recall elections for local officials are authorized in around half of U.S. states. In California these have become a regular occurrence. Term limits in a growing number of U.S. localities have also prevented incumbents from holding on to safe seats. Finally, referenda are a more regular feature of local politics in much of the United States than in any country other than Switzerland. Although resort to direct democracy varies widely by state and region, voting now plays a major role in transportation, infrastructure and public finance in such states as California,

Ohio and Washington State. Canada also has a long tradition of referenda (Hahn 1968). With the exception of three-year council terms, these practices set both countries apart from fellow former colonies Australia and New Zealand.

Participation in local elections is relatively low, conforming to the international trend of higher voter turnout for elections at higher levels. This tendency is particularly pronounced in the United States where electoral turnout has been lower than it is in other countries affiliated with the Organisation for Economic Co-operation and Development (OECD). Local election turnout as a proportion of the eligible pop-

## Table 5 — Local Democracy

| | Local councils | | | Local executive | | | | Direct democracy |
|---|---|---|---|---|---|---|---|---|
| | Proportional/ majority rule | Constituencies | Term | Mode of selection | Term | Collegial / unitary | Recall | |
| Australia | preferential or plurality systems (4 states), preferential or proportional representation (2), proportional representation (1) | One | 3-4 years | Mostly popular election, some indirectly election | 3-4 years | Unitary | No | Infrequent |
| Canada | Generally, plurality | Multiple | 3 years, 4 years or 2-3 years | Direct election (8 provinces), indirect election (2) | 3 years, 4 years or 2-3 years | Unitary | No | Frequent: for taxes, planning |
| New Zealand | Plurality | Multiple | 3 years | Direct election | 3 years | Unitary | No | Occasional, infrastructure and electoral rules |
| United States | Mostly plurality, some multimember districts and single nontransferable vote systems | Multiple, one and mixed | 3.3 years on average | Direct election (50%), indirect election (50%), | Generally 2-4 years (3 on average) | Collegial (5%), Otherwise unitary | Authorized in half of states, occasionally used | Frequent or very frequent: revenues, infrastructure, annexation issues |

**Sources:** *Bush (1995); Commonwealth Local Government Forum (2002a, 2002b); International City/County Management Association (1997); McManus (1999); Mouritzen and Svara (2002); United Nations Economic and Social Commission for Asia and the Pacific (2002a, 2002b); Zimmerman 1997; Canadian provincial and territorial local government acts.*

ulation has been estimated as low as 10% (Hajnal and Trounstine 2005). A study of five major U.S. metropolitan areas from 1996 to 2003 showed an average turnout of 29% for municipal elections, compared with an average turnout of 57% for the presidential election of 2000 (Sellers and Latner 2006). In Canada, where the only available measures are for the major cities, local election turnout since the 1990s ranged between 41% and 49% of the eligible population in general election years, and between 31% and 39% in off-year elections.

The traditional New England town meeting, a legislative assembly of citizens themselves, survives today in only a very small proportion of U.S. local governments. But citizen commissions and boards remain a regular feature of local government throughout Canada and the United States, and several municipalities have adopted innovative new forms of citizen participation in recent years. Several larger cities of Canada and the United States have adopted systems of neighborhood-level councils with elected representatives (Berry et al . 1993; Rivard and Collin 2006: 7). Most of these councils have been confined to advisory powers. In a few cases, such as the borough system of New York City and the neighborhood councils of San Antonio, sub-municipal councils of this sort also exercise governmental powers. A few Canadian municipalities have also experimented with such innovations as participatory budgeting. New practices in such functional areas as planning have also included consultations with neighborhood associations and even individual residents in the preparation of local development plans.

*Representation of racial and ethnic minorities continues to pose problems in both countries.*

### IV.5. Choice of Localities to Determine the Shape of Their Own Institutions

In Canada and the United States, local governments have historically exercised considerable authority over the shape of their institutions. General laws governing municipal government in the provinces and states offer a choice among a variety of different legal forms, as well as discretion to choose different voting systems, executive forms, and other electoral processes. As a practical matter, choices vary only moderately among a limited number of standard types, often depending on population size and the rural or urban character of a jurisdiction. Especially in the areas of later European settlement –outside the northeastern region of the United States, for example– state laws for annexation and municipal incorporation facilitate the formation of new local governments as well as the public annexation of land. Throughout the U.S. and in a number of Canadian cities, many larger city governments have been maintained through a specifically legislated charter under the state government. This leads to even more distinctive institutional arrangements for each such city. A charter of this kind enables higher-level governments to establish the local government's structure, fiscal authority and other powers for each city. Local authority of this kind is unusual in Europe, or even Australia and New Zealand, although it is fairly common in developing regions.

### IV.6. Local Political Representation

Representation of women in local government has increased in recent decades. In a 2001 survey by the U.S National League of Cities, 28% of city council members were female, two percent more than in 1989 (Svara 2003, p. 5). In the city councils of large cities, as well as 'liberal' states like New York, the number has risen to more than 30% (ibid.; Anthony Center: 2006). In 2002, 17% of mayors in cities with populations of 30,000 or more were women (Conway 2005: 60). Female representation was highest, 44%, on local school boards (ibid.). In Canada the proportion is somewhat lower. A 2004 national survey by the Federation Canadian of Municipalities reported that only 21.7% of municipal councilors were women (Federation of Canadian Municipalities 2004: 9), with much lower representation of women from minority ethnicities.

Representation of racial and ethnic minorities continues to pose problems in both countries. In the United States, with the rise of majority-minority jurisdictions in many central cities, African-American, Latino and Asian-American representatives have in many places acquired a significant or even predominant role in local councils. In cities of all sizes – especially in the largest ones – surveys indicate that minority representation doubled from 1979 to 2001 (Svara 2003: p. 7). But studies continue to show under-representation of minorities in relation to their numbers, a situation often linked to low electoral turnout and other factors (Hajnal and Trounstine 2005). Similarly, a 1998 analysis of council members in Montreal showed only 29% from the ethnic minority groups that comprised 43% of the total population (Simard 2000: p. 17).

## IV.7. Traditional Institutions

In particular regions in both countries, indigenous populations from the years before European settlement continue to maintain traditional institutions that can alter or replace the workings of other local governments. In some cases, relations between indigenous local practices and local government have become enmeshed in renewed debates about indigenous claims to land title and forms of sovereignty (Langton et al. 2004). Wider systems for providing services and maintaining infrastructure have also had to be modified to accommodate local self government through traditional institutions.

In Canada, where there are some 1500 indigenous tribes, a series of treaties since the 1970s has established the right of First Nations to self-government (Morse 2004). The need for cooperation with the local governments has led First Nation treaty

negotiators for British Columbia to agree to a protocol that guarantees local government representatives a place in treaty negotiations.

On the 550 Indian reservations in the United States, the tribal government is the local government authority. Reservations are exempt from certain taxes, such as state sales taxes, and often maintain their own tribal courts. The isolation and poverty of many reservations makes settlements some of the poorest in the country (Kalt and Cornell 2000).

## IV.8. Decentralization and Oversight of Local Government

Adhering to the British system that influenced the early development of these countries, higher-level governments in Canada and the United States do not rely on the territorial representation of a prefect, or a comparable general representative at the local level. In the federal systems of the two countries, separate departments of the states, provinces and territories provide general oversight. In Canadian provinces and territories, Ministries or Departments of Local Government provide this function. In the U.S. states, the Secretaries of State generally have this responsibility. In both countries, the oversight activities include supervision of local elections, administrative records, and other requirements including those for balanced budgets.

National governments in both countries have, for several decades scaled back direct intervention into municipal affairs. Canada eliminated its federal ministry of urban affairs in the 1970s; the Department of Housing and Urban Development (HUD) in the U.S., has also reduced its role. However, the national governments have undertaken some initiatives in recent decades, intervening directly in local affairs. In Canada, the creation of a Minister of State for Infrastructure and Communities in 2004, which became the Minister for Transport, Infrastructure. In certain areas, such as grants for housing or community de-

*In some cases, relations between indigenous local practices and local government have become enmeshed in renewed debates about indigenous claims to land title and forms of sovereignty*

velopment or the administration of national parks in the United States, direct intervention of this sort bypasses officials of state and provincial governments. In areas like transportation planning or regulation of air and water pollution, the federal government in the United States has enlisted state governments in national regulatory schemes, and sometimes works alongside state officials at the local level.

Higher-level governments, therefore, do retain some broad powers to oversee local affairs, and to intervene in local government activities. Canadian provincial ministers responsible for local government, in addition to broad oversight and approval powers, can go so far as to dissolve local councils and appoint administrators to carry out local government functions. In the United States as well, state governments are generally empowered to take over administration of local governments that default on financial obligations or otherwise fail. This has occurred, for instance, in the takeover of the urban Philadelphia school district by the state of Pennsylvania. These powers are also typical of higher level governments in other systems with British colonial legacies, including, once more, Australia and New Zealand.

Among politicians, the holding of multiple electoral mandates offices for local and state or national office is rare, and is largely, if not entirely, prohibited by conflict of interest laws. Although politicians have often moved between offices at different levels, they do so through a succession of posts. In U.S. states, where term limits have increasingly restricted the number of mandates a politician can serve, moving between state office and local office has become increasingly common.

### IV.9. Public Opinion on Local Government

As in most advanced industrial democracies with longstanding institutions, skepticism about public officials and politicians has increased. In both the United States and Canada, however, the public opinion of local government appears to be somewhat more positive.

Since the 1970s in the United States, the public has placed growing trust in local government, particularly in comparison with government at higher levels. In 1972, a Gallup survey showed that 12% placed "a great deal" and 51% "a fair amount" of trust in local government – a total of 63%. In 2005, 23% expressed "a great deal" of trust and 47% "a fair amount" – a total of 70%. From 2001 to 2004, the proportion in both categories averaged 5 % higher than trust in state government, and eleven percent higher than trust in the federal government.

In Canada as well, a recent survey showed skepticism about the performance of the federal government, but positive assessments of the performance of local government in facing local issues (Infrastructure Canada 2006). Fifty three percent of respondents rated local governments "excellent" or "good" in addressing these issues. This compared with 37% for provincial governments, and 32% for the federal government.

### IV.10. Local Government Associations

As in other countries with highly developed systems of local governance, national associations of local governments and local government officials play diverse roles. The Federation of Canadian Municipalities (FCM) began in 1901 as the Union of Canadian Municipalities. In the United States, the National League of Cities (NLC) was founded in 1924, and the United States Conference of Mayors in 1932. Much of local government legislation is a matter of state or provincial and territorial law. Local government associations formed within these intermediate levels of government are also very active and influential. Associations of local professionals, such as the International City/County Management Association, have also been a major factor.

*Since the 1970s in the United States, the public has placed growing trust in local government, particularly in comparison with government at higher levels*

One of the most important roles that these organizations have served is as corporate representatives of the interests of local governments in national and state or provincial policymaking. The U.S. Conference of Mayors (USCM), for instance, emerged in the 1930s from the first successful efforts by a coalition of mayors to secure a package of federal financial aid targeted to city governments during The Depression. The Canadian Federation of Municipalities (FCM) has increasingly gained recognition as a voice for protection of the rights of municipalities in national debates. By contrast, the U.S. national organizations have in recent decades scaled back efforts to influence national policy. State or provincial organizations of municipal governments are often more active at these lower levels of government, where most policies and frameworks for local governments are crafted.

### IV.11. National Organizations Also Take on Other Roles

Documenting and disseminating best practices and information about local government has been a goal for all of these associations. This role has been especially prominent among the national associations in the United States. The National League of Cities (NLC) maintains a database of local government practices, and a Municipal Reference Service that collects information on local government activities around the country. Both the NLC and the International City/County Managers Association regularly conduct surveys of local governments. Their surveys have become the most important source of information on broad trends at the local level. In the U.S., national forums linked to the USCM and the NLC bring local officials together regularly to discuss issues of common concern. Networking both domestically and internation-

ally among local governments has also been an important element of these activities. As part of its initiatives for local capacity building, the FCM has established the Center for Sustainable Community Development (CSCD). The FCM also maintains a Green Municipal Fund (GMF), a unique $550 million endowment from the federal government devoted to environmental sustainability and local capacity building. Since 1987, Canadian municipalities have authorized an International Center for Municipal Development to represent the FCM in international work. In both countries, international partnerships have proliferated outside as well as within the auspices of national associational activities.

## V. Conclusion

In both Canada and the United States, local government has evolved quite far from its original British colonial legacy. Their parallel evolution has given these settler nations a distinctive type of local government that can be understood only partly through comparison with contemporary British local government, or even with local government in other former British colonies. Long-standing features of these systems include limited legal status, comparative local fiscal autonomy, a modest municipal role in overall public finance, a strong role in local civic action, and an emphasis on local democracy. By comparison with Europe and East Asia, these systems may seem to embody a limited role for local government. But that role is also much more institutionalized and robust than in many newly decentralizing countries, and less subject to supervision from above than in most of the developed North.

Within both countries, but especially within the United States, considerable variety continues to mark local governance. Local government remains subject to different legal frameworks by state or province, and even by individual city. Informal and formal inter-local arrangements also differ widely, even across a single metropolitan area. Such common trends as the growth of local government, the shifting of responsibilities to the local level, and the search for new inter-local and public-private arrangements for governance show few signs of abating.

In the United States, local government has thrived even as it has confronted widespread decentralization, greater supervision, intergovernmental fragmentation and an increasingly limited role in national policy. Local government powers in some states include general authorizations like those of Northern Europe, and overall, local government has one of the highest proportions of public employment in the world. Both this proportion and the local government portion of public spending continue to rise. The growing trust of citizens in local government suggests that this growth will continue.

Canadian local governments traditionally possess more limited powers and fiscal resources than do those in many U.S. states, but this may be changing. Local government representatives have lobbied for strengthening these powers. New governmental units, and planning at the metropolitan level have taken hold, and the trust of citizens in local government remains high.

*In both Canada and the United States, local government has evolved quite far from its original British colonial legacy*

# Metropolitan governance

Jefferey Sellers
Vincent Hoffmann-Martinot

## I. Introduction

Worldwide, metropolitan regions (also referred to as "urban regions" or "city regions") are rapidly becoming the predominant form of human settlement. In 1800 only 2% of the world's population lived in urban areas. Five years from today –most likely when a villager somewhere in Asia or Africa moves to an urban center there– the majority of the world's population will be urban. Thereafter, humankind will be, indisputably, an urban species.

With the industrial revolutions of the 19th and early 20th Centuries, urban regions became the predominant form of settlement throughout most of the global North. This process of urbanization is now increasingly the rule in the global South as well. For example, most of Latin America is now urbanized. The United Nations predicts that from 2005 to 2030, 90% of all global population growth will take place in urban regions of the global South (UNCHS 2005).

The size and form of metropolitan regions differ considerably, both within countries and between global North and global South regions. The size of today's largest urban regions is unprecedented in world history. In 1950 only one city had a population of more than 10 million. By 1975 there were five cities of this size, three of them in the developing world. By 2000 there were 16 cities with populations over 10 million, twelve of them in the developing world. However, such megacities like these present only part of the story. Cities with populations in excess of one million are proliferating worldwide, and the number of cities with more than five million inhabitants is also increasing. As more people are drawn into expanding urban regions (UNCHS 2005), the world's metropolises grow more extensive, more diverse and more fragmented.

Simultaneously, changes in the governance, economics and societies continue to transform the spatial and social structures of urban regions. Diverse service sectors in both the South and the North have grown into dominant components of metropolitan economies. As economic globalization has increasingly linked urban regions to each other, and cities to their peripheries and hinterlands, competition among cities and regions has intensified. At the same time, widespread decentralization has encouraged high-level governments to abandon local governments within metropolitan regions to the myriad consequences of the ongoing demographic, economic and social changes.

Social scientists have for many years linked urbanization with economic development, education and other components of "modernization" (Ingram 1997). Of course, cities are still the centers of economic and social activity worldwide, but in important ways the dynamics of modernization have changed. It is increasingly clear that today's metropolitan regions face unprecedented governance challenges. The size of modern cities, their continued growth, their social and spatial fractures, their distinctive economic characteristics, and their institutional dimensions present hitherto unanticipated dimensions of governance. As expanding metropolitan regions cope with the new facts of governance, governments at higher levels must also acknowledge and address metropolitan issues. Nor is it likely that solutions will be simple. Solutions for one region may not pertain in another. Each metropolitan setting, North and South, is in important respects unique.

## II. Conditions of Metropolitan Governance

Worldwide urbanization has given rise to the global phenomenon of geographically extended metropolitan regions. This chapter focuses on governance of these settings, governance being defined as "actions and institutions within an urban region that regulate or impose conditions for its political economy" (Sellers 2002, p. 9). Despite the many forms that metropolitan governments take, they confront common challenges shaped by parallel shifts in politics, economics and

*The size of today's largest urban regions is unprecedented in world history*

*As markets for residence and employment in metropolitan areas diversify, affluent households seize the opportunity to sort themselves into areas with superior amenities and a better quality of life*

society. Still, fundamental differences between Northern and Southern cities make governance a significantly different proposition above and below the equator.

Urban growth means territorial expansion as well as population growth. De facto metropolitan borders push thus farther and farther out into the surrounding rural area. At the same time, improved transportation and communication technologies have greatly increased the mobility of employers and residents. Especially in developed countries, clear dichotomies between city and countryside have given way to dispersed, polycentric patterns of settlement and economic activity. Many developing areas, such as the Pearl River Delta of China, manifest a similar evolution.

The problem of horizontal governance across an extended area confronts all of these urban regions. Settlement and economic activity frequently expand across institutionalized boundaries, and beyond the reach of stable, pre-existing governance arrangements. This phenomenon presents several potential problems:

- **Absence of territorial controls and guidance:** Urban spread can be limited and restricted only by co-operative action among the affected urban areas. Local governments must look beyond their parochial vision and strategy, and make at least a minimal effort to acknowledge and accommodate this crucial spillover dimension;

- **Shortcomings in management capabilities and experience:** Small government units find it difficult to attract and develop the administrative and technical resources required for territorial management. Pooling resources could provide increased efficiency and economies of scale;

- **Lack of structural consultation for solving common problems:** Collective action by local governments is still the exception.

Yet when the social and economic structures within a metropolitan region are interconnected, decisions and actions taken by one community can easily affect or even undermine the choices made in a neighboring one. This interconnectedness of metropolitan communities stands at the core of the metropolitan problem.

Partly for these reasons, metropolitan governance requires vertical as well as horizontal relations among governments. The social and economic problems that the higher-level governments of both developed and developing countries confront – from economic development to reducing pollution – are also increasingly the problems of metropolitan regions. Opportunities for governance within these regions are often provided by national policies and institutions. For example, transportation policy determined at a higher level of government can be coordinated with local decisions about economic development. Similarly, implementation of national or regional pollution laws can be facilitated by appropriate local planning; or an overarching social welfare policy can be coordinated with local educational policy.

Other social and economic dynamics in metropolitan areas compound the need for metropolitan governance. Recent research points to growing socio-economic disparities within many contemporary metropolitan regions (e.g., Fainstein 2001; Segbers et al. 2007). As markets for residence and employment in metropolitan areas diversify, affluent households seize the opportunity to sort themselves into areas with superior amenities and a better quality of life. Poor households gravitate toward areas with the lowest housing costs. Especially where the boundaries between affluence and poverty correspond to boundaries between governmental entities, such as villages or towns, heightened differences in the number and quality of public services can reinforce social disparities. Without public measures to equilibrate the fiscal disparities among locales, governance arrangements can reinforce spatial advantages and disadvantages.

Even beyond the boundaries of metropolitan settlement itself, increased mobility and communication have intensified social and economic links between urban centers and outlying areas. Metropolitan regions, like most central cities, function as centers of production and distribution for the surrounding regions. However, they are also centers of consumption for outlying areas, providing a strong cultural economy for intellectual life, education and tourism. Indeed, growth in the metropolis often comes at the expense of rural economies, triggering a population influx from rural areas.

## Differences between northern and southern metropolitan regions

Within these broad commonalities, urban regions in the developed North and those in the developing South have distinctive characteristics and face markedly different challenges.

In parts of the South, especially in Asia and Africa, urban regions are growing at unprecedented rates, faster even than cities grew at the onset of urbanization in the North. Flight from the countryside is driven by rural environmental degradation, disappearing job opportunities and poverty. So dire are conditions in many rural areas that growth in southern metropolitan regions is simply explosive. Although current rates of growth among cities in the North vary widely, they are generally lower. In much of Europe, declining birth rates and migration present new problems among declining urban populations.

The populations and forms of peripheral settlement also differ. In most of the North, middle class and affluent residents have led a migration from the central cities (Hoffman-Martinot and Sellers 2005). In most of the South, however, urban regions remain generally more concentrated and dense, and poor residents typically predominate on the urban periphery.

Concentrations of poverty and slums may still be found in major metropolitan areas in the United States and in a number of European countries. In many Southern metropolitan regions, however, poverty predominates. The latest survey data suggest that 25% of the urban population is below the poverty line in India, 15% in Brazil, 30% in Tanzania, 19% in Ghana, 13% in Jamaica, 57% in Sierra Leone and approximately 7% in Vietnam (UNFPA:2006). If poverty in the South were measured by the same standards applied in developed countries, at least half of the urban population in many developing countries would be categorized as poor. In developing nations, the urban figure is usually less than the proportion of households below the relevant poverty line in the rural areas (UNFPA: 2007).

The most recent UN figures also suggest that one third of the world's urban population – 90% of city dwellers in the developing world – live in slums, defined as areas with inadequate provision of infrastructure such as sewers, running water and electricity (UNFPA: 2007).

For urban residents in the South, a notable measure of informality characterizes employment and housing (cf. Gilbert 1998; Segbers et al. 2007). While their legal status varies with local circumstance, these settlements by definition lie outside the formal planning and legal system, and are usually built on land that the inhabitants do not own. Such residential areas come in many forms and sizes, and most attain de facto acceptance by local authorities. Local municipal politicians often use their residents as sources of patronage and electoral support. One result of this acknowledged but unofficial status has been the appearance of a full-fledged underground housing market with properties (usually shacks) being unofficially bought and sold. Because most settlement residents can not afford to "own" property, even under such quasi-legal conditions, there is also a strong rental market.

In many developed countries, local governments, planning regimes, property laws and welfare states institutionalized at the

*Concentrations of poverty and slums may still be found in major metropolitan areas in the United States and in a number of European countries*

*The growth*

*patterns*

*of metropolitan*

*regions are most*

*usefully viewed as*

*products of both*

*government and*

*private-sector*

*policies*

national level have provided powerful instruments to steer metropolitan settlement and address resource inequalities. In the South, however, even where comparable mechanisms exist, they are apt to be less extensive and less effective.

In confronting rapid urbanization and the challenges of metropolitan governance in the 21st Century, Southern metropolitan areas can find guidance in the growing number and range of global institutional models. These models incorporate international expertise about policy in specific sectors, and accumulated lessons about metropolitan management garnered from previous experience with urbanization. But the sheer size and extent of the largest urban regions, as well as the growing influence of outside forces and metropolitan interconnectedness, frequently give rise to unforeseen circumstances and daunting complexities.

The growth patterns of metropolitan regions are most usefully viewed as products of both government and private-sector policies. Intentionally or not, even the most diverse and expansive metropolitan areas achieved certain aspects of their present form partly as a result of governmental choices. Such governmental efforts include extending transportation systems, such as motorways, trains and other forms of mass transport, designating locations for businesses and residents, providing incentives through tax abatements and other subsidies, and planning suburban habitats. At the same time, individual businesses and consumer housing preferences exert powerful, ongoing influences on growth patterns.

## III.  Key Challenges of Governing Metropolitan Areas

The governance of metropolitan areas is particularly difficult for a number of reasons. Whatever the institutional arrangements or the peculiarities of the surrounding region, metropolitan governance must address increasingly extended, diverse, and divided

spaces. Many metropolitan areas must deal with continued demographic expansion. Many others must also overcome institutional fragmentation due to the lack of a central, encompassing regulatory authority. Most, to some degree, also have to cope with new and sometimes intense local conflicts.

### III.1.  Social and Territorial Diversity

The shape of metropolitan regions today marks a clear departure from the traditional form of cities. Especially in Europe, urban settlement has long been understood to follow an agglomerative concentric model. Within fortifications, behind gates and along great boulevards, the European city developed a distinct economy and way of life. Beyond the city walls lay the economically and administratively separate sphere of rural settlement. Modern metropolitan regions, however, have far more complex patterns of territorial diversity that often blend urban and rural elements. Such new patterns are reinforced by social diversity that frequently outstrips that of urban regions in centuries past.

Though it may seem counterintuitive, today the fastest growth often occurs in the rural communities on the fringes of urban areas. In the developed countries of the North, this growth is fed by young families looking for homes with more space. Many of these "new rural dwellers" left denser urban neighborhoods or even established suburbs to live in outlying villages. Though they move farther from the center of the city, these families typically remain dependent on the city for employment and public amenities.

In the developing countries of the South, especially in Brasilia and Mexico City, middle class and affluent households are also moving away from the center of metropolitan regions. However, an even larger number of new arrivals are poor residents of rural areas and poor urban dwellers seeking affordable housing.

As the urban fabric spreads and stretches, the notion of 'conurbation' – a continuous network of built-up urban areas – has increasingly failed to capture the fluid and ambiguous nature of peri-urban regions. It has given way to measures of commuting intensity or patterns of migration toward a central city. Significantly, geographers and urban planners have even invented special terms to describe the new entities that are taking shape around large cities: City-archipelago, emerging town, megalopolis, metapolis and metropolitan area are a few examples of recent additions to the urban-studies lexicon (Ascher 1996; Gottman 1961; Mongin 1998; Veltz 1995).

Growing social diversity in many urban regions has contributed to the increase in ground-level territorial diversity. The largest urban regions in developed countries generally feature higher levels of social and economic segregation by residence. In Europe and North America, many such regions have also absorbed the largest proportions of new immigrants, including those from developing countries. Growing economic and social diversity has often compounded metropolitan segregation. Although middle class areas predominate in the largest metropolitan regions of the developed world, it is usually possible to find both exclusive affluent localities or neighborhoods and concentrations of poverty and social disadvantage. Overall levels of territorial segregation vary widely among metropolitan regions, but range higher in the United States than in most of Western Europe or Japan.

In most southern cities, the incidence of poverty is determined primarily by the local labor market. The income, security, and benefits linked to employment remain the primary means by which households can avoid impoverishment. Industrial firms are the major employers in the urban centers of the South, though in some places the service sector has been replacing them. Street trading and the informal job sector have become a major source of employment for those not in the formal sector. The proportion of jobs in this sector varies between cities but often accounts for upwards of 20% of those in employment.

## III.2. Governmental Fragmentation

Another challenge for governance stems from the organizational fragmentation of local governments in extended metropolitan regions. Much of this fragmentation is geopolitical. As more people move into an increasing number of communities surrounding central cities, more local governments are drawn into problems that beset the entire metropolitan region.

Data from the 476 metropolitan regions in the International Metropolitan Observatory (Hoffmann-Martinot and Sellers 2005) offer the most systematic current overview of governmental fragmentation in OECD countries; data for several additional cases are provided as well. Measured by the proportion of the central city population in areas of more than 200,000 inhabitants, Israel is one of the most fragmented countries from a geopolitical point of view, along with Switzerland (30%), Germany (31%), the United States (34%) and France (36%). In the Netherlands, about half the population lives in central city neighborhoods, but in the other countries studied, the bulk of the population continues to reside in central towns rather than traditional suburbs.

The number of communities with approximately 100,000 inhabitants is a second widely accepted measure of this kind of political-institutional fragmentation (e.g., Brunn and Ziegler 1980) in metropolitan areas. The higher this indicator is for a metropolitan area, the greater the fragmentation. In a majority of the countries in the International Metropolitan Observatory (IMO) project, this measure of institutional fragmentation is low, having a value lower than five. Such a low score invariably indicates that municipalities in the region have been merged, as they were recently in Canada (1). Sweden and the Netherlands (2), Poland and Israel (3), and Norway (4), also merged their metropolitan municipalities comparatively recently. In Spain, the exurban parts of metropolitan areas have only developed in recent years, accounting for that country's low level of

*The largest urban regions in developed countries generally feature higher levels of social and economic segregation by residence*

*As measured by this index, France appears as the most territorially fragmented country in Europe*

institutional fragmentation (3). The highest values appear in countries where pre-industrial municipal boundaries largely survive, such as France (32), the Czech Republic and Switzerland (21), Germany (18), the United States (15) and Hungary (12). It may seem surprising that these values are much higher in Hungary and in the Czech Republic, former communist countries, than in Poland (3) or in other post-communist countries such as Slovak Republic. This higher level of fragmentation is a result of planned programs for municipal disaggregation carried out by the Czech and Hungarian national governments.

A geopolitical fragmentation index developed by Brunn and Zeigler (1980) combines the two previous indicators into a single measurement. This enables a summary comparison among the IMO countries.

As measured by this index, France appears as the most territorially fragmented country in Europe with a value of 11. This indicates considerably more fragmentation than the average for the United States (7), which is more or less the level for Switzerland. International comparison of the Zeigler and Brunn scale shows that there is no uniform North American model: Canadian metropolitan areas are institutionally very different from those in the United States, and recent consolidation reforms have placed Canada closer to the Northern European model. Similarly, it is not possible to put all countries in Eastern Europe in the same bracket. While they were all subject to waves of mergers during the communist period, the fragmentation of the post-communist Czech Republic (3) presents a completely different profile from Hungary (1.7) or Poland (0.6). Because of a recent, less-pronounced metropolitanization process, Spain (0.5) appears to be closer to the Netherlands (0.5), Sweden (0.3) and Norway (0.8) than to neighboring France. Germany (6) is highly fragmented, and has higher levels in eastern metropolitan areas, as well as some western metropolitan areas, including Koblenz.

Overall, the IMO data show geopolitical fragmentation to be highest in those developed countries where metropolitanization has proceeded amid continued legacies of older town and village settlement and administration (France, Germany, Switzerland, the eastern portions of the United States). Fragmentation is also progressing rapidly in a number of other countries where metropolitanization is relatively new, such as the Czech Republic, Hungary, Spain and Israel. By contrast, far-reaching reforms have succeeded spectacularly in reducing fragmentation in Scandinavia, Canada, and the United Kingdom.

Other than South Africa, which is included in the IMO project, no comparable data are as yet available to measure geopolitical fragmentation in the developing and transitional countries of the South. However, South Africa provides a dramatic example of governmental restructuring in the South. Post-apartheid reforms in South Africa effectively eliminated geopolitical fragmentation by reconfiguring municipal boundaries to correspond with the economic and social outline of the major metropolitan areas.

Similar moves toward metropolitan consolidation took place earlier in other developing countries during the period when governmental consolidation was fashionable in Northern Europe. In 1973, the Brazilian military regime created nine metropolitan regions that are still functioning today. In Republic of Korea, the regime instituted metropolitan regional governments for Seoul and several other cities. Many Southern countries also established some form of metropolitan territorial authority for their capital city regions.

In the South, these consolidation efforts have generally failed to eliminate the problem of geopolitical fragmentation. There as in the North, the problem remains especially evident in the largest urban regions. Laqian, in a recent survey of governance in Asian metropoles, calls political and administrative fragmentation "[t]he most serious problem that many of them face" (2007, p. 145). In some former colonies, structures of colonial administration still define local district boundaries outside central cities. Elsewhere, as with the Indian panchayat or the Philippine barangay, indigenous settlements shape municipal jurisdictions. Where metropolitan governments are in place, spatial expansion often continues beyond the formal administrative boundaries into surrounding localities. Metropolitan governments now administer 50% of the metropolitan population in Mexico City, 71% in Sao Paulo, 45% in Seoul and 38% in Johannesburg.

Even where the jurisdiction of metropolitan governmental authority extends over the entire metropolitan area, other forms of fragmentation can frustrate effective governance. In Bangkok, Manila, and Mumbai, for instance, metropolitan authorities have secured extensive geopolitical jurisdiction, yet effectiveness is often limited by political and administrative interference. To some extent local or high-level governments can formally restrict the power of metropolitan institutions. A further dilution of metropolitan authority occurs where agencies or offices charged with different sectoral tasks, such as roads, housing, and transit, resist directives from the metropolitan government.

## III.3.  Economic Globalization and Competitiveness

Increasingly, in both the North and the South, metropolitan regions have been recognized as key nodes for national economic strategies. They are also regarded as vital hubs for mobilization for rapid economic development. Alongside the globalization of trade and production networks, the shift to service and high-technology business has reinforced this transformation of metropolitan commerce.

Most literature on "global cities" initially centered on the largest cities of the North, and sought to analyze urban regions according to global hierarchies based on their position in international finance, corporate governance, elite travel, and communication (e.g., Sassen 1991; Taylor 2003). Other work on "global city regions" points instead to the role of regional economic clusters in the high-technology and advanced service components of modern industrial economies (e.g., Scott 2001). In developed countries, a range of smaller and mid-size urban regions have also managed to stimulate growth by attracting high technology, corporate branch offices, and educational or administrative services (Markusen, Lee and DiGiovanna 1999). This new round of economic competitiveness has not pushed growth in just one direction. Increasingly, metropolitan centers find that there is considerable commercial allure in a vibrant urban environment and the cultural amenities found there (Glaeser, Kolko and Saiz 2000). Such new regional economic dynamics further reinforce demands for more regional collective action.

In the South, development has been comparatively uneven. Despite greater pressures there to pursue economic prosperity, governance of metropolitan regions in the South presents challenges that are similar to those in the North. For the first half of the 20th Century, cities in Asia and Latin America focused almost exclusively on industrial development and modernization. In much of Latin America, as well as in the Asian countries of Thailand and Republic of Korea, cities absorbed much of this industrialization and commanded correspondingly large proportions of national resources. Aggravated by conditions of authoritarian rule in many of these countries, urban primacy had the demonstrated effect of reducing the potential for overall national development (Ades and Glaeser 1994).

Since the 1970s, however, much of the new manufacturing capacity in the developing world has been built outside urban centers, usually in surrounding towns. New industrial parks and high-technology centers have also been situated on the periphery of major urban centers, such as Campinas in the Sao Paulo region (Markusen, Lee and DiGiovanna) and the HITEC Center outside of Hyderabad (Kennedy 2007). In the face of the underdevelopment and declining fortunes of the countryside, new centers of

*Since the 1970s, however, much of the new manufacturing capacity in the developing world has been built outside urban centers, usually in surrounding towns*

*Services, high technology activities and commercial development have increasingly replaced traditional manufacturing as the objects of metropolitan economic recruitment*

development in the South continue to rely on the infrastructure, capital, and other advantages conferred by proximity to the largest urban concentrations. This stands in contrast with the North where more disparate, smaller urban regions, including Austin, Montpellier, Raleigh-Durham and Toulouse, have seen significant growth in high technology and service development (Sellers 2002).

A corresponding consequence of global economic shifts has been a general increase in inequality. According to Sassen (1991), the increase in disparities between the elite in service businesses and the underpaid, immigrant work force employed by those businesses, results in an increase in social and spatial polarization. Regional strategies associated with globalization are often geared more toward attracting economic development than to addressing these new disparities. In more dynamic regions, public expenditure tends to support physical infrastructure that facilitates growth and new economic activities. Especially when accompanied by the fragmentation of many metropolitan regions, such strategies can compound disparities in the provision of local public services.

### III.4. Socio-Political Conflicts

The emergence of metropolitan regions has some of its most far-reaching implications for territorial conflicts. Especially in much of the North, as the monopolistic position of central cities has declined, increasingly fierce economic and political competition pits urban centers against surrounding municipalities that refuse to be relegated to suburbs or satellites. Experiments in inter-local redistribution of resources in Europe and North America have largely arisen out of intensified arguments over fiscal exploitation between ex-urban communities and cities.

As the localities within metropolitan regions have coalesced into distinctive demographic and income clusters, tensions over the territorial distribution of resources and responsi-

bilities have increased. Conflicts now focus routinely on the financing of collective goods and services, from public transportation to cultural facilities to sewage treatment. Even within a consolidated jurisdiction, territorial polarization between neighborhoods or other parts of cities can generate growing conflicts. In the wake of decentralization and democratization in Southern cities, metropolitan leaders in such diverse settings as Brazil, South Africa and India have all had to address tensions of this kind.

The socio-economic dimension of conflict can transcend territorial bases. A classic example is the perennial clash between the interests of capital and those of the workforce and local residents. Conflicts of this type hark back to the mercantile origins of cities, yet they still drive debates over metropolitan governance institutions. Proponents of metropolitan governance, regardless of whether they are themselves local chambers of commerce or business representatives, often portray economic development as a primary objective. But in the South as well as the North, the arguments about this objective have shifted. Services, high technology activities and commercial development have increasingly replaced traditional manufacturing as the objects of metropolitan economic recruitment. In the North, local businesses now mobilize regularly alongside governments around local initiatives to bring these activities (Sellers 2002; Jouve and Lefèvre 2002). In much of the North partisans of growth limits or growth management also regularly contest the untrammeled pursuit of regional growth (Clark and Goetz 1994). In the South, environmental groups usually exercise less influence, but are becoming more active.

Ethnicity and religion present another source of conflict that can cross territorial boundaries in metropolitan regions. In both the North and South, ethnic, racial and religious divisions often reinforce existing barriers between the haves and have-nots. Where minorities, especially immigrants, move into areas dominated by residents with a different ethnicity or race, the integration of the newcomers can give rise to conflicts with a national majority, as well as between the new minority and the resident majority. Immigration and citizenship issues have thus provoked both populist backlashes and resurgences in minority-rights movements in the cities of Europe, Japan and the United States. In the growing number of large cities with pervasive ethnic or racial divisions, such as Mumbai or Los Angeles, group identity regularly furnishes flashpoints for social tensions, political clashes and inter-group violence.

A fourth element of the new urban strife is partisan conflict over ideologies, programs and strategies. The influence of distinct parties and coalitions differs considerably, depending on location and context. Reflecting, at least in part, trends in other dimensions of conflict, political parties have also developed new forms. In many countries the number of parties and political groups represented in local assemblies has grown substantially. In Europe new ecological and populist parties have appeared. In the South decentralization and the establishment of local democracy has helped foster new interest groups in the local partisan landscape. Partisan organizations traditionally have exerted only limited control over local politics in many Southern cities. Now upstart religious and ethnic parties compete openly and with some success with the established parties. As in Europe, these new groups threaten traditional single – or two-party domination, and further complicate the already fragmented local party system.

## IV.  Institutional Alternatives for Governance within Metropolitan Areas

In early 20th Century North America, widespread suburbanization created some of the most extensive and dispersed urban regions ever seen. Under conditions of high geopolitical fragmentation, a debate emerged that to this day continues to shape choices about institutional designs for metropolitan governance. At the beginning of the 1940s, one of the leading representatives of the Chicago School of urban studies, Louis Wirth (1942), called for formal institutional consolidation: "We live in an era which dissolves boundaries, but the inertia of antiquarian lawyers and lawmakers, the predatory interests of local politicians, real estate men, and industrialists, the parochialism of suburbanites, and the myopic vision of planners have prevented us from a full recognition of the inescapable need for a new planning unit in the metropolitan region."

Up to the 1970s academic opinion throughout the global North reflected this view. The wave of reorganization of local government in the 1960s and 1970s in Europe, North America and parts of the South drew on these critiques. Two arguments were essential to the case against fragmentation. First, the essential tasks and responsibilities of governance – from infrastructure to social equity – spilled over fragmented jurisdictional boundaries in ways that demanded consolidated institutions. The second, opposing, concept posits that larger governmental units could take advantage of economies of scale, providing public services at lower cost than smaller governments.

Applied to vastly different regional, national and socio-political contexts, a decades-old argument has coalesced around two general strategies: supra-community reformation and territorial polycentrism.

### IV.1.  Supra-Community Reform

To those in favor of creating overarching metropolitan governments to replace a multitude of existing local authorities, a salient failing of the multi-government model is its weak performance as a democratic institution. This is evidenced by a decline in local political and electoral participation in many countries. In addition, many local governments are perceived as inefficient and disconnected from the expectations of their citizens.

*In many countries the number of parties and political groups represented in local assemblies has grown substantially*

*There is a perceptible lack of collective will among those who might effect broad changes in metropolitan boundaries*

The weakness of a multitude of local governments preoccupied with only local concerns is a perceived unwillingness to act on issues that affect the entire region. This was the argument advanced, for example, by the Quebec government in their White Book on municipal reorganization (2000:20): "The limited size of the municipalities is sometimes presented as an advantage in terms of the exercising of democracy because it allows for an administration that is more attuned to residents' needs. However, insofar as the fragmentation of the municipalities limits their ability to deal with the often important issues that transcend their territories, e.g. land use planning, the environment, public transportation, and economic development, there is instead a risk that residents will be less interested in participating in municipal life."

The significance of these arguments needs to be understood in light of the highly decentralized states where they were put forth. In North America, the fragmentation of local authorities, including municipalities and districts established for education and other services, contributes to great disparities in the services different communities receive. In some cases these differences are caused by variations in local skills and in the professionalism of municipal bureaucracies. In the United States and Canada, those in favor of integrated forms of metropolitan government have generally stressed the need to reduce intra-metropolitan area socio-economic disparities in such services as education and security (Dreier, Mollenkopf and Swanstrom 2004). Reform was also held out as a better way to address problems that require coordinated collective action throughout a metropolitan area, in such sectors as water supply, waste management and air pollution.

## IV.2. Territorial Polycentrism

It was ultimately in more centralized Northern European countries, for example the United Kingdom, where successive waves of communal consolidation came closest to realizing the goals of supra-community reform nationwid.. In the United States, a counter-

movement emerged to defend decentralized metropolitan arrangements. To counter the arguments of reformers, those against the formation of metropolitan governments criticized their red tape, their high operating costs and their remoteness from their citizens.

The supporters of the political-economic approach known as Public Choice have provided the main inspiration for arguments in favor of small local units as the main units for governance in metropolitan areas (Ostrom, Bish and Ostrom 1988). This approach analogizes local governments competing for residents to privately owned companies competing for the production or sale of goods. Proponents argue that it is more efficient and democratic for the localities within a metropolitan area to compete among themselves for the production or sale of public services than to leave those services to one monolithic government entity. They argue further that the coexistence of different government units with different combinations of services and taxes offers inhabitants a wider choice of residential areas. Residents can thus select the community within the metropolitan area that best corresponds to the level of public service they seek. Resources needed by the separate metropolitan towns can be shared through agreements about specific functional sectors, such as transportation, education and health (Marks and Hooghe 2003).

Beyond such operational concerns, there is a perceptible lack of collective will among those who might effect broad changes in metropolitan boundaries. Middle classes in many countries have shown little desire to contribute financially to the reduction of intra-metropolitan wealth disparities, and to the quest for fiscal equity. There has thus been only limited middle-class support for a key principle underlying the push for metropolitan integration.

## IV.3. The "New Regionalism"

Given the imposing realities of life in large metropolitan areas, a practical compromise may be found in a flexible solution with a variable scale of inter-municipal cooperation. In this case results can be manifested in different ways. The advantages of such quasi-formal cooperation have been emphasized in many empirical studies.

By the end of the 1970s, disenchantment with conurbation institutions became apparent in many countries. In Great Britain the suppression of urban counties and the Greater London Council took place in 1986; the same year saw the dissolution in the Netherlands of the Rotterdam and Eindhoven conurbation bodies. At about the same time, Australian authorities acknowledged the failure of repeated federal and state attempts to consolidate local authorities, and in Spain metropolitan governments in Valencia and Barcelona were dismantled. The French called an early halt to an urban communities' institutionalization process, the Italian effort to create metropolitan areas failed to get off the ground and in Germany consolidation experiments such as the Umland Verband Frankfurt and the Kommunalverband Ruhrgebiet proved disappointing.

However, the concept of metropolitan area government itself has substantially changed in the past 20 years. Most of the models envisaged or experimented with in the 1980s are now seen from the perspective of governance, rather than government. Moreover, governance is no longer confined to the built-up areas of distinct urban conurbations; it now extends to vast multi-polar urban regions that continue to expand and change.

This new trend toward a more flexible, polycentric form of governance, described in North America as new regionalism, is firstly associated with the global decentralization process. This approach seeks to strengthen local authorities at the expense of large, supra-municipal organizations, especially in areas of the world that are on the path to democracy. At the same time, the form, pace and scale of contemporary metropolitan transformations has made

traditional forms of metropolitan government seem increasingly inadequate.

It is therefore not appropriate to speak of simple replacement or of the substitution of one model by another over time. Rather it is more useful to envision increased differentiation among a variety of mixed systems of government. This movement can be observed in most countries, both in the North and in the South.

How can these new forms of metropolitan governance be characterized? Analysis of recent institutional experience reveals five particularly significant aspects:

- Pragmatic responsiveness in execution. State governments tend not to impose their ideas any more; instead they take great care to consult, listen, put into perspective, harmonize and reconcile. Rather than propose a single institutional model for all urban areas, they work carefully on a "made-to-measure" solution. Decisions to undertake reform respond to specific challenges related to the management of urban growth (Downs 1994).

This view makes it easier to understand the changes in governance of the Tokyo region. The Tokyo Metropolitan Government (TMG), became one of many players – prefectures, regional ministerial offices, Japan Railway, private companies – involved in regional governance. In a similar fashion, the recently created Greater London Assembly appears to be a relatively superficial mechanism. It cannot exercise any real influence except in strict collaboration with the boroughs, privately owned public service companies (special purpose agencies), two regional development agencies, and several central government departments. Canada, throughout the second half of the 20th Century a leader in integration of metropolitan governments, has now turned toward a polycentric neo-regionalism. This shift comes in the wake of spectacular de-fusion measures following referenda among municipalities

*Governance is no longer confined to the built-up areas of distinct urban conurbations; it now extends to vast multi-polar urban regions that continue to expand and change*

grouped within metropolitan areas. The development of "lighter" governance structures built around regional districts and metropolitan municipalities has followed.

- The adaptation of existing territorial units and governments above the municipal level to manage emerging challenges of metropolitan regions. For large urban regions, such as Tokyo, Paris and Sao Paulo, a regional or federal unit of government provides administration at a scale beyond the local government itself. Similarly, in the United States county governments, which are a higher level than local municipalities, often provide a more encompassing administrative framework for carrying out planning or providing social services across municipal boundaries. American advocates of metropolitan governance increasingly look to coalitions among representatives of cities and suburbs in the legislative and policymaking arenas of state and federal governments as a source of metropolitan policy (Dreier, Mollenkopf and Swanstrom 2004).

- Strengthening democratic legitimacy. For the supporters of new forms of metropolitan governance, direct popular election of legislators and government executives has a double purpose: enhancing local autonomy and strengthening the link between citizens and their political representatives (responsiveness). The direct election of the leadership for Metro Toronto began in 1988. In Stuttgart, when the political parties offered lists of candidates for election to the Stuttgart Regional Community (Verband Region Stuttgart) founded in 1994, party leaders took care to include the smallest possible number of local representatives. This tactic limited political ties to parties in existing local governments, further empowering the regional assembly. Since 2000, the Greater London Assembly and the mayor are elected directly by the people. Unlike the former Greater London Council, the GLA has adopted a strategy to encourage competition and social cohesion rather

*Metropolitan governments can usefully be classified by the amount of territory where they have jurisdiction, their institutional depth, and their democratic intensity*

than simply to supply services directly (Harloe 2003).

- The primacy of mission over management. The metropolitan administration is committed above all to planning, coordinating and integrating policies set by metropolitan area local authorities. True management tasks remain limited. As a consequence, expert and scientific analysis of the metropolitan problem is more nuanced and pluralistic than it was 20 years ago. Rather than agencies of strategic direction, the new structures of metropolitan governance are necessarily lighter: The Greater London Authority has little more than 600 employees.

- Close association with the private sector. At all stages in the process of institutional maturity, the strong influence of private sector leaders and organizations can be seen. In Europe as well as the United States, chambers of commerce and associations of enterprises are particularly prevalent. In some countries, the role of the private sector is determined by legislation.

## V. Panorama of Existing Metropolitan Governance Arrangements

Worldwide there is great variety in metropolitan governance. As illustrated in Table 1, metropolitan governments can usefully be classified by the amount of territory where they have jurisdiction, their institutional depth, and their democratic intensity. The position of metropolitan regional governments in the overall governmental hierarchy, including national and other systems, also influences the effectiveness and significance of metropolitan governance. Additionally, the specific governmental functions assumed by the institutions of metropolitan governance reveal global similarities and contrasts, as do any trans-national arrangements that address the challenges of de facto international metropolitan governance.

| Table 1 | Dimensions of Governance Institutions in Metropolitan Areas |
|---------|-------------------------------------------------------------|

|  | **Lower** | **Moderate** | **Higher** |
|---|---|---|---|
| **INTERNAL** | | | |
| **Spatial coverage** | Fraction of the metropolitan area | Majority of the metropolitan area | The entire metropolitan area |
| **Institutional thickness** | Inter-community co-operation | Authority for metropolitan development or specific sector | Metropolitan town |
| **Democratic intensity** | Local democracy only | Multi-level democracy | Compound metropolitan democracy |
| **EXTERNAL** | | | |
| **Centrality to higher level policymaking** | Intra-metropolitan divisions<br>Inter-metropolitan divisions<br>Limited representation<br>for metropolitan interests | Regional capital<br>National alliance of urban regions<br>Sector-specific integration | Prime urban region<br>National capital |

## V.1. Spatial Coverage

Existing institutions may cover all of a metropolitan territory, or only part of it. Consequently, their ability to regulate, manage and affect residents necessarily varies. Especially under conditions of rapid growth, the fluid functional and demographic boundaries of metropolitan regions make spatial coverage a constant challenge.

Most metropolitan governments have to make adjustments to accommodate changes in their official territory. In some cases, the metropolitan government at its inception did not encompass its entire modern region; others have seen their region grown well beyond their official boundaries. For example, Metro Toronto was created in 1953, but by 1991 still covered only 54% of the Toronto metropolitan area. Similarly, the Greater Bombay Municipal Corporation (GBMC) covers only 67% of the population in the Mumbai metropolitan region, even though it serves 12 million of the region's 18 million inhabitants. More recently, the reform that created metropolitan governments for South African urban regions succeeded in bringing only 38% of the total population in the Johannesburg metropolitan region under the single central metropolitan government there.

Many metropolitan governance arrangements are confined to limited, often socially and spatially distinct portions of metropolitan areas. In Argentina, the Northern Metropolitan Region, a consortium created in 2000, encompasses just a portion of the mainly affluent municipalities in the Buenos Aires metropolitan area (San Fernando, Vicente Lopez, San Isidro, Tigre). In the same manner, the minimal coordination of public policy among 39 different towns in the Sao Paulo metropolitan area appears to affect just seven of them. All seven, Diadema, Sao Caetano do Sul, Sao Bernardo do Campo, Santo Andre, Maua, Ribeirao Pires and Rio Grande da Serra, operate within the Camara Regional do Grande APC. It is symptomatic that the central town, Sao Paulo, is not a member of this consortium.

## V.2. Institutional Thickness

The governance of metropolitan areas can be more or less institutionally concentrated and integrated, both territorially and functionally.

### a) New town or metropolitan town
It is relatively rare for a single authority to exercise general and multifunctional authority over an entire metropolitan territory. It occurs where a merger of all component communities has taken place.

*The metropolitan level of governance can take any one of several forms: a metropolitan development council, a metropolitan development authority, or a fully empowered metropolitan government*

When this happens, the metropolitan area is likely to be structured around the metropolitan town that provides most services. The Bangkok Metropolitan Administration (BMA), for example, was created by merging Bangkok and Thonburi. Similar absorption of at least some functions and responsibilities of lesser towns has occurred in Seoul, Kuala Lumpur, Surabaya and Jakarta. The Seoul Metropolitan Government is run by a mayor and an assembly that is more or less elected directly by the people, and encompasses 25 districts called Gu. The Chinese government created metropolitan towns directed by powerful mayors who are appointed by the state in Beijing, Shanghai, Guangzhou, Chongqing and Tianjin. On the infra-metropolitan level, districts still exist, but with reduced authority and budgets. This sometimes leads to friction between the metropolitan level and the affected areas.

A series of mergers between communities belonging to two-level metropolitan systems has taken place at the instigation of Canadian provinces. In 1970, the New Democratic Party, having a majority in the Manitoba provincial parliament, decided to combine the Corporation of Greater Winnipeg and its districts into a single town, Winnipeg. The hope was that the merger would alleviate socio-economic and financial difficulties in the central town by including its wealthier suburbs in the region's resource pool. The Ontario government in 1998 employed a similar merger strategy to forge the new Town of Toronto. Two years after that, the province of Quebec created the new, enlarged municipal areas of Montreal and Quebec.

One of the world's most striking recent experiments with metropolitan governance is taking place in South Africa. By its nature, the old apartheid regime with its institutionalized segregation prevented any type of metropolitan organization. The abolition of apartheid in the 1990s led in a very short time to the appearance of metropolitan towns. Pressure for this change came primarily from the dominant party, the

ANC, which saw in metropolitan government the most effective vehicle for territorial reform and for reduction of socio-economic inequities. In December 1998, the Local Government Municipal Structures Act officially recognized the formation of metropolitan towns, whose boundaries would be defined by a commission called the Municipal Demarcation Board before the 2000 local elections. There are now six such towns: Cape Town, Ethekwini, Johannesburg, Ekurhuleni, Tshwane, and Nelson Mandela (Cameron and Alvarez 2005). It is still too early to draw firm conclusions from this unique effort. So far, however, the creation of metropolitan towns appears to have improved the lives of residents in some places but had mixed or even disappointing results in others.

**b) Co-existence of local governments with metropolitan structures**

This formula combines proximity between local authorities and their citizens with transfers of responsibility for metropolitan issues to a specific supra-community entity. In principle, the federal logic underlying such an arrangement precludes any hierarchical or subordinate relationship between the two territorial levels. The Canadian provinces of Ontario, Manitoba, Quebec and British Columbia created such structures for all of their metropolitan areas in the 1950s and 1960s; for a long time Metro Toronto (1953-1997) was the government prototype. Similar metropolitan governance structures also play a role in Metro Manila, Sao Paulo, Lima, Rio de Janeiro, Bombay and Calcutta.

The metropolitan level of governance can take any one of several forms: a metropolitan development council, a metropolitan development authority, or a fully empowered metropolitan government.

The metropolitan development council guarantees the retention of power by component local governments. Members of the local government designate their mayor, or some other local official, as their council member. These council members in turn select a council executive from among their number. Advisory councils with this type of structure can be found in most metropolitan areas in the United States, For example, the Metropolitan Washington Council of Governments (WASHCOG), was created in 1957 for the Washington metropolitan area. The same structure is also found in El Salvador in the Council of Mayors for the Metropolitan Area of San Salvador (COAMSS: Consejo de Alcaldes del Área Metropolitana de San Salvador).

The Metro Manila Development Authority (MMDA) was created by Filipino legislation in 1995. The council is made up of state representatives and 17 mayors (seven towns with extended powers, and 10 municipalities). It replaced the Manila Metropolitan Authority, which in 1990 had in turn replaced the Metropolitan Manila Commission, which was set up in 1975 with relatively important powers. The MMDA is not a territorial collective. It is a specific public body placed under the direct control of the President of the Philippines. The MMDA is responsible for planning, monitoring and co-ordination tasks, but its budgetary resources remain limited. It is considered not well suited to regulating the policies of its component parts because of the weakness of its integration instruments. The MMDA appears to be caught between the power of the state authorities and the desire of the 17 municipal authorities to escape from any direction or restriction imposed by higher authorities. (Laquian 2001).

Compared with a metropolitan development council, a metropolitan development authority concentrates more on technocratic functions than on political methods of governance. This model has been adopted by many Indian metropolitan areas, including New Delhi, Bombay, Karachi and Colombo.

The model of a metropolitan government superimposed on local authorities provides more functional integration, and its leadership is often elected directly by the people. This is the case in Tokyo and in Toronto.

Tokyo's TMG was created in 1943 by a merger of the City of Tokyo and the Prefecture of Tokyo. Today, it is a metropolitan prefecture consisting not only of the central town and its districts, but also the Tama area, which includes 39 municipalities, 26 towns, 5 localities and 8 villages. It appears that the TMG gives priority to running the services and development of 23 districts of the City of Tokyo guided by a system of financial equalization, while running the western part of its territory (Tama) in a more detached manner (Vogel 2001).

The degree of institutional thickness depends on a metropolitan structure's financial autonomy. The Chinese central government has given metropolitan areas significant scope in taxation and the management of their own resources, including buying and selling of land, tariffs and license fees and securing loans in China and abroad. In France, the communautés urbains are responsible for large budgets that correspond to their expanded areas of authority. The Communauté Urbaine de Bordeaux (CUB) budget is twice the size of the budget of the City of Bordeaux, in part because the CUB carries both compulsory and optional missions associated with the production of large facilities, the modernization of urban services and the development of the local economy.

*The degree of institutional thickness depends on a metropolitan structure's financial autonomy*

### c) Intercommunity co-operation
Governing metropolitan areas can also be carried out by means of agreements between and among municipalities. Legislation can prescribe or simplify such arrangements in designated sectors or services. An intermunicipal agreement, which is the most popular arrangement worldwide, can operate even in the absence of a specific metropolitan institution. Such cooperative agreements have been established in quasi-official form within the metropolitan areas of Sydney (Kübler 2005), Australia, and also in Lima-Callao, Santiago du Chile, and Santa Fe de Bogota in South America. They also foster mutual support between large Russian towns and their surrounding oblasts (regions) and among

*Flexible structures*

*to coordinate local*

*participation*

*around targeted*

*initiatives are*

*common, and have*

*become more so*

*over the past few*

*years*

many municipalities and counties in United States metropolitan regions.

Under these types of agreements, territorial fragmentation persists, but specific sector-based integration overcomes it in the performance of specific, sometimes narrowly defined sectors, such as water and sanitation, electricity, transportation and waste processing. The resulting arrangements are expected to realize economies of scale for the management of capital-intensive services.

The two main agencies of Metro Manila are the Metropolitan Waterworks and Sewerage System, and the Light-Rail Transit Authority. The Karachi Metropolitan Corporation specializes in economic development projects in the largest of Pakistan's cities, the Karachi Development Authority manages property and infrastructure and the Karachi Water Supply and Sewerage Boards preside over their respective tasks. Another example of inter-community cooperation is seen in the Dhaka metropolitan area of Bangladesh. There specialized agencies operate in parallel both in the City of Dhaka, and with a set of municipalities (pourashavas) and 42 state services. Among these, the most important are RAJUK (Capital Development Authority), the Dhaka City Corporation and the partly state-controlled Dhaka Water and Sewerage Authority. Similar arrangements may be found in other major metropolitan regions from Los Angeles to Sao Paulo (see Appendix).

Flexible structures to coordinate local participation around targeted initiatives are common, and have become more so over the past few years. The State of Sao Paulo, for instance, has initiated a number of these arrangements since the 1990s. In conjunction with an NGO, the Metropolitan Forum for Public Safety created the institute "Sao Paulo Contra a Violência." The state also established a system of governance for river watersheds, incorporating a variety of local stakeholders (Abers and Keck 2006).

Especially in the South, many metropolitan areas have weak intra-metropolitan coordi-

nation: in some cities there, none at all. Lack of sufficient local autonomy or capability often contributes to this problem. In Nigeria, Ethiopia and Tanzania, the urban authorities have rarely experienced a level of autonomy that would allow them to manage their own policies, much less forge cooperative agreements with neighboring local governments. In Nigeria, disputes over the proper application of existing governmental and professional skills have impeded intra-city cooperation. It was only in 2003 that the decentralization begun by Ethiopian state authorities gave Addis-Ababa a new charter with the express aim of ending a century of centralized development. In Tanzania, decentralization in the 1970s was simply a de-concentration exercise. Dar el-Salaam's new municipal structure, operational since February, 2000, followed a long period of technocratic and centralized management of the town. In all three of these African metropolitan towns, territorial parceling through the creation of new administrative units contrasts with the unification process seen in South Africa.

Intervention by higher level governments can also supplant metropolitan cooperation. In Israel, for instance, despite the high proportion of its population living in the four metropolitan areas of Tel Aviv, Jerusalem, Haifa and Beer Sheva, there are very few metropolitan governance mechanisms. In the Tel-Aviv metropolitan area most inter-community efforts are organizationally weak. At least in part, this is because central authorities maintain strict control over territorial development, transport and regional infrastructures (Razin and Hazan 2005).

## V.3. Democratic Depth

The citizens' role in the appointment and control of metropolitan authorities varies widely. Although electoral institutions alone are rarely sufficient to ensure responsiveness or democracy, recent local electoral reforms in many countries have been intended to extend opportunities for electoral participation. The growing size, complexity and territorial connectedness of metropolitan regions increasingly poses what Devas (2005) calls a tradeoff between "scale" and "voice" in governance. The larger the scale of governance, the more difficult it is to provide effectively for the participation of local units, neighborhoods, civil societies or individual citizens.

Indeed, integrated metropolitan structures have frequently been imposed by authoritarian central governments. Alongside technocratic efficiency in urban management, non-democratic governments have used metropolitan administration to control politically "sensitive" urban regions; that is, those suspected of having potential to breed opposition. For example, in 1973 it was the Brazilian military regime that created the nine metropolitan regions of Belém, Fortaleza, Recife, Salvador, Belo Horizonte, Rio de Janeiro, Sao Paulo, Curitiba and Porto Alegre. Though initially supported and tightly controlled by the government, only vestiges of this system remained at the start of the 1990s. By then, a new democratization and decentralization process was well underway. Similarly, the Metropolitan Manila Commission was created by the Marcos dictatorship in 1975, its leadership entrusted to Imelda Marcos.

Association with authoritarian regimes may explain why metropolitan governance has to a certain extent been neglected in some countries. In metropolitan governance systems that are based on the functions of specialized agencies, management is mainly carried out by technicians or bureaucrats. This necessarily reduces democratic control, and with it, legitimacy. Appointed by the President of the Philippines, the MMDA executive is often politically impotent in the presence of the 17 directly elected mayors of the towns in the metropolitan area. These mayors provide financial contributions to the metropolitan authority's budget.

Direct election of a metropolitan executive, as in Tokyo, Bangkok and Jakarta Raya, can enhance the legitimacy of metropolitan political institutions. South African metropol-

itan towns are run either by mayors (Johannesburg, Ekurhuleni, Tshwane, and Nelson Mandela) or by executive colleges (Cape Town and Ethekwini). Although the latter are not directly elected by the people, they are appointed by the parties according to their electoral score. In some cases, only some of the representatives are elected by the people. The council of Bombay's GBMC, for instance, is elected, but its executive is appointed by the state of Maharashtra.

Democracy can be organized on an infra-metropolitan scale. Sub-municipal elected governments play an especially important role when the municipal government is large. Thus, South African legislation allows provincial authorities to create either sub-councils or ward committees. The sub-councils, made up of municipal councilors and councilors from adjacent wards, perform a consultative role for the municipal council, which can delegate specific powers to them. Ward committees, made up of the ward municipal councilor and representatives of the people, function as instruments of participative democracy. Sixteen, then 20 sub-councils have been created in Cape Town. Ward committees have been set up in Johannesburg, Ekurhuleni, Tshwane and Nelson Mandela. As in many such instances of sub-municipal participation, municipal authorities have generally been hesitant to transfer power to these bodies. Initial assessments of their operation show only modest participation by local people (Cameron 2005).

In the case of the Tokyo TMG, arrangements for sub-metropolitan democracy have recently provided greater democratic depth. The mayors of the TMG districts have since 1974 been elected directly by the people. Since then, the districts have been transformed from administrative entities into special urban governments that carry out a portion of metropolitan government services. A reform to devolve financial functions and skills to the districts was adopted in 1998 and took effect in 2000. The metropolitan authority remains responsible for fire-fighting services as well as water and sanitation.

*Electoral institutions alone are rarely sufficient to ensure responsiveness or democracy, recent local electoral reforms in many countries have been intended to extend opportunities for electoral participation*

The depth of democracy refers to an aspiration that may never be entirely met. Nonetheless, governance structures that come closest are those that go beyond multi-level participation procedures and provide real empowerment to make participation meaningful at each level, from neighborhoods to metropolitan councils. Mechanisms that allow public participation in routine governmental planning and budgeting can also deepen democracy. Since the emergence of metropolitan areas as a widespread form of settlement, democratic theorists have advocated compound democratic forms of this nature (Dahl 1969).

## V.4. Relations with Higher-Level Governments

The politics of metropolitan governance plays out at higher levels of government, as well as within metropolitan regions themselves. From the perspective of leaders in metropolitan regions, effective governance often depends upon bringing wider regional and national organizations and resources to bear. As urban regions have become increasingly extended and connections with the hinterlands have grown, a better understanding is needed of the changing dynamics of intergovernmental relations between large cities and other surrounding regions.

It can not be surprising that relations between metropolitan regions and higher levels of government vary widely. At one end of the spectrum are urban regions that have secured a central position in the national political process. Such cities contain the bulk of a nation's urban population, economic activity and cultural production. The metropolitan region of Seoul, for instance, contains 47% of the Republic of Korean population; metropolitan Lima contains 32% of the population of Peru; metropolitan Buenos Aires has 32% of the Argentine population. The demographic weight of such cities often goes along with economic, political and cultural centrality. In the smaller countries of the North, the growth of cities into inter-connected regions has

sometimes created metropolitan regions with a similar kind of primacy. In the Netherlands, for instance, the national economy revolves around the Randstad region that encompasses Amsterdam, Rotterdam and the Hague. Even with a smaller proportion of the national population, status as a national capital can enhance the position of an urban region in the national economy and in the shaping of national policy.

In the South, the political dominance of major cities in the middle of the 20th Century provoked criticism that "urban bias" in policymaking had rewarded the urban elite at the expense of citizens living in smaller settlements and in rural areas (Lipton 1977; Bates 1983). Although cities, especially the largest, remain more prosperous than rural areas, recent analyses have rejected such a broad conclusion. The increasing prosperity of cities small and large, the growth of poverty within cities, the democratization of national and local governments, and the growing inter-dependency of city and countryside have fundamentally altered underlying assumptions of that early analysis (Corbridge and Jones 2005). Moreover, accumulating evidence shows that policy intervention can alter economic and social disparities between cities, as well as between cities and the countryside (Overman and Venables 2005). National development in much of the South now hinges on the exploitation of joint advantages in cities, in the countryside and in the rapidly growing zones in between.

By comparison with other metropolitan regions, those with a favored position in national politics can benefit from advantages in policymaking as well as in economic and cultural life. Paris, for instance, has been a repeated site of major planning initiatives since the 19th Century. Similar initiatives in many smaller French cities began only in the 1970s. Latin American capital cities such as Bogota and Santiago, as well as Bangkok, Manila and Seoul in Asia, have been leaders in efforts to build metropolitan governmental institutions.

However, some metropolitan regions, especially in the largest nations, lack a notable degree of socio-economic and political centrality. Under these conditions, metropolitan regions can still find a voice at higher levels of government, and secure crucial support for governance at the metropolitan level. In federal countries, metropolitan dominance within one of the federal states can secure similar resources. The Sao Paulo region in Brazil, for instance, dominates the larger state of Sao Paulo; the Mumbai region is the metropole for the Maharashtra state in India. Officials and activists from the Sao Paulo region helped secure state-level legislation for water basin governance that created new possibilities at the metropolitan level (Abers and Keck 2006). Similarly, public companies and officials from Maharashtra state have played an important role in the development plans of localities in metropolitan Mumbai.

In specific sectors of policy-making, state ministries or other specific organizations representing higher-level governments may contribute to metropolitan governance in ways that need not implicate those governments as a whole. National and state environmental agencies, for instance, often play active roles in antipollution initiatives. Organizations such as the Metropolitan Region Development Authorities in Karachi and Mumbai can mobilize higher-level government resources and authority on behalf of local development. (See Annex 1.)

At the national level, disparate metropolitan regions can form alliances to represent collective interests. Politically influential organizations of urban representatives, such as the German Staedtetag or the Nordic local government associations, provide examples of this potential (Sellers and Lidström 2007). In other countries such as the United States, urban representatives have faced growing marginalization in national political processes (Dreier, Mollenkopf and Swanstrom 2005).

The increasingly dispersed, fragmented and divided nature of metropolitan regions in many developed countries poses new problems for effective political and intergovernmental representation of this sort. At the same time, political and economic divergences between metropolitan regions can frustrate alliances in pursuit of common metropolitan interests. Intra-metropolitan and inter-metropolitan political divisions are now a recurrent feature of governance in the United States, and recently have begun to emerge in such countries as Canada, France, Switzerland and the United Kingdom (Hoffmann-Martinot and Sellers 2005).

## V.5. Sectoral Diversity and Limited Convergence

As Hooghe and Marks (2003) have observed, governance arrangements for local cooperation in specific policy sectors – roads, education, and pollution regulation – departs from the traditional hierarchical model of relations between higher-level and local governments. By and large, such arrangements for governing metropolitan regions reflect a global convergence around this more sector-specific, flexible approach, which is consistent with the "new regionalism." To a degree not seen in the earlier U.S. debates over polycentric and supra-communal arrangements, higher-level governments have played decisive roles in many sectors. But the main international commonalities in organizational practices correspond to differences between distinct sectoral domains.

A look at the main organizations involved in metropolitan governance in six major metropolitan regions provides illustrative examples of several distinctive patterns. (See Appendix.) The two examples from the developed world present both centralized and decentralized models. Los Angeles has relatively decentralized governing arrangements under a federal state, whereas Paris relies on a more centralized pattern under a unitary state. The remaining cases include Seoul, which has experienced recent transitions resulting from industrialization and democratization, and the Southern metropolises of Johannesburg, Mumbai and Sao Paulo. These six examples include two national capitals (Paris and Seoul), two capitals of federal states

*The increasingly dispersed, fragmented and divided nature of metropolitan regions in many developed countries poses new problems for effective political and intergovernmental representation*

(Mumbai and Sao Paulo), and two metropolises that are neither state nor national capitals (Johannesburg and Los Angeles). The comparative table of the Appendix focuses on the main organizations charged with carrying out policy implementation in nine sectoral domains, including the distribution of public and private responsibilities.

Regional geopolitical fragmentation by itself imposes similar problems for all of these different governmental structures. As is typical of other metropolises, the central city in these cases contains between 19% and 67% of the metropolitan population. In every case – even Johannesburg in the wake of the recent metropolitan reforms– the local governments across the metropolitan area divide into multiple units. If we include the infra-local district governance in Johannesburg, then every configuration of general-purpose governments includes both some local units and a second layer of units that takes the obligations of the entire metropolitan area into account. In each case, under both unitary and federal states, an intermediate unit of government at the regional level stands between the national level and these local arrangements.

Even more striking similarities among metropolitan institutions emerge from the breakdown of specific sectors of policy. For example, a similar configuration of agencies and firms addressing needs at national, metropolitan and local levels carries out transit services. Roads administration is also divided among national agencies responsible for big state and national roads, local governments charged with maintaining local roads and other governments for the roads in between. Municipal and inter-local arrangements manage most trash collection and land use planning sectors. Against a backdrop of national legislation in all six countries, local or metropolitan governments are often given the job of implementing environmental policies. These common trends reflect a transnational understanding of best practices, as well as common influences at work within each sector.

Of course, there are significant contrasts. In Seoul and in the Southern metropolitan areas, the examples demonstrate how public corporations tied to national or other higher-level governments play a more pervasive role in many areas. National public companies in all of these countries exercise exclusive control over all airports. National or state-held development companies play a leading role in land-use planning and roads. National or provincial governments carry out secondary and – except in Mumbai – primary education. Even where local governments bear much of the responsibility, there is less evidence of active inter-local arrangements or local initiatives in French and U.S. metropolitan areas. Especially in the rapidly developing areas outside the main urban centers, local government capacities remain weak.

The metropolitan regions of Los Angeles and Paris contrast with their counterparts in the South in their reliance on stronger local institutions, particularly those commanding the greater resources available to towns outside the urban centers. Yet Los Angeles and Paris differ significantly in their patterns of organizational fragmentation. To a far greater degree than that seen in Los Angeles, the 1584 communal governments of metropolitan Paris exemplify a polycentric model espoused by Public Choice proponents of territorial fragmentation. In trash collection, water or sewage and land-use planning, inter-governmental arrangements in Paris have proliferated more or less in ways that Public Choice theory would prescribe. Even in these domains, however, multiple municipalities often depend on unified centralized agencies or companies. Before the decentralization of the 1980s in France, even land use and planning were carried out by national field offices.

By comparison, the 180 municipalities and five counties of greater Los Angeles present a less fragmented organizational landscape of general purpose local governments. However, numerous sectors that are centralized in France are decentralized

*The metropolitan regions of Los Angeles and Paris contrast with their counterparts in the South in their reliance on stronger local institutions, particularly those commanding the greater resources available to towns outside the urban centers*

and fragmented here. Primary and secondary schools present perhaps the biggest contrast. Unlike any other metropolitan region, in the Los Angeles area a patchwork of local districts operating almost independently share the primary responsibility for this area. Ownership of the area's airports similarly belongs to four different local governments, although the central city owns the largest airport, Los Angeles International, and one other. Land-use planning lacks the coordinating intervention that has typified planning at the regional level in Paris and in other metropolitan regions. Even pollution regulation is the responsibility of metropolitan-level district organizations created by the state government, rather than being subject to direct intervention by higher-level governments. The result is an organizational landscape that is in important respects more fragmented than metropolitan Paris. Private contracting, a widespread practice in greater Los Angeles for trash collection, adds to the organizational fragmentation of local service delivery.

A full comparison of metropolitan governance would include other elements that would be difficult to categorize without more detailed comparative case analysis. These include legal norms, fiscal relations between different levels of government, the role of private factors, and the dynamics of leadership. Organizational comparison nonetheless demonstrates both broad global similarities in the practical form that governance takes and strong contrasts that stand out boldly only when differences between sectors of governance and policy are taken into account.

## VI. Conclusion: The Emerging Metropolitan Agenda

To a significant degree, the governance of 21st-Century metropolitan regions poses similar questions both for the established metropolis of the North and for the emerging ones of the South. The extension and increasing diversity of metropolitan settlement has imposed new conditions for governance in the metropolitan areas of both regions. In both, arrangements for governance present parallel dilemmas of fragmentation and coordination. North and South, the formal institutional alternatives for metropolitan governance share similar dimensions. Metropolitan governance presents common problems of accommodating an array of diverse, conflicting interests and influences. In both the North and the South, growing mobility and the influence of trans-local and trans-national connections are reshaping the possibilities as well as the imperatives for metropolitan governance.

In important respects, however, the problems of metropolitan governance in Southern urban regions still differ from those in Northern ones. The growth of Southern metropolitan regions has created the largest metropolitan areas in the world. More compact, denser and less geographically fragmented, Southern metropolises are more likely to be driven by security concerns born of great disparities between affluent and poor neighborhoods. Southern metropolitan areas also have fewer economic and administrative resources to bring to bear on far more pressing and massive problems.

### VI.1. Multi-Level Governance

As urban regions have become increasingly extended, and connections with their hinterlands have proliferated, a better understanding is needed of the changing dynamics of intergovernmental relations between cities and their surrounding regions. Metropolitan regions in both the South and the North are not only crucial to the realization of national policy in numerous domains, but can take an active role in influencing policies at higher levels.

## VI.2. Participation in Metropolitan Governance

Participation in metropolitan governance presents important issues for the realization of democracy as well as for effective decision-making processes. Whatever institutional form it takes, governance at the metropolitan level confronts the problem of incorporating the participation of a growing number of increasingly diverse interests. Understanding the informal as well as the formal dimensions of participation is crucial. The challenges surrounding participation are particularly acute for marginalized groups, such as the urban poor and ethnic and racial minorities.

## VI.3. Ecological Sustainability

Environmental policy in many domains depends on effective implementation at the local level, and in turn on the efficacy of metropolitan governance. The provision of adequate water resources and water quality, especially in the South, presents some of the most far-reaching challenges. Global and national efforts to assure air quality and carbon conservation depend on sustainable transportation as well as solid regulatory and energy policies at the local level. Metropolitan initiatives are critical to these efforts.

## VI.4. Social and Spatial Inequalities

Addressing the legal informality and poverty of Southern cities is one of the highest priorities for metropolitan governance. Concentrations of the disadvantaged often require more intervention and public expenditure to combat related problems, such as crime, inadequate education and health needs (Pack 1993; Chernick and Reschovsky 1995). In diverse, segregated metropolitan regions, fragmented governance can exacerbate the disadvantages of the poor in obtaining public services (Alesina, Baqir and Easterly 1997). Similarly, extended, diverse metropolitan regions can offer affluent communities opportunities and incentives to segregate themselves from the rest of society. This process can also undermine collective efforts to provide goods to the entire metropolis.

*Metropolitan governance presents common problems of accommodating an array of diverse, conflicting interests and influences*

## Annex 1 — Examples of Metropolitan Organization, by Tasks

| Metropolitan area | Los Angeles | Paris | Seoul | Sao Paulo | Mumbai | Johannesburg |
|---|---|---|---|---|---|---|
| Population (per km²) | 196 per km² | 927 per km² | 1929 per km² | 2.314 per km² | 4.089 per km² | 1.692 per km² |
| Percent in central city | 22.29% | 19.00% | 44.94% | 57.32% | 66.90% | 38.23% |
| Sub-national governments | State (1), counties (5), municipalities (180), regional councils of governments (11) (advisory) | Regions (1), departements (7), communes (1.584) City of Paris | Province (1), metropolitan local governments (2), other municipalities (20) | State (1), Metropolitan Regions (3), municipalities (139) | State (1), municipal corporations (7), municipal councils (13), state districts (4), villages (900) | Metropolitan or district municipalities (3) |
| Transit | Amtrak (national rail company), Metrolink (joint authority of transit agencies), separate county transit authorities (5), interlocal authorities (6), municipal systems (39), private lines | SNCF (national railway), RATP (public company with metro, bus, regional rail), OPTILE (network of 39 public, private lines), STIVO (network of public and private lines) | Korail (national railway), Seoul Metropolitan government, Seoul Metro Subway Corporation and Seoul Metro Rapid Transit Corporation (city-owned companies), provincial transit authorities, municipal systems and private lines, national ministries | State Secretariat for Metropolitan Transports, Sao Paulo Transporte, SA, (private company), Companhia do Metropolitano de Sao Paulo Metro, Companhia Paulista de Trens Metropolitanos, and Empresa Metropolitana de Transportes Urbanos (state companies), numerous private firms by concession | Indian Railways (national public company), State Road Transport Corporation, Mumbai Metropolitan Region Development Authority (state agency with participation by central city), other state agencies, interlocal and municipal bus services | Spoornet (national railway), Metrobus (central city-owned company); municipal governments; provincial Department of Public Transport, Roads, and Works |
| Roads | Federal Highway Administration (national roads), State Transportation Department, Regional Council of Governments (advisory), counties, municipalities (local roads | Infrastructure ministry field offices (region, department); departments, municipalities (local roads) | Ministry of Construction and Transportation, Special Metropolitan City Government, Provincial/City/County/District Government, public corporations (Korea Construction Management Corporation, Korea Expressway Corporation) | Federal Transportation Ministry (federal roads), State Department of Roads, municipalities (local roads), private companies by concession | National Highways Authority, Mumbai Metropolitan Region Development Authority (state agency), City Industrial Development Co. (state company), municipal governments | National Roads Agency (national roads), Johannesburg Roads (central city-owned company), municipal governments |
| Trash collection | Private contracting (42), municipal governments (13), some interlocal cooperation | Municipal and a limited number of intercommunal agencies: 65+ (collection), 30+ (treatment) | Municipal governments and private contracting. Some interlocal cooperation | Municipal governments (mostly), limited use of private contracting, municipal firms | Municipal governments, limited private contracting | Pikitup (central city-owned company), other municipal governments |
| Water/sewage | Numerous county, municipal and interlocal utilities or agencies, private contractors | Municipal and a limited number of intercommunal agencies, private contractors | Municipal governments, national public corporations (Environment Management Cooperation (EMC), ENVICO (Korea Environment & Resources Corporation)) and interlocal cooperation directed by Ministry of Environment | Basic Sanitation Company of the State of Sao Paulo (SABESP) (state-owned company), state government, basin committees of local officials and others | Municipal governments, City Industrial Development Co. and Maharashtra Industrial Development Co. (state companies) | Johannesburg Water (city-owned company), other municipal governments, private contractors |

## Annex 1 — Examples of Metropolitan Organization, by Tasks (Cont.)

| Metropolitan area | Los Angeles | Paris | Seoul | Sao Paulo | Mumbai | Johannesburg |
|---|---|---|---|---|---|---|
| **Airports** | Five (two owned by central city, others by separate municipal or county governments) | Two (owned by Paris Airports (national public company)) | Two (owned by Korea Airport Corporation (national public company)) | Three (owned by INFRAERO (National public company)) | Two (both under Airport authority of India, one managed by private firm) | Five (owned by Airports Company South Africa (national public corporation)) |
| **Land use planning** | Municipal governments, counties, advisory council of governments | Municipal governments, interlocal cooperation, private contracting | Municipal governments advised by Korea Land Corporation (national public company) and Ministry of Construction and Transportation, Seoul Metropolitan Development Corporation (city owned company) | Municipal governments, private contracting, Empresa Municipal de Urbanizacao company) | Mumbai Metropolitan Region Development Authority (state agency with central city participation), City Industrial Development Co. (state company), other state agencies, municipal governments | Municipal governments, advised by provincial government |
| **Air pollution** | Air quality districts established by state (2), governed by boards of local officials | National government agency field offices | Municipal governments and interlocal cooperation led by Ministry of Environment | State Environment Ministry, State Environment Agency (CETESB) | State pollution control board, municipal governments | Municipal governments |
| **Water pollution** | Water quality districts established by state (3), governed by boards of local officials | National government agency field offices | Metro government and municipal agencies and public corporations, Ministry of Construction and Transportation, K-Water (Korean Water Resources Corporation (national public company), nationally designated water test centers (usually public institutions) | State Environment Ministry, State Environment Agency (CETESB), basin committees of local officials and others | State pollution control board, municipal governments | Municipal governments |
| **Primary and secondary education** | Local school districts (172) | National ministry of education | National ministry of Education | State Secretary of Education (elementary and secondary), municipalities (elementary) | State government (secondary), local governments (primary), private schools | Provincial government Department of Education |

**Sources:** *Abers and Keck 2006; Metropolis 2007; Segbers et al. 2007; and governmental and organizational websites.*

# CONCLUSION

## Decentralization and Democracy: A Global Perspective in 2007

### Tim Campbell

The purpose of the First World Report on Decentralization and Local Democracy – and of this overview – is neither normative nor prescriptive[1]. Rather, the aim is to provide a balanced view of the state of decentralization and local democracy in the world.

The opening section of these conclusions provides an overview of trends. The section also frames the major issues –the policy objectives and component issues– that virtually all states must engage to achieve decentralized democracy, noting outstanding areas of progress as well as areas of concern. The succeeding section then reviews each of six central policy issues, analyzed from the perspective of their contribution to decentralized democracy. Next, are emerging sets of global issues, selected Millennium Development Goals – climate change, land use, health, and gender – are directly relevant to local governments and will require more attention in the future. Another emerging issue, though not an MDG, concerns metropolitan governance. Suggestions for next steps to address the state of inter-governmental relations and democracy are included in the closing section.

Though the regional reports provide a central source of information for this synthesis, additional perspectives are brought in from a variety of local, national, independent, and supra-national organizations. In addition, recent research from a sampling of academic literature complement and round out the discussion.

## I. The Many Faces of Decentralization and Democracy

The nations covered in this report present a wide variety of experiences, most of them leading toward decentralized governance in some form. The fact that so many states have chosen to move along the path of decentralization constitutes a remarkable phenomenon, the impetus for which must connect with deep underlying structural factors felt around the globe.

Among the more frequently mentioned drivers of change are the exhaustion of the central state model after the collapse of the Soviet Union and the realization that a new departure towards state development was required, one that relied on a broader-based pyramid of legitimacy and state presence. Meanwhile in Europe, the process of regionalization was encouraged by the European Union and many countries were confronting the emergence of regionalist demands (Spain, Italy, Scotland, and Northern Ireland). At virtually the same time, and for similar reasons, the spread of democracy was a palpable form of reconnecting citizens and governments, and many actors and grass roots movements pushed for deeper democratization

1.  The author wishes to acknowledge the extensive and detailed contributions of the World Secretariat of UCLG to the preparation of this report. The present analysis draws from regional chapters from time to time. Reference is made to the respective chapter whenever necessary.

in the countries of Africa, Asia and Latin America (Haggard, 1994; Campbell 2003).

In a related sphere, and about the same time, liberalization of trade and the dramatically increased velocity of global transactions suddenly thrust states into a more vulnerable, more competitive environment, as compared to just decades earlier (Swyngedouw, E. A. 1992; Amin and Tomaney, 1995). One consequence of the globalized economy has been the rise of cross-state corporate connections. As national borders began to lose their importance as markers of comparative advantage, regions and cities became the next distinguishing feature on the economic landscape (Harris, 2003; Taylor and Watts, 1995). Some authors point to the "...opposing forces of horizontal competition imposing market based disciplines in Europe... constrained by within-country redistributive tendencies and mobility-based competition." (Salmon, 2007). Accordingly, a regional perspective on economic development began to assume an important place in both the process and the outcome of decentralization.

## Snapshot of the Regions

In short, looking across an extremely diverse set of nations grappling with a complicated field of issues, nations have moved on decentralization in a half dozen distinct directions, and have not held close to any single normative framework to guide the formulation and implementation of decentralized governance.

- European countries seem to have embarked on a new phase of territorial reforms. Not all states are similarly affected by this development, with some in fact remaining outside of it. In essence, the reforms are concerned with strengthening the municipal and intermunicipal framework, a trend to regionalization, and the problems related to organizing urban areas.

- In North America, higher-level governments have shifted more of the responsibility for financing activities to the local level, often cutting back on fiscal support from above. New substantive mandates and procedural requirements for accountability have often accompanied these shifts. To varying degrees local governments operate under less regulatory restrictions than in other regions and have sought new modes of service delivery through privatization and public-private partnerships. Various innovations have introduced elements of interlocal cooperation or territorial consolidation.

- In Africa, implementation of the decentralization process has rarely been properly planned. Many countries, especially south of the Sahara, have undertaken reforms in the field of organization of the state and public life, particularly by adopting decentralization policies. These countries have organized local elections, which have seen local authorities emerging as new public authority figures alongside the national authorities. In almost all these countries, this splitting of public authority has caused problems, as this major institutional change has not yet been reflected in the behavior of most national authorities. But in West and Central Africa, apart from Mali, Senegal and Burkina Faso, there is no real plan to implement decentralization, which seems to rest on policy announcements. And in North African countries the autonomy of local government is still restricted overall in relation to the central state.

- In Eurasia, the main idea of the reforms was to separate the state from local self-government. Legal reforms have been approved, but for the most part the functions of local authorities are not clearly defined. The Soviet system of sub-national government forms a legacy that continues to influence the evolution of decentralization. The principle of local autonomy has often come into collision with that of regional autonomy and nowhere more than in the Russian Federation from the early 1990s onwards. It is possible to distinguish three groups of countries. In the first – Armenia, Azerbaijan and Russia – local governments could be seen as independent institutions. Whereas in the second group – Georgia, Kyrgyz Republic, Moldova and Ukraine – the process of the formation of local self-government is still not concluded. Reforms can hardly be implemented, or simply could not be achieved until now. The third group is composed of the states of Central Asia (Kazakhstan, Tajikistan, Turkmenistan, Uzbekistan) where local issues in this region are vested in local state organs subordinate to central government.

- In Latin America, the three biggest nations (Argentina, Brazil, Mexico) all federal systems, focused mainly on strengthening the intermediate levels of government, although Brazil shifted more weight to the municipal level. In República Bolivariana de Venezuela, also a federal country, contradictory reforms are actually taking place that could affect the nature of local institutions. In the Andean countries, decentralization has taken place through far-reaching constitutional and legislative reforms, in relatively brief processes. Colombia and Bolivia produced comprehensive visions of reforms in the early 1990s. But economic and political crisis altered their coherence and slowed the pace of their implementation. In Peru, the process of decentralization restarted after 2000 following a reversal of direction in the 1990s. The unitary states of the Southern Cone – Chile, Uruguay and Paraguay – have also carried out reforms shaped by their respective characteristics. Central American countries have enacted laws on decentralization, and their main challenge is to achieve their implementation.

- In the Middle East and Western Asia, in spite of the ceaseless political, military, and religious tensions, some advances deserve recognition: the first local elections in Saudi Arabia, the holding of democratic local elections in the West Bank and Gaza, the restoration of the mayoral elections by universal suffrage in Jordan, and the 2002 constitutional reforms in Bahrain. In Turkey, three new laws favourable to decentralization were adopted in 2004-2005. Decentralization is one of the criteria for membership of the European Union.

- In Asia Pacific, decentralization has become a major theme of governance reform over the past decade and decentralization has for the most part been accompanied by enhanced local democracy. But the forms and patterns of local governance have varied widely, as have the outcomes, reflecting the diversity of country contexts. While there are clearly a great many weaknesses in the current arrangements for decentralized governance, and while further reforms will undoubtedly be required, it is hard to imagine that any wholesale return to a centralized system of governance would be either appropriate or politically acceptable.

## Framework of Issues

In short, decentralization has been pursued by different countries with different objectives – some political, others more economic, still others give more weight to better services or democracy. Furthermore, states have placed emphasis on different combinations of the half dozen strategic areas which must be engaged to decentralize successfully. These include national policy, state organization, responsibilities of local governments, intergovernmental finance, mechanisms of participation, and capacity strengthening. Taken together, the objectives and strategic areas constitute a framework for understanding the breadth and depth of the decentralization experience.

To illustrate, from the snapshot of cases, political reforms were mixed with economic restructuring in some regions, notably in the transition states in Eastern Europe, the former Soviet Union, and China and Vietnam. Still others centered on democracy and modernization of the state as in Africa, Latin America and in some countries in Asia (e.g. Indonesia, Philippines). Improved services were perhaps a more notable priority in North America, Australia and New Zealand. And though this categorization is far from neat, pursuit of policy and practice, especially in political reforms, economic development, and finance, has strayed even further afield from the avowed objectives of many states.

## Velocity of Change

Turning to the pace of change in decentralization, the nations covered in the reports can be classified very broadly in three groups. At one extreme, are those countries (many of them higher income GDP) where decentralization has advanced quite far, having built on 50 years or more of consolidated local government. In many countries of this group (and some countries in other groups, as noted below), deliberate if not measured progress has been made on policy and technical issues in a search for what must be called a dynamic balance in power sharing. Shifting political preference is complicated by gradual improvement in institutional capacity and occasional shifts in technological possibilities, all of which can move the fulcrum of balance in central/local relations.

At another extreme, mainly but not entirely in the Middle East, are those countries that are taking a long, slow take-off, mostly in the direction of improving participation at the local level. A few countries are making good faith efforts and show promise to be sources of

advice and counsel for their neighbors in the region. Reviewing the uneven record, Cheema and Rondonelli (2007) point to ineffectiveness in implementation, as opposed to weaknesses in the concept of decentralization itself. They also caution about the use of parallel administrations at the subnational level, a ploy that is ultimately self-defeating. The most troubled cases, from the point of view of power-sharing and democracy, are those countries afflicted by armed conflict or oil wealth. They present understandable sluggishness, even resistance.

In the middle, a disparate collection of countries that, with few exceptions, are in an active tug of war over the state of decentralized democracy. Some detailed examples, below, are drawn from the regional chapters.

- The most exemplary case in this respect is South Africa, where the end of the Apartheid regime imposed a new approach to governance based on decentralization and involving the entire population in public management at all levels. In most francophone countries of Africa, the profusion of statutes complicates the implementation of decentralization and slows things down, causing substantial delays between approval of laws and their actual enforcement (delays of 10 years are common). In countries of North Africa, the pace of decentralization is uneven.

- In Latin America, some countries, such as Bolivia, Brazil, Chile, Colombia, Peru, and República Bolivariana de Venezuela started early and, with Argentina and Ecuador, went further than others in the devolution of functions and resources. Peru and República Bolivariana de venezuela reversed some of the decentralization reforms begun in the 1980-90s. Mexico has moved forward with a "new federalism," but progress is slower at the municipal level. Other countries are evolving to a lesser extent.

- In Eurasia, particularly in Eastern Europe, reforms were taken quickly to dismantle the former system and move toward local self-government, and at present the countries have attained different levels of institutional development. In some countries local self-government exists as an independent institution, while in others reform has not been implemented.

- In Asia-Pacific, Indonesia, the Philippines, and India provide the most dramatic examples of major reform for enhanced local government autonomy. Countries such as China and Vietnam have adopted decentralization strategies within the context of strongly centralized political ruling systems. In some other countries, like Pakistan, there has been a noticeable cyclical movement to and fro between periods of centralization and decentralization. By contrast, in Bangladesh and Malaysia resistance from the center has impeded any substantial decentralization that would strengthen the political role of local government. Finally, the OECD countries in the region, Australia, Japan, the Republic of Korea and New Zealand, also emphasize decentralization as part of their ongoing administrative reform processes.

With these two perspectives – on strategic objectives and on velocity of change – we turn now to explore how the nations and local governments have approached the organization of the state. To what extent have policy frameworks guided the design and implementation of decentralized governance? What changes have been made in assigning functions, in providing adequate finance, and arranging for participation and democracy? How closely have governments adhered to international expectations and standards as expressed in the UN Habitat *Guidelines on Decentralization and the Strengthening of Local Authorities* and the *European Charter of Local Self-Government*?

## II. Progress and Pitfalls: Six Core Issues

Though the preceding introduction may be rhetorically useful for grasping a glimpse of the global state of affairs, it is not a tidy categorization and has limitations in terms of understanding the tactical issues in implementation. Countries are in various degrees of engagement with the six areas of policy 1) national policy and strategy, 2) organizational units, 3) responsibilities, 4) financing, 5) mechanisms of participation and accountability, and 6) institutional capacity. This section reviews the six core issues, noting trends across or within regions, and spotting promising areas of progress where lessons may be useful in a wider setting.

### Policy and Strategy

This review of countries and regions reveals a wide spectrum of policy positions and organizational strategies for local governments. Though few countries have full-blown strategies, as we note below, most make some reference to the *European Charter* and *Guidelines on Decentralization* (see Box 1, below). Both documents refer to principles that have been widely discussed, synthesized and generally accepted by the international community. The *European Charter* was published in 1985. UN Habitat in close collaboration with local authorities produced *Guidelines on Decentralization*.

Only a handful of nations have framed a comprehensive policy on decentralization, blending political reform (power-sharing), economic development, and democratic choice-making with capacity-strengthening and financing in order to produce a long term solution. As noted above, Bolivia, South Africa, and Indonesia have each mounted comprehensive elements, but not a complete strategy. Bolivia and South Africa produced comprehensive visions (in 1992 and 1994, respectively), and though Bolivia recently reaffirmed its intentions (Government of Bolivia 2006), neither go-

## Box 1    Guidelines and Charter of Europe

### UN Habitat Guidelines on Decentralization and the Strengthening of Local Authorities

- The principle of subsidiarity constitutes the rationale underlying the process of decentralization. According to that principle, public responsibilities should be exercised by those elected authorities, which are closest to the citizens.
- In many areas powers should be shared or exercised concurrently among different spheres of government. These should not lead to a diminution of local autonomy or prevent the development of local authorities as full partners.
- National, regional and local responsibilities should be differentiated by the constitution or by legislation, in order to clarify the respective powers and to guarantee access to the resources necessary for the decentralized institutions to carry out the functions allocated to them
- As far as possible, nationally determined standards of local service provision should take into account the principle of subsidiarity when they are being drawn up and should involve consultation with local authorities and their associations.
- Local authorities should freely exercise their powers, including those bestowed upon them by national or regional authorities, within the limits defined by legislation. These powers should be full and exclusive, and should not be undermined, limited or impeded by another authority except as provided by law.

### European Charter of Local Self-Government

- Basic powers and responsibilities of local authorities shall be prescribed by the constitution or by statute
- Local authorities shall, within the limits of the law, have full discretion to exercise their initiative
- Public responsibilities shall generally be exercised, in preference, by those authorities which are closest to the citizen.
- Powers given to local authorities shall normally be full and exclusive.
- Where powers are delegated to them by a central or regional authority, local authorities shall, insofar as possible, be allowed discretion in adapting their exercise to local conditions.

vernment has been able to sustain coherent effort to implement its strategy.

Indonesia's sudden "Big Bang" of reform is notable for the scope of change (transferring several million public sector workers to local authorities), but not for the integrated, long term solution needed. None of these countries has developed a comprehensive decentralization plan, a blue print with concrete objectives and milestones to guide the decentralization process, including local capacity strengthening and a central agency to see through the entire process. Even when piecemeal legislation is in place, sluggish regulation drags down the speed and limits the reach of implementation.

International institutions – financial, technical, and political – have had no shortage of normative frameworks to recommend to governments, yet neither do they fully address the practical issues of implementation most governments face. The international

financial assistance organizations like the World Bank and the regional development banks adhere to a market-based approach, seeking to introduce quasi-market mechanisms to guide supply and demand of public goods. The Asian Development Bank does not have a specific policy paper on decentralization. Instead, it focuses on good governance and corruption.

The Inter-American Development Bank (IDB) published its public sector strategy in 1996 and last year issued a companion policy paper on the issues of implementing decentralization (IDB 1996, 2002). Like most development banks, the IDB policy starts with the fiscal imperative of macroeconomic stability. Guarding against excessive debt, and particularly sub-national debt held by domestic banks and even suppliers, is not merely to keep the banks in line with their primary stakeholders, national governments. It is also to safeguard exposure to risk and increased cost of borrowing on international capital markets.

A companion principle in the international finances institutions (IFI) framework is management of economic systems free from distortions (for instance, due to interference in local decision-making). Efficient resource allocation places a premium on expression of demand, especially at the local level. The banks also recommend clarity in the division of labor among levels of government. All of the development banks espouse a similar line in connection with reform of the state.

The World Bank recently cast decentralization issues in terms of poverty alleviation and services for the poor. Building on earlier work devoted to reform of the state (World Bank 1995), the World Bank's *World Development Report* (WDR) of 2000 dedicated a chapter to decentralization, and the 2004 report focuses on services to the poor, arguing that politicians, providers and the poor must be brought into tighter juxtaposition with one another in order to improve provision of and access to basic health-care and education. A key mechanism is "local voice." Expression of demand at the local level goes hand in glove with the idea of participatory democracy. The Bank points out that local government plays a key role in certain circumstances, for instance, when local populations are more or less homogeneous and when services are easy to monitor. These tests could prove useful in evaluating policies of nations and roles of local governments.

Thus, governments have the benefit of several international sources on general principles. We shall see in the ensuing discussion that more practical strategies of implementation might be useful. Before moving on, note should be taken of important areas that have been largely ignored and should be addressed in the future. One gap is the calculation of the cost to the nation of decentralizing in a piecemeal or haphazard way. None of the regional chapters speak of the economic and social costs of burdens being transferred to local authorities in the shape of half-baked or under-financed decentralization schemes imposed on poorly-equipped local governments.

## Organization of the State

The inchoate nature of national decentralization policies is mirrored by piecemeal measures, either explicit or tacit, to organize administration of the state at the local level. This may be partly due to the dual nature of governmental units. Governments have both **territorial** and **functional** aspects. They are put in place to connect to citizens **and** they operate to deliver services. Decentralization experiences sometimes get wrapped up with these multi-dimensional features – federal, unitary, territorial, functional – producing a system of governance which is incomplete or out of sync.

Many federated systems accord to states, with their own constitutions or legal statues or both, the powers to govern, regulate, sometimes even create, lower tier, municipal governments. For the most part federated systems have been adopted in large territories, as for instance in Russia, Brazil, and India, and often, national governments like Argentina, USA and India have left many issues for the states to decide. This can either compound or help to solve problems, depending on the system in question, i.e., states can help coordinate, but as the regional reports have shown, they can also introduce confusion and interfere with national policy on both functional and representational issues.

Some states were more inclined to respond to a clamor for representation, as in the majority of African, some Latin American and some Asian countries in the 1990s. Most states in Eurasia have created or extended local government units to accommodate regional or ethnic groups. Other countries (New Zealand, Germany) focus on the functional side, aiming to improve the extension or efficiency of services. This sometimes means a diminution of numbers

| Figure 1 | Local Governments and Population Percentage Distribution, LAC |
|---|---|

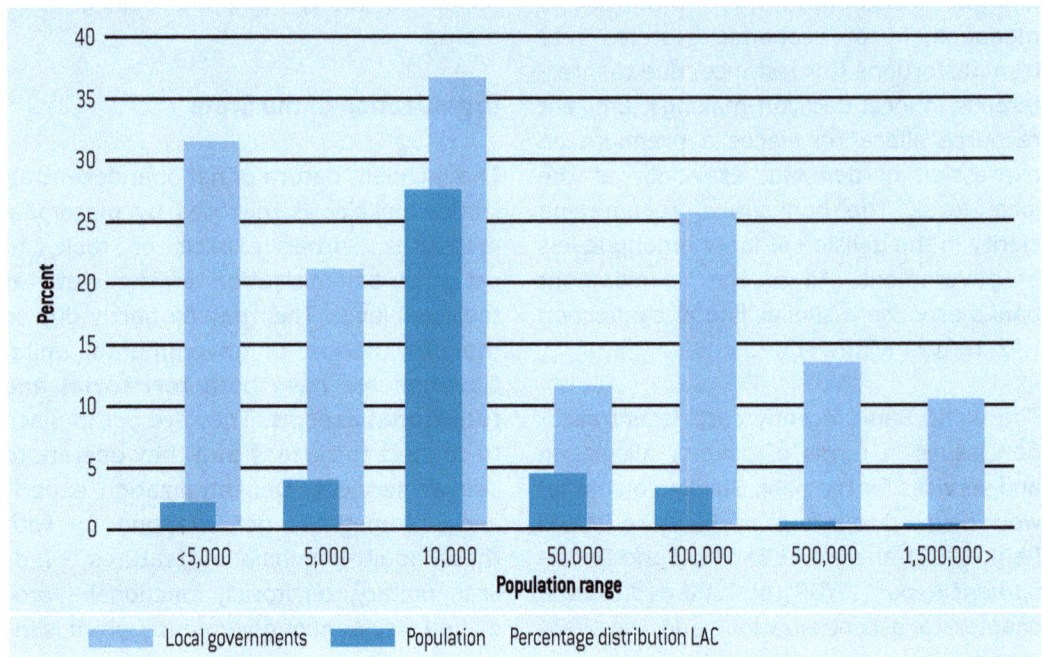

Local governments — Population — Percentage distribution LAC

**Source:** IDB 2006.

in local government units. In OECD countries, a wave of amalgamation is taking place to reduce the sheer number of local government units in the interest of improving efficiency. OECD Countries such as the UK, Belgium, and Greece, among others have reduced the numbers of governmental units by substantial fractions. Where local units were weak in the past (Hungary, France, Italy), new tiers have been created to handle new tasks.

The wide range of organizational approaches, and even conceptions of local government, makes head to head comparisons between nations not just difficult, but also ultimately unproductive. Nevertheless, it is useful to gain an appreciation for the variations in approaches taken by states in different regions.

Many countries are experiencing problems where units of government overlap in dense urban areas. Countries have explored various kinds of partnerships among

local units –a step that is frequently allowed in national legislation. North American local governments have fewer constraints imposed upon them about cooperating across boundaries, both horizontal and vertical (with states). The US is unusual also in having developed a large number of special districts; governmental units with high target finance and a tightly focused mandate (for instance in primary education, environmental controls or fire safety).

Outside Europe and North America, Japan is the only country that provides examples of policies of amalgamation of municipalities. Horizontal cooperation among first tier units of government is taken up again in a later section of this paper on metropolitan governance.

It should be noted that the sheer numbers of small local governments implies a policy dilemma. The weak institutional capacity of many small local governments affects a

| Box 2 | Subsidiarity—an issue at the heart of autonomy—is viewed in different ways by academics, political organizations, and development institutions |
|---|---|
| **Oates, 1972** | "Assign to the lowest level of government possible, those local public goods and services which can best be delivered at that level." |
| **World Bank** 2004, p. 189 | "The lowest tier of government that can internalize the costs and benefits of the service." |
| **European Charter** Art. 4.3 | "Public responsibilities shall generally be exercised, in preference, by those authorities which are closest to the citizen." |

minor share of the population, while a few strong local governments of big cities hold an important share of the population (see Figure 1). Take the example of Latin America, a region with 16,400 units of local government and a population (2005) of nearly 550 million. Less than 5 % of local governments – those in big cities – contain more than half the population, while more than 53 % of local governments in small towns and rural areas cover less than a tenth of the population. Similar proportions are found in most regions (see Figure 1).

In a nutshell, the issue of organizing local government units is one of balancing a tension between two imperatives. Effective representation is needed to serve democracy, but this tends to require more units of government. Against this expansionary push is a constricting pull to reduce the number of units, or fold them into higher tier governments in order to achieve economies of scale and more efficient service delivery. Virtually all countries in the middle and many in the advanced stages are engaged at some level with this issue.

## Responsibilities

The logic of assigning responsibilities to local governments is to achieve efficacy or efficiency in delivery of local goods and services to citizens. And though the guideline principles of subsidiarity and autonomy provide a normative standard for gov-

ernments, in practice, states find many dilemmas when implementing subsidiarity (See Box 2).

States also face many temptations to push the limits, like shifting responsibilities to local governments with little or no consultation and without corresponding financial resources. The issues related to responsibilities can be summed up as follows: a) clarity and consistency in observing subsidiarity and autonomy of choice; b) achieving efficiency in allocation and in delivery of services, an issue that involves public and/or private provision of service; and c) the impact of technology.

***Subsidiarity and Autonomy in Choice.*** Most countries have devolved a core set of local functions, and many countries gradually adjust these, as circumstances require. On the one extreme are China's big cities that handle supra-local functions like judiciary, pensions, and economic development. A more typical arrangement involves local public services, like water connections, streets, solid waste, local markets, urban and land use planning, and primary care in health and often education, social policy and sometimes economic development and housing.

In Europe the most important variations relating to powers and responsibilities occur in the fields of education, health, and social security or benefits. Broadly, local governments are responsible for such services in the Nordic countries and to a large extent in the United Kingdom. Others restrict assignments to be either exclusive (land-use controls in many countries) or shared, such as primary education in most countries and in others, police and security. Still others share responsibilities. Turkey provides an example of a modus vivendi in which municipalities and the Special Provincial Administrations (SPAs) share public services, including education (maintenance of school buildings).

None of these variations necessarily violates the principles of subsidiarity and autonomy. The problem comes, as regional reports frequently show, when assignments are shifted in a way that is unclear, is ambiguous, or is unreasonable, arbitrary, or inconsistent. For instance, in the US, recent devolution of Home Security responsibilities suddenly imposed severe financial constraints on many cities. Another example is found in Eurasia, where in most countries the functions of local authorities are not clearly defined by law, largely because of an unending process of redistribution of powers between different levels of government. In the Middle East, on the other hand, many countries designate local services in national law, but these are sometimes ambiguously worded, contradicted, or ignored. The report on the Middle East notes that formal assignments are "highly idealized and out of step with reality..." (of local authorities and institutional capacity).

In Africa, while public assertion of the new nominal powers of local governments is widespread, the actual transfer of real executive and operational powers is still rare. In Northern Africa, national ministries typically retain control of local services, or delegate them to the private sector. This tendency can also be observed in West and Central Africa, although basic services there for education, health, water, sanitation and transportation are generally acknowledged as local concerns. In several eastern and southern African countries, like Ghana, South Africa and Uganda, cen-

tral government defines strategic guidelines for sectoral policies regarding health, water and education and local governments are responsible for implementation.

Direct intervention by higher levels is another form of disturbing subsidiarity and violating the principle of choice. Ambiguous or overlapping jurisdictions sometimes lead to "end run" practices –nominal decentralization coupled with direct delivery by central government. This represents a significant slippage in the way governments should work. Serious problem arose in Latin America in the 1990s when central governments either delivered directly to local citizens, as a means of gaining political support, or simply fell short on coordination, meaning that both central and local governments were spending on redundant services, resulting in the increase of economic costs to the nation (Peterson, 1997). Similar problems have been detected in Russia.

Intervention from higher levels of government in Europe is currently the focus of debate in connection with the European Community Laws on public service management subject to competition rules. The issue is the extent to which, in seeking to provide certain services, national powers effectively limit local self government. The position of local governments is that they should enjoy complete freedom to choose the modality of service provision that best reflects the needs of their communities.

The uncertainty and lack of definition illustrated in these examples – examples which are a few among many cited in the regional reports – effectively rob the subsidiarity principle of its virtues and limit the choice of local governments.

***Efficiency in Allocation and Production.*** A second aspect of the assignments issue is efficiency. Two distinct functions are involved: 1) deciding on what is needed (allocation efficiency) and 2) actually delivering the services (production efficiency). Allocation efficiency is one of the principal economic rationales for decentralization. It is to ensure public sector decisions are made close to the citizens who use (and may need to pay for) infrastructure and services. For this reason, participation in choice-making – in voicing preferences and voting in local elections – is important. These topics are covered in a more organic way in a subsequent section, below, having to do with participation and choice.

One of the front edge issues in the delivery of services is whether and how much to contract out, to privatize, or to delegate. In the case of the Middle East, mentioned earlier, so-called "external solutions" include joint service councils for infrastructure in small rural areas and neighborhood committees. A survey of North American local governments in 2003 showed that as many as two-thirds of the municipalities had tried privatization of some kind, although this trend has declined in this decade. New Zealand and Australia have followed a steadily expanding privatization policy. In other countries, the reform process that has been reliant on the private sector has led to a reduction of local government competencies (UK, Holland and Sweden).

In the 1990s, public-private-partnerships (PPP) were advanced by the international financial assistance agencies (World Bank, Asian Development Bank, International Finance Corporation) as a promising solution to lagging investment and poor management by public agencies. PPPs promised a practical alternative for financing the ever-growing demand for services. The argument reached the point of suggesting that local governments should limit themselves to a strictly "enabling function," leaving service provision in the hands of a competitive private sector (European Commission). In hindsight, the promise of private sector investment in infrastructure was overestimated. A World Bank report shows that private participation in infra-

structure represented a small and decreasing proportion of the total in local public and urban infrastructure in the 1990s (Annex 2006).

**Technology.** Finally, few if any assignments of functional responsibilities will hold for all time because of shifting preferences, political agendas, and administrative capacity in government. Changing technology also plays a role. Technological change in such fields as distributed solar power, health care diagnostics, distance-learning in education, and water purification can affect the placement of responsibilities. Furthermore, the time cycles of change – either of decentralizing functions or bringing new technologies on line – have similar life cycles. This means that a well-intentioned country might, say, centralize diagnostic aspects of health care and take three or four years to accomplish it, only to find that during the period of implementation, technological progress now permits sophisticated diagnoses to be done virtually anywhere. For these technological and other reasons, the assignment of responsibilities is probably best viewed as a moving target.

## Financing Decentralized Systems

When assignments change, so should finance. Inter-governmental finance is inextricably linked with decentralization because the vast majority of states on the planet have more than one level or tier, and lower tiers of government are rarely, if ever, financially self-sufficient. In fact, it is worth noting that the notion of pure financial autonomy for local governments is illusory. Even the richest countries, for instance those in the G-8, support half or more of local government expenditures through revenue transfers of some sort. Constraints on many local governments in the south – for instance limited or no ability to set rates, raise taxes, or borrow – make the idea of financial autonomy even more remote.

| Figure 2 | Local Government Expenditures, Sample Countries |
|---|---|

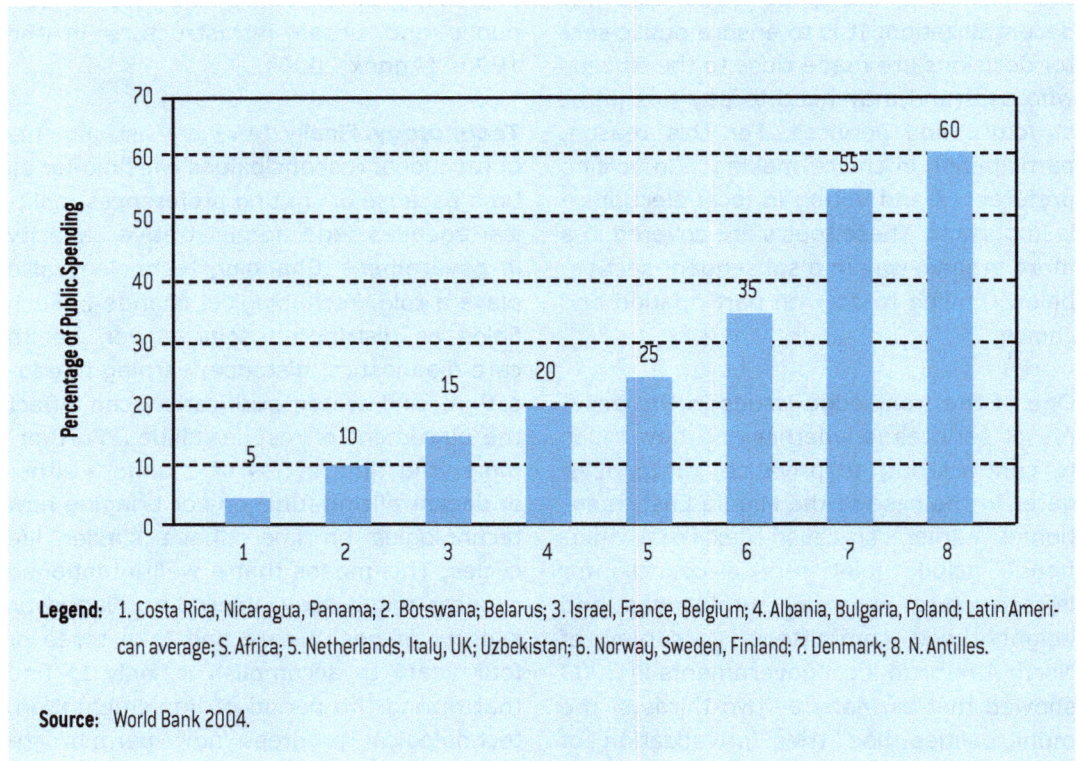

**Legend:** 1. Costa Rica, Nicaragua, Panama; 2. Botswana; Belarus; 3. Israel, France, Belgium; 4. Albania, Bulgaria, Poland; Latin American average; S. Africa; 5. Netherlands, Italy, UK; Uzbekistan; 6. Norway, Sweden, Finland; 7. Denmark; 8. N. Antilles.

**Source:** World Bank 2004.

National governments structure many ways to finance local investment and services, and almost all of them involve issues of tax (and rate setting), borrowing (or private involvement), and revenue sharing. But each of these singly and in combination entails issues of policy and practice, including mechanisms of control, capacity constraints and problems of transparency and discretion. The question is how have current practices around the globe engaged and solved these issues?

Though regional reports document a widespread growth in the share of spending by local governments relative to central government spending, the share is small in all but a few cases. Denmark and the Netherlands Antilles are the only two countries where municipal spending is over 50 percent of the total sub-national spending.

Figure 2 shows spending by all subnational tiers. Municipal-level spending ranges widely and on the whole is on an upward trend over the past few decades. At the low end of the spectrum are some Caribbean islands (zero) and a number of countries in the Middle East, which range in a few percentage points of total government spending. The chapter on Africa reports a range of five to 10 percent in 30 African countries. Most of Latin America is under 20 percent, but it is notable that this proportion has increased from 11% to 18% in the past two decades. On the high end are countries like Denmark, Switzerland, Finland and Sweden. More than anything, these figures suggest that many formulas for spending are in use.

On the income side, central governments are in the habit of restricting the income potential of local governments. In Latin America, local governments depend on the executive or legislative branches and sometimes the states in federated systems to set taxes and, in some instances, to set tariffs. Fiscal power in the Middle East, Africa, and Eurasia is even more limited or nonexistent, with very low levels of revenue (excluding Turkey, Zambia and South Africa). More than half the countries in the Asia-Pacific region have own-source revenues above 30% of the total. The same pattern holds in North America and Europe (around 40%).

Perhaps the most troubling trend is the tendency of central governments to impose spending responsibilities on local governments without loosening the constraints on income. These unfunded mandates are a burning issue in high income countries and some southern countries. Virtually all of the regional reports mention (but did not quantify) increasing burdens on local governments.

Non-tax sources of income – borrowing and private finance – have been tightly circumscribed in most countries. In the first place, only a small fraction of local governments are credit worthy. Some countries (Chile) flatly prohibit borrowing; others (Philippines) are experimenting with graduated systems of indebtedness. In the European Union, the newer states enjoy fewer restrictions on borrowing. Often, the potential for revenue mobilization varies directly with city size, and the distinctive advantage of larger cities echoes an earlier discussion about the possible practical advantages of managing decentralization by size class of city.

Even when credit worthiness can be established, national governments face moral hazard issues of sovereign guarantees. India has begun to experiment with syndicated subnational borrowing by packaging loans to groups of local governments. European countries are discussing municipal credit, somewhat along the lines of the Swedish and former Belgian municipal funds. Municipal bonds are common in the US. They are approved by voters at elections and enjoy tax advantages, but these arrangements would be of dubious feasibility in lower income countries. Depending upon the state of capital markets, credit worthiness, and

the willingness of national governments to offer sub-sovereign guarantees, bond financing can be feasible for a handful of well-managed local governments.

Transfers from central government, in grants or revenue sharing, are the most common way to cover local government costs (the so-called "vertical gap"). They are also useful in helping less advantaged regions ("horizontal gap"). Intergovernmental finance specialists have a multitude of tools – automatic, formula-driven revenue sharing, block grants, and conditional grants, for instance, that have matching requirements and other refinements. Fiscal specialists are learning about the multiplier effects of conditional grants (Shah 2007) and the importance of hard budget constraints (Rodden, Eskeland and Litvack 2003).

A tension in financial imbalance is discernible in virtually every report. The theory of intergovernmental finance is not the problem. The problem arises more with ambiguous or changing rules (Latin America), lack of transparency (Middle East), and excessive discretion (Africa) on the part of central governments in implementing revenue sharing programs. Wescott (2005) provides a review of these arrangements and the questions they raise for nations and the Asian Development Bank in the case of several Asia-Pacific countries.

One more point deserves emphasis. For the most part, intergovernmental transfers are formulated, promulgated, and defended by central governments, often on advice from international financial institutions (IFIs). The point of view of local governments is rarely given equal weight in adjusting the system. In the case of Latin America, constant tinkering with transfer formulas left local governments perpetually in the dark about prospective income from year to year (Peterson, 1997). An added problem is imprecision of data. The regional reports speak of a fiscal squeeze in which local governments have more responsibilities without the financial means with which to discharge them. None of the regional reports contains data to measure the magnitude of this squeeze. Indeed, many reports call attention to the need for reliable, time-series data to document financial and other issues (for instance, personnel). Even fewer countries have accurate numbers on the costs of delivering local services. Objective cost and expenditure data are vital to help decision makers formulate and defend policies on finance and spending.

## Local Democracy: Participation and Accountability

One of the signal features of decentralization, and one of its bright spots, is the renewed connection between citizens and government. The regional reports document a growing tendency of involving citizens in the decision-making process. This is important for economic reasons – the allocative efficiency discussed earlier – and for political reasons of legitimizing local government and holding elected leaders accountable for their actions. In practice, governments employ many modes of participation and choice-making.

The range of issues considered in the participatory dimension of decentralization includes:
a) elections and electoral rules;
b) the focus on chief executives and councils at the local level; and
c) modalities of voice, participation, and choice.

***Elections.*** The very fact that elections are taking place at the local level in most regions of the world is by itself a notable achievement. The regional reports note "important gains" in Europe and that, "undeniable progress" has been made in Africa, LAC, Asia, Eurasia, and MEWA. Several reports refer to political parties and election rules in connection with local democratic choice-making. The Eurasia report notes that elections are "increasingly competitive," and in Asia-Pacific, that "multi-party democracy is thriving" and is the norm. In LAC, the regional report notes that "plural-

ism is taking hold" and the North America report notes an independence from partisanship. Further, in North America "...single-member electoral districts, frequent elections, direct democracy, and greater local choice set local institutions in these countries apart" from others with British traditions like Australia and New Zealand.

Yet a number of concerns persist in connection with local elections. One issue signaled in several regions is the tendency for national partisan issues to crowd out local concerns. Some observers feel that local and national elections should be staggered in time in order to prevent local elections from becoming miniature battles of national issues. A second issue is low turnout of voters in local elections. With some exceptions, turnouts are in decline in North America, Europe and Eurasia and decreasing in some parts of East Asia and the Pacific.

Still another issue, one that requires much more scrutiny, concerns the rules of elections, not just the timing, but also how winners are declared (first past the post versus majority or slate lists) and the issues of direct and indirect elections, the periods of office (often short, three to four or five years), and whether electoral rules allow for self-succession in re-election. Short periods and prohibitions on re-election make it difficult to design and implement significant programs at the local level.

***Executive and Legislative.*** Much of the focus of local democracy has been on the city or municipal executive – mayor, principal officer, or municipal president. Selection of chief executives is not always direct. Countries have structured indirect means to select second tier executives or to accommodate minority parties at the local level. But direct elections appear to have increased accountability (in Europe). Some countries – for instance Indonesia and Vietnam – are beginning to relax the rules on candidacy. In Asia-Pacific and Latin America, big city mayors are a well-known stepping stone to higher political office. On the other hand, more than half the North American cities have adopted a council manager form of executive, separating political functions from the day to day operations of running a large city. City managers bring certified, professional skills to handle the complexities of modern city management. The disadvantage of the manager (or in Russia the hired manager) system, is that this arrangement puts the CEO of the city one step further away from direct electoral accountability, since most managers are hired by, and are accountable to, the city council.

**Modes of Participation.** Modes of participation by local citizens – i.e., expressing voice and making choice – are the most colorful and innovative spots in the unfolding story of decentralization and democracy. Perhaps the most refreshing message in the reports is that many countries in Africa (for instance, Ghana, Niger, and Uganda) in Asia (India and Pakistan) in East Asia (Philippines) and in Latin America draw on tradition and custom, making creative use of village councils to hear citizen opinion and deliberate. A good example is the *Gram Sabha* in rural India, a mandatory meeting of registered voters called to decide important issues. Table 1 illustrates the many ways that citizens at the local level take part in planning, implementing and monitoring local government activities.

However, evaluative research reports that participation by itself does not mean that governance or services are better or that poverty is any more quickly reduced, or even that local autonomy is safeguarded. One tricky issue concerns interventions by central state actors on behalf of disadvantaged people at the local level (Johnson et al 2005 in India; Tendler 1997 in Brazil). Other studies have focused on the conditions of successful participation. Crook and Manor (1998), suggest that in the cases of South Asia and Africa, the impact of participation depends on pre-existing conditions and the type of participation employed (see Table 1).

Still others argue for the importance of connecting participation to the deeper issue

| Table 1 | Sample Mechanisms of Participation and Their Functions |

| Participatory mechanism | Area of effectiveness | | | |
| | Policy and planning | Demand preferences and budgeting | Implementation and oversight | Accountability |
| --- | --- | --- | --- | --- |
| Tapping into grassroots opinion | Gram Sabha, India; neighborhood councils (Africa, Middle East) | | | |
| Mobilizing grassroots groups | Participatory budgeting (several countries in LAC, Philippines, Europe). | | Neighborhood work gangs, many countries | *Comités de Vigilancia* (Bolivia) |
| Beneficiary contributions | | Mayor's funds (Chile) | Bond measures in US | |
| Citizens initiated contact | | | Voluntary neighborhood organizations in Japan | Rating systems India, US |
| Electoral and voting process | Programmatic campaign (Colombia) | | | Referenda in US, Europe, and Eurasia (permitted but not used). |
| Legal and judicial system | | | | Impeachment, LAC, US, Canada |

**Source:** Adapted from Campbell 2003.

of citizenship and citizen rights (Hickey and Mohan, 2005). Local leadership, central monitoring, an articulate civil society, and the right kinds of information are all necessary, though not a guarantee that government services will work better (Devas and Grant 2003). Several of the regional reports speak of serious issues in the free flow of information and the need to ensure the availability of information, as represented in legislation on freedom of information (Philippines, UK, US).

A somewhat deeper modality of participation, one that relies on the instigation of citizens, is in such tools as the ballot initiative, referenda, and recall elections (see Campbell 2003 and Cabrero 2007). These are widespread in North America and Japan, and though permitted in many countries of Eurasia, not used. They are "seeping down" in Europe and Latin America. The LAC region has its own innovative uses of participation, in the form of participatory budgeting. As the name implies, the practice involves community and neighborhood groups taking part in semi-formal planning sessions to determine the mix and scale of capital investment.

## Capacity

The second most important problem after financial shortfalls, (again, except for many OECD countries) is the yawning gap in proficiency of administration and management in local government. The range of issues covered includes a) the sheer numbers of qualified staff, b) contracting and management systems, c) the need for merit based reforms and d) corruption, where it occurs.

In the first place, the majority of regional reports note that local governments are undermanned and their personnel under paid and in many places poorly qualified. In purely numerical terms, the reports from regions frequently cite local public sector workers as a proportion of total public sector (often ignoring differences across countries in responsibilities assigned to local governments).

A somewhat more useful ratio is the number of local government personnel in relation to the population. This figure, compiled from the regional reports, runs from 2 per 1000 population in West Africa to over 43 per 1000 population in the US (see Table 2).

Another way to normalize the data is to express municipal staff in relation to the responsibilities of local government, for instance, per capita public expenditures at the local level (column 2 in Table 2). The range here is €5.6 in West Africa to €348 in Japan. The implications of these ratios are clear. A municipal government of 100,000 in West Africa would have no more than six professional staff to look after a spending program of € 1 million. Increased decentralization or increased assistance to African cities or both, imply a need to improve these ratios. The numbers of qualified personnel per capita, would need to move ahead of public expenditure (the denominator) in order to expect national governments to deepen decentralization. But the data are sketchy. Moreover, time series data are rarely available. Nickson (1995) is a notable exception.

But the regional reports are clear about the discouraging, vicious circle of local employees. In several regions, for instance, the Middle East and Africa, there is little career prospect for municipal employees. As a result, qualified professionals do not seek positions in local government. One consequence noted in Lebanon, admittedly an extreme case because of the war, is that the average age of municipal workers is 55. Another consequence is that governments turn to contract workers. Turkey has reverted to a short term contract system. Elsewhere, the prospects for rent seeking begin to appear in the system. The perception is that corruption has increased in China and Indonesia, and a survey in the Ukraine

| Table 2 | Local Government Personnel and Spending in Selected Countries | |
|---|---|---|

| Country | Personnel per 1000 population | Expenditure/cap/staff (euros) |
|---|---|---|
| Africa (5)* 3 West 2 North | 2 | 5.6 |
| Eurasia (5) | 2.5 | Na |
| N. America (US) | 43.8 | 31.6 |
| Canada | 28.3 | 36.4 |
| Europe | Na | Na |
| Asia-Pacific (4 low income) | 6.75 | Na |
| Indonesia | 12.8 | 4.84 |
| Malaysia | 2.3 | 67.4 |
| Australia | 7.5 | 36.8 |
| New Zealand | 5.5 | 69.1 |
| Japan | 11.1 | 348.5 |
| LAC | 4.9 | Na |

* Uses per capita expenditures from West African Economic and Monetary Union.

**Source:** Compiled by author from Regional reports, Nickson (1995), OECD.

established that 60 % of the respondents had "faced one fact of corruption" in the previous year and in Turkey, the confidence level is only 5.2 on a scale of 10.

Different systems of management – public law, civil service, and private contract law – can all be made to work. Public law is still the predominant career employment structure in Europe. Russia has recently taken this step (Art 86 of its public framework law of March 2007). Some countries are in the process of extending the national civil service to local levels (ex: in LAC Colombia, Brazil, Costa Rica, Nicaragua, El Salvador.). It should be noted that the civil service is only one solution of many. Certification systems are beginning to appear in Mexico and Thailand. In the US, certification is managed by professional associations of municipal employees, not by government. The issue is not so much the nature of legal framework, but rather that few governments have established a unified system of merit-based public employment that offers career professional employment and mobility.

Other hopeful signs of progress include the new public administration (NPA) reforms that have begun to influence thinking and policy in several regions, though according to the Europe chapter it is "running out of steam." Many countries have launched initiatives to improve professional competence of local public officials or to explore alternatives to direct service (such as increased private provision with local public supervision), for instance, public transport in Europe, the US, and Latin America and the swapping of national and local employees, as in Republic of Korea, Germany, and Japan, so that national officials might see the world from the shoes of local officials.

Only a small handful of countries in the south have framed a long term strategy to build capacity at the local level. These circumstances leave local governments weak and provide a convenient justification for nations to hold position in the stalemated tug of war.

## III. Metropolitan Governments

Cities that are comprised of more than one local governmental unit are of special concern to decentralization and democracy. Virtually every regional report, in addition to the dedicated chapter on metropolitan governance, calls attention to the special problems of large, multi-jurisdictional cities. National strategies and actions are hobbled by the lack of understanding about feasible approaches to horizontal cooperation among governments in large cities. The changing global environment, coupled with rapid city growth, have often made institutional arrangements obsolete soon after they are promulgated.

### Definition: Numbers and Growth

Much attention has been paid to the growing urban population, and to the peak cities in the demographic pyramid –the so-called mega-cities of 10 million or more in population. More attention needs to be paid to the growth in the number of large cities – those of a million or more in population. Cities in this size-class numbered around 200 in the latter part of the 20th century. They will reach more than 500 by 2015 (Table 3). These are all metropolitan cities in the sense that they are either of great economic importance (Douala, Cameroon) in their countries; or are centers of cultural heritage or religious tradition; or because they are national capitals (Rabat), or all of these things. Many cities have special regimes (Abuja), but not a metropolitan government. Virtually all cities in this group are comprised of more than one municipality, and often involve many units of local government. Only about a quarter of metro cities are in advanced economies.

### Emerging Features of Metro Cities: Flatter, More Fragmented, In Competition

Three features about growing metropolitan areas add new challenges to decentralized governance and democratic choice-making. First, metro cities are spreading out. Angel et al (2005) have recently reported that average densities are falling in cities around the globe, and particularly in the developing regions. Angel's data are

| Table 3 | Cities by Population Size, 2015 | | |
|---|---|---|---|
| Size range | World total | Less developed | More developed |
| 10 M > | 21 | 17 | 4 |
| 5-10 M | 37 | 31 | 6 |
| 1-5 M | 496 | 378 | 118 |
| 0.5-1 M | 507 | 400 | 107 |
| Total >500.000 | 1.061 | 826 | 235 |

**Source:** National Research Council 2003.

drawn from side-by-side comparisons of 1990 and 2000 satellite images of a representative sample of 120 cities. His team calculated that average density decrease is a direct function of spreading city perimeters. These observations are corroborated by the chapter on metropolitan governance and by data from East Asia (e.g. Webster 2003, Laquian 2005).

Second, as settlements move beyond established administrative and jurisdictional boundaries, they stretch the customary definitions of city limits and often lead to new municipalities, contributing to a fragmentation of the metro area. The Africa report provides a comprehensive illustration of the large number of municipal jurisdictions in Africa's major cities. A well-known example of this spreading urban region is the Boston-Washington corridor, a megalopolitan region with a population of 50 million, which extends more than 600 km, far beyond the prospective planning competence of any of the more than 50 metropolitan areas in the region.

The significance of spreading urban regions is not just the growing territorial expansion, but also the increasing social distance implied in these developments. Though many low income populations still settle in and around the urban core of metro cities, increasingly, low income settlements take up residence on low-cost land where property values are suppressed because of distance or due to clouded title, poor conditions of slope or flood. At the same time, wealthy settlements spring up in nearby places, formed as self-contained enclaves protected by security walls. Both the poor and emerging middle classes require services of health, education, water, and roads outside the established perimeters of the city. These settlement patterns translate into fragmented political units and uncoordinated actions. Metro cities increase the importance of inter-jurisdictional coordination in planning, infrastructure investment, and services delivery.

A third feature of metropolitan centers is that they have entered a more competitive environment. Liberalization of trade leaves cities much more exposed to outside competition because the elimination of protectionist trade regimes no longer shields city industries from competitors. Also, the increasing velocity of international transactions – in trade, exchange of capital, and investment – means that metropolitan cities must move quickly to retain industries as well as to attract new ones. Beaverstock et al (1999) have developed indicators which measure the growing extent to which metropolitan centers are connected to global places of doing business.

## Policy Challenges

The policy challenges for cities spanning more than one jurisdiction or sprawling into outlying regions fall into three familiar areas:

1) substantive issues of growth, poverty, and environment;
2) institutional issues of powers, organization, and finance;
3) issues of democratic representation.

City regions have always been the centers of national GDP. For example, the cities of Rio and Sao Paulo in Brazil accounted for around 40 percent of the nation's US$800 billion dollar economy in the early 2000s. This made the economies of those two cities approximately equal in size to the economic importance of all five Andean countries, combined. And although cities in decentralized regimes all around the world are handling much more public spending, few nations have found the solutions and tools to manage infrastructure and services in metro cities.

Handling spillovers, both positive and negative, is a defining feature of metropolitan areas. Smaller cities or units of government cannot generate the economies of scale that are typical of production in metropolitan cities. On the other side of the coin, major cities generate negative spillovers in pollution and congestion. The challenge is made sharper by the need to incorporate large regional hinterlands.

Few organizational models seem to hold up under the pressures of changing economic and political circumstances. Virtually all the European countries are engaged in the question of metropolitan organization. Turkey has addressed the problem directly with reforms that link municipal, metropolitan and national tiers in planning and functions and the direct election of a metropolitan mayor. Russian and some former Soviet states have given capital cities special legal or financial status, as is the case with many capitals, particularly special districts, for instance, Brasilia, Canberra, and Abuja (Nigeria). These enjoy special spending or planning status, often linked directly to central government budgets. Cities in Europe, Canada, the US, and Republic of Korea have all undergone a variety of configurations with mixed success. Many of the cities – London, Montreal, and Toronto, for example – have reversed field, going from regional councils or area-wide governments to facilitate planning and investment of large scale infrastructure, back to small governance units, and back again to larger areas in a quest to capture a wider tax base. In the US, the policy battle has been over whether there is an economic payoff to cities with regional authorities (Nelson and Foster 1999).

## Recent Trends

The chapter on metropolitan governance points out that recent trends are toward cooperative pragmatism at the regional level. Governments are recognizing that no normative solution will fit the rapidly changing political and economic circumstances of the globalizing world, and that metropolitan governance needs to start with solutions for basic problems and have degrees of flexibility as it moves to more complex arrangements, as they have in Republic of Korea

and Peru. Cooperative regionalism might describe the problem-solving approach and give-and-take arrangements for large regions in Europe and the ad hoc intergovernmental agreements in the US, like Seattle's King County. An example of flexible arrangements is the growing use of "convenios" (agreements) in Brazil, having grown from a handful in the 1990s to hundreds today (Spink 2005), or the mancomunidades (associated municipalities).

## IV. Role of Associations

Virtually every region reports a flowering of regional and sometimes professional associations involving local governments. In Latin America, 28 associations are listed, the oldest (in Ecuador) dating from 1940, but 16 having been formed since 1990. Further, many regions report a parallel growth of associations of local government professionals, for instance, of mayors, of finance officials and engineers. For these groups, the most common denominators functionally are:

1) representing interests of local governments in national policy;
2) advocating for local governments;
3) building capacity to strengthen local governments.

They also create a platform for exchange of views and experience about policy and practice. Very few countries do not have associations, but some, for instance in Africa, have very limited resources.

At the apex of national and regional groupings is the Union of Cities and Local Governments (UCLG), formed from the World Federation of United Cities and the International Union of Local Authorities and Metropolis. UCLG came into being officially in 2004 and counts on various regional affiliates (known as sections), a network of regional associations which is growing in numbers and strength. For instance, in Africa, the United Cities and Local Governments of Africa, a Pan-African local government organization, arose from three local government organizations previously divided along linguistic lines. The founding congress in 2005 marked a starting point for a unified African municipal movement.

National associations have had mixed success in mobilizing political movement to solve the many problems faced by local government. A combination of approaches has been tried and needs deepening; they include focused educational activities on selected topics for local and national governments to assist national associations to do their job, documentation of good practice approaches and techniques, and a system of learning and information exchange between and among local governments across nations and regions.

## V. Global Challenges

New evidence is coming to light about the impact of decentralization on the Millennium Development Goals (MDGs) and related issues. Besides poverty, gender, health, technology and culture, the MDGs have brought out the importance of environmentally sustainable development. But climate change, particularly the production of greenhouse gasses, moves this issue to a much higher and more urgent plane. Similarly, some infectious and communicable diseases threaten to become global problems.

Local governments have a front line position in the battle against poverty, through social inclusion, access to basic services, and participation. But environmental issues are increasingly at the top of the agenda: fighting greenhouse gasses, for instance, land use and transportation, building standards, density controls, solid waste recycling, and many other aspects of urban growth that frequently fall under local government jurisdiction. Hundreds of cities have taken action to improve environmental sustain-

ability of urban growth following Local Agenda 21 and the Aalborg Charter of 1994, that addresses climate change agendas and action plans. Scores of European cities have developed detailed plans to achieve a smaller "carbon footprint," that is, more sustainable settlements. In the US, mayors are joining a coalition to achieve or surpass Kyoto protocol targets. More than 500 US mayors have signed a climate protection agreement.

Recent evidence reported by Angel et al (2005) shows a trend towards decreased density in cities, signalling an alarming move in a direction away from sustainable urban living. Brazil and China have begun to focus on urban remedies to the problems of rapid conversion of land into the urban fabric. Brazil has recently enacted legislation requiring local governments to meet a higher standard in land-use planning and has created land-swapping tools to do so.

As for the MDGs, local governments have an important role to play in managing growth for health and safety. Effective action in these spheres would strengthen the rationale for governments to mobilize lower tiers to address these issues. WHO has recently signaled the importance of the social determinants of health, pointing particularly to issues of safety, violence, and prevention of at risk buildings in urban settings. WHO's contribution adds to the already large body of work on local level action to address communicable diseases like HIV/AIDs, malaria and tuberculosis (Kjellstrom, et al 2007). In health and climate change, local governments have a critical role to play.

On other MDG issues, gender, culture, and technology, local governments are again on the front line. More than a few countries – Africa, Middle East, Asia-Pacific are notable examples among many – speak of quotas to involve woman in local government. Special status is accorded to women in Africa; 30 to 40 % of council seats are held by women in Eurasia, and India has set aside 30 % of local government elected positions for women and scheduled castes. Cultural issues, in heritage, buildings, and inter-cultural dialog, are areas where cities have shown promise and have great potential, for example in city to city exchanges, in cultural understanding, and in informal alliances around issues of sport and festivals. New information technology holds great promise for local governments in a variety of fields – management, information for citizens, and education to name a few. In all of these areas, the agenda is wide and promising.

## VI. Next Steps

In this final conclusion we have attempted to summarize the main points and findings of the *World Report*, while also introducing new elements and insights that may enhance reflection. Quite possibly, the study does not always provide precise, conclusive answers to the issues and questions raised in the introduction of the *Report* regarding the principles of local self-government and subsidiarity.

The discussion remains open. Only through the sustained practice of running local governments and continued interaction with their citizens and other levels of government will concrete solutions be found.

Therefore, the *Report* essentially concludes with a call for initiatives that develop and deepen local democracy. In effect, the objective should be to apply these core principles of local self-government, subsidiarity and participation to the praxis, particularly by:

- Underpinning policies favorable to decentralization. The *Guidelines on Decentralization* approved by UN Habitat are important instruments for advancing in this direction. It is necessary for UCLG and local government

associations to disseminate this *Report* and to encourage the implementation of the *Guidelines* both at national levels and among international and regional organizations, e.g. African Union through the African Conference on Decentralization and Local Development (CADDEL), the Organization of American States (OAS) and its Inter-American High Level Network on Decentralization (RIAD).

- Strengthening policy-making capacities of local government. In effect, UCLG, through the Global Observatory on Local Democracy and Decentralization (GOLD), should develop indicators, recognized by national and international institutions, to monitor processes of decentralization and the implementation of the *Guidelines*; and contribute to local capacity for policy dialog vis-à-vis national governments and international organizations. These indicators should be used to shape and inform local development policies and national strategies for poverty reduction.

- Enhancing local finance systems. Local access to adequate funding is key to development. In view of the fiscal weaknesses observed at local level, UCLG should continue to promote proposals and initiatives to strengthen local finances and to draw up plans, in consultation with governments and regional and international financial institutions, for new national systems in order to keep pace with urban explosion, growing demands for basic services and mounting environmental challenges.

This list of initiatives could, without a doubt, be extended further to include equally as important initiatives such as local government capacity building, upgrading service provision and urban policy for sustainable development.

Local governments have an integral role to play in the international development agenda not only to articulate their own needs and have them met, but also to play a role in reaching the MDGs and fighting climate change. The sustained efforts of local governments to integrate their needs in the international development agenda for the fulfillment of the MDGs and fight against climate change will continue to guide these actions.

Quite plainly, change and transformation cannot be brought about without the direct involvement and determination of local governments around the world.

# POSTFACE

## Essay on the clarification of some key concepts and methodical problems

**Gérard Marcou[1]**

The *World Report* offers, for the first time, the possibility of clarifying the meaning of words used to address the term "local". Via the different situations and developments analyzed, the words often seem closely related but not accurately synonymous. In addition, the choice of linguistic equivalents when translating may involve nuances of meaning or presuppose differences which, in fact, are merely differences in terminology. The interest of the *World Report* is that it puts key notions into context by comparing political and legal discourse from many countries on all continents. The definitions arrived at could then acquire legitimacy from the fact that they are not self-centered. The convergences we have found are not alien to the socio-political reality of each of the countries concerned, even though mimetic effects may still exist, and at times arise from prescriptions imposed by international organizations. These convergences can be considered as positive effects of globalization.

However, convergence at the level of ideas does not necessarily imply that the same occurs at institutional or practical levels. On the contrary, factors of differentiation remain, resulting from very diverse socio-political and economic realities, which should not be overlooked. The very notion of "local" varies considerably from one country and one continent to another and with it varies the definition of the territories constituting the framework of local self-government, and the concept of local-state relations. The sociology of local institutions is dependent on the importance of the social structures. The role of local democracy in decentralization depends on the state's political system. The scope of decentralization depends on the political weight and human and financial resources available to local authorities. **Decentralization does not exist outside the state but it ceases to exist even within where local authorities are no more than the executors of policies determined by higher authorities.** These are the extreme positions that limit the space of local self-government; this is the space within which the equilibrium of decentralization must be created in each country depending on the conditions[2].

The *World Report* refers explicitly to two notions: decentralization and local democracy. These two terms should be clarified together with their status in the political and legal systems of states. A distinction should also be made between them and similar or correlated notions. This clarification must be contextual and comparative, i.e. based as much as possible on the accepted concepts used by states in the various regions of the world, depending on their history and institutions. But at the same time, these notions are part of global debates fostered by international organizations and a number of states, contributing to the convergence of ideas under discussion by providing terms of common reference.

Firstly, a distinction can be made between three separate semantic fields: decentralization, self-governance and democracy.

1. The text below is a part of the synthesis chapter submitted by the author to UCLG under the title: "Decentralization and local democracy at the age of globalization".
2. In what follows, the information quoted comes from chapters in the World Report, unless other sources are indicated by notes.

The first of these three terms refers to relations between the various levels of power, the second to the status of the authorities and the third to the way in which power is exercised. We will not address the expressions of these semantic fields relating to federalism or to regional autonomies. The comparison between these three fields shows a convergence at the level of political ideas and legal notions; even though some major states have remained outside this tendency.

## I. Decentralization

The notion of decentralization is understood today in very different ways depending on the author and institution, which leads to misunderstanding and confusion. Sometimes, overly broad definitions of decentralization become confused with governance, a notion which in itself is already not very precise. This is the case in a report published by the UNDP on decentralized governance *à propos* the services which ought to be provided to poor populations: "Conceptually, decentralization relates to the roles of, and the relations between, central and sub-national institutions, whether they are public, private or civic. Improved governance will require not only strengthened central and local governments but also the involvement of other actors from civil society organizations and the private sector in partnerships with government at all levels"[3]. According to this definition, the relations between the state or local government and private companies or NGOs are part of the problem concerning decentralization.

The report then distinguishes four types of decentralization: administrative decentralization, in which local authorities are accountable to higher authorities; political decentralization, in which local authorities are theoretically independent of the state, invested with powers and elected; budgetary decentralization, which refers to the transfer of the resources necessary for the exercise of the transferred powers and responsibilities; and lastly, divestment or market decentralization, which entails a transfer of functions to the private sector (companies, NGOs...), including planning and administration, previously held by public institutions.

However, the argument slips from decentralization to governance. We recognize that improved governance might indeed call for the involvement of private actors, but this applies to all levels of government and not just to relations between local powers and higher authorities. This idea is also represented in a recent book with contributions from various United Nations experts. Globalization would necessitate an enlarged vision of decentralization within the framework of the new concept of governance. According to these authors, decentralization cannot be devised any longer as the devolution of powers within government, and rather embraces resource and power sharing in policy making in society as a whole. The enlarged concept of "governance decentralization" suggests a new decentralization category, in addition to the traditional ones: "economic decentralization", including "market liberalization, deregulation, privatization of public enterprises and public-private partnerships"[4].

3.  Work, R. (2002), *The Role of participation and partnership in decentralized governance: a brief synthesis of policy lessons and recommendations of nine countries on service delivery for the poor*, UNDP, New York, p.3.
4.  G. Shabbir Cheema / Dennis A. Rondinelli (2007), "From government decentralization to decentralized governance", p.6 in: G. Shabbir Cheema / Dennis A. Rondinelli (eds), *Decentralizing governance*, Brookings Institution Press / Ash Institute for Democratic Governance and Innovation.

This approach is not really all that new. It comes from a critique of the "Welfare state", developed in particular in the 1980s. Such lines of thinking advocated market competition as an alternative for the provision of services that the public powers could no longer provide, as well as decentralization so that fiscal competition would exercise pressure to reduce public expenditure and so better satisfy the collective preferences of the electorate through competition between local authorities[5]. Hence, a distinction could be made between "economic", "administrative" and "political" decentralization. "Economic decentralization" refers to economic decisions (decentralized when they result diffusely from the play of market forces, centralized if they are decisions made by the government); "administrative decentralization" refers instead to the degree of dispersion or concentration of public decisions; and, finally, "political decentralization" which refers to the authorities with the capacity to make political choices[6].

In this framework, it has been possible to propose a classification of all systems of decentralization based on two dimensions: the method of allocating resources (pure market and state controlled economies represent the two extremes) and the levels of political and administrative organization to which the resources are allocated (central, local or intermediate). Obviously, all real systems are mixed systems but they are situated somewhere between four extreme theoretical models as follows: the centralized public model, the centralized market model, the decentralized public model and the decentralized market model[7]. These models make it possible to assess the characteristics of real systems and to compare their relative positions.

Despite its heuristic value, this global theory of decentralization may be criticized for leading to a degree of confusion. Firstly, the relations between the public powers and the relations between the public powers and the economy are not the same; unlike the pu-blic powers, the decisions of economic agents are not subject to democratic procedures. In addition, the fact of turning to the market to produce or supply a good or a service does not mean that the public authority, local or otherwise, is no longer competent. If the responsibility of the public authority is to ensure that a good or a service is offered to the population and it is allowed by law to chose the method or form of provision, it can then assess whether it is preferable to set up a public organization, to conclude public procurement contracts or to proceed to delegate the public service to the private. However, the public authority remains responsible in the eyes of the law and the citizens for the provision of the service under the conditions it has defined. The case would be different, of course, if privatization is decided on by the state and the consequences affect the local authorities, or if the law obliged them to resort to the private sector, even when the local authority continues to exercise powers of control and organization. It is then paradoxical to use the expression "decentralization" to characterize measures which result in a reduction of the role and responsibilities of the local authorities.

**This is why it is preferable to reserve the notion of decentralization for the relations between the public powers, some of which are placed under the control of others, and not for the relations between the public powers and the economy or society in general.** This is not to ignore, for all that, the importance of relations with the economy, and they may be addressed in an analysis of governance, but they do not come under what is normally called decentralization.

Even within these boundaries, the notion of decentralization is still likely to be understood in two different ways: a broad meaning, which relates to the public economy or to the sociology of organizations, or a narrow meaning, of a legal and political nature. The former has become the general or commonplace meaning; the lat-

5.  See amongst basic texts on the subject: Tiebout, C.M. (1956), "A pure theory of local expenditure", Journal of Political Economy, vol.64, p.416; Buchanan, J.M. / Tullock, G. (1962), The calculus of consent: Logical foundations of constitutional liberty, University of Michigan Press, Ann Harbor.

6.  Wolman, H. (1990), "Decentralization: What it is and why we should care", p.29-42 in: Bennett, R.J. (ed), Decentralization, local governments and markets. Towards a post-welfare agenda, Oxford, Clarendon.

7.  Bennett, R.J. (1990), "Decentralization, intergovernmental relations and markets: towards a post-welfare agenda?", pp.1-26 in: Bennett, R.J. (ed), op. cit.; Bennett, R.J. (1994), "An overview of developments in decentralization", pp.11-37 in: Bennett, R.J. (ed.), Local government and market decentralization. Experiences in industrialized, developing and former Eastern Bloc countries, United Nations University Press.

ter, more exact, is the only one, as we will see, which has a normative scope. Decentralization should also be distinguished from related notions: *devolution*, originally an English concept, and *deconcentration*, which is of French origin and the notion of delegation.

In its broadest sense, decentralization expresses a quality of the relations between levels of authority one of which is under the control of the other. We say that these relations are more or less decentralized, depending on whether the inferior power benefits more or less from freedom of action in the exercise of its attributions under the control of the superior power. The notion of decentralization can thus apply both to the relations between the federal power and the member states (for example Austrian or Australian types of federalism are said to be more centralized than those in the USA or Canada) and to the relations between the state and local authorities in a unitary state, or between the federated entities and the local authorities which they comprise, or even to the internal relations in a company or a group of companies considered as an organization.

In the narrow sense, decentralization means that local authorities are established by the law, have a legal personality and are administered by bodies through which they exercise, with a degree of liberty, the powers and responsibilities they obtain from the law under the control of the state. This notion was first asserted in France. According to an English variant found in many countries influenced by British tradition, the law confers the legal personality and powers not on the communities but on the bodies; since the 90s, it is this concept which has been followed, with certain differences, by Russian legislation and that of other former Soviet Union countries. Decentralization understood in this way, depending on the variant, has resulted in quite different regimes from the point of view of local institutions and the self-governance left to local

authorities. But it still signifies, and this is the basis of its unity, an institutional and political differentiation between the state and the local authorities, and the legitimacy of representation at local level of public interests distinct from those for which the state is responsible.

From decentralization in its narrowest sense, we must compare and distinguish the English notion of *devolution*, which one hesitates to translate as *"dévolution"* in French. It is a relatively imprecise notion which appeared at the end of the 19th century as an attempt to respond to the Irish independence movement through an internal regime of extensive self-government (*Home Rule*). *Devolution* corresponds to the transfer of wide-ranging powers to a political assembly for the management of internal affairs. The word was used to designate the projects in the 70s and the reforms of 1998, which transferred important powers and means to regional bodies. But it is also used, today, in a broader sense, particularly outside the UK, to designate transfers of power to local or regional communities.

The meaning of the word *devolution* thus seems akin to a distinction commonly made today between political decentralization and administrative decentralization. But the criterion of the distinction is far from clear. In the typology of decentralization proposed in the UNDP report referred to above, administrative decentralization is characterized by the fact that the local authorities are accountable to the higher authority. This corresponds to what one could call de-concentration or delegation (depending on the cases - cf. infra). **This control relation (*accountability*) with the higher authority does not exist in political decentralization nor in *devolution*, which implies a total transfer of powers and responsibilities, decision-making power and resources, including the power to procure resources**[8]. However, *devolution* does not necessarily imply that the local authority

8.  *Op. cit. p.4.*

POSTFACE

results from election, just as decentralization also does not necessarily entail the election of local authorities.

However, the distinction between political and administrative decentralization is more currently based on other criteria. A few examples follow. Political decentralization corresponds to the exercise of political power, as in the case of federated governments in the framework of a federal state; whereas administrative decentralization only consists of the institutionalization of the legal entities responsible for managing local interests[9]. It is therefore the exercise of legislative power by sub-national territorial units which is considered as the expression of political decentralization, in contrast with the classical case of the unitary state in which the unity of legislation is the expression of the unity of power[10]. Or again, political decentralization presupposes the dispersion of political decision-making power, i.e., a degree of freedom of action as to the determination of policies, the capacity to mobilize resources and the freedom to use them[11]. But some definitions of administrative decentralization do not differ greatly from this latter concept: according to Maurice Hauriou, it is the need for political freedom rather than administrative needs, which justifies decentralization[12]; according to Charles Eisenmann, administrative decentralization "consists of giving to locally competent authorities powers of action, therefore firstly of decision-making, independent of the central authorities"[13].

But today, over and above these theoretical approaches, another criterion must be added, that of the election of local authorities. Although, from a theoretical point of view, the notions of decentralization and *devolution* do not necessarily imply the election of local authorities, the fact is that today territorial decentralization is inseparable from the democratic legitimacy of local authorities, and in all countries the institution of locally elected councils is the rule. Even in the Arab Gulf states, local

elections have been held over the last few years with the exception of the United Arab Emirates. **If the classical idea of decentralization accepts the autonomy of local authorities in the framework of the law, the modern view of decentralization is today inseparable from the democratic norm,** and no one disputes this even if its transposition and implementation are often criticised.

As soon as universal suffrage applies for the designation of local authorities, it becomes inevitable that decentralization will take on a political dimension, even though, in certain countries, political parties are not allowed to participate in local elections, and even though the official vocabulary continues to speak of "administrative" decentralization, or "administrative" elections à propos local elections. This is so, given that elections imply a form of responsibility of those elected vis-à-vis their electorate even if the higher authority exercises a form of supervision. This is the meaning (the direction) of *accountability* which makes the difference, as shown in the UNDP report: no longer towards the state but towards the electorate.

In this case, *devolution* is not distinguished from decentralization through its political dimension but by its possible scope. In point of fact, the idea of *devolution* has no limit on the transfers which may carried out, other than the point at which the transfers would mean independence; on the contrary, the idea of decentralization is inseparable from the idea of the unity of power. Decentralized entities administer themselves without ceasing to be an integrated part of the state and without the state conceding to them part of its constitutional functions. Extended to the transfer of legislative powers, political decentralization corresponds in fact to a different notion of decentralization in its strictest sense. This results in the fact that, apart from this hypothesis, *devolution* and decentralization may be considered as synonymous particularly for local authorities at

9. Bourjol, M. (1975), La réforme municipale, Paris, Berger-Levrault, pp.56-58.
10. Aja, E. (1999), El Estado autonómico. Federalismo y hechos diferenciales, Madrid, Alianza Editorial, pp.23 et suiv.
11. Wolman, H., op. cit. pp.29-30.
12. Hauriou, M. (1919), Précis de droit administratif, Paris, Sirey, preface.
13. Eisenmann, Ch. (1982), Cours de droit administratif, Paris, LGDJ, tome 1 p.278 (cours de 1966-1967).

municipal level for which there is never a transfer of legislative powers.

On the other hand, a clear distinction must be made between *deconcentration* and decentralization and the former must not be assimilated to a restrictive application of the idea of decentralization as is proposed within a broad concept of decentralization. Deconcentration is originally a French notion which applies to the relations between the central administration and their local-level offices that depend on the delegation of powers to the latter. **Deconcentration is the opposite of decentralization in that it governs the relations within an administrative hierarchy, whereas decentralization excludes any hierarchical relations between the state and local authorities**. Deconcentration comprises two elements:

i) the existence of territorially competent services within the state administration;

ii) delegation of powers to these services.

But the term *delegation* may also be used to designate an intermediate situation: state powers and responsibilities are delegated to a decentralized authority (i.e., resulting from an election and not from nomination by a higher authority) and are exercised on behalf of the state and for which the decentralized authority is accountable to the state. This situation is most often designated by the expression: "delegated powers and responsibilities". Depending on the case, it may be that elective legitimacy weakens the control of the higher authority or, on the contrary, that the weight of the delegated powers and responsibilities weakens decentralization because of the control exercised by the higher authority.

These distinctions lead to a preference for a strict definition of decentralization which marks the difference from related notions. **Decentralization is thus characterized by the existence of locally elected authorities, distinct from the state's administrative authorities, and exercising, in the framework of the law, their own powers and responsibilities for which they have a degree of self-government, under the control of the state. As understood in this way, decentralization in its modern meaning is inseparable from the idea of local self-government and the democratic principle.** But the volume of responsibilities exercised is not sufficient to assess the level of decentralization in a given country; that depends also on the regime under which the responsibilities are to be found and the control effectively exercised by the state.

In its broadest sense, decentralization exists in almost all countries although it has very different characteristics. But strictly defined, decentralization is lacking in very many countries. Hence, when article 96 of the constitution of the China states that "local congresses of the people at different levels are the organs of the state's power", this is a form of decentralization in its broadest, and not strictest, sense. This was the concept in the Soviet Union, abandoned today under article 12 of the constitution of the Russian Federation. But some states, formerly part of the Soviet Union, still adhere more or less explicitly to this concept (in general the states of Central Asia and Belarus). In Cuba, although assemblies of people's power are characterized in the constitution as the "higher local bodies of state power", it is however recognized that they fulfil specific functions other than the assistance they provide in realizing the ultimate goals of the state (art.102 and 103). Other political concepts may also lead to principles excluding decentralization of the local administration. This is the case in Saudi Arabia, in Oman and in Qatar; in other Arab countries and in Islamic Republic of Iran some moves have been made towards decentralization in recent laws and constitutions. Yet the Iranian constitution, which sets up locally elected councils, subjects them to the principles of the Islamic regime and envisages their "subordination" to central government authority (article 100)[14]. Despite this, there is a tendency towards the diffusion of the model of decentralization and the recognition of a sphere of responsibility specific to local authorities, at least regarding the principles, even in countries which seem far removed from these principles.

## II. Self-Government (Autonomy)

Autonomy literally means the power to set for oneself the rules by which one is governed. However, this notion may also be understood in at least two different ways. In the sense of political autonomy, it is a demand for sovereignty which stops at the limit of independence, from which it is distinct. Understood as administrative self-government, it expresses the possibility for the local authority to govern its own affairs and those which the law entrusts to it. It is in this second sense that it is generally understood as local self-government. The regional autonomy statutes in different European countries (e.g. in Spain or in the UK) and on other continents (for example the autonomy of Karakalpakstan in Uzbekistan, or that of Aceh in Indonesia) come under the first meaning. The French constitution today accepts both meanings but applies them to entities of a different nature: the first to "overseas countries" (New Caledonia, French Polynesia) (art.74), and the second to territorial communities (art.72). The European Charter for Local Self-government as well as the "Guidelines" recently adopted by the Governing Council of UN Habitat both refer to the second meaning. This self-government also has a political dimension but it results from elections not from the statute of the local authorities.

**Local self-government, as understood above, is more and more widely recognized on the different continents.** The exceptions are states which do not refer to decentralization in the legal meaning of the word and also a few countries which attribute a political status to municipal self-government.

Local self-government is expressed in sometimes differently coined legal notions but which are, in general, similar in content. In certain European countries, reference is formally made to the notion of "autonomy" in the constitutions (Italy: art.5; Spain: art.140; Portugal: art.6; Romania: art.120; Greece: art.102.2; "administrative autonomy"). In all the other European countries, the term used corresponds literally to the German expression *Selbstverwaltung* (Fundamental Law: art.28.2), defined as "the right to govern, under one's own responsibility, all the affairs of the local authority", which corresponds to the notion of *"libre administration"* in the French constitution (art.72), and the English notion of *self-government*[15]. This latter expression could however be distinguished insofar as its material content derives only from the provisions of the law, but this limitation is receding both in the United Kingdom and in the USA and Australia (constitution of certain federated states in the latter two countries), and by the link with a degree of freedom of organization at local level (*home rule*).

This notion of "self-government" (*"libre administration"* in French) is to be found in the 1993 Russian constitution (*mestnoe samoupravlenie*, art.130 to 133), including the freedom of organization in law 131/2003), the Ukrainian constitution of 1996 (*mitzeve samovriaduvania*, art.140) or the Polish constitution of 1997 (*samorzad terytorialny*: art.163 et seq.). In Latin America, the word "autonomy" is usually preferred, both in unitary states (Colombia: art.287) and in federal states (Argentina: art.123, ensuring municipal autonomy is a duty of the provincial constitutions; see for example that of La Rioja: art.154). In Asia, countries which were under British colonial rule have retained the British concept of

14. Jalali, M. (2005), "Iran: une décentralisation en trompe l'œil? Les fondements essentiels de la décentralisation en Iran", Revue iranienne de Droit constitutionnel, summer 2005, n°4, pp.74-86.

15. In this sense: Breuillard, M. (2000), L'administration locale en Grande-Bretagne, entre centralisation et régionalisation, L'Harmattan, coll. « GRALE » Paris.

*local government* and of *local self-government*, including the restoration of traditional methods of local organization (not only Australia and New Zealand, but also India, Pakistan, Malaysia) but other countries refer rather to the wording "local autonomy" (Japan, Indonesia, Republic of Korea, Philippines).

One can see however that these differences in terminology and sometimes conceptualization have no impact on the real content of "autonomy" or "self-government". There is nothing that allows us to assert that the reference to "local autonomy" corresponds to a degree of decentralization greater than the reference to the principle of "self-government", if one compares institutions, powers and responsibilities. Municipalities in Germany or France do not benefit from less extensive decentralization than municipalities in Italy or Portugal; decentralization is no more advanced in the Republic of Korea than in India. But decentralization is essential as a reference standard for local government. This standard is being developed by the *European Charter for Local Self-government* and the UN Habitat *Guidelines for Decentralization*.

This general tendency has however a few nuances. In African countries, the concepts which the constitutions and national laws reflect follow those of the former colonial power. However, this conception has been dominated since independence by the wish to ensure the unity of the state, which has upheld a centralized system and an essentially instrumental vision of decentralization. However, for a number of years, the reforms undertaken in a certain number of states bring them closer to the general trend by giving to decentralization a more substantial content of local self-government (for example: South Africa, Uganda, Zambia, Burkina Faso, Niger, Senegal).

Lastly, a few countries stand out, conversely, by the affirmation of a concept of municipality which makes it a component of the state or the framework of an expression of sovereignty. Sweden is the only European country whose constitution declares that "self-management of local communities" contributes to the realization of "national sovereignty" (1:1). The constitution of the Ukraine also states that the people's sovereignty is exercised by the organs of power of the state and by the bodies of local self-government (art.5), but this formula recalls the former adherence of local bodies to the state power. In Brazil, the 1988 constitution, in principle, confers on the municipalities (*municipio*) political self-government: the *municipios*, as with federated states, are part of the components whose "indissoluble unity" forms the Federal Republic of Brazil (art.1), and the federal constitution defines the bases of their organization and their powers and responsibilities (art.29 to 31). The practical scope of this concept seems, however, limited[16]. In Indonesia, the introduction of the reference to "autonomy" in the laws of 1999 and later laws, corresponds on the other hand to a change of concept, with the transfer of wide-ranging powers, responsibilities and resources and the direct election of the local executive.

**Local self-government is a constituent element of decentralization. The terms "local autonomy", "*libre administration*" and "self-government" do indeed correspond to one and the same notion. It presupposes freedom of action and organization for the local authority in the context of the laws; this freedom may be more or less extensive but this does not affect the notion itself.**

## III. Democracy

The classical notion of decentralization does not necessarily imply democracy; an organization may be decentralized

16. Franck Moderne (2006), "Le municipio comme entité politique dans l'organisation territoriale fédérale du Brésil", pp.347-363 in: Mélanges en l'honneur de Jean-Claude Douence. La profondeur du droit local, Paris, Dalloz.

without being based on democratic principles[17]. Conversely, an organization based on democratic principles may be centralized.

Now, the link between decentralization and democracy has become narrower and more direct, as in the past in Europe, the link between parliamentary government, arising out of the census system, and democracy. **Decentralization, understood in its strictest sense as a method of organization, today implies democracy. It presupposes the self-government of local authorities in the framework of the law, but it is democracy which is the basis for local self-government.** Democracy effectively allows citizens to express collective preferences which direct the exercise of power held by local authorities by law. This has not always been the case: property ownership as a requirement for voting or the recognized authority of the traditional elite have in the past constituted the basis, or the driving force, for decentralization.

This has not completely disappeared. On the contrary, in certain countries, the institutions give community leaders or religious chiefs a controlling role in civil society and the law sometimes gives them a place in the representative bodies exercising public powers (for example:

Ghana, Uganda, Niger, South Africa...). In certain Middle Eastern countries, the authority of members of the local aristocracy is influential even though there are elections (UAE, Saudi Arabia and Bahrain).

Despite these surviving customs, the general trend is towards the election of local government bodies and to the development of instituted forms of popular participation. Even if the election is not disputed, it is considered to be essential for the authority and the legitimacy of the local authorities and one can see that legislation tends to introduce a degree of possibility of choice or influence for electors (Vietnam, 2004 local elections; China at village or district committee level).

In conclusion, it is obvious that a system of reference for decentralization is being consolidated which includes recognizing local self-government and calls for representative elected institutions and participatory institutions by which the people may express their collective preferences and interests. We should underline that this system of reference is not found everywhere, but it is challenged by any other reference system and continues to spread. Without question, its strength lies in its ability to take form in a wide variety of institutional models.

17. A renowned French legal expert, Charles Eisenmann, wrote: "decentralization is a system without a given political colour; it can be equally undemocratic and democratic"; all that is required is that the designation of local authority be "independent of central authority" (op. cit. p.277).

# Africa

Banque Mondiale, 2003, *Résultats de recherches menées par la Banque Mondiale sur l'expérience de décentralisation de 30 pays africains,* http://www.worldbank.org/afr/findings.

Belaid, N., 1999, *Autonomie locale et mutations récentes dans les finances municipales,* ENA-CREA, Tunis.

Ben Salah, H. and Marcou G., (sous dir.), 1998, *Décentralisation et démocratie en Tunisie,* IORT, L'Harmattan, coll. Logiques juridiques. Paris, Tunis.

Bureau d'Appui à la Coopération Canadienne pour le Développement International (Bacdi), Avril 2005, *Etat des lieux de la décentralisation au Sénégal.*

Club du Sahel / Partenariat pour le Développement Municipal (PDM), 2000, *Rapport sur le financement du développement locale en Afrique de l'Ouest,* par Gagnon Gérard.

Crook, R. and Manor J., 2001, *Local Government and Decentralization in Zambia,* Final Report to SNV, MoLGH and the Donor Reference Group, Lusaka.

Cordelier, S and Didiot B., 2005, *Etat du monde 2006 : annuaire économique géopolitique mondiale* ( 25 éme éd. Paris , la Découverte).

Momaniat, I., 2001, *Fiscal Decentralization in South Africa,* http://www.worldbank.org/decentralization/afrlip/Momoniat.

Kessey, K.D., (April 2006), *Traditional Leadership Factor in Modern Local Government System in Ghana: Policy Implementation, Role Conflict and Marginalization.* Journal of Science and Technology, Kwame Nkrumah University of Science and Technology Kumasi, Ghana. Volume 26.

*Mémorandum Union des Associations des Elus locaux, 2006,* Union des Associations des Elus Locaux du Sénégal.

Nach Mback, Ch., 2003, *Démocratisation et décentralisation « Genèse et dynamiques comparés des processus de décentralisation en Afrique subsaharienne »,* Karthala-PDM, Paris.

Ouazzani Chahdi, H., 2003, *Droit administratif,* imprimerie Najah el Jadida, Casablanca.

Partenariat pour le Développement Municipal (PDM), 2003, *Etat de la décentralisation,* Karthala.

Partenariat pour le Développement Municipal (PDM), "Observatoire des Finances locales", *Données sur les finances locales 2000 à 2004.*

Rapport du Comité Paritaire Etat/ Communes, 2005, *Suivi du transfert des compétences aux Communes du Béni*n, décembre.

Roubaud, F., 2000, *Identité et transition démocratique : l'exception malagasy ?* L'Harmattan, Paris.

Smoke, P., 2003, *Decentralization in Africa: goods, dimensions, myths and challenge.* Public administration and development, Volume 23, p. 7-16.

Steytler, N., 2005, *Local Government in South Africa: Entrenching Decentralized Government.*

Yatta, F. P., 2006, *Villes et développement économique en Afrique,* Economica, Paris.

## Asia-Pacific

ADB, 2004, *Devolution in Pakistan*. Manila: Asian Development Bank, World Bank and Department for International Development.

ADB, 2006, *Urbanization and Sustainability: Case Studies of Good Practice*. Manila: Asian Development Bank.

ADB, 2006, *Indonesia 2006 – 2009: Country Strategy and Program*. Manila: Asian Development Bank.

Alatas, V., Pritchett, L., and Wetterberg, A., 2002, *Voice lessons: local government organizations, social organizations and the quality of local governance*. Washington DC: World Bank Policy Research Working Paper 2981, 49 pages.

Asquith, A., 2007, New Zealand Country *Fact Sheet on the State of Decentralization and Local Democracy in the Asia Pacific Region.*

Bambang, P. , Brodjonegero, S. and Swasono F., 2007, *Indonesia Country Fact Sheet on the State of Decentralization and Local Democracy in the Asia Pacific Region.*

Blair, H., 2000, *Participation and accountability at the periphery: Democratic local governance in six countries*, World Development 28(1): 21-39.

Boston, J., 1996, *The use of contracting in the public sector: Recent New Zealand experience*, Australian Journal of Public Administration 53 (Sept.): 105-110.

Brillantes, A., 2001, *Public Sector Reform and Poverty Reduction in Developing Asia*. Manila: Economics and Development Research Center, Asian Development Bank.

Brillantes, A., 2006, *Decentralization Imperatives: Lessons from some Asian Countries*. Meiji University International Exchange Programs Guest Lecture Series.

Chandra-nuj, M., 2007, *Thailand Country Fact Sheet on the State of Decentralization and Local Democracy in the Asia Pacific Region.*

Cheema, A., Khwaja, A. and Qadir, A., 2006, *Local Government Reforms in Pakistan: Context, Content and Causes*, in Bardhan, P. and Mookherjee, D. (eds.) "Decentralization and Local Governance in Developing Countries: A Country Perspective". Cambridge, MA and London: MIT Press (pp. 257-284).

Citypopulation, *List of metropolitan areas by population*, http://www.citypopulation .de/world.html.

CLGF, 2005, *Commonwealth Local Government Handbook 2005*. London: Commonwealth Local Government Forum.

Devas, N. et al., 2004, *Urban Governance, Voice and Poverty in the Developing World*. London: Earthscan.

Devas, N., 2005, *Metropolitan Governance and Urban Poverty*, Public Administration and Development. Vol 25 (pp. 351-361).

Gao Xiao Ping., 2007, *China Country Fact Sheet on the State of Decentralization and Local Democracy in the Asia Pacific Region.*

Hairong, L., 2004, *Semi-competitive elections at township level in Sichuan province*, China Perspectives, Vol.51 (January-February).

Hofman, B. and Kaiser, K., 2006, *Decentralization, Democratic Transition and Local Governance in Indonesia*, in Bardhan, P. and Mookherjee, D. (eds.), "Decentralization and Local Governance in Developing Countries: A Country Perspective". Cambridge, MA and London: MIT Press (pp. 81-124).

International Monetary Fund, 2006, *Government Finance Statistics 2006*. Washington DC: International Monetary Fund.

Lee, D., 1998, *Local Government Reforms in Korea: A Transition from a Marionnette Performance Toward an Elementary Class Day*, in Nakamura, A. (ed.), "Reforming Government: New Concepts and Practices in Local Public Administration", Tokyo: EROPA Local Government Center (pp. 65-82).

National Tax Service of the Republic of Korea, *Korean Taxation 2006*. http://www.nta.go.kr/engdefault.html. Date accessed: 9 July 9 2007.

OECD, 2001, *Revenue Statistics of Member Countries, 1965-2000*. Paris: Organisation for Economic Co-operation and Development.

OECD, 2005, *OECD in figures*. Paris: Organisation for Economic Co-operation and Development.

Park, I., 2007, *Republic of Korea Country Fact Sheet on the State of Decentralization and Local Democracy in the Asia Pacific Region*.

Qiao, J., 2005, *La réforme de l'administration chinoise face aux rites confucéens, thesis*. Paris: University Paris 1 (unpublished).

Rakodi, C, 2004, *Urban Politics: Exclusion or Empowerment*, in Devas, N. et al.: "Urban Governance, Voice and Poverty in the Developing World". London: Earthscan.

Rao, G. and Singh, N., 2003, *How to Think About Local Government Reform in India*, in Kalirajan, K. (ed.), Economic Reform and the Liberalisation of the Indian Economy: Essays in Honour of Richard T. Shand. Cheltenham: Edward Elgar (pp. 335-390).

Sagawa, Y., 2007, *Japan Country Fact Sheet on the State of Decentralization and Local Democracy in the Asia Pacific Region*.

Schubert, G., 2003, *Democracy under one party rule?*, China Perspectives Vol. 46 (March-April).

Seong, K., 1998, *Delayed decentralization and incomplete consolidation of democracy: The case of Korean local autonomy*, paper presented at the Hoover Conference on Institutional Reform and Democratic Consolidation in Korea, 8-9 January 1998.

Sethi, G. (ed.), 2004, *Fiscal decentralization to rural governments in India*. Washington, DC: World Bank and Oxford University Press.

Singh, A. and Matthew, J., 2007, *India Country Fact Sheet on the State of Decentralization and Local Democracy in the Asia Pacific Region*.

Sproats, K., 2003, *Local Governments in Asia and the Pacific: A Comparative Analysis of Fifteen Countries*, in Brillantes, A. et al. "Decentralization and Power Shift: An Imperative for Good Governance". Quezon City: Center for Local and Regional Governance, National College of Public Administration and Governance, University of the Philippines (pp. 25-62).

Teehankee, J., 2002, *Electoral politics in the Philippines*, in Croissant, A. (ed.) Electoral politics in Southeast and East Asia. Singapore: Friedrich Ebert Stiftung.

UNDESA, 2006, *Urban and Rural Areas 2005*. New York: United Nations Department of Economic and Social Affairs, Population Division.

UNDP, 2006, *Human Development Report 2006*. New York: Palgrave Macmillan.

UNDP, 2006, *Local democracy in Asia: Representation in decentralized governance*. Bangkok: United Nations Development Programme Regional Centre in Bangkok.

UNESCAP, 2005, *State of women in urban local government in Australia,* http://www.unescap.org/huset/women/reports/australia.pdf, United Nations Economic and Social Commission for Asia and the Pacific.

UNESCAP, 2005, *State of women in urban local government in New Zealand,* http://www.unescap.org/huset/women/reports/newzealand.pdf, United Nations Economic and Social Commission for Asia and the Pacific.

UNESCAP, *Local Government in Asia and the Pacific*, http://www.unescap.org/huset/lgstudy/country/malaysia/malaysia.html, date accessed: 12 July 2007.

UNESCAP, *Country Reports on Local Government Systems: Republic of Korea*, pp. 9-10, http://www.unescap.org/huset/lgstudy/new-countrypaper/RoK/RoK.pdf, date accessed: 12 July 2007.

Weist, D., 2001, *Thailand's Decentralization: Progress and Prospects* (Paper prepared for the KPI Annual Congress III on Decentralization and Local Government in Thailand held on 10-11 November 2001). http://www1.worldbank.org/wbiep/decentralization/eaplib/weist.pdf, date accessed 17 July 2007.

Weist, D. (ed.), 2004, *India Urban Finance and Governance Review*. Washington, DC: World Bank Report No. 32253-IN, vol. 1 (executive summary and main report).

Wettenhall, R. and Aulich, C., 2007, *Australia Country Fact Sheet on the State of Decentralization and Local Democracy in the Asia Pacific Region*.

World Bank, 2004, *Village Justice in Indonesia*. Case Studies on Access to Justice, Village Democracy and Governance. Jakarta: World Bank Social Development Unit, 117 pages.

Yunus, A., 2007, *Malaysia Country Fact Sheet on the State of Decentralization and Local Democracy in the Asia Pacific Region*.

# Eurasia

Administrativnaya reforma v Rossii. M., 2006.

Aksenenko Yu. N. Municipal'naya social'naya politika:Stanovlenie, puti I factory realizacii. Saratov, 1999.

Babich A. M., Pavlova L. N. Gosudarstvennye i municipal'nye financy. M., 2000.

Babichev I. V. Subyekty mestnogo samoupravleniya i ikh vzaimodejstvie. M., 2000.

Babun P. B., Mullagaleyeva Z. Z. Voprosy municipal'noj ekonomiki. M., 2000.

Bazhinov M.A. Mestnoe samoupravlenie kak faktor stanovleniya grazhdanskogo obshhestva v sovremennoj Rossii. M., 2004.

Bajmuratov M. A. Evropejskie standarty lokal'noj demokratii I mestnoe samoupravlenie v Ukraine. Kh., 2000.

Berkovich E. F. Zakonnost' i mestnoe samoupravlenie v Rossijskoj Federacii M., 2005.

Cherkasov A. Spraviteln'noe mestnoe upravlenie: teoriya I praktika. M., 2005.

Chikhladze L.T. Mestnoe samoupravlenie i mestnoe upravlenie v Gruzii: tradicii I opyt. M., 2005.

Filippow V. Yu., Avdeyeva T. T. Osnovy razvitiya mestnogo khozyajstva. M., 2000.

Grazhdan, zakon I publichnaya vlast'. M., 2005

Grigoyev V. A. Stanovlenie mestnogo samoupravleniya v Ukraine. Odessa, 2000.

Dementyev A. N. Ustanovlenie granic territorij I preobrazovanie municipal'nykh obrazovanij. M., 2004.

Eremin A. R. Realizaciya prava cheloveka I grazhdanina na mestnoe samoupravlenie v Rossiiskoj Federacii: Konstitucionnye voprosy. Saratov, 2003.

Iginatyuk N. A., Zamotayev A. A., Pavlushin A. V. Municipal'noe pravo. Uchebnik. Moscow, 2004.

Ivanov D. V. Pravotvorchestvo predstavitel'nykh organov mestnogo samoupravleniya: Na materialakh Ural'skogo regiona. Chelyabinsk, 2004.

Khabrieva T. Ya. Sovremennaya konstituciya i mestnoe samoupravlenie // zhurnal rossijskogo prava. 2005 4.

Khabrieva, T. Ya. O razgranichenii predmetov vedeniya I polnomochij mezhdu gosudarstvennymi organami I organami mestnogo samoupravleniya // Administrativnoe pravo: teoriya I praktika. M., 2002.

Koveshnikov E. M. Gusudarstvo I mestnoe samoupravlenie v Rossii: teoretiko-pravovye osnovy vzaimodejstviya. M., 2002.

Kompetenciya organov gosudarstvennoj vlasti subyektov Rossijstkoj Federacii. Orenburg, 2000.

Kutafin O. E., Fadeyev V. I. (2006) Municipalnoe pravo Rossijskoj Federacii.; M.
Malye goroda i mestnoe samoupravlenie. A. M. Kuzancev, V. P. Lenyshin, A. E. Murashov, E. A. Suslova; pod. red. E. A. Suslovaya. M., 2004.

Makhmutova M. Sistema mestnogo samoupravleniya v Respublike Kazakhstan // Razrabotka novykh pravil igry v starykh usloviyakh. Pod red. I.Muntyanu I V.Popa. – Budapesht: Institut otkrytogo obshhestva,

Programma reformirovaniya mestnogo samoupravleniya i kommunal'nogo khozyajstva, 2001.

Mestnoe samoupravlenie v Kazakhstane: osobennosti situacii I perspektivy razvitiya. Materialy mezhdunarodnoj konferencii I rapochego seminara regionalnykh centrov obucheniya gosudarstvennykh centrov obucheniya gosudarstvennykh sluzhhikh. M., 2003.

Mestnoe samoupravlenie v Rossii: preblemy razvitiya, stanovleniya, funkcionirovaniya. Perm, 1999.

Mestnoe samoupravlenie: Otechestvennyj i zarubeznyj opyt. Uchebnoe posobie / Pod red. S.Yu. Naumova. Saratov, 2001.

Mestnye soobshhestva v mestnom samoupravlenii M., 2000.

Mokryj V. S. Samoupravlenie v Rossijskoj Federacii kak institute publichnoj vlasti v grazhdanskom obshhestve. Samara, 2003.

Municipal'noe pravo Respubliki Armeniya. Uchebnoe posobie dlya vuzov. Arutyunyan A. Sh. Yerevan 2004, - 359 st.

Municipal'nyj menedzhment v Rossijskoj Federacii M., 2001.

Naumov C. Yu. Mestnoe samoupravlenie v sisteme publichnoj vlasti: Rossijskij i mirovoj opyt: cb. Nauch. Tp. Saratov, 2004.

Nechaev V. D. Territorial'naya organizaciya mestnogo samoupravleniya v regionakh Rossii: genesis I institucional'nye effekty. Kursk, 2004.

Osnovy Evropejskoj Khartii mestnogo samoupravleniya: metodicheskoe posobie / otv. red.  I.A.Volodin. M., 1999.

Penkova-Lyujer P., Pagozina L. Social'naya politika municipal'nykh obrazovanij: soderzanie prioritety, mekhanizmy osushhestvleniya. M., 2000.

Pravovoe obespechenie nacional'nykh interesov: materialy mezhdunarodnoj

nauchno-prakticheskoj konferencii (Moskva, 25-26 Oktyabrya 2005 g.) / pod obshh. red. T. Ya. Khabrievoj. M., 2005.

Pylin V. V.   Narodovlastie v sisteme mestnogo samoupravleniya. SPB, 1998.

Ragulin D. D. Obshhie principy organizacii mestnogo samoupravleniya v Gosudarstvakh Sodruzhestva. Yurist., 1998 9.

Ragulin D. D.   Territorial'nye osnovy mestnogo samoupravleniya v zarubezhnykh stranakh CNG I Baltii // Pravo i zhizn'. 1998. 14.

Regulirovanie voprosov organizacii mestnogo samoupravleniya zakonami subyektov Rossijskoj Federacii i municipal'nymi pravovymi aktam. M, 2004.

Salomakin A. A. Mestnoe samiupravlenie v sel'skikh peselenyakh Rossii: voprosi teorii I praktiki. Chekyabinsk, 1999.

Sergeyev P.V. Mestnoe samoupravlenie na sele: voprosy terii I praktiki. Kursk, 2003.

Shirokov A. N., Yurkova C. N. Mestnoe samoupravlenie v Rossijskoj Federacii: osnovnye ponyatiya, terminy I polozheniya federal'nogo zakonodatel'stva. M., 2004.

Shvecov A. A.   Ekonomicheskie resurcy municipal'nogo razvitiya: Financy, imushhestvo, zemlya. M., 2004.

Sivickii V. A.  Regulirovanie otvetstvennosti v sfere mestnogo samoupravleniya // Konstitucionnye I zakonodatel'nye osnovy mestnogo samoupravleniya v Rossijsoj Federacii M., 2004.

Social'noe zakonodatel'stvo. Nauchno-prakticheskoe posobie. M., 2005.

Social'nye osnovy mestnogo samoupravleniya v Rossijskoj Federacii. M.,1998.

Spravitel'noe konstitucionnoe pravo / Pod red. Chirkina V.E. – M., 1996. M., 2004.

Sudebnaya zashhita organov mestnogo samoupravleniya v Rossijskoj Federacii. M., 1998.

Uchastie naceleniya v osushhestvlenii mestnogo samoupravleiya. M., 2004.

Upravlenie municipal'nym khozyajstvom i mestnymi financami. M., 2004.

Vasilyev V. I. Zakonodatel'naya osnova municipal'noj reform. Moscow, 2005.

Vestnik Central'noj izbiratel'noj komissii Rossijskoj Federacii. 2006 2 (193).

Voronenko A. M. Mestnoe samoupravlenie v krupnykh gorodakh zarubezhnykh stran. M., 1990.

Zaslavskaya L. V. Byudzhetnyj process v municipal'nom obrazovanii kak odna iz stadij upravleniya finansami. M., 1999.

**Country reports:**

- Armenia: Rafaelian, V.V., Kazinian, A.G., Chatirian, E.E.
- Azerbaijan: Safarov, N.
- Belarus: Vasilevitch, G.A.
- Kazakhstan: Januzakova, L.T.
- Central Asia (Kazakhstan, Kyrgyz Republic, Tajikistan, Turkmenistan, Uzbekistan): Saïdov, A.X.
- Uzbekistan: Saïdov, A.X.
- Russia: IZAK
- Ukraine: Batanov, A.

## Europe

Bäck, H., Heinelt, H., Magnier, A. (eds.), 2006, *The European mayor,* VS Verlag "Urban and Regional Research International", Wiesbaden.

Baldersheim, H., Illner, M., Wollmann, H. (eds.), 2003, *Local Democracy in Post-Communist Europe*, VS Verlag "Urban and Regional Research International", Wiesbaden.

Bennett, R. (ed.), 1989, *Territory and Administration in Europe*, London.

Berg, R., Rao, N. (eds.), *Transforming local Political Leadership*, 2005, Houndmills, Palgrave.

Bloomfield, J., 2006, *Counselling, Cajoling or Coordinating: Central Governments' Policy Approaches toward Local Government on the Issues of Performance and Cost-Effectiveness.* Brussels, CCRE/CEMR.

Comité des Régions [Committee of the Regions], 2002, *Les pouvoirs locaux et régionaux en Europe* [Local and regional authorities in Europe], volumes 1 et 2, Luxembourg.

Comité des Régions, 2003, *Le processus de décentralisation dans les Etats membres et les pays candidats* [The decentralization process in the member states and applicant countries], Luxembourg.

Conseil de l'Europe (années diverses) [Council of Europe (various years)], *La démocratie locale et régionale, collection de brochures par pays* [Local and regional democracy, collection of brochures by country], Strasbourg.

Coulson, A., Campbell, A. (eds.), 2006, *Local Government in Central and Eastern Europe*, Local Government Studies, Vol. 32 No. 5, November, special edition.

Council of Europe, *Effective democratic governance at local and regional level*, Budapest, Open Society Institute, 2005 (reports by Gérard Marcou and Ken Davey on the Stability Pact countries of South-East Europe).

Centre National de la Fonction Publique Territoriale [National center for territorial civil service], 2005, *Les fonctions publiques locales en Europe. Décentralisation et réforme des conditions d'emploi des agents publics dans l'Europe élargie, Rapport final* [Local civil service in Europe. Decentralization and reform of the employment conditions of civil servants in the widened Europe, Final report], 195 pages, Paris.

Dafflon, B., 2002, *Local Public Finance in Europe*, Cheltenham, Edward Elgar.

Delcamp, A., Loughlin, J. [dir. (ed.)], 2002, *La décentralisation dans les Etats de l'Union européenne* [Decentralization in the European Union States], La Documentation française, Paris.

Denters, B., Rose, L. E. (eds.), 2004, *Comparing Local Governance*, Palgrave.

Dexia, 2004, *Les finances locales dans l'Europe à 25* [Local finances in the Europe of the 25], Dexia Editions, Paris.

Gabriel, O. W., Hoffmann-Martinot, V. (eds.), 1999, *Démocraties urbaines* [Urban democracies], Paris, L'Harmattan.

Goldsmith, M., 2002, *Central Control over Local Government – A Western European Comparison*, Local Government Studies, vol. 28 , no.3, 91-112.

Goldsmith, M., Klausen, K. (eds.), 1997, *European Integration and Local Government*, London, Edward Elgar 1997.

Guérin-Lavignotte, E., Kerrouche, E., 2006, *Les élus locaux en Europe. Un statut en mutation* [Local authority elected officials in Europe. A changing status.], La Documentation Française « Etudes », 158 pages.

Haus, M. et al., (ed.) 2005, *Urban Governance and Democracy*, Routledge.

Hesse, J.-J. (ed.), 1991, *Local Government and Urban Affairs in International Perspective*, Baden-Baden, Nomos.

Hoffmann-Martinot, V. and Sellers, J. J. (eds.), 2005, *Metropolitanization and Political Change*, VS Verlag "Urban and Regional Research International", Wiesbaden.

John, P., 2001, *Local Governance in Western Europe*, London, Sage.

Kandeva, E. (ed.), 2001, *Stabilization of Local Governments* (2 vols). Local Government and Public Service Reform Initiative, Budapest.

Kersting, N., Vetter, A. (eds.), 2003, *Reforming Local Government in Europe. Closing the Gap between Democracy and Efficiency*, VS Verlag "Urban and Regional Research International", Wiesbaden.

Lazijn , F. et al., (eds.), 2007, *Local Government Reforms in Countries in Transition. A Global Perspective.* Lexington Press (forthcoming).

Le Galès, P., 2002, *European Cities*, Oxford, Oxford University Press.

Lorrain, D., Stoker, G. (eds.), 1996, *The Privatization of Urban Services*, London, Pinter.

Marcou, G., 2002, *Les structures régionales dans les pays candidats et leur compatibilité avec les fonds structurels (Europe centrale et orientale)* [Regional structures in the applicant countries and their compatibility with the structural funds (central and eastern Europe)], "Rapport au Parlement européen" [Report to the European Parliament], Luxembourg, Parlement européen, Direction générale des Etudes, STOA 105 FR, septembre 2002, 150 pages.

Marcou, G., 2003, *Les régions entre l'Etat et les collectivités locales. Etude comparative de cinq Etats européens à autonomies régionales ou à constitution fédérale (Allemagne, Belgique, Espagne, Italie, Royaume-Uni)* [The regions between state and local authorities. Comparative study of five European states with self-governing regions or a federal constitution (Germany, Belgium, Spain, Italy, UK)], Ministère de l'Intérieur [Ministry of the Interior], Travaux et Recherches du Centre d'Etudes et de Prévision [Research and work of the Center for Studies and Forecasting], Ministère de l'Intérieur, Paris, 2003, 237 pages.

Marcou, G., 2007, *L'étendue et la nature des compétences des collectivités locales dans les Etats membres du Conseil de l'Europe* [Scope and nature of the powers and responsibilities of local authorities in the member states of the Council of Europe], Rapport pour le CDLR (Comité directeur des pouvoirs locaux et régionaux) [Report for the Steering Committee on local and regional authorities], Conseil de l'Europe, Strasbourg, 102 pages (à paraître).

Marcou, G., Verebelyi, I. (eds.), 1993, *New trends in local government in Western and Eastern Europe*, International Institute of Administrative Science, Bruxelles.

Marcou, G. and Wollman, H. (eds.), *Annuaire des Collectivités locales, éditions annuelles avec une chronique internationale thématique* [Local authority yearbook with international thematic articles], CNRS Editions Paris.

Meligrana, J. (ed.), *Redrawing Local Government Boundaries*, 2004, UBC Press, Vancouver, Toronto.

Norton, A., 1993, *International Handbook on local and regional government. A comparative analysis of advanced democracies,* Edward Elgar, London.

Sellers, J. M., 2002, *Governing from Below, Urban Regions and the Global Economy,* Cambridge U Press.

Szücs, S., Strömberg, L. (eds.), 2006, *Local Elites, Political Capital and Democratic Development. Governing Leaders in Seven European Countries*. VS Verlag "Urban and Regional Research International", Wiesbaden.

Travers, T., 2005, *International Comparisons of Local Government Finance: Propositions and Analysis*. London School of Economics and Political Science.

## Latin America

**A) Books and reviews:**

Aghón, G., *Los retos pendientes de la descentralización fiscales América Latina y el Caribe*, 2000.

Alburquerque, F., *Desarrollo económico local y descentralización en América Latina*, Revista de la CEPAL, núm. 82, abril de 2004. ¡Desarrollo Económico Local y Distribución del Progreso Técnico!. ILPES/-CEPAL, Santiago de Chile, 2006.

Banco Interamericano de Desarrollo, *Informe Sobre la Situación del Servicio en América Latina*, Washington, IADB, 2006.

Burki, S. J. and others. *La Descentralización del Estado*. World Bank, Washington, 1999.

Carbonell, M. (ed.), *Derecho constitucional* (Memoria del Congreso Internacional de Culturas y Sistemas Jurídicos Comparados), México, UNAM, 2004.

Cetrangolo, O., *Descentralización y Federalismo Fiscal: aspectos teóricos y prácticos en América Latina*. Arequipa, Perú, 2006.

Conam GTZ Ecuador, *Línea de Referencia Descentralización en Argentina, Bolivia, Brasil, Chile, Colombia, Ecuador, Perú y Venezuela*. Quito, 2000.

European Commission, *Informe Estratégico Regional Sobre América Latina*, april, 2002.

Espitia, G., *Descentralización Fiscal en América Latina*. El Salvador. CONFEDELCA, Diputación de Barcelona, GTZ. Octubre 2004.

Finot, I., *Descentralización en América Latina: teoría y práctica*, Santiago de Chile, CEPAL-ILPES, 2001.

——. *Descentralización, transferencias territoriales y desarrollo local*, Revista de la CEPAL, núm. 86, agosto 2005.

——. *La descentralización fiscal y transferencias intergubernamentales en América Latina,* CEPAL-ILPES, 2004. "Teoría económica de la descentralización y procesos latinoamericanos", octubre de 2006.

Fix Z., Carmona H. and V., Salvador, Derecho constitucional y comparado, 4 ed. México, Porrúa, 2005.

Foschiatto, P. and Stumpo, G. (ed.), *Políticas municipales de micro crédito. Un instrumento para la dinamización de los sistemas productivos locales*. Estudios de caso en América Latina, Santiago de Chile, CEPAL-Cooperazione Italiana, 2006.

Kliksberg, B., *Más Ética, Más Desarrollo*. Editorial Temas, Buenos Aires, 2004.

Licha, I. (ed.), *Citizens in charge. Managing local budgets in East Asia and Latin America*, Inter-American Development Bank, 2004.

Lora, E. and Cárdenas, M., *Reforma de las instituciones fiscales en América Latina*, IADB, 2006.

María Hernández, A., *Derecho municipal*, México, UNAM, 2003.

Martín, J. and Martner, R. (ed.) *El estado de las finanzas públicas: América Latina y El Caribe*, CEPAL-ILPES, 2004.

United Nations (UNDP), *Informe Sobre Desarrollo Humano 2005*, Ediciones Multiprensa, 2005.

Nickson, A., *Tendencias actuales de las finanzas en América Latina*, http://www.lagniks.net/lagniks/c.php?e=FILEFRAME andid=436155651668.mhtandaction, consulted: July 2006.

Palomino Manchego, J., *Regiones y municipios del Perú. Marco constitucional actual*, in "El municipio en México y el mundo", México, UNAM, 2005.

Piazze, A. and Flaño, N., *Diálogo Social en América Latina*, IADB, 2005.

United Nations Development Programme (UNDP), *La Democracia en América Latina. Hacia una democracia de ciudadanos y ciudadanas*, 2004. http://democracia.undp.org/default.asp.

Rodlauer, M. and Schipke, A., *América Central: Integración mundial y cooperación regional*, Washington, IMF, 2005.

Rojas, E., Cuadrado, J. and Fernández, J. M., *Gobernar las metrópolis,* IADB-Universidad de Alcalá de Henares, 2005.

Rosales, M., *Los Secretos del Buen Alcalde.* Universidad Virtual del Tecnológico de Monterrey, México, 2000.

——. *El Buen Gobierno Local,* Universidad Bolivariana de Chile. Santiago, 2005.

Rosas Aispuro, J.; Cienfuego, D. (ed.), *El Municipio en Iberoamérica, México*, Edit. Laguna, 2003.

Rousset, M., *L'action international des collectivités locales*, Paris. Librairie Générale de Droit de jurisprudence. EJA, 1998.

Serna de la Garza, J.M., *La reforma del estado en América Latina: Los casos de Argentina, Brasil y México, México*, UNAM, 1998.

Valadés, D. and Serna, J. M. (Coord.) *El gobierno en América latina*, México, UNAM; 2000.

Valencia Carmona, S., *Derecho Municipal*, México, Porrúa, 2003, El Municipio en México y en el mundo. "Primer Congreso Internacional de Derecho Municipal", México, UNAM; 2005.

Varios autores, *Los sistemas constitucionales Iberoamericanos*, Madrid, Dykinson, 1992.

Vasquez Baquero, A., *Desarrollo Económico Local y Descentralización en América Latina*. CEPAL, Santiago de Chile. 2000.

Wiesner, E., *La descentralización, la estabilidad macroeconómica y la integración económica regional: Enlaces de política y mecanismos de transmisión*, Bogotá BID-Instituto para la Integración de la América y El Caribe, 2003.

**B) Latin American constitutions:**

Cited constitutions, compiled by the Department of Legislation and Jurisprudence, UNAM Legal Research Institute: http://www.juridicas.unam.mx.

**C) Websites:**

Centro Latinoamericano de Administración para el Desarrollo (CLAD). http://www.clad.org.ve/.

e-local.gob.mx. http://www.e-local.gob.mx/wb2/.

Economic Commission for Latin America and the Caribbean (ECLAC). http://www.eclac.cl/.

Federación de mujeres municipalistas de América Latina y el Caribe. http://www.femum.org.

Federación Latinoamericana de Ciudades, Municipios y Asociaciones. http://www.flacma.org/.

Fundación para el Desarrollo Local y el Fortalecimiento Municipal e Institucional de Centroamérica y el Caribe (DEMUCA). http://www.demuca.or.cr/.

Human Development Reports. http://hdr.undp.org/reports/global/2005/espanol/.

Inter-American Agency for Cooperation and Development (IACD). http://oeamejorespracticas.axesnet.com/default.asp.

Latin American Governance Network Information and Knowledge System. http://www.lagniks.net/lagniks/c.php?e=HOME.

Latinobarómetro. http://www.latinobarometro.org/.

Municipium / Servicio de Asistencia y Capacitación para el Desarrollo Local (SACDEL). http://www.municipium.cl/.

Observatorio Latino Americano de la descentralización. http://www.observatorio-flacma.org/.

PNUD Mexico - United Nations Development Program in Mexico. http://www.undp.org.mx/.

Political Data base of the Americas. http://pdba.georgetown.edu/spanish.html.

Red de Investigación y Acción para el Desarrollo Loca (RIADEL). http://www.riadel.cl/default.asp.

Sistema Económico Latinoamericano y del Caribe – SELA. http://www.sela.org/sela/index.asp.

Transparency International. http://www.transparency.org/regional_pages/americas/introduccion.

UCLG - Global Observatory on Local Democracy and Decentralization. http://www.cities-localgovernments.org/gold/list.asp?region=8andL=en.

United Cities and Local Governments. http://www.cities-localgovernments.org/uclg/index.asp?L=ES.

United States Agency for International Development (USAID) - Latin America. http://www.usaid.gov/espanol/.

Zevallos V., *Micro, pequeñas y medianas empresas en América Latina.* http://www.cepal.org/.

Zovatto, D. and Burdman, J., *Balance Electoral Latinoamericano 2003–2004*, working paper of the Observatorio Electoral. http://www.observatorioelectoral.org/.

## Middle East and West Asia

### Enactments:

**Saudi Arabia:**
- Saudi Constitution (Basic Law), 1992.
- Law on the provinces (Saudi Arabia), 1 March 1992.
- Law on municipal elections, 2004.
- Royal decree no. A/276 of 08 October 1395 H[1] on the creation of the Ministry of Rural and Municipal Affairs (Saudi Arabia).

**Bahrain:**
- Bahraini Constitution, 2002.

**Islamic Republic of Iran:**
- Iranian Constitution, 1979.
- Law of 25 June 1949 establishing municipalities and town and village councils.
- Law of 2 July 1955 concerning municipalities.
- Law of 5 July 1979 establishing local councils.
- Law of 28 September 2003 amending the law on « les structures, les attributions et l'élection des conseils islamiques du pays et l'élection des maires » of 23 May 1996.
- Implementing decree of 20 December 1998 concerning the election of councils in towns and small towns.
- Implementing decree of 20 December 1998 concerning the election of village and district councils.

**Iraq:**
- Constitution du gouvernement intérimaire irakien, 1990.
- Constitution proposée par les partis d'opposition, in Al-Mutamar no. 305 of 23 May 2005, pp. 14-15. (Iraq).

**Jordan:**
- Jordanian Constitution.
- Law on municipalities, 1995, and 2007.

**Kuwait:**
- Kuwaiti Constitution, 1962.

1. *Hegiric calendar. 14th October 1975 in the Gregorian calendar.*

**Lebanon:**
- Lebanese Constitution.
- Legislative decree no. 118, 1977 on municipalities.
- Taëf Accords (Pacte national de Taëf), 22 October 1989.
- Law on administrative organization (décret-loi n° 111 du 12/06/1960).
- Law on the mokhtar of 27 November 1947.

**Oman:**
- Omani Constitution, 1996 (Basic Law).

**Qatar:**
- Qatari Constitution, 2003.

**Syria:**
- Syrian Constitution, 1973.

**Turkey:**
- Turkish Constitution, 1982, substantially amended in 2001.

**West Bank and Gaza**
- Law on 'Palestinian local council elections', December 1996, partially amended in 2005.
- Law on local life, September 1997.

**Yemen:**
- Yemeni Constitution, 1991, amended in 1994.

**Articles and reports:**

Al Jordi, H., *Power and the municipalities*, Centre National de Recherches, p. 20, 1998.

Al Khalil, Y., *The role of municipalities in economic and rural development*, Id., in Municipalités et administration locale, n°2, p. 45, Centre d'Etudes et de Recherches sur le Moyen-Orient contemporain.

Bédar, S., *The Greater Middle East: a worldwide post-colonial project?*, Diplomatie n°3, May-June 2003.

Imad, A., *Municipal elections*, Jarrous Press, p. 20.

Municipalités et administration locale n°1, *Centre d'Etudes et de Recherches sur le Moyen-Orient contemporain*, 2000.

SARROUH E., *Decentralized Governance for Development in the Arab States*, report presented during a forum on the governance of the Arab states, Sana'a, 6-9 September 2003.

*Saudi Elections in Regional Perspective : The Shiite 'Threat' Theory*, Policy Watch no. 970, 9 March 2005, The Washington Institute for Near-East Policy.

Zubai, K., 2006. *Local Administration and its integrative relations with the central authorities of the modern state*. The proceedings of the third conference of big cities administration. (June 4-6) Amman, Jordan.

**Main websites :**

http://www.citymayors.com

World Bank: http://www.worldbank.org

Program on governance in the Arab Region: http://www.pogar.org

UNDP: http://www.undp.org

Transparency International: http://www.transparency.org

**Government websites**

Lebanese Finance Ministry: http://www.finance.gov.lb

Lebanese Ministry of the Interior and of Municipalities: http://www.interior.gov.lb

## North America

Saudi Ministry of Rural and Municipal Affairs: http://www.momra.gov.sa

Jordanian Ministry of Rural and Municipal Affairs and the Environment: http://www.nis.gov.jo

Jordanian Finance Ministry: http://www.mof.gov.jo

Bahraini Finance Ministry: http://www.mofne.gov.bh

Qatari Ministry of Municipal Affairs and Agriculture: http://www.baladiya.gov.qa

Syrian Ministry of the Economy and Finance: http://www.syrecon.org

Ammons, David N., 2003, *Urban Services*. In John P. Pelissero (ed.), "Cities, Politics, and Policy" (pp. 254-282). Washington, D.C.: CQ Press.

Berner, M., 2001. *Citizen Participation in Local Government Budgeting*. Popular Government, Spring 2001, 23-30.

Berry, J. M., Portney, K. E., and Thomson, K., 1993. *The Rebirth of Urban Democracy*. Washington, D.C.: The Brookings Institution.

Bibby, J. F., 1999. *State and Local Parties in a Candidate-Centered Age*. In R. E. Weber and P. Brace (eds.), "American State and Local Politics: Directions for the 21st Century". New York: Seven Bridges Press.

Blatter, J.K., 2001. *De-bordering a world of states: towards a multi-level system in Europe and a multi-polity system in North-America? Insights from border regions*. European Journal of International Relations 7, 2 (2001): 175-209.

Bureau of Indian Affairs, 2006, BIA Website. Retrieved June 28, 2006, http://www.doi.gov/bureau-indian-affairs.html.

Canadian Federation of Municipalities, 2004. *Increasing Representation of Women in Municipal Decision-making Processes*. Ottawa: Canadian Federation of Municipalities. Retrieved July 3, 2007, http://www.fcm.ca/english/policy/women.html.

Center for American Women and Politics, 2006. New Brunswick, N.J.: *Eagleton Institute of Politics*, Rutgers, The State University of New Jersey, Retrieved on August 10, 2006, http://www.cawp.rutgers.edu/Facts/Officeholders/stleg.pdf.

CIA World Factbook, 2006. Retrieved July 4, 2006, http://www.cia.gov/cia/publications/factbook/fields/2056.html.

City Mayor, 2006, *Canada Offers Its People an Array of Local Governments*, Retrieved June 26, 2006, http://www.citymayors.com/canada/canada_locgov.html.

Commonwealth Local Government Forum, 2002, Canada. Retrieved July 6, 2006 http://www.clgf.org.uk/index_profiles.htm.

Cornell, S. and Kalt, J. P., 2000, *Sovereignty and Nation-Building: The Development Challenge in Indian Country Today*. Unpublished paper, John F. Kennedy School of Government, Cambridge, MA.

Coursey, D., 2005, *E-Government: Trends and Challenges*. In The Municipal Year Book (pp. 14-21), Washington, D.C.: International City/County Management Association.

Diaz, A., 2003, *Shifting of service responsibilities between provincial and local governments*. Ottawa: Statistics Canada.

Elections Canada (n.d.), Retrieved July 25, 2006, http://www.elections.ca/scripts/OVR2004/default.html.

Electronic Government 2004. (2004). Washington, D.C.: International City/County Management Association.

Fisher P. S., 1982, *Regional Tax-Base Sharing: An Analysis and Simulation of Alternative Approaches*. Land Economics, 58(4), 497-515.

Freyss, S. F., 1995, *Municipal Government Personnel Systems: A Test of Two Archetypical Models*. Review of Public Personnel Administration 15: 69-93.

Gallup, 2006, *Trust in Government*. Retrieved June 12, 2006, 2006, www.gallup.com.

Hahn, H., 1968, *Voting in Canadian Communities: A Taxonomy of Referendum Issues*. Canadian Journal of Political Science 1(4): 462-469.

Hajnal, Z.L. and Trounstine, J., 2005, *When turnout matters: The consequences of uneven turnout in city elections*, Journal of Politics 67(2): 515-535.

Hajnal, Z. L., and Lewis, P. G., 2003, *Municipal Institutions and Voter Turnout in Local Elections*. Urban Affairs Review, 38(5), 645-668.

Hajnal, Z. L., Lewis, P. G., and Louch, H., 2002, *Municipal Elections in California: Turnout, Timing, and Competition*. San Francisco: Public Policy Institute of California.

Hesse, J.J. and Sharpe , L.J., 1991, *Conclusions*. In "Local Government and Urban Affairs in International Perspective", ed. J.J. Hesse. Baden-Baden: Nomos, 603-621.

Hill, M. B. (n.d.), *State Laws Governing Local Government Structure and Administration*, Institute of Government/University of Georgia.

Infrastructure Canada, 2006, *Public Opinion Research*. Ottawa: Government of Canada. Retrieved December 21, 2006 at http://www.infrastructure.gc.ca/communities-collectivites/pub_opinion/.

International City/County Management Association, 2001, *Municipal Form of Government*. Washington, D.C.: International City/County Management Association.

International City/County Management Association, 1997, *Municipal Forms of Government*, 1996. Washington, D.C.: International City/County Management Association.

Internet Center for Corruption Research. (n.d.). Retrieved July 25, 2006, http://www.icgg.org/corruption.cpi_2005.html.

Judd, D., and Swanstrom, T., 1994, *City Politics: Private Power and Public Policy*. New York: HarperCollins College Publishers.

Laubach, T., 2005, *Fiscal Relations across Levels of Government in the United States.* OECD Economics Department Working Paper No. 462. Retrieved July 4, 2005, http://www.olis.oecd.org/olis/2005doc.nsf/43bb6130e5e86e5fc12569fa005d004c/da360144bb5dbe5ec12570c8005c0cfd/$FILE/JT00195165.PDF.

Leland, S.M. and Thurmaier, K. (eds.), 2004, *Case Studies of City-County Consolidation.* Armonk, NY: M.E. Sharpe.

McManus, S., 1999, *The Resurgent City Councils.* In Ronald E. Weber and Paul Brace (eds.), "American State and Local Politics" (pp. 166-193). New York: Chatham House Publishers.

MacManus, S. A., and Bullock, C. S., 2003, *The Form, Structure, and Composition of America's Municipalities in the New Millennium.* In Municipal Year Book (Vol. 2003, pp. 3-18). Washington, D.C.: International City/County Management Association.

Maher, M. and Jay S., 2005, *Production Market Competition and Economic Performance in Canada.* OECD Economic Department Working Papers No. 421. Retrieved August 17, 2006, http://www.olis.oecd.org/olis/2005doc.nsf/43bb6130e5e86e5fc12569fa005d004c/c62110dffb4a9cdcc1256fd9007d0670/$FILE/JT00181345.PDF#search=%22eCO%2FWKP(2005)49%3A%208%22.

Meligrana, J.F., 2000, *Toward a process model of local government restructuring: Evidence from Canada,* Canadian Journal of Regional Science 23(3).

Morse, B. W., 2004, *Indigenous-Settler Treaty Making in Canada.* In M. Langton, M. Tehan, L. Palmer and K. Shain (eds.), "Honour Among Nations?" Melbourne: Melbourne University Press.

Mouritzen, P. E. and Svara, J. H., 2002, *Leadership at the Apex: Politicians and Administrators in Western Local Governments.* Pittsburgh, PA: University of Pittsburgh Press.

OECD, 2001, *Revenue Statistics of Member Countries, 1965-2000.* Washington, D.C.: OECD.

OECD, 2003, Public and Territorial Development Directorate - Country Factsheets. Retrieved July 19, 2006 from http://www.oecd.org.

OECD, 2005, *OECD in Figures-2005 Edition.* August 1, 2006, from http://www.oecd.org/document/62/0,2340,en_2649_37405_2345918_1_1_1_37405,00.html.

OECD, 2006, *Statistical Profile of Canada-2006.* Retrieved July 25, 2006 from http://stats.oecd.org/WBOS/ViewHTML.aspx?QueryName=177andQueryType=ViewandLang=en.

OECD, 2006, *Statistical Profile of United States-2006.* Retrieved July 25, 2006 from http://stats.oecd.org/WBOS/ViewHTML.aspx?QueryName=203andQueryType=ViewandLang=en.

OECD, 2003, *Metropolitan Governance in OECD Countries.* Retrieved July 25, 2006 from http://www.oecd.org/dataoecd/59/40/6100078.pdf.

OECD Observer, 2003, *OECD Territorial Review of Montreal.* Retrieved July 25, 2006 from http://www.oecd.org/dataoecd/35/11/26010229.pdf.

Post, S. S., 2005, *Metropolitan Area Governance and Institutional Collective Action.* In Feiock, Richard C. (Ed.), "Metropolitan Governance: Conflict, Competition, and Cooperation" (67-92). Washington, D.C.: Georgetown Press.

Reece, B., 2006, *E-Government Design and Equity.* Ph.D. Dissertation, University of Southern California, Los Angeles.

Richardson, J., Gough, M. and Puentes, R., 2003, *Is Home Rule the Answer? Clarifying the Effect of Dillon's Rule on Growth Management.* Washington, D.C.: Brookings Institution.

Rivard, M. and Collin, J.-P., 2006, *Factsheet: Canada.* Paris: Global Observatory on Local Democracy and Decentralization.

Ross, B. H. and Levine, M. A., 2001, *Urban Politics: Power in Metropolitan America.* Itasca, Illinois: F.E. Peacock Publishers.

Saffell, D. C. and Basehart, H., 1997, *Governing States and Cities.* New York: McGraw-Hill Companies Inc.

Sbragia, A. 1988, *Debt Wish.* Pittsburgh, University of Pittsburgh Press.

Sellers, J.M., 2006, *Comparing local governance in developed democracies: Selected indicators.* Working paper available online at http://www.usc.edu/dept/polsci/sellers/Publications/publications.htm.

Sellers, J.M. and Latner, M.L., 2006, *The Political Ecology of the U.S. Metropolis: An Interim Report.* Paper presented at International Political Science Association and American Political Science Association Annual Meetings, Fukuoka, Japan and Philadelphia, PA.

Sellers, J.M., 2007, *The Decentered State.* Manuscript in process.

Sellers, J.M. and Lidström, A.L., 2007, *Decentralization, local government and the welfare state.* Governance (forthcoming).

Simard, C., 2000, *Ethnic Minority Political Representation in Montreal.* Paper presented at National Metropolis Conference, Montreal.

Simpson, D. M., 2005, *Use of Web Technology by U.S. Planning Agencies: Results from a National Benchmarking Survey.* In Municipal Year Book (Vol. 2005, pp. 22-26). Washington, D.C.: International City/County Management Association.

United States Census Bureau, Statistical Abstract of the United States. (Jan. 04, 2006). Retrieved July 4, 2006 from http://www.census.gov/prod/www/statistical-abstract-2001_2005.html.

Public Sector Statistics: Supplement 2006, Statistics Canada, 2006, Ottawa: Ministry of Industry.

Stephens, G. R. and Wikstrom, N., 2000, *Metropolitan Government and Governance: Theoretical Perspectives, Empirical Analysis, and the Future.* New York: Oxford University Press.

Svara, J. H., 2003, *Two Decades of Continuity and Change in American City Councils,* National League of Cities.

Silva, L., 2005, *Escaping from the Straightjacket that Baffled Houdini: An Analysis of the Myths and Realities of Empowering Toronto Through a City Charter,* Master of Public Administration, University of Western Ontario.

Anthony Center, 2006, *Women Lag as Local Leaders.* Rochester, NY: Anthony Center. Retrieved December 12, 2006 at http://www.rochester.edu/SBA/PDFs/WomenLag2006.pdf.

Turnbull, G. K., 2002, *Local Tax Sharing: An Incentive for Intergovernmental Cooperation.* Fiscal Research Program No. 75. Andrew Young School of Policy Studies: Georgia State University.

U.S. Advisory Commission on Intergovernmental Relations (USACIR), 1993, *State Laws Governing Local Government Structure and Administration.* DC: U.S. Advisory Commission on Intergovernmental Relations.

U.S. Bureau of the Census, 1992, *Census of Governments,* 1(1) Government Organization. Retrieved July 28,2006 from http://www.census.gov/govs/www/cog92.html.

U.S. Bureau of the Census, 1997, *Government Organization. 1997 Census of Governments,* Vol. 1 Government Organization. Retrieved July 28, 2006 from http://www.census.gov/govs/www/cog.html.

U.S. Bureau of the Census, 2002, *Government Organization,* 1(1) Government Organization. Retrieved July 28, 2006 from http://www.census.gov/govs/www/cog 2002.html.

U. S. Bureau of the Census, 2002, *Government Finances. 2002 Census of Government* 4(5). Retrieved July 4, 2006 from http://www.census.gov/prod/2005pubs/gc024x5.pdf.

U.S. Bureau of the Census, 2006, *2005 Public Employment,* Data: Local Governments. In "Statistical Abstract of the United States".

World Bank, 2006, *GRICS: Governance Research Indicator Country Snapshot Comparison within Canada for all Six Governance Indicators. Governance and Anti-Corruption.* Retrieved July 28,2006 from http://www.worldbank.org/wbi/governance/.

World Bank, 2006, *GRICS: Governance Research Indicator Country Snapshot Comparison within United States for all Six Governance Indicators. Governance and Anti-Corruption.* Retrieved July 28,2006 from http://www.worldbank.org/wbi/governance/.

Zahra, S.A. et al., 2000, *Privatization and entrepreneurial transformation: Emerging issues and a future research agenda,* The Academy of Management Review 35(3): pp 509-524.

Zimmerman, J. F., 1997, *The Recall: Tribunal of the People.* Westport, Connecticut. Praeger Publishers.

## Metropolitan Governance

Abers, R. N. and Keck, M., 2006, *Muddy Waters: The Political Construction of Deliberative River Basin Governance in Brazil,* International Journal of Urban and Regional Research 30(3): 601-622.

Ades, A. F. and Glaeser, E. L., 1995, *Trade and Circuses: Explaining Urban Giants,* Quarterly Journal of Economics 110(1): 195-227.

Alesina, A., Baqir, R. and Easterly, W., 1999, *Public Goods and Ethnic Divisions,* Quarterly Journal of Economics 114(4): 243-84.

Ascher, F., 1995, *Metapolis ou l'avenir des villes.* Paris: Odile Jacob.

Banfield, E. C. and Grodzins, M., 1958, *Government and Housing in Metropolitan Areas,* New York: McGraw-Hill.

Blankart, C. B. and Pommerehne, W. W., 1979, *Les économies d'échelle dans les services urbains,* "Revue Économique", vol. 30, n°2.

Cameron, R. G., 2005, *Metropolitan restructuring (and more restructuring) in South Africa,* Public Administration and Development 25(4): 329-339.

Cameron, R. and Alvarez, A., 2005, *Metropolitanisation and political change in South Africa,* in: Hoffmann-Martinot, V. and Sellers, J. (eds.), "Metropolitanization and Political Change", Wiesbaden: VS-Verlag (Urban Research International, 6): 373-394.

Chernick, H. and Reschovsky, A., 2001, *Lost in the Balance: How State Policies Affect the Fiscal Health of Cities,* Working Paper, La Follette School of Public Affairs.

Clark, T. N. and Goetz, E. G., 1994, *The anti-growth machine: Can city governments control, limit or manage growth?* In Clark, Terry N. (ed.) "Urban innovation", pp 105-145. Thousand Oaks, CA: Sage.

Cobridge, S. and Jones, G. A., 2005, *The Continuing Debate About Urban Bias*. Working Paper, Department of Geography and Environment, London School of Economics.

Dahl, R., 1969, *The city in the future of democracy,* American Political Science Review 61: 953-970.

Davis, M., 2006, *Planet of Slums*. London: Verso.

Devas, N., 2005, *Metropolitan Governance and Poverty,* Public Administration and Development 25: 351-361.

Downs, A., 1994, *New Visions for Metropolitan America*, Washington, D.C.: The Brookings Institution.

Dreier, P., Mollenkopf, J. and Swanstrom, T., 2004, *Place Matters*, Lawrence, KS: University of Kansas Press.

Dupuy, G., 1997, *Préface*, in: Dubois-Taine, G. and Chalas, Y. (eds.), "La ville émergente", Paris, Editions de l'Aube, p. 5-9.

Fainstein, S., 2001, *Inequality in Global City-Regions*, in: Allen J. Scott (ed.), "Global City-Regions", New York : Oxford University Press, pp 285-98.

Frederickson, H. G., 1999, *The Repositioning of Public Administration*, *PS:* Political Science and Politics 32(4): 701-711.

Gilbert, A., 1998, *The Latin American City*, revised edition, London: Latin American Bureau.

Glaser, E., Kolko, J. and Saiz, A., 2001, *Consumer City*, Journal of Economic Geography 1, pp. 27-50.

Gottmann, J. 1961, *Megalopolis: The Urbanized Northeastern Seaboard of the United States*. New York: The Twentieth Century Fund.

Haddad, L., Ruel, M.T. and Garrett, J.L., 1999, *Are Urban Poverty and Undernutrition Growing?* Some Newly Assembled Evidence, World Development 27(11): pp. 1891-1904.

Harloe M., 2003, *Le nouveau gouvernement métropolitain de Londres: vers la terre promise*, Revue Française d'Administration Publique n° 107: 319-332.

Hoffmann-Martinot, V. and Sellers, J. (eds.), 2005, *Metropolitanization and Political Change*, Wiesbaden: VS-Verlag (Urban Research International, 6).

Hoffmann-Martinot, V., 2005, *Towards an Americanization of French Metropolitan Areas?*, in Hoffmann-Martinot, V. and Sellers, J. (eds.) (2005), "Metropolitanization and Political Change", Wiesbaden: VS-Verlag.

Huang, Jingnan, Xi Xi Lu and Sellers, J., 2008, *A Global Comparative Analysis of Urban Form*, Landscape and Urban Planning (forthcoming).

Ingram, G., 1997, *Patterns of Metropolitan Development: What Have We Learned?* Washington, D.C.: World Bank.

Jouve, B. and Lefèvre, C. (eds.), 2002, *Local power, territory, and institutions in European metropolitan regions*, London: Frank Cass.

Kennedy, L. 2007, *Regional Industrial Policies Driving Peri-Urban Dynamics in Hyderabad, India,* Cities 24(2): 95-109.

Kübler, D., 2005, *Problems and prospects of metropolitan governance in Sydney: towards 'old' or 'new' regionalism?*, City Futures Research Centre, University of New South Wales, 43 p.

Laquian Aprodicio A., 2001, *Metro Manila: Participation and Inclusion in A City of Villages*, in: Blair A. Ruble, Richard E. Stren, Joseph S. Tulchin and Diana H. Varat (eds.), "Urban Governance Around the World", Washington, D.C.: Woodrow Wilson International Center for Scholars: 74-110.

Laquian, Aprodicio A., 2005, *Beyond Metropolis: The Planning and Governance of Asia's Mega-Urban Regions*, Baltimore, MD: Johns Hopkins University Press.

Lipton, M., 1977, *Why Poor People Stay Poor: Urban Bias and World Development*, Avebury, UK: Aldershot.

Marcuse, P. and Van Kempen, R. (eds.), 2000, *Globalizing Cities: A New Spatial Order*, London: Blackwell.

Marks, G. and Hooghe, L., 2003, *Unraveling the Central State, But How? Types of Multi-Level Governance*, American Political Science Review 97(2): 233-43.

Markusen, Ann R., Lee, Y. S. and Dibiovanna, S. (eds.), 1999, *Second Tier Cities* (Minneapolis, MN: University of Minnesota Press).

Martinotti, G., 1997, *The New Social Morphology of Cities*, UNESCO-MOST, Discussion Paper Series No.16, Paris, UNESCO.

METROPOLIS, 2005, *Politique-cadre pour les régions métropolitaines proposée par le secrétariat régional Métropolis-Amérique du Nord*, Montréal, April 2005.

METROPOLIS, 2005, *Rapport de la Commission permanente présenté au 8ème Congrès de Metropolis*, Berlin, 11-15 May.

METROPOLIS, 2007, *Information on Metropolises*, retrieved June 15, 2007 at http://www.metropolis.org/index.php?action=mostrar_contenidoandid_seccion=88andtemplate=interior.

Mollenkopf, J., 1983, *The Contested City*. Princeton: Princeton University Press.

Mongin, O., 1998, *La Ville émergeante*. Paris: Presses Universitaires de France.

Ostrom, E., 2000, *The Danger of Self-Evident Truths*, PS: Political Science and Politics Vol. 33, No. 1 (March): 33-44.

Ostrom, V., Bish, V. and Ostrom, E.,1988, *Local Government in the United States*, San Francisco: ICS (Institute for Contemporary Studies) Press.

Overman, H. G. and Venables, A. J., 2005, *Cities in the Developing World*, Centre for Economic Performance Discussion Paper No. 695. London: Centre for Economic Performance, London School of Economics and Political Science.

Pack, J. R., 1998, *Poverty and Urban Public Expenditures*, Urban Studies 35(11): 1995-2019.

Rakodi, C. with Lloyd-Jones, T. (eds.), 2002, *Urban Livelihoods: A People-Centred Approach to Reducing Poverty*, London: Earthscan.

Razin, E. and Hazan, A., 2005, *Metropolitanization and Political Change in Israel*, in: Hoffmann-Martinot, V. and Sellers, J. (eds.), 2005, "Metropolitanization and Political Change", Wiesbaden : VS-Verlag (Urban Research International, 6): 395-423.

Sancton A., 2005, *The Governance of Metropolitan Areas in Canada*, Public Administration and Development Vol. 25, No. 4, October: pp 317-327.

Sancton A., 2001, *Canadian Cities and the New Regionalism*, Journal of Urban Affairs Vol. 23, No. 5: 543-555.

Sassen, S., 1991, *The Global City*. Oxford: Oxford University Press.

Satterthwaite, D., 2004, *The Underestimation of Urban Poverty in Low and Middle-income Nations*. IIED Poverty Reduction in Urban Areas Series Working Paper 14. London: IIED.

Segbers, K. (ed.), 2007, *The Making of Global City Regions*. Baltimore: Johns Hopkins University Press.

Sellers, J., 2002, *Governing From Below: Urban Regions and the Global Economy*. Cambridge: Cambridge University Press.

Sellers, J., 2005, *Metropolitanization and Politics in the United States: From Single Model to Multiple Patterns*, Hoffmann-Martinot, V. and Sellers, J., "Metropolitanization and Political Change", Wiesbaden: VS Verlag.

Sellers, J. and Lidström, A., 2007, *Decentralization, Local Government and the Welfare State*, *Governance* (forthcoming).

Souza C., 2005, *Brazilian Metropolitan Regions: Regime Change and Governance Vacuum*, Public Administration and Development Vol. 25, No. 4, October: 341-350.

Stren R. and Cameron, R., 2005, *Metropolitan Governance Reform: An Introduction*, Public Administration and Development Vol. 25, No. 4, October: 275-284.

Taylor, P. J., 2003, *World City Network*, New York: Routledge.

UNCHS, 2003, *The Challenge of Slums. Global Report on Human Settlements 2003*. Earthscan: London.

UNCHS, 2005, *World Urbanization Prospects: The 2005 Edition*. New York: United Nations Economic and Social Division. Retrieved online January 20, 2007 at http://www.un.org/esa/population/publications/WUP2005/2005wup.htm.

Veltz, P. 1996, *Mondialisation, villes et territoires*, Paris: Presses Universitaires de France

Vogel R. K., 2001, *Reforming Tokyo Metropolitan Government*, in: Ruble, B. A., Stren, R. E., Tulchin, J. S. and Varat , D. H. (eds.), "Urban Governance around the World", Washington, D.C.: Woodrow Wilson International Center for Scholars: pp. 114-148.

Wirth, L., 1942, *Proceedings, National Conference on Planning*, 1942. Chicago: American Society of Planning Officials: pp. 141-151.

Wood, R. C., 1964, *1,400 Governments: The Political Economy of the New York Region*, Garden City: Doubleday Anchor.

Zeigler, D. J. and Brunn, S. D., 1980, *Geopolitical Fragmentation and the Pattern of Growth and Need*, in Brunn, S. D. and Wheeler, J. O. (Eds.), *The American Metropolitan System: Present and Future*, New York: John Wiley, Scripta Series in Geography (with Don J. Zeigler): pp. 77-92.

## Conclusion

Aalborg C., 1994, *Charter of European Cities and Towns Towards Sustainability,* Agreement approved by the participants at the European Conference on Sustainable Cities and Towns in Aalborg, Denmark on 27 May 1994.

Amin, A. and Tomaney, J., 1995, *The Regional Dilemma in a Neo-liberal Europe,* in European Urban and Regional Studies No. 2: 171-188.

Shlomo, A., Sheppard, S. and Civico, D., 2005, *The Dynamics of Global Urban Expansion.* Transport and Urban Development Department. World Bank, Washington D.C., September.

Annez, P., 2006, *Urban Infrastructure Finance from Private Operators: What Have We Learned from Recent Experience?,* World Bank Research Working Paper 4045.

Beaverstock, J, Smith, R. and Taylor, P., 1999, *A Roster of World Cities,* Cities *16* (6): 445-458.

Boadway, R. and Shah, A. (ed.), 2007, *Intergovernmental Fiscal Transfers.* Principles and Practice. Public Sector Governance and Accountability Series. Washington, DC: World Bank. 572 p.

Cabrero, E., 2007, *Government Decentralization and Decentralized Governance in Latin America: The Silent Revolution at the Local Level?* pp. 156-169 in Cheema, S. and Rondinelli, D., "Decentralizing Governance. Emerging Concepts and Practices".

Campbell, T., 2003, *Decentralization and the Rise of Political Participation in Latin American Cities.* "The Quiet Revolution". Pittsburgh: University of Pittsburgh Press.

Cheema, G. S. and Rondinelli, D. A, (eds.), 2007, *Decentralizing Governance. Emerging Concepts and Practices.* Washington, DC: Brookings Institution Press and the Ash Institute for Democratic Governance and Innovation. 326 pp.

Cohen, J. and Peterson, S., 1999, *Administrative Decentralization.* Strategies for Developing Countries. West Hartford, CT: Kumarian Press. 207 p.

Council of Europe, 1985, *European Charter of Local Self-Government.* Strasbourg, France. October.

Crook, R. and Manor, J., 1998, *Democracy and Decentralization in South Asia and West Africa.* Participation, Accountability and Performance. Cambridge: Cambridge University Press. 348 p.

Devas, N. and Grant, U., 2003, *Local Government Decision-Making—Citizen Participation And Local Accountability: Some Evidence From Kenya And Uganda,* Public Administration and Development 23 (4): 307-316.

Edralin, J. S., (ed.) 1998, *Metropolitan Governance in Asia and the Pacific.* Tokyo: UN Center for Regional Development, Nagoya, Japan.

Ehtisham, A. and Tanzi, V. (eds.), 2002, *Managing Fiscal Decentralization.* London: Routledge.

Friedmann, J., 2001, *Intercity Networks in a Globalizing Era.* pp. 119-136 in Scott, A. (ed.), "Global City Regions: Trends, Theory, Policy". Oxford: Oxford University Press.

Government of Bolivia, 2006, *Strategy of Fiscal Decentralization.* Framework for Action. Office of the President and Ministry of Hacienda. La Paz, Bolivia.

Harris, N., 2003, *The Return of Cosmopolitan Capital.* Globalization, the State, and War. London: I.B. Tauris.

Haggard, S. and Webb, S., 1994, *Voting for Reform.* Democracy, Political Liberalization, and Economic Adjustment. Washington, DC: World Bank.

Hickey, S. and Mohan, G., 2005, *Relocating Participation within Radical Politics of Development,* Development and Change 36 (2): 237–262.

Inter-American Development Bank, 2002, *Making Decentralization Work in Latin America and the Caribbean.* A background paper for the subnational development strategy. Sustainable Development Department, Inter-American Development Bank. Washington, DC: IDB.

———. 1996, *Frame of Reference for IDB Action in Programs for Modernization of the State and Strengthening of Civil Society.* GN-1883-5. Strategic Planning and Operational policy department. Washington, DC: IDB.

Johnson, C., Priya, D. and Start, D., 2005, *Grounding the State: Devolution and Development in India's Panchayats,* Journal of Development Studies 41 (6): 937–970.

Kaufmann, D., Kraay, A. and Mastruzzi, M., 2007, *Governance Matters VI: Governance Indicators for 1996-2006,* July 2007, World Bank Policy Research Working Paper No. 4280. Available at SSRN: http://ssrn.com/abstract=999979.

Kjellstrom, T., Ercado, S., Sami, M., Havermann, K. and Iwao, S., 2007, *Achieving Health Equity in Urban Settings,* Journal of Urban Health 84 (3): 1-6.

Laquian, A., 2005, *Beyond Metropolis.* The Planning and Governance of Asia's Mega-Urban Regions. Washington, DC: Woodrow Wilson Center. 488 p.

National Research Council, 2003, *Cities Transformed.* Demographic Change and Its Implications in the Developing World. Washington, DC: US National Academies of Science. 529 p.

Nelson C. A. and Foster, K. A., 1999, *Metropolitan Governance Structure and Income Growth,* Journal of Urban Affairs 21 (3): 309-324.

Nickson, A., 1995, *Local Government in Latin America.* London: Lynn Reiner Publishers. 315 p.

Oates, W., 1972, *Fiscal Federalism.* New York: Harcourt Brace Jovanovich.

Panniza, U. and Yanezs, M., 2006, *Why Are Latin Americans so Unhappy about Reforms?,* IDB Research Department Working Paper No. 567. Inter-American Development Bank. Washington, DC.

Peterson, G., 1997, *Learning by Doing: Decentralization and Policy in Latin America and the Caribbean.* Discussion Series, Latin America Technical Department. Washington, DC: World Bank.

Rodden, J., Eskeland, G. and Litvack, J., 2003, *Fiscal Decentralization and the Challenge of Hard Budget Constraints.* Cambridge, MA: MIT Press. 476 p.

Rojas, E., Cuadrado-Roura, J. and Fernández Güell, J. M. (eds.), 2005, *Gobernar las metrópolis.* Washington, DC: Inter-American Development Bank.

Rothblatt, D. N. and Sancton A. (eds.), 1993, *Metropolitan Governance-American/Canadian Intergovernmental Perspectives.* Volume One, North American Federalism Project. Institute of Governmental Studies, University of California, Berkeley.

Salmon, P., 2002, *Decentralization and Supranationality: The Case of the European Union,* in Ehtisham, H. and Tanzi, V., "Managing Fiscal Decentralization". London: Routledge.

Smoke, P., 2007, *Fiscal Decentralization and Intergovernmental Relations in Developing Countries: Navigating a Viable Path to Reform.* In *Decentralized Governance: Emerging Concepts and Practice,* Cheema, G. S. and Rondinelli, D. (eds.), Washington, DC: The Brookings Institution.

———. 2003, *Decentralization and Local Governance in Africa,* Special Issue. Public Administration and Development 23 (4): 7–16.

Spink, P. K., 2005, *Growing Use of Convenios, in Metropolitan Governance of Brazil.* Paper presented at University of Texas, Austin Conference on Metropolitan Governance. March.

Stren, R. and Cameron, R., 2005, *Metropolitan Governance Reform: An Introduction,* Public Administration and Development 25 (4): 275–284. Special Issue: Metropolitan Governance Reform.

Swyngedouw, E. A., 1992, *The Mammon Quest. 'Globalization', Interspatial Competition, and the Monetary Order: The Construction of New Scales,* pp. 39-67 in Dunford, M. and Kafkalas, G. (eds.), "Cities and Regions in the New Europe," London: Belhaven Press.

Tendler, J., 1997, *Good Governance in the Tropics.* Baltimore: Johns Hopkins University Press.

Wescott, C., 2005, *Fiscal Devolution in East Asia.* Asian Development Bank, Regional and Sustainable Development Department. Manila: ADB.

Wescott, C. and Porter, D., 2002, *Fiscal Decentralization and Citizen Participation in East Asia,* Paper prepared for the Asian Development Bank INDES workshop on Fiscal Decentralization and Citizen Participation in East Asia.

World Bank, 2003, *Making Services Work for Poor People.* World Development Report 2004. London: World Bank and Oxford University Press.

World Bank, 1997, *World Development Report 1997: The State in a Changing World.* Oxford: Oxford University Press. 354 pages.

www.ingramcontent.com/pod-product-compliance
Lightning Source LLC
Chambersburg PA
CBHW050615290326
41929CB00063B/2910